Poetry:
Theory and Practice

Laurence Perrine

SOUTHERN METHODIST UNIVERSITY

Under the General Editorship of
David Levin
Stanford University

HARCOURT, BRACE & WORLD, INC.   NEW YORK · BURLINGAME

808.1
P42 p

51939
Jan. '66

COPYRIGHTS AND ACKNOWLEDGMENTS

CAMBRIDGE UNIVERSITY PRESS —from *The Name and Nature of Poetry* by A. E. Housman. By permission of the Cambridge University Press, London and New York, 1937. For *The Poet's Way of Knowledge* by C. Day Lewis, 1957, by arrangement with the Cambridge University Press.

CHATTO & WINDUS LTD. —from *Poetry: Direct and Oblique*, by E. M. W. Tillyard, 1945.

THE CLARENDON PRESS —from Jowett's translation of *The Dialogues of Plato*.

J. M. DENT & SONS LTD. —for "Fern Hill" from *The Collected Poems of Dylan Thomas*, 1953.

FABER AND FABER LTD. —for "In Memory of W. B. Yeats" from *Another Time* by W. H. Auden, "The Love Song of J. Alfred Prufrock" from *Collected Poems 1909–1935* by T. S. Eliot, and "The Social Function of Poetry" from *On Poetry and Poets* by T. S. Eliot.

FARRAR, STRAUS & CUDAHY, INC. —for "The Social Function of Poetry" reprinted from *On Poetry and Poets* by T. S. Eliot, by permission of Farrar, Straus & Cudahy, Inc. Copyright © 1957 by T. S. Eliot.

HARCOURT, BRACE & WORLD, INC. —for "A Haunted House" from *A Haunted House and Other Stories* by Virginia Woolf, copyright, 1944, by Harcourt, Brace & World, Inc. and reprinted with their permission. "For the New Railway Station in Rome" from *Things of This World* © 1956 by Richard Wilbur. Reprinted by permission of Harcourt, Brace & World, Inc. "if up's the word" © 1958 by E. E. Cummings. Reprinted from *95 Poems* by E. E. Cummings by permission of Harcourt, Brace & World, Inc. "What Does Poetry Communicate?" from *The Well Wrought Urn*, copyright, 1947, by Cleanth Brooks. Reprinted by permission of Harcourt, Brace & World, Inc. "The Love Song of J. Alfred Prufrock" from *Collected Poems 1909–1935* by T. S. Eliot, copyright, 1936, by Harcourt, Brace & World, Inc. and reprinted with their permission. "Salem" from *Lord Weary's Castle*, copyright, 1944, 1946, by Robert Lowell. Reprinted by permission of Harcourt, Brace & World, Inc.

HOLT, RINEHART AND WINSTON, INC. —for "Fog" from *Chicago Poems* by Carl Sandburg. Copyright 1916 by Holt, Rinehart and Winston, Inc. Copyright renewed 1944 by Carl Sandburg. Reprinted by permission of Holt, Rinehart and Winston, Inc. "Farewell to barn and stack and tree" from *A Shropshire Lad*—Authorised Edition—from *Complete Poems* by A. E. Housman. Copyright © 1959 by Holt, Rinehart and Winston, Inc. Reprinted by permission of Holt, Rinehart and Winston, Inc. "The Figure a Poem Makes," "Stopping by Woods on a Snowy Evening," and "Not to Keep" from *Complete Poems of Robert Frost*. Copyright 1923, 1949 by Holt, Rinehart and Winston, Inc. Copyright renewed 1951 by Robert Frost. Reprinted by permission of Holt, Rinehart and Winston, Inc.

HOUGHTON MIFFLIN COMPANY —for "Ars Poetica" from *Collected Poems 1917–1952* by Archibald MacLeish. Reprinted by permission of Houghton Mifflin Company.

ALFRED A. KNOPF, INC. —for "Six Significant Landscapes" and "Negation" reprinted from *The Collected Poems of Wallace Stevens*, by Wallace Stevens, by permission of Alfred A. Knopf, Inc. Copyright 1931, 1954 by Wallace Stevens.

LITTLE, BROWN & COMPANY —for "After great pain a formal feeling comes" from *The Complete Poems of Emily Dickinson*, 1960, by permission of Little, Brown & Co. Copyright 1929 by Martha Dickinson Bianchi. "A bird came down the walk" from *The Complete Poems of Emily Dickinson*, 1960. "Lion" from *Poems: 1947–1957*, William Jay Smith, by permission of Little, Brown & Co. Copyright © 1956 by William Jay Smith.

THE MACMILLAN COMPANY —for "The Symbolism of Poetry" from *Essays and Introductions* by W. B. Yeats. © Mrs. W. B. Yeats, 1961. Used with permission of The Macmillan Company. "The Darkling Thrush" from *The Collected Poems of Thomas Hardy*. Copyright 1925 by The Macmillan Company, and used with their permission. "Eros Turannos" from *The Collected Poems of Edwin Arlington Robinson*. Copyright 1916 by E. A. Robinson, renewed 1944 by Ruth Nivison. Used with permission of The Macmillan Company. "In Waste Places" from *Collected Poems* by James Stephens. Copyright 1915 by The Macmillan Company, renewed 1943 by James Stephens. Used with permission of The Macmillan Company. "Poetry" from *Collected Poems* by Marianne Moore. Copyright 1935 by Marianne Moore. Used with permission of The Macmillan Company. "Sailing to Byzantium" from *The Collected Poems of W. B. Yeats*. Copyright 1928 by The Macmillan Company, renewed 1956 by Georgie Yeats. Used with permission of The Macmillan Company.

MACMILLAN & CO. LTD. —for "Poetry for Poetry's Sake" from A. C. Bradley's *Oxford Lectures on Poetry* by permission of St Martin's Press, Inc., The Macmillan Co. of Canada, Ltd. and Macmillan & Co. Ltd. "The Darkling Thrush" from *The Collected Poems of Thomas Hardy* by permission of the Trustees of the Hardy Estate, The Macmillan Co. of Canada Ltd. and Macmillan & Co. Ltd. "In Waste Places" from *Collected Poems*, by James Stephens, by permission of Mrs. Iris Wise, The Macmillan Co. of Canada Ltd. and Macmillan & Co. Ltd.

NEW DIRECTIONS —for "Fern Hill" from *The Collected Poems of Dylan Thomas*. Copyright © 1957 by New Directions. Reprinted by permission of New Directions, Publishers.

OXFORD UNIVERSITY PRESS, INC. —for "The Windhover" from *Poems of Gerard Manley Hopkins*, third edition, edited by W. H. Gardner. Copyright 1948 by Oxford University Press, Inc., and reprinted by permission.

PARTISAN REVIEW —for "The Making of a Poem" by Stephen Spender, from *Partisan Review*, Summer, 1946. Reprinted by permission.

RANDOM HOUSE, INC. —for "Pure and Impure Poetry" copyright 1943 by Robert Penn Warren. Reprinted from *Selected Essays of Robert Penn Warren* by permission of Random House, Inc. "In Memory of W. B. Yeats" copyright 1940 by W. H. Auden. Reprinted from *The Collected Poetry of W. H. Auden* by permission of Random House, Inc. "The Fly" copyright 1942 by Karl Shapiro. Reprinted from *Poems 1940–1953*, by Karl Shapiro, by permission of Random House, Inc.

SATURDAY REVIEW —for "Poetry in the Theatre" by Christopher Fry, from *Saturday Review*, March 21, 1953. Taken from an address given by Mr. Fry over the BBC.

CHARLES SCRIBNER'S SONS —for "Lion" (Copyright 1951 May Swenson). Reprinted with the permission of Charles Scribner's Sons from *Poets of Today I, Another Animal: Poems* by May Swenson. From "Forms and Citizens" reprinted with the permission of Charles Scribner's Sons from *The World's Body* by John Crowe Ransom. Copyright 1938 Charles Scribner's Sons.

THE SOCIETY OF AUTHORS —for "Farewell to barn and stack and tree" reprinted by permission of The Society of Authors as the literary representative of the Estate of the late A. E. Housman, and Messrs. Jonathan Cape, Ltd, publishers of A. E. Housman's *Collected Poems*, 1959.

ALAN SWALLOW —for "A Foreword" reprinted from *In Defense of Reason* by Yvor Winters by permission of the publisher, Alan Swallow. Copyright 1947 by Yvor Winters.

THE UNIVERSITY OF KENTUCKY PRESS —for "The Concrete Universal" from *The Verbal Icon* by W. K. Wimsatt, Jr., 1954.

A. P. WATT & SON —for "Sailing to Byzantium" reprinted from *Collected Poems of W. B. Yeats*. Reprinted by permission of A. P. Watt & Son, Mrs. W. B. Yeats and The Macmillan Company of Canada Ltd. "The Symbolism of Poetry" by W. B. Yeats from *Essays and Introducions*. Reprinted by permission of A. P. Watt & Son, Mrs. W. B. Yeats and The Macmillan Company of Canada Ltd.

EDMUND WILSON —for "Is Verse a Dying Technique?" from *The Triple Thinkers* by Edmund Wilson, Oxford University Press, 1948. Reprinted by permission of the author.

LEONARD WOOLF —for "A Haunted House" by Virginia Woolf reprinted from *A Haunted House and Other Stories*. Reprinted by permission of Leonard Woolf.

Foreword

The purpose of *Poetry: Theory and Practice* is to bring together materials to support a number of writing projects on the nature and criticism of poetry. The materials include (1) a selection of theoretical and critical essays on poetry, ranging from Plato to the present, (2) a selection of English and American poetry, ranging from medieval ballads and lyrics to the present, and (3) four specimens of writing that lie in the ambiguous territory between prose and poetry. Various kinds of writing projects are thus possible: the essays may be compared with each other, ideas in the essays may be tested against the poems and prose selections, or poems may be compared with each other. Bibliographical information and the pagination of the editions cited, often the original editions, are given for all the essays so that fully documented papers may be prepared. A list of suggested topics for writing is included in the back.

Contents

Part Three: Between Prose and Poetry   225

PART ONE

Essays

PLATO

from the *Ion* and the *Republic*

[The pupil of Socrates, Plato (427?–347 B.C.) gave up a political career after the execution of his mentor in 399 B.C. and, after a period of travel, returned to Athens and in about 387 B.C. founded the Academy, where he spent the remainder of his life as a teacher and philosopher. Plato cast his writings into the form of dialogues, many of which have Socrates—whose own teachings were entirely oral—as their principal speaker. By thus using Socrates as spokesman, Plato indicated his indebtedness, but he undoubtedly modified and extended Socrates' teaching to express his own thought. His most extensive remarks about poets and poetry are contained in the *Ion,* composed about 390 B.C., and in Book X of the *Republic,* composed about 373 B.C. The following excerpts are from *The Dialogues of Plato,* translated by B. Jowett in 1871 and reprinted here from the revised fourth edition (Oxford, 1953), Volumes I (*Ion*) and II (*Republic*).]

FROM THE *Ion*

Ion. I cannot deny what you say, Socrates. Nevertheless I am conscious in my own self, and the world agrees with me, that I do speak better and have more to say about Homer than any other man; but I do not speak equally well about others. After all, there must be some reason for this; what is it?

Soc. I see the reason, Ion; and I will proceed to explain to you what I imagine it to be. The gift which you possess of speaking excellently about Homer is not an art, but, as I was just saying, an inspiration; there is a divinity moving you, like that contained in the stone which Euripides calls a magnet, but which is commonly known as the stone of Heraclea. This stone not only attracts iron rings, but also imparts to them a similar power of attracting other rings; and sometimes you may see a number of pieces of iron and rings suspended from one another so as to form quite a long chain: and all of them derive their power of suspension from the original stone. In like manner the Muse first of all inspires men herself; and from these

inspired persons a chain of other persons is suspended, who take the inspiration. For all good poets, epic as well as lyric, compose their beautiful poems not by art, but because they are inspired and possessed. And as the Corybantian revellers when they dance are not in their right mind, so the lyric poets are not in /107/ their right mind when they are composing their beautiful strains: but when falling under the power of music and metre they are inspired and possessed; like Bacchic maidens who draw milk and honey from the rivers when they are under the influence of Dionysus but not when they are in their right mind. And the soul of the lyric poet does the same, as they themselves say; for they tell us that they bring songs from honeyed fountains, culling them out of the gardens and dells of the Muses; they, like the bees, winging their way from flower to flower. And this is true. For the poet is a light and winged and holy thing, and there is no invention in him until he has been inspired and is out of his senses, and reason is no longer in him: no man, while he retains that faculty, has the oracular gift of poetry.

Many are the noble words in which poets speak concerning the actions of men; but like yourself when speaking about Homer, they do not speak of them by any rules of art: they are simply inspired to utter that to which the Muse impels them, and that only; and when inspired, one of them will make dithyrambs, another hymns of praise, another choral strains, another epic or iambic verses, but not one of them is of any account in the other kinds. For not by art does the poet sing, but by power divine; had he learned by rules of art, he would have known how to speak not of one theme only, but of all; and therefore God takes away reason from poets, and uses them as his ministers, as he also uses the pronouncers of oracles and holy prophets, in order that we who hear them may know them to be speaking not of themselves, who utter these priceless words while bereft of reason, but that God himself is the speaker, and that through them he is addressing us. And Tynnichus the Chalcidian affords a striking instance of what I am saying: he wrote no poem that anyone would care to remember but the famous paean which is in everyone's mouth, one of the finest lyric poems ever written, simply an invention of the Muses, as he himself says. For in this way God would seem to demonstrate to us and not to allow us to doubt that these beautiful poems are not human, nor the work of man, but divine and the work of God; and that the poets are only the interpreters of the gods by whom they are severally possessed. Was not this the lesson /108/ which God intended to teach when by the mouth of the worst of poets he sang the best of songs? Am I not right, Ion? . . . /109/

FROM THE *Republic,* BOOK X
[*The interlocutors are Socrates
and Glaucon.*]

Of the many excellences which I perceive in the order of our State, there is none which upon reflection pleases me better than the rule about poetry.

To what do you refer?

To our refusal to admit the imitative kind of poetry, for it certainly ought not to be received; as I see far more clearly now that the parts of the soul have been distinguished.

What do you mean?

Speaking in confidence, for you will not denounce me to the tragedians and the rest of the imitative tribe, all poetical imitations are ruinous to the understanding of the hearers, unless as an antidote they possess the knowledge of the true nature of the originals.

Explain the purport of your remark.

Well, I will tell you, although I have always from my earliest youth had an awe and love of Homer which even now makes the words falter on my lips, for he seems to be the great captain and teacher of the whole of that noble tragic company; but a man is not to be reverenced more than the truth, and therefore I will speak out.

Very good, he said.

Listen to me then, or rather, answer me.

Put your question.

Can you give me a general definition of imitation? for I really do not myself understand what it professes to be.

A likely thing, then, that I should know.

There would be nothing strange in that, for the duller eye may often see a thing sooner than the keener.

Very true, he said; but in your presence, even if I had any faint notion, I could not muster courage to utter it. Will you inquire yourself?

Well then, shall we begin the inquiry at this point, following our usual method: Whenever a number of individuals have a common name, we assume that there is one corresponding idea or form:—do you understand me? /468/

I do.

Let us take, for our present purpose, any instance of such a group; there are beds and tables in the world—many of each, are there not?

Yes.

But there are only two ideas or forms of such furniture—one the idea of a bed, the other of a table.

True.

And the maker of either of them makes a bed or he makes a table for our use, in accordance with the idea—that is our way of speaking in this and similar instances—but no artificer makes the idea itself: how could he?

Impossible.

And there is another artificer,—I should like to know what you would say of him.

Who is he?

One who is the maker of all the works of all other workmen.

What an extraordinary man!

Wait a little, and there will be more reason for your saying so. For this is the craftsman who is able to make not only furniture of every kind, but all that grows out of the earth, and all living creatures, himself included; and besides these he can make earth and sky and the gods, and all the things which are in heaven or in the realm of Hades under the earth.

He must be a wizard and no mistake.

Oh! you are incredulous, are you? Do you mean that there is no such maker or creator, or that in one sense there might be a maker of all these things but in another not? Do you see that there is a way in which you could make them all yourself?

And what way is this? he asked.

An easy way enough; or rather, there are many ways in which the feat might be quickly and easily accomplished, none quicker than that of turning a mirror round and round—you would soon enough make the sun and the heavens, and the earth and yourself, and other animals and plants, and furniture and all the other things of which we were just now speaking, in the mirror. /469/

Yes, he said; but they would be appearances only.

Very good, I said, you are coming to the point now. And the painter too is, as I conceive, just such another—a creator of appearances, is he not?

Of course.

But then I suppose you will say that what he creates is untrue. And yet there is a sense in which the painter also creates a bed? Is there not?

Yes, he said, but here again, an appearance only.

And what of the maker of the bed? were you not saying that he too makes, not the idea which according to our view is the real object denoted by the word bed, but only a particular bed?

Yes, I did.

Then if he does not make a real object he cannot make what *is*, but only some semblance of existence; and if any one were to say that the work of the maker of the bed, or of any other workman, has real existence, he could hardly be supposed to be speaking the truth.

Not, at least, he replied, in the view of those who make a business of these discussions.

No wonder, then, that his work too is an indistinct expression of truth.

No wonder.

Suppose now that by the light of the examples just offered we inquire who this imitator is?

If you please.

Well then, here we find three beds: one existing in nature, which is made by God, as I think that we may say—for no one else can be the maker?

No one, I think.

There is another which is the work of the carpenter?

Yes.

And the work of the painter is a third?

Yes.

Beds, then, are of three kinds, and there are three artists who superintend them: God, the maker of the bed, and the painter?

Yes, there are three of them.

God, whether from choice or from necessity, made one bed /470/ in nature and one only; two or more such beds neither ever have been nor ever will be made by God.

Why is that?

Because even if He had made but two, a third would still appear behind them of which they again both possessed the form, and that would be the real bed and not the two others.

Very true, he said.

God knew this, I suppose, and He desired to be the real maker of a real bed, not a kind of maker of a kind of bed, and therefore He created a bed which is essentially and by nature one only.

So it seems.

Shall we, then, speak of Him as the natural author or maker of the bed?

Yes, he replied; inasmuch as by the natural process of creation He is the author of this and of all other things.

And what shall we say of the carpenter—is not he also the maker of a bed?

Yes.

But would you call the painter an artificer and maker?

Certainly not.

Yet if he is not the maker, what is he in relation to the bed?

I think, he said, that we may fairly designate him as the imitator of that which the others make.

Good, I said; then you call him whose product is third in the descent from nature, an imitator?

Certainly, he said.

And so if the tragic poet is an imitator, he too is thrice removed from the king and from the truth; and so are all other imitators.

That appears to be so.

Then about the imitator we are agreed.

And what about the painter?—Do you think he tries to imitate in each case that which originally exists in nature, or only the creations of artificers?

The latter.

As they are or as they appear? you have still to determine this.

What do you mean?

I mean to ask whether a bed really becomes different when /471/ it is seen from different points of view, obliquely or directly or from any other point of view? Or does it simply appear different, without being really so? And the same of all things.

Yes, he said, the difference is only apparent.

Now let me ask you another question: Which is the art of painting designed to be—an imitation of things as they are, or as they appear—of appearance or of reality?

Of appearance, he said.

Then the imitator is a long way off the truth, and can reproduce all things because he lightly touches on a small part of them, and that part an image. For example: A painter will paint a cobbler, carpenter, or any other artisan, though he knows nothing of their arts; and, if he is a good painter, he may deceive children or simple persons when he shows them his picture of a carpenter from a distance, and they will fancy that they are looking at a real carpenter.

Certainly.

And surely, my friend, this is how we should regard all such claims: whenever any one informs us that he has found a man who knows all the arts, and all things else that anybody knows, and every single thing with a higher degree of accuracy than any other man—whoever tells us this, I think that we can only retort that he is a simple creature who seems to have been deceived by some wizard or imitator whom he met, and whom he thought all-knowing, because he himself was unable to analyse the nature of knowledge and ignorance and imitation.

Most true.

And next, I said, we have to consider tragedy and its leader, Homer; for we hear some persons saying that these poets know all the arts; and all things human; where virtue and vice are concerned, and indeed all divine things too; because the good poet cannot compose well unless he knows his subject, and he who has not this knowledge can never be a poet. We ought to consider whether here also there may not be a similar illusion. Perhaps they may have come across imitators and been deceived by them; they may not have remembered when they saw their works that these were thrice removed from the truth, and could easily be made without any knowledge of the truth, because they are appearances only and not realities? Or, after /472/ all, they may be in the right, and good poets do really know the things about which they seem to the many to speak so well?

The question, he said, should by all means be considered.

Now do you suppose that if a person were able to make the original as well as the image, he would seriously devote himself to the image-making branch? Would he allow imitation to be the ruling principle of his life, as if he had nothing higher in him?

I should say not.

But the real artist, who had real knowledge of those things which he chose also to imitate, would be interested in realities and not in imitations; and would desire to leave as memorials of himself works many and fair; and, instead of being the author of encomiums, he would prefer to be the theme of them.

Yes, he said, that would be to him a source of much greater honour and profit.

Now let us refrain, I said, from calling Homer or any other poet to account regarding those arts to which his poems incidentally refer: we will not ask them, in case any poet has been a doctor and not a mere imitator of medical parlance, to show what patients have been restored to health by a poet, ancient or modern, as they were by Asclepius; or what disciples in medicine a poet has left behind him, like the Asclepiads. Nor shall we press the same question upon them about the other arts. But we have a right to know respecting warfare, strategy, the administration of States and the education of man, which are the chiefest and noblest subjects of his poems, and we may fairly ask him about them. "Friend Homer," then we say to him, "if you are only in the second remove from truth in what you say of virtue, and not in the third—not an image maker, that is, by our definition, an imitator—and if you are able to discern what pursuits make men better or worse in private or public life, tell us what State was ever better governed by your help? The good order of Lacedaemon is due to Lycurgus, and many other cities great and small have been similarly benefited by others; but who says that you have been a good legislator to them and have done them any good? Italy and Sicily boast of Charondas, and there is Solon who is renowned among us; but what city has anything to say about you?" Is there any city which he might name? /473/

I think not, said Glaucon; not even the Homerids themselves pretend that he was a legislator.

Well, but is there any war on record which was carried on successfully owing to his leadership or counsel?

There is not.

Or is there anything comparable to those clever improvements in the arts, or in other operations, which are said to have been due to men of practical genius such as Thales the Milesian or Anacharsis the Scythian?

There is absolutely nothing of the kind.

But, if Homer never did any public service, was he privately a guide or teacher of any? Had he in his lifetime friends who loved to associate with him, and who handed down to posterity an Homeric way of life, such as was established by Pythagoras who was especially beloved for this reason and whose followers are to this day conspicuous among others by what they term the Pythagorean way of life?

Nothing of the kind is recorded of him. For surely, Socrates, Creophylus, the companion of Homer, that child of flesh, whose name always makes us laugh, might be more justly ridiculed for his want of breeding, if what is said is true, that Homer was greatly neglected by him in his own day when he was alive?

Yes, I replied, that is the tradition. But can you imagine, Glaucon, that if Homer had really been able to educate and improve mankind—if he had been capable of knowledge and not been a mere imitator—can you imagine, I say, that he would not have attracted many followers, and been honoured and loved by them? Protagoras of Abdera, and Prodicus of Ceos, and a host of others, have only to whisper to their contemporaries: "You will never be able to manage either your own house or your own State until you appoint us to be your ministers of education"—and this ingenious device of theirs has such an effect in making men love them that their companions all but carry them about on their shoulders. And is it conceivable that the contemporaries of Homer, or again of Hesiod, would have allowed either of them to go about as rhapsodists, if they had really been able to help mankind forward in virtue? Would they not have been as unwilling to part with them as with gold, and have compelled them to stay at home with them? Or, if the /474/ master would not stay, then the disciples would have followed him about everywhere, until they had got education enough?

Yes, Socrates, that, I think, is quite true.

Then must we not infer that all these poetical individuals, beginning with Homer, are only imitators, who copy images of virtue and the other themes of their poetry, but have no contact with the truth? The poet is like a painter who, as we have already observed, will make a likeness of a cobbler though he understands nothing of cobbling; and his picture is good enough for those who know no more than he does, and judge only by colours and figures.

Quite so.

In like manner the poet with his words and phrases may be said to lay on the colours of the several arts, himself understanding their nature only enough to imitate them; and other people, who are as ignorant as he is, and judge only from his words, imagine that if he speaks of cobbling, or of military tactics, or of anything else, in metre and harmony and rhythm, he speaks very well—such is the sweet influence which melody and rhythm by nature have. For I am sure that you know what a poor appearance the works of poets make when stripped of the colours which art puts upon them, and recited in simple prose. You have seen some examples?

Yes, he said.

They are like faces which were never really beautiful, but only blooming, seen when the bloom of youth has passed away from them?

Exactly.

Come now, and observe this point: The

imitator or maker of the image knows nothing, we have said, of true existence; he knows appearances only. Am I not right?

Yes.

Then let us have a clear understanding, and not be satisfied with half an explanation.

Proceed.

Of the painter we say that he will paint reins, and he will paint a bit?

Yes. /475/

And the worker in leather and brass will make them?

Certainly.

But does the painter know the right form of the bit and reins? Nay, hardly even the workers in brass and leather who make them; only the horseman who knows how to use them— he knows their right form.

Most true.

And may we not say the same of all things?

What?

That there are three arts which are concerned with all things: one which uses, another which makes, a third which imitates them?

Yes.

And the excellence and beauty and rightness of every structure, animate or inanimate, and of every action of man, is relative solely to the use for which nature or the artist has intended them.

True.

Then beyond doubt it is the user who has the greatest experience of them, and he must report to the maker the good or bad qualities which develop themselves in use; for example, the flute-player will tell the flute-maker which of his flutes is satisfactory to the performer; he will tell him how he ought to make them, and the other will attend to his instructions?

Of course.

So the one pronounces with knowledge about the goodness and badness of flutes, while the other, confiding in him, will make them accordingly?

True.

The instrument is the same, but about the excellence or badness of it the marker will possess a correct belief, since he associates with one who knows, and is compelled to hear what he has to say; whereas the user will have knowledge?

True.

But will the imitator have either? Will he know from use whether or no that which he paints is correct or beautiful? or will he have right opinion from being compelled to associate with another who knows and gives him instructions about what he should paint? /476/

Neither.

Then an imitator will no more have true opinion than he will have knowledge about the goodness or badness of his models?

I suppose not.

The imitative poet will be in a brilliant state of intelligence about the theme of his poetry?

Nay, very much the reverse.

And still he will go on imitating without knowing what makes a thing good or bad, and may be expected therefore to imitate only that which appears to be good to the ignorant multitude?

Just so.

Thus far then we are pretty well agreed that the imitator has no knowledge worth mentioning of what he imitates. Imitation is only a kind of play or sport, and the tragic poets, whether they write in iambic or in heroic verse, are imitators in the highest degree?

Very true.

And now tell me, I conjure you,—this imitation is concerned with an object which is thrice removed from the truth?

Certainly.

And what kind of faculty in man is that to which imitation makes its special appeal?

What do you mean?

I will explain: The same body does not appear equal to our sight when seen near and when seen at a distance?

True.

And the same objects appear straight when looked at out of the water, and crooked when in the water; and the concave becomes convex, owing to the illusion about colours to which the sight is liable. Thus every sort of confusion is revealed within us; and this is that weakness of the human mind on which the art of painting in light and shadow, the art of conjuring, and many other ingenious devices impose, having an effect upon us like magic.

True.

And the arts of measuring and numbering and weighing come to the rescue of the human understanding—there is the beauty of them—with the result that the apparent greater or less, or /477/ more or heavier, no longer have the mastery over us, but give way before the power of calculation and measuring and weighing?

Most true.

And this, surely, must be the work of the calculating and rational principle in the soul?

To be sure.

And often when this principle measures and certifies that some things are equal, or that some are greater or less than others, it is, at the same time, contradicted by the appearance which the objects present?

True.

But did we not say that such a contradiction is impossible—the same faculty cannot have contrary opinions at the same time about the same thing?

We did; and rightly.

Then that part of the soul which has an opinion contrary to measure can hardly be the same with that which has an opinion in accordance with measure?

True.

And the part of the soul which trusts to measure and calculation is likely to be the better one?

Certainly.

And therefore that which is opposed to this is probably an inferior principle in our nature?

No doubt.

This was the conclusion at which I was seeking to arrive when I said that painting or drawing, and imitation in general, are engaged upon productions which are far removed from truth, and are also the companions and friends and associates of a principle within us which is equally removed from reason, and that they have no true or healthy aim.

Exactly.

The imitative art is an inferior who from intercourse with an inferior has inferior offspring.

Very true.

And is this confined to the sight only, or does it extend to the hearing also, relating in fact to what we term poetry?

Probably the same would be true of poetry.

Do not rely, I said, on a probability derived from the analogy /478/ of painting; but let us once more go directly to that faculty of the mind with which imitative poetry has converse, and see whether it is good or bad.

By all means.

We may state the question thus:—Imitation imitates the actions of men, whether voluntary or involuntary, on which, as they imagine, a good or bad result has ensued, and they rejoice or sorrow accordingly. Is there anything more?

No, there is nothing else.

But in all this variety of circumstances is the man at unity with himself—or rather, as in the instance of sight there was confusion and opposition in his opinions about the same things, so here also is there not strife and inconsistency in his life? Though I need hardly raise the question again, for I remember that all this has been already admitted; and the soul has been acknowledged by us to be full of these and ten thousand similar oppositions occurring at the same moment?

And we were right, he said.

Yes, I said, thus far we were right; but there was an omission which must now be supplied.

What was the omission?

Were we not saying that a good man, who has the misfortune to lose his son or anything else which is most dear to him, will bear the loss with more equanimity than another?

Yes, indeed.

But will he have no sorrow, or shall we say that although he cannot help sorrowing, he will moderate his sorrow?

The latter, he said, is the truer statement.

Tell me: will he be more likely to struggle and hold out against his sorrow when he is seen by his equals, or when he is alone in a deserted place?

The fact of being seen will make a great difference, he said.

When he is by himself he will not mind saying many things which he would be ashamed of any one hearing, and also doing many things which he would not care to be seen doing?

True.

And doubtless it is the law and reason in him which bids him resist; while it is the affliction itself which is urging him to indulge his sorrow? /479/

True.

But when a man is drawn in two opposite directions, to and from the same object, this, as we affirm, necessarily implies two distinct principles in him?

Certainly.

One of them is ready to follow the guidance of the law?

How do you mean?

The law would say that to be patient under calamity is best, and that we should not give way to impatience, as the good and evil in such things are not clear, and nothing is gained by impatience; also, because no human thing is of serious importance, and grief stands in the way of that which at the moment is most required.

What is most required? he asked.

That we should take counsel about what has happened, and when the dice have been thrown, according to their fall, order our affairs in the way which reason deems best; not, like children who have had a fall, keeping hold of the part struck and wasting time in setting up a howl, but always accustoming the soul forthwith to apply a remedy, raising up that which is sickly and fallen, banishing the cry of sorrow by the healing art.

Yes, he said, that is the true way of meeting the attacks of fortune.

Well then, I said, the higher principle is ready to follow this suggestion of reason?

Clearly.

But the other principle, which inclines us to recollection of our troubles and to lamentation, and can never have enough of them, we may call irrational, useless, and cowardly?

Indeed, we may.

Now does not the principle which is thus inclined to complaint, furnish a great variety of materials for imitation? Whereas the wise and calm temperament, being always nearly equable, is not easy to imitate or to appreciate when imitated, especially at a public festival when a promiscuous crowd is assembled in a theatre. For the feeling represented is one to which they are strangers.

Certainly.

Then the imitative poet who aims at being popular is not /480/ by nature made, nor is his art intended, to please or to affect the rational principle in the soul; but he will appeal rather to the lachrymose and fitful temper, which is easily imitated?

Clearly.

And now we may fairly take him and place him by the side of the painter, for he is like him in two ways: first, inasmuch as his creations have an inferior degree of truth—in this, I say, he is like him; and he is also like him in being the associate of an inferior part of the soul; and this is enough to show that we shall be right in refusing to admit him into a State which is to be well ordered, because he awakens and nourishes this part of the soul, and by strengthening it impairs the reason. As in a city when the evil are permitted to wield power and the finer men are put out of the way, so in the soul of each man, as we shall maintain, the imitative poet implants an evil constitution, for he indulges the irrational nature which has no discernment of greater and less, but thinks the same thing at one time great and at another small—he is an imitator of images and is very far removed from the truth.

Exactly.

But we have not yet brought forward the heaviest count in our accusation:—the power which poetry has of harming even the good (and there are very few who are not harmed), is surely an awful thing?

Yes, certainly, if the effect is what you say.

Hear and judge: The best of us, as I conceive, when we listen to a passage of Homer or one of the tragedians, in which he represents some hero who is drawling out his sorrows in a long oration, or singing, and smiting his breast—the best of us, you know, delight in giving way to sympathy, and are in raptures at the excellence of the poet who stirs our feelings most.

Yes, of course I know.

But when any sorrow of our own happens to us, then you may observe that we pride ourselves on the opposite quality—we would fain be quiet and patient; this is considered the manly part, and the other which delighted us in the recitation is now deemed to be the part of a woman.

Very true, he said. /481/

Now can we be right in praising and admiring another who is doing that which any one of us would abominate and be ashamed of in his own person?

No, he said, that is certainly not reasonable.

Nay, I said, quite reasonable from one point of view.

What point of view?

If you consider, I said, that when in misfortune we feel a natural hunger and desire to relieve our sorrow by weeping and lamentation, and that this very feeling which is starved and suppressed in our own calamities is satisfied and delighted by the poets;—the better nature in each of us, not having been sufficiently trained by reason or habit, allows the sympathetic element to break loose because the sorrow is another's; and the spectator fancies that there can be no disgrace to himself in praising and pitying any one who while professing to be a brave man, gives way to untimely lamentation; he thinks that the pleasure is a gain, and is far from wishing to lose it by rejection of the whole poem. Few persons ever reflect, as I should imagine, that the contagion must pass from others to themselves. For the pity which has been nourished and strengthened in the misfortunes of others is with difficulty repressed in our own.

How very true!

And does not the same hold also of the ridiculous? There are jests which you would be ashamed to make yourself, and yet on the comic stage, or indeed in private, when you hear them, you are greatly amused by them, and are not at all disgusted at their unseemliness;—the case of pity is repeated;—there is a principle in human nature which is disposed to raise a laugh, and this, which you once restrained by reason because you were afraid of being thought a buffoon, is now let out again; and having stimulated the risible faculty at the theatre, you are betrayed unconsciously to yourself into playing the comic poet at home.

Quite true, he said.

And the same may be said of lust and anger and all the other affections, of desire and pain and pleasure, which are held to be inseparable from every action—in all of them poetry has a like effect; it feeds and waters the passions instead /482/ of drying them up; she lets them rule, although they ought to be controlled if mankind are ever to increase in happiness and virtue.

I cannot deny it.

Therefore, Glaucon, I said, whenever you meet with any of the eulogists of Homer declaring that he has been the educator of Hellas, and that he is profitable for education and for the ordering of human things, and that you should take him up again and again and get to know him and regulate your whole life according to him, we may love and honour those who say these things—they are excellent people, as far as their lights extend; and we are ready to acknowledge that Homer is the greatest of poets and first of tragedy writers; but we must remain firm in our conviction that hymns to the gods and praises of famous men are the only poetry which ought to be admitted into our State. For if you go beyond this and allow the honeyed Muse to enter, either in epic or lyric verse, not law and the reason of mankind, which by common consent have ever been deemed best, but pleasure and pain will be the rulers in our State.

That is most true, he said.

And now since we have reverted to the subject of poetry, let this our defence serve to show the reasonableness of our former judgement in sending away out of our State an art having the tendencies which we have described; for reason constrained us. But that she may not impute to us any harshness or want of politeness, let us tell her that there is an ancient quarrel between philosophy and poetry; of which there are many proofs, such as the saying of "the yelping hound howling at her lord," or of one "mighty in the vain talk of fools," and "the mob of sages circumventing Zeus," and the "subtle thinkers who are beggars after all"; and there are innumerable other signs of ancient enmity between them. Notwithstanding this, let us assure the poetry which aims at pleasure, and the art of imitation, that if she will only prove her title to exist in a well-ordered State we shall be delighted to receive her—we are very conscious of her charms; /483/ but it would not be right on that account to betray the truth. I dare say, Glaucon, that you are as much charmed by her as I am, especially when she appears in Homer?

Yes, indeed, I am greatly charmed.

Shall I propose, then, that she be allowed to return from exile, but upon this condition only—that she make a defence of herself in some lyrical or other metre?

Certainly.

And we may further grant to those of her defenders who are lovers of poetry and yet not poets the permission to speak in prose on her behalf: let them show not only that she is pleasant but also useful to States and to human life, and we will listen in a kindly spirit; for we shall surely be the gainers if this can be proved, that there is a use in poetry as well as a delight?

Certainly, he said, we shall be the gainers.

If her defence fails, then, my dear friend, like other persons who are enamoured of something, but put a restraint upon themselves when they think their desires are opposed to their interests, so too must we after the manner of lovers give her up, though not without a struggle. We too are inspired by that love of such poetry which the education of noble States has implanted in us, and therefore we shall be glad if she appears at her best and truest; but so long as she is unable to make good her defence, this argument of ours shall be a charm to us, which we will repeat to ourselves while we listen to her strains; that we may not fall away into the childish love of her which captivates the many. At all events we are well aware that poetry, such as we have described, is not to be regarded seriously as attaining to the truth; and he who listens to her, fearing for the safety of the city which is within him, should be on his guard against her seductions and make our words his law.

Yes, he said, I quite agree with you.

Yes, I said, my dear Glaucon, for great is the issue at stake, greater than appears, whether a man is to be good or bad. And /484/ what will any one be profited if under the influence of honour or money or power, aye, or under the excitement of poetry, he neglect justice and virtue?

Yes, he said; I have been convinced by the argument, as I believe that anyone else would have been. . . . /485/

ARISTOTLE
from the *Poetics*

[Aristotle (384–322 B.C.) at the age of seventeen became a pupil at Plato's Academy and studied there until Plato's death twenty years later. After a twelve-year interlude, half of which he spent as tutor to Alexander at the Macedonian court, Aristotle in 335 B.C. founded the Lyceum in Athens, where most of his extant writings were delivered as lectures. The *Poetics*, composed between 335 and 322 B.C., is thought by some critics to be the draft or summary of a lecture, or a later abridgment of the original work. The extant portion is concerned mainly with tragedy but deals in parts with poetry in general. The following excerpts are taken from the corrected fourth edition of *Aristotle's Theory of Poetry and Fine Art*, by S. H. Butcher (London, 1911). The first edition of Butcher's translation appeared in 1895.]

I

I propose to treat of Poetry in itself and of its various kinds, noting the essential quality of each; to inquire into the structure of the plot as requisite to a good poem; into the number and nature of the parts of which a poem is composed; and similarly into whatever else falls within the same inquiry. Following, then, the order of nature, let us begin with the principles which come first.

Epic poetry and Tragedy, Comedy also and Dithyrambic poetry, and the music of the flute and of the lyre in most of their forms, are all in their general conception modes of imitation. They differ, however, from one another in three respects,—the medium, the objects, the manner or mode of imitation, being in each case distinct.

For as there are persons who, by conscious art or mere habit, imitate and represent various objects through the medium of colour and form, or again by the voice; so in the arts above mentioned, taken as a whole, the imitation is produced by rhythm, language, or "harmony," either singly or combined. /7/

Thus in the music of the flute and of the lyre, "harmony" and rhythm alone are employed; also in other arts, such as that of the shepherd's pipe, which are essentially similar to these. In dancing, rhythm alone is used without "harmony"; for even dancing imitates character, emotion, and action, by rhythmical movement.

There is another art which imitates by means of language alone, and that either in prose or verse—which verse, again, may either combine different metres or consist of but one kind—but this has hitherto been without a name. For there is no common term we could apply to the mimes of Sophron and Xenarchus and the Socratic dialogues on the one hand; and, on the other, to poetic imitations in iambic, elegiac, or any similar metre. People do, indeed, add the word "maker" or "poet" to the name of the metre, and speak of elegiac poets, or epic (that is, hexameter) poets, as if it were not the imitation that makes the poet, but the verse that entitles them all indiscriminately to the name. Even when a treatise on medicine or natural science is brought out in verse, the name of poet is by custom given to the author; and yet Homer and Empedocles have nothing in common but the metre, so that it would be right to call the one poet, the other physicist rather than poet. . . . /9/

II

Since the objects of imitation are men in action, and these men must be either of a higher or a lower type (for moral character mainly answers to these divisions, goodness and badness being the distinguishing marks of moral differences), it follows that we must represent men either as better than in real life, or as worse, or as they are. It is the same in painting. Polygnotus depicted men as nobler than they are, Pauson as less noble, Dionysius drew them true to life.

Now it is evident that each of the modes of imitation above mentioned will exhibit these differences, and become a distinct kind in imitating objects that are thus distinct.

Such diversities may be found even in dancing, flute-playing, and lyre-playing. So again in language, whether prose or verse unaccompanied by music. Homer, for example, makes men better than they are; Cleophon as they are; Hegemon the Thasian, the inventor of parodies, and Nicochares, the author of the Deiliad, worse than they are. The same thing holds good of Dithyrambs and Nomes; here too one may portray different types, as /11/ Timotheus and Philoxenus differed in representing their Cyclopes. The same distinction marks off Tragedy from Comedy; for Comedy aims at representing men as worse, Tragedy as better than in actual life.

III

There is still a third difference—the manner in which each of these objects may be imitated. For the medium being the same, and the objects the same, the poet may imitate by narration—in which case he can either take another personality as Homer does, or speak in his own person, unchanged—or he may present all his characters as living and moving before us.

These, then, as we said at the beginning, are the three differences which distinguish artistic imitation—the medium, the objects, and the manner. So that from one point of view, Sophocles is an imitator of the same kind as Homer—for both imitate higher types of character; from another point of view, of the same kind as Aristophanes—for both imitate persons acting and doing. Hence, some say, the name of "drama" is given to such poems, as representing action. . . . /13/

IV

Poetry in general seems to have sprung from two causes, each of them lying deep in our nature. First, the instinct of imitation is implanted in man from childhood, one difference between him and other animals being that he is the most imitative of living creatures, and through imitation he learns his earliest lessons; and no less universal is the pleasure felt in things imitated. We have evidence of this in the facts of experience. Objects which in themselves we view with pain, we delight to contemplate when reproduced with minute fidelity: such as the forms of the most ignoble animals and of dead bodies. The cause of this again is, that to learn gives the liveliest pleasure, not only to philosophers but to men in general; whose capacity, however, of learning is more limited. Thus the reason why men enjoy seeing a likeness is, that in contemplating it they find themselves learning or inferring, and saying perhaps, "Ah, that is he." For if you happen not to have seen the original, the pleasure will be due not to the imitation as such, but to the execution, the colouring, or some such other cause.

Imitation, then, is one instinct of our nature. Next, there is the instinct for "harmony" and rhythm, metres being manifestly sections of rhythm. Persons, therefore, starting with this natural gift developed by degrees their /15/ special aptitudes, till their rude improvisations gave birth to Poetry.

Poetry now diverged in two directions, according to the individual character of the writers. The graver spirits imitated noble actions, and the actions of good men. The more trivial sort imitated the actions of meaner persons, at first composing satires, as the former did hymns to the gods and the praises of famous men. A poem of the satirical kind cannot indeed be put down to any author earlier than Homer; though many such writers probably there were. But from Homer onward, instances can be cited,—his own Margites, for example, and other similar compositions. The appropriate metre was also here introduced; hence the measure is still called the iambic or lampooning measure, being that in which people lampooned one another. Thus the older poets were distinguished as writers of heroic or of lampooning verse.

As, in the serious style, Homer is preeminent among poets, for he alone combined dramatic form with excellence of imitation, so he too first laid down the main lines of Comedy, by dramatising the ludicrous instead of writing personal satire. His Margites bears the same relation to Comedy that the Iliad and Odyssey do to Tragedy. But when Tragedy and Comedy came to light, the two classes of poets still followed their natural bent: the lampooners became writers of Comedy, and the Epic poets were succeeded by Tragedians, since the drama was a larger and higher form of art. . . . /17/

VI

Tragedy, then, is an imitation of an action that is serious, complete, and of a certain magnitude; in language embellished with each kind of artistic ornament, the several kinds being found in separate parts of the play; in the form of action, not of narrative; through pity and fear effecting the proper purgation of these emotions. . . . /23/

VII

Again, a beautiful object, whether it be a picture of a living organism or any whole composed of parts, must not only have an orderly arrangement of parts, but must also be of a certain magnitude; for beauty depends on magnitude and order. Hence an exceedingly small picture cannot be beautiful; for the view of it is confused, the object being seen in an almost imperceptible moment of time. Nor, again, can one of vast size be beautiful; for as the eye cannot take it all in at once, the unity and sense of the whole is lost for the spectator; as for instance if there were one a thousand miles long. As, therefore, in the case of animate bodies and organisms a certain magnitude is necessary, and a magni- /31/ tude which may be easily embraced in one view; so in the plot, a certain length is necessary, and a length which can be easily embraced by the memory. The limit of length in relation to dramatic competition and sensuous presentment, is no part of artistic theory. For had it been the rule of a hundred tragedies to compete together, the performance would have been regulated by the water-clock, —as indeed we are told was formerly done. But the limit as fixed by the nature of the drama itself is this:—the greater the length, the more beautiful will the piece be by reason of its size, provided that the whole be perspicuous. . . . /33/

VIII

Unity of plot does not, as some persons think, consist in the unity of the hero. For infinitely various are the incidents in one man's life, which cannot be reduced to unity; and so, too, there are many actions of one man out of which we cannot make one action. Hence the error, as it appears, of all poets who have composed a Heracleid, a Theseid, or other poems of the kind. They imagine that as Heracles was one man, the story of Heracles must also be a unity. But Homer, as in all else he is of surpassing merit, here too—whether from art or natural genius —seems to have happily discerned the truth. In composing the Odyssey he did not include all the adventures of Odysseus—such as his wound on Parnassus, or his feigned madness at the mustering of /33/ the host—incidents between which there was no necessary or probable connexion: but he made the Odyssey, and likewise the Iliad, to centre round an action that in our sense of the word is one. As therefore, in the other imitative arts, the imitation is one when the object imitated is one, so the plot, being an imitation of an action, must imitate one action and that a whole, the structural union of the parts being such that, if any one of them is displaced or removed, the whole will be disjointed and disturbed. For a thing whose presence or absence makes no visible difference, is not an organic part of the whole.

IX

It is, moreover, evident from what has been said, that it is not the function of the poet to relate what has happened, but what may happen,—what is possible according to the law of probability or necessity. The poet and the historian differ not by writing in verse or in prose. The work of Herodotus might be put into verse, and it would still be a species of history, with metre no less than without it. The true difference is that one relates what has happened, the other what may happen. Poetry, therefore, is a more philosophical and a higher thing than history: for poetry tends to express the universal, history the particular. By the universal I mean how a person of a certain type will on occasion speak or act, according to the law of probability or necessity; and it is this universality at which poetry aims in the names she attaches to the personages. The particular is—for example—what Alcibiades did or suffered. . . . /35/

It clearly follows that the poet or "maker" should be the maker of plots rather than of verses; since he is a poet because he imitates, and what he imitates are actions. And even if he chances to take an historical subject, he is none the less a poet; for there is no reason why some events that have actually happened should not conform to the law of the probable and possible, and in virtue of that quality in them he is their poet or maker.

Of all plots and actions the epeisodic are the worst. /37/ I call a plot "epeisodic" in which the episodes or acts succeed one another without probable or necessary sequence. Bad poets compose such pieces by their own fault, good poets, to please the players; for, as they write show pieces for competition, they stretch the plot beyond its capacity, and are often forced to break the natural continuity. . . . /39/

XXII

The perfection of style is to be clear without being mean. The clearest style is that which uses only current or proper words; at the same time it is mean:—witness the poetry of Cleophon and of Sthenelus. That diction, /81/ on the other hand, is lofty and raised above the commonplace which employs unusual words. By unusual, I mean strange (or rare) words, metaphorical, lengthened,—anything, in short, that differs from the normal idiom. Yet a style wholly composed of such words is either a riddle or a jargon; a riddle, if it consists of metaphors; a jargon, if it consists of strange (or rare) words. . . . A certain infusion, therefore, of these elements is necessary to style; for the strange (or rare) word, the metaphorical, the ornamental, and the other kinds above mentioned, will raise it above the commonplace and mean, while the use of proper words will make it perspicuous. But nothing contributes more to produce a clearness than the lengthening, contraction, and alteration of words. For by deviating in exceptional cases from the normal idiom, the language will gain distinction; while, at the same time, the partial conformity with usage will give perspicuity. The critics, therefore, are in error who censure these licenses of speech, and hold the author up to ridicule. Thus Eucleides, the elder, declared that it would be an easy matter to be a poet if you might lengthen syllables at will. He caricatured the practice in the very form of his diction, . . . /83/ To employ such license at all obtrusively is, no doubt, grotesque; but in any

mode of poetic diction there must be moderation. Even metaphors, strange (or rare) words, or any similar forms of speech, would produce the like effect if used without propriety, and with the express purpose of being ludicrous. . . . /85/

Again, Ariphrades ridiculed the tragedians for using phrases which no one would employ in ordinary speech: . . . It is precisely because such phrases are not part of the current idiom that they give distinction to the style. This, however, he failed to see.

It is a great matter to observe propriety in these several modes of expression as also in compound words, strange (or rare) words, and so forth. But the greatest thing by far is to have a command of metaphor. This alone cannot be imparted by another; it is the mark of genius, for to make good metaphors implies an eye for resemblances.

Of the various kinds of words, the compound are best adapted to dithyrambs, rare words to heroic poetry, metaphors to iambic. In heroic poetry, indeed, all these varieties are serviceable. But in iambic verse, which reproduces, as far as may be, familiar speech, the most appropriate words are those which are found even in prose. These are,—the current or proper, the metaphorical, the ornamental.

Concerning Tragedy and imitation by means of action this may suffice. /87/

XXIII

As to that poetic imitation which is narrative in form and employs a single metre, the plot manifestly ought, as in a tragedy, to be constructed on dramatic principles. It should have for its subject a single action, whole and complete, with a beginning, a middle, and an end. It will thus resemble a living organism in all its unity, and produce the pleasure proper to it. It will differ in structure from historical compositions, which of necessity present not a single action, but a single period, and all that happened within that period to one person or to many, little connected together as the events may be. For as the sea-fight at Salamis and the battle with the Carthaginians in Sicily took place at the same time, but did not tend to any one result, so in the sequence of events, one thing sometimes follows another, and yet no single result is thereby produced. Such is the practice, we may say, of most poets. Here again, then, as has been already observed, the transcendent excellence of Homer is manifest. He never attempts to make the whole war of Troy the subject of his poem, though that war had a beginning and an end. It would have been too vast a theme, and not easily embraced in a single view. If, again, he had kept it within moderate limits, it must have been overcomplicated by the variety of the incidents. As it is, he detaches a single portion, and admits as episodes many events from the general story of the war—such as the Catalogue of the ships and others—thus diversifying the poem. All other poets take a single hero, a single period, or an action single indeed, but with a multiplicity of parts. Thus did the /89/ author of the Cypria and of the Little Iliad. For this reason the Iliad and the Odyssey each furnish the subject of one tragedy, or, at most, of two; while the Cypria supplies materials for many, and the Little Iliad for eight—the Award of the Arms, the Philoctetes, the Neoptolemus, the Eurypylus, the Mendicant Odysseus, the Laconian Women, the Fall of Ilium, the Departure of the Fleet. /91/

XXIV

Homer, admirable in all respects, has the special merit of being the only poet who rightly appreciates the part he should take himself. The poet should speak as little as possible in his own person, for it is not this that makes him an imitator. Other poets appear themselves upon /93/ the scene throughout, and imitate but little and rarely. Homer, after a few prefatory words, at once brings in a man, or woman, or other personage; none of them wanting in characteristic qualities, but each with a character of his own. . . .

Accordingly, the poet should prefer probable impossibilities to improbable possibilities. The tragic plot must not be composed of irrational parts. Everything /95/ irrational should, if possible, be excluded; or, at all events, it should lie outside the action of the play (as, in the Oedipus, the hero's ignorance as to the manner of Laius' death); not within the drama,—as in the Electra, the messenger's account of the Pythian games; or, as in the Mysians, the man who comes from Tegea to Mysia and is still speechless. The plea that

otherwise the plot would have been ruined, is ridiculous; such a plot should not in the first instance be constructed. But once the irrational has been introduced and an air of likelihood imparted to it, we must accept it in spite of the absurdity. Take even the irrational incidents in the Odyssey, where Odysseus is left upon the shore of Ithaca. How intolerable even these might have been would be apparent if an inferior poet were to treat the subject. As it is, the absurdity is veiled by the poetic charm with which the poet invests it.

The diction should be elaborated in the pauses of the action, where there is no expression of character or thought. For, conversely, character and thought are merely obscured by a diction that is over brilliant.

XXV

With respect to critical difficulties and their solutions, the number and nature of the sources from which they may be drawn may be thus exhibited.

The poet being an imitator, like a painter or any other artist, must of necessity imitate one of three objects,—things as they were or are, things as they are said or thought to be, or things as they ought to be. The vehicle of expression is language,—either current terms or, it may be, rare words or metaphors. There are also many modifications of language, which we /97/ concede to the poets. Add to this, that the standard of correctness is not the same in poetry and politics, any more than in poetry and any other art. Within the art of poetry itself there are two kinds of faults,—those which touch its essence, and those which are accidental. If a poet has chosen to imitate something, <but has imitated it incorrectly> through want of capacity, the error is inherent in the poetry. But if the failure is due to a wrong choice—if he has represented a horse as throwing out both his off legs at once, or introduced technical inaccuracies in medicine, for example, or in any other art—the error is not essential to the poetry. These are the points of view from which we should consider and answer the objections raised by the critics.

First as to matters which concern the poet's own art. If he describes the impossible, he is guilty of an error; but the error may be justified, if the end of the art be thereby attained (the end being that already mentioned),—if, that is, the effect of this or any other part of the poem is thus rendered more striking. A case in point is the pursuit of Hector. If, however, the end might have been as well, or better, attained without violating the special rules of the poetic art, the error is not justified: for every kind of error should, if possible, be avoided.

Again, does the error touch the essentials of the poetic art, or some accident of it? For example,—not to know that a hind has no horns is a less serious matter than to paint it inartistically.

Further, if it be objected that the description is not /99/ true to fact, the poet may perhaps reply,—"But the objects are as they ought to be": just as Sophocles said that he drew men as they ought to be; Euripides, as they are. In this way the objection may be met. If, however, the representation be of neither kind, the poet may answer,—"This is how men say the thing is." This applies to tales about the gods. It may well be that these stories are not higher than fact nor yet true to fact: they are, very possibly, what Xenophanes says of them. But anyhow, "this is what is said." Again, a description may be no better than the fact: "still, it was the fact"; as in the passage about the arms: "Upright upon their butt-ends stood the spears." This was the custom then, as it now is among the Illyrians.

Again, in examining whether what has been said or done by some one is poetically right or not, we must not look merely to the particular act or saying, and ask whether it is poetically good or bad. We must also consider by whom it is said or done, to whom, when, by what means, or for what end; whether, for instance, it be to secure a greater good, or avert a greater evil. . . . /101/

In general, the impossible must be justified by reference to artistic requirements, or to the higher /105/ reality, or to received opinion. With respect to the requirements of art, a probable impossibility is to be preferred to a thing improbable and yet possible. Again, it may be impossible that there should be men such as Zeuxis painted. "Yes," we say, "but the impossible is the higher thing; for the ideal type must surpass the reality." To justify the irrational, we appeal to what is commonly said to be. In addition to which, we urge that the irrational sometimes does not violate reason; just as "it is probable that a thing may happen contrary to probability." . . . /107/

SIR PHILIP SIDNEY

from *The Defense of Poesy*

[Sir Philip Sidney (1554–1586), poet, soldier, and statesman, was educated at Oxford, served at the court of Queen Elizabeth I, was appointed Governor of Flushing, and received a fatal bullet wound at the Battle of Zutphen in the Netherlands, fighting against the Spanish. Of a generous and chivalric nature, Sidney is generally accounted the fullest English embodiment of the Renaissance ideal of the perfect gentleman. As an author he is most famous for *Astrophel and Stella*, a series of love sonnets; *Arcadia*, a pastoral romance in prose; and *The Defense of Poesy*. The last work, written probably between 1581 and 1584, partly as a reply to Stephen Gosson's *The Schoole of Abuse* (1579), circulated extensively in manuscript for several years. It was published in 1595 by two publishers under different titles: *An Apologie for Poetrie* and *The Defence of Poesie*. The following excerpts are from *The Defense of Poesy*, by Sir Philip Sidney, edited by Albert S. Cook (Boston, 1898). Professor Cook has modernized spelling and punctuation.]

And first, truly, to all them that, professing learning, inveigh against poetry, may justly be objected that they go very near to ungratefulness, to seek to deface that which, in the noblest nations and languages that are known, hath been the first light-giver to ignorance, and first nurse, whose milk by little and little enabled them to feed afterwards of tougher knowledges. And will they now play the hedgehog, that, being received into the den, drave out his host? Or rather the vipers, that with their birth kill their parents? Let learned Greece in any of her manifold sciences be able to show me one book before Musæus, Homer, and Hesiod, all three nothing else but poets. Nay, let any history be brought that can say any writers were there before them, if they were not men of the same skill, as Orpheus, Linus, and some other are named, who, having been the first of that country that made pens deliverers of their knowledge to their posterity, may justly challenge to be called their fathers /2/ in learning. For not only in time they had this priority—although in itself antiquity be venerable—but went before them as causes, to draw with their charming sweetness the wild untamed wits to an admiration of knowledge. So as Amphion was said to move stones with his poetry to build Thebes, and Orpheus to be listened to by beasts,—indeed stony and beastly people. So among the Romans were Livius Andronicus and Ennius; so in the Italian language the first that made it aspire to be a treasure-house of science were the poets Dante, Boccace, and Petrarch; so in our English were Gower and Chaucer, after whom, encouraged and delighted with their excellent foregoing, others have followed to beautify our mother-tongue, as well in the same kind as in other arts.

This did so notably show itself, that the philosophers of Greece durst not a long time appear to the world but under the masks of poets. So Thales, Empedocles, and Parmenides sang their natural philosophy in verses; so did Pythagoras and Phocylides their moral counsels; so did Tyrtæus in war matters, and Solon in matters of policy; or rather they, being poets, did exercise their delightful vein in those points of highest knowledge which before them lay hidden to the world. For that wise Solon was directly a poet it is manifest, having written in verse the notable fable of the Atlantic Island which was continued by Plato. And truly even Plato whosoever well considereth, shall find that in the body of his work though the inside and strength were philosophy, the skin as it were and beauty depended most of poetry. For all standeth upon dialogues; wherein he feigneth many honest burgesses of Athens to speak of such matters that, if they had been set on the rack, they would never have confessed them; besides his poetical describing the circumstances of their meetings, as the /3/ well-ordering of a banquet, the delicacy of a walk, with interlacing mere tales, as Gyges' Ring and others, which who knoweth not to be flowers of poetry did never walk into Apollo's garden.

And even historiographers, although their

lips sound of things done, and verity be written in their foreheads, have been glad to borrow both fashion and perchance weight of the poets. So Herodotus entitled his history by the name of the nine Muses; and both he and all the rest that followed him either stole or usurped of poetry their passionate describing of passions, the many particularities of battles which no man could affirm, or, if that be denied me, long orations put in the mouths of great kings and captains, which it is certain they never pronounced.

So that truly neither philosopher nor historiographer could at the first have entered into the gates of popular judgments, if they had not taken a great passport of poetry, which in all nations at this day, where learning flourisheth not, is plain to be seen; in all which they have some feeling of poetry. . . . /4/

But since the authors of most of our sciences were the Romans, and before them the Greeks, let us a little stand upon their authorities, but even so far as to see what names they have given unto this now scorned skill. Among the Romans a poet was called *vates*, which is as much as a diviner, foreseer, or prophet, as by his conjoined words, *vaticinium* and *vaticinari*, is manifest; so heavenly a title did that excellent people bestow upon this heart-ravishing knowledge. And so far were they carried into the admiration thereof, that they thought in the chanceable hitting upon any such verses great foretokens of their following fortunes were placed; whereupon grew the word of *Sortes Virgilianæ*, when by sudden opening Virgil's book they lighted upon some verse of his making. Whereof the Histories of the Emperors' Lives are full: as of Albinus, the governor of our island, who in his childhood met with this verse,

Arma amens capio, nec sat rationis in armis,
[To arms I rush in frenzy—not that good cause is shown in arms,]

and in his age performed it. Although it were a very vain and godless superstition, as also it was to think that spirits were commanded by such verses—whereupon this word charms, derived of *carmina* [verses], cometh—so yet serveth it to show the great reverence those wits were held in, and altogether not without

ground, since both the oracles of Delphos and Sibylla's prophecies were wholly delivered in verses; for that same exquisite observing of number and measure in words, and that high- /5/ flying liberty of conceit proper to the poet, did seem to have some divine force in it.

And may not I presume a little further to show the reasonableness of this word *vates*, and say that the holy David's Psalms are a divine poem? If I do, I shall not do it without the testimony of great learned men, both ancient and modern. But even the name of Psalms will speak for me, which, being interpreted, is nothing but Songs; then, that it is fully written in metre, as all learned Hebricians agree, although the rules be not yet fully found; lastly and principally, his handling his prophecy, which is merely poetical. For what else is the awaking his musical instruments, the often and free changing of persons, his notable prosopopœias, when he maketh you, as it were, see God coming in His majesty, his telling of the beasts' joyfulness and hills' leaping, but a heavenly poesy, wherein almost he showeth himself a passionate lover of that unspeakable and everlasting beauty to be seen by the eyes of the mind, only cleared by faith? But truly now having named him, I fear I seem to profane that holy name, applying it to poetry, which is among us thrown down to so ridiculous an estimation. But they that with quiet judgments will look a little deeper into it, shall find the end and working of it such as, being rightly applied, deserveth not to be scourged out of the church of God.

But now let us see how the Greeks named it and how they deemed of it. The Greeks called him ποιητήν, which name hath, as the most excellent, gone through other languages. It cometh of this word ποιεῖν, which is "to make"; wherein I know not whether by luck or wisdom we Englishmen have met with the Greeks in calling him a maker. Which name how high and incomparable a title it is, I had rather were known by marking the scope of other sciences than by any partial /6/ allegation. There is no art delivered unto mankind that hath not the works of nature for his principal object, without which they could not consist, and on which they so depend as they become actors and players, as it were, of what nature will have set forth. So doth the astronomer look upon the stars, and, by that he seeth, set down what order nature hath taken therein. So do the geometrician and arithmetician in their divers sorts of quantities. So doth the musician in times tell you which by nature agree, which not. The natural philosopher thereon hath his name, and the moral philosopher standeth upon the natural virtues, vices, and passions of man; and "follow nature," saith he, "therein, and thou shalt not err." The lawyer saith what men have determined, the historian what men have done. The grammarian speaketh only of the rules of speech, and the rhetorician and logician, considering what in nature will soonest prove and persuade, thereon give artificial rules, which still are compassed within the circle of a question, according to the proposed matter. The physician weigheth the nature of man's body, and the nature of things helpful or hurtful unto it. And the metaphysic, though it be in the second and abstract notions, and therefore be counted supernatural, yet doth he, indeed, build upon the depth of nature.

Only the poet, disdaining to be tied to any such subjection, lifted up with the vigor of his own invention, doth grow, in effect, into another nature, in making things either better than nature bringeth forth, or, quite anew, forms such as never were in nature, as the heroes, demi-gods, cyclops, chimeras, furies, and such like; so as he goeth hand in hand with nature, not enclosed within the narrow warrant of her gifts, but freely ranging within the zodiac of his own wit. Nature never set forth the earth in so rich tapestry as divers poets have /7/ done; neither with pleasant rivers, fruitful trees, sweet-smelling flowers, nor whatsoever else may make the too-much-loved earth more lovely; her world is brazen, the poets only deliver a golden.

But let those things alone, and go to man—for whom as the other things are, so it seemeth in him her uttermost cunning is employed—and know whether she have brought forth so true a lover as Theagenes; so constant a friend as Pylades; so valiant a man as Orlando; so right a prince as Xenophon's Cyrus; so excellent a man every way as Virgil's Æneas? Neither let this be jestingly conceived, because the works of the one be essential, the other in imitation or fiction; for any understanding knoweth the skill of each artificer standeth in that idea, or fore-conceit of the work, and not in the work itself. And that the poet hath that idea is manifest, by delivering them forth in such excellency as he hath imagined them. Which delivering forth, also, is not wholly imaginative, as we are wont to say by them that build castles in the air; but so far substantially it worketh, not only to make a Cyrus, which had been but a particular excellency, as nature might have done, but to bestow a Cyrus upon the world to make many Cyruses, if they will learn aright why and how that maker made him. Neither let it be deemed too saucy a comparison to balance the highest point of man's wit with the efficacy of nature; but rather give right honor to the Heavenly Maker of that maker, who, having made man to His own likeness, set him beyond and over all the works of that second nature. Which in nothing he showeth so much as in poetry, when with the force of a divine breath he bringeth things forth far surpassing her doings, with no small argument to the incredulous of that first accursed fall of Adam,—since our erected wit maketh us know what perfection is, and yet our infected will keepeth us from /8/ reaching unto it. But these arguments will by few be understood, and by fewer granted; thus much I hope will be given me, that the Greeks with some probability of reason gave him the name above all names of learning.

Now let us go to a more ordinary opening of him, that the truth may be the more palpable; and so, I hope, though we get not so unmatched a praise as the etymology of his names will grant, yet his very description, which no man will deny, shall not justly be barred from a principal commendation.

Poesy, therefore, is an art of imitation, for so Aristotle termeth it in his word μίμησις, that is to say, a representing, counterfeiting, or figuring forth; to speak metaphorically, a speaking picture, with this end,—to teach and delight.

Of this have been three general kinds. The chief, both in antiquity and excellency, were they that did imitate the inconceivable excellencies of God. Such were David in his Psalms; Solomon in his Song of Songs, in his Ecclesiastes and Proverbs; Moses and Deborah in their Hymns; and the writer of Job; which, beside other, the learned Emanuel Tremellius and Franciscus Junius do entitle the poetical part of the Scripture. Against these none will speak that hath the Holy Ghost in due holy reverence. In this kind, though in a full wrong divinity, were Orpheus, Amphion, Homer in his Hymns, and many other, both Greeks and Romans. And this poesy must be used by whosoever will follow St. James' counsel in singing psalms when they are merry; and I know is used with the fruit of comfort by some, when, in sorrowful pangs of their death-bringing sins, they find the consolation of the never-leaving goodness.

The second kind is of them that deal with matters philosophical: either moral, as Tyrtæus, Phocylides, and /9/ Cato; or natural, as Lucretius and Virgil's Georgics; or astronomical, as Manilius and Pontanus; or historical, as Lucan; which who mislike, the fault is in their judgment quite out of taste, and not in the sweet food of sweetly uttered knowledge.

But because this second sort is wrapped within the fold of the proposed subject, and takes not the free course of his own invention, whether they properly be poets or no let grammarians dispute, and go to the third, indeed right poets, of whom chiefly this question ariseth. Betwixt whom and these second is such a kind of difference as betwixt the meaner sort of painters, who counterfeit only such faces as are set before them, and the more excellent, who having no law but wit, bestow that in colors upon you which is fittest for the eye to see,—as the constant though lamenting look of Lucretia, when she punished in herself another's fault; wherein he painteth not Lucretia, whom he never saw, but painteth the outward beauty of such a virtue. For these third be they which most properly do imitate to teach and delight; and to imitate borrow nothing of what is, hath been, or shall be; but range, only reined with learned discretion, into the divine consideration of what may be and should be. These be they that, as the first and most noble sort, may justly be termed *vates;* so these are waited on in the excellentest languages and best understand-ings with the foredescribed name of poets. For these, indeed, do merely make to imitate, and imitate both to delight and teach, and delight to move men to take that goodness in hand, which without delight they would fly as from a stranger; and teach to make them know that goodness whereunto they are moved:—which being the noblest scope to which ever any learning was directed, yet want there not idle tongues to bark at them. /10/

These be subdivided into sundry more special denominations. The most notable be the heroic, lyric, tragic, comic, satiric, iambic, elegiac, pastoral, and certain others, some of these being termed according to the matter they deal with, some by the sort of verse they liked best to write in,—for indeed the greatest part of poets have apparelled their poetical inventions in that numberous kind of writing which is called verse. Indeed but apparelled, verse being but an ornament and no cause to poetry, since there have been many most excellent poets that never versified, and now swarm many versifiers that need never answer to the name of poets. For Xenophon, who did imitate so excellently as to give us *effigiem justi imperii*—the portraiture of a just empire under the name of Cyrus (as Cicero saith of him)—made therein an absolute heroical poem; so did Heliodorus in his sugared invention of that picture of love in Theagenes and Chariclea; and yet both these wrote in prose. Which I speak to show that it is not riming and versing that maketh a poet—no more than a long gown maketh an advocate, who, though he pleaded in armor, should be an advocate and no soldier—but it is that feigning notable images of virtues, vices, or what else, with that delightful teaching, which must be the right describing note to know a poet by. Although indeed the senate of poets hath chosen verse as their fittest raiment, meaning, as in matter they passed all in all, so in manner to go beyond them; not speaking, table-talk fashion, or like men in a dream, words as they chanceably fall from the mouth, but peizing [weighing] each syllable of each word by just proportion, according to the dignity of the subject.

Now therefore it shall not be amiss, first to weigh this latter sort of poetry by his works, and then by his parts; and if in neither of these anatomies he be condemnable, I hope we shall obtain a more favorable sen- /11/ tence. This purifying of wit, this enriching of memory, enabling of judgment, and enlarging of conceit, which commonly we call learning, under what name soever it come forth or to what immediate end soever it be directed, the final end is to lead and draw us to as high a perfection as our degenerate souls, made worse by their clay lodgings, can be capable of. This, according to the inclination of man, bred many-formed impressions. For some that thought this felicity principally to be gotten by knowledge, and no knowledge to be so high or heavenly as acquaintance with the stars, gave themselves to astronomy; others, persuading themselves to be demi-gods if they knew the causes of things, became natural and supernatural philosophers. Some an admirable delight drew to music, and some the certainty of demonstration to the mathematics; but all, one and other, having this scope:—to know, and by knowledge to lift up the mind from the dungeon of the body to the enjoying his own divine essence. But when by the balance of experience it was found that the astronomer, looking to the stars, might fall into a ditch, that the inquiring philosopher might be blind in himself, and the mathematician might draw forth a straight line with a crooked heart; then lo! did proof, the over-ruler of opinions, make manifest, that all these are but serving sciences, which, as they have each a private end in themselves, so yet are they all directed to the highest end of the mistress-knowledge, by the Greeks called ἀρχιτεκτονική, which stands, as I think, in the knowledge of a man's self, in the ethic and politic consideration, with the end of well-doing, and not of well-knowing only:—even as the saddler's next end is to make a good saddle, but his further end to serve a nobler faculty, which is horsemanship; so the horseman's to soldiery; and the soldier not only to have the skill, but to perform the /12/ practice of a soldier. So that the ending end of all earthly learning being virtuous action, those skills that most serve to bring forth that have a most just title to be princes over all the rest; wherein, if we can show, the poet is worthy to have it before any other competitors.

Among whom as principal challengers step forth the moral philosophers; whom, me thinketh, I see coming toward me with a sullen gravity, as though they could not abide vice by daylight; rudely clothed, for to witness outwardly their contempt of outward things; with books in their hands against glory, whereto they set their names; sophistically speaking against subtility; and angry with any man in whom they see the foul fault of anger. These men, casting largess as they go of definitions, divisions, and distinctions, with a scornful interrogative do soberly ask whether it be possible to find any path so ready to lead a man to virtue, as that which teacheth what virtue is, and teacheth it not only by delivering forth his very being, his causes and effects, but also by making known his enemy, vice, which must be destroyed, and his cumbersome servant, passion, which must be mastered; by showing the generalities that contain it, and the specialities that are derived from it; lastly, by plain setting down how it extendeth itself out of the limits of a man's own little world, to the government of families, and maintaining of public societies?

The historian scarcely giveth leisure to the moralist to say so much, but that he, loaden with old mouse-eaten records, authorizing himself for the most part upon other histories, whose greatest authorities are built upon the notable foundation of hearsay; having much ado to accord differing writers, and to pick truth out of partiality; better acquainted with a thousand years ago than with the present age, and yet better knowing how this world goeth than how his own wit runneth; curious for /13/ antiquities and inquisitive of novelties, a wonder to young folks and a tyrant in table-talk; denieth, in a great chafe, that any man for teaching of virtue and virtuous actions is comparable to him. "I am *testis temporum, lux veritatis, vita memoriæ, magistra vitæ, nuntia vetustatis* [the evidence of time, the light of truth, the life of memory, the directress of life, the herald of antiquity]. The philosopher," saith he, "teacheth a disputative virtue, but I do an active. His virtue is excellent in the dangerless Academy of Plato, but mine showeth forth her honorable face in the battles of Marathon, Pharsalia, Poitiers, and Agincourt. He teacheth virtue by certain abstract considerations, but I only bid you follow the footing of them that have gone before you. Old-aged experience goeth beyond the fine-witted philosopher; but I give the experience of many ages. Lastly, if he make the song-book, I put the learner's hand to the lute; and if he be the guide, I am the light." Then would he allege you innumerable examples, confirming story by story, how much the wisest senators and princes have been directed by the credit of history, as Brutus, Alphonsus of Aragon—and who not, if need be? At length the long line of their disputation maketh a point in this,—that the one giveth the precept, and the other the example.

Now whom shall we find, since the question standeth for the highest form in the school of learning, to be moderator? Truly, as me seemeth, the poet; and if not a moderator, even the man that ought to carry the title from them both, and much more from all other serving sciences. Therefore compare we the poet with the historian and with the moral philosopher; and if he go beyond them both, no other human skill can match him. For as for the divine, with all reverence it is ever to be excepted, not only for having his scope as far beyond any of these as eternity exceedeth a moment, but even for passing each of these in themselves. And /14/ for the lawyer, though *Jus* [Law] be the daughter of Justice, and Justice the chief of virtues, yet because he seeketh to make men good rather *formidine pœnæ* [from fear of punishment] than *virtutis amore* [from love of virtue]; or, to say righter, doth not endeavor to make men good, but that their evil hurt not others; having no care, so he be a good citizen, how bad a man he be; therefore, as our wickedness maketh him necessary, and necessity maketh him honorable, so is he not in the deepest truth to stand in rank with these, who all endeavor to take naughtiness away, and plant goodness even in the secretest cabinet of our souls. And these four are all that any way deal in that consideration of men's manners, which being the supreme knowledge, they that best breed it deserve the best commendation.

The philosopher therefore and the historian are they which would win the goal, the one by precept, the other by example; but both not having both, do both halt. For the philosopher, setting down with thorny arguments the bare rule, is so hard of utterance and so misty to be conceived, that one that hath no other guide but him shall wade in him till he be old, before he shall find sufficient cause to be honest. For his knowledge standeth so upon the abstract and general that happy is that man who may understand him, and more happy that can apply what he doth understand. On the other side, the historian, wanting the precept, is so tied, not to what should be but to what is, to the particular truth of things and not to the general reason of things, that his example draweth no necessary consequence, and therefore a less fruitful doctrine.

Now doth the peerless poet perform both; for whatsoever the philosopher saith should be done, he giveth a perfect picture of it in some one by whom he presupposeth it was done, so as he coupleth the general notion with the particular example. A perfect picture, I say; /15/ for he yieldeth to the powers of the mind an image of that whereof the philosopher bestoweth but a wordish description, which doth neither strike, pierce, nor possess the sight of the soul so much as that other doth. For as, in outward things, to a man that had never seen an elephant or a rhinoceros, who should tell him most exquisitely all their shapes, color, bigness, and particular marks; or of a gorgeous palace, an architector, with declaring the full beauties, might well make the hearer able to repeat, as it were by rote, all he had heard, yet should never satisfy his inward conceit with being witness to itself of a true lively knowledge; but the same man, as soon as he might see those beasts well painted, or that house well in model, should straightways grow, without need of any description, to a judicial comprehending of them: so no doubt the philosopher, with his learned definitions, be it of virtues or vices, matters of public policy or private government, replenisheth the memory with many infallible grounds of wisdom, which notwithstanding lie dark before the imaginative and judging power, if they be not illuminated or figured forth by the speaking picture of poesy.

Tully taketh much pains, and many times not without poetical helps, to make us know the force love of our country hath in us. Let us but hear old Anchises speaking in the midst of Troy's flames, or see Ulysses, in the fulness of all Calypso's delights, bewail his absence from barren and beggarly Ithaca. Anger, the Stoics said, was a short madness. Let but Sophocles bring you Ajax on a stage, killing and whipping sheep and oxen, thinking them the army of Greeks, with their chieftains Agamemnon and Menelaus, and tell me if you have not a more familiar insight into anger, than finding in the schoolmen his genus and difference. See whether wisdom and temperance in Ulysses and Diomedes, valor in Achilles, /16/ friendship in Nisus and Euryalus, even to an ignorant man carry not an apparent shining. And, contrarily, the remorse of conscience in Œdipus; the soon-repenting pride of Agamemnon; the self-devouring cruelty in his father Atreus; the violence of ambition in the two Theban brothers; the sour sweetness of revenge in Medea; and, to fall lower, the Terentian Gnatho and our Chaucer's Pandar so expressed that we now use their names to signify their trades; and finally, all virtues, vices, and passions so in their own natural states laid to the view, that we seem not to hear of them, but clearly to see through them.

But even in the most excellent determination of goodness, what philosopher's counsel can so readily direct a prince, as the feigned Cyrus in Xenophon? Or a virtuous man in all fortunes, as Æneas in Virgil? Or a whole commonwealth, as the way of Sir Thomas More's Utopia? I say the way, because where Sir Thomas More erred, it was the fault of the man, and not of the poet; for that way of patterning a commonwealth was most absolute, though he, perchance, hath not so absolutely performed it. For the question is, whether the feigned image of poesy, or the regular instruction of philosophy, hath the more force in teaching. Wherein if the philosophers have more rightly showed themselves philosophers than the poets have attained to the high top of their profession,—as in truth,

> Mediocribus esse poetis
Non Dii, non homines, non concessere columnæ,—
[Mediocrity in poets is condemned by gods and men, aye, and booksellers too,—]

it is, I say again, not the fault of the art, but that by few men that art can be accomplished.

Certainly, even our Saviour Christ could as well have given the moral commonplaces of uncharitableness and humbleness as the divine narration of Dives and Laz- /17/ arus; or of disobedience and mercy, as that heavenly discourse of the lost child and the gracious father; but that his through-searching wisdom knew the estate of Dives burning in hell, and of Lazarus in Abraham's bosom, would more constantly, as it were, inhabit both the memory and judgment. Truly, for myself, me seems I see before mine eyes the lost child's disdainful prodigality, turned to envy a swine's dinner; which by the learned divines are thought not historical acts, but instructing parables.

For conclusion, I say the philosopher teacheth, but he teacheth obscurely, so as the learned only can understand him; that is to say, he teacheth them that are already taught. But the poet is the food for the tenderest stomachs; the poet is indeed the right popular philosopher. Whereof Æsop's tales give good proof; whose pretty allegories, stealing under the formal tales of beasts, make many, more beastly than beasts, begin to hear the sound of virtue from those dumb speakers.

But now may it be alleged that if this imagining of matters be so fit for the imagination, then must the historian needs surpass, who bringeth you images of true matters, such as indeed were done, and not such as fantastically or falsely may be suggested to have been done. Truly, Aristotle himself, in his Discourse of Poesy, plainly determineth this question, saying that poetry is φιλοσοφώτερον and σπουδαιότερον, that is to say, it is more philosophical and more studiously serious than history. His reason is, because poesy dealeth with καθόλου, that is to say with the universal consideration, and the history with καθ᾽ ἕκαστον, the particular. "Now," saith he, "the universal weighs what is fit to be said or done, either in likelihood or necessity—which the poesy considereth in his imposed names; and the particular only marketh whether Alcibiades did, or suffered, this or that;" thus /18/ far Aristotle. Which reason of his, as all his, is most full of reason.

For, indeed, if the question were whether it were better to have a particular act truly or falsely set down, there is no doubt which is to be chosen, no more than whether you had rather have Vespasian's picture right as he was, or, at the painter's pleasure, nothing resembling. But if the question be for your own use and learning, whether it be better to have it set down as it should be or as it was, then certainly is more doctrinable the feigned Cyrus in Xenophon than the true Cyrus in Justin; and the feigned Æneas in Virgil than the right Æneas in Dares Phrygius; as to a lady that desired to fashion her countenance to the best grace, a painter should more benefit her to portrait a most sweet face, writing Canidia upon it, than to paint Canidia as she was, who, Horace sweareth, was foul and ill-favored.

If the poet do his part aright, he will show you in Tantalus, Atreus, and such like, nothing that is not to be shunned; in Cyrus, Æneas, Ulysses, each thing to be followed. Where the historian, bound to tell things as things were, cannot be liberal—without he will be poetical—of a perfect pattern; but, as in Alexander, or Scipio himself, show doings, some to be liked, some to be misliked; and then how will you discern what to follow but by your own discretion, which you had without reading Quintus Curtius? And whereas a man may say, though in universal consideration of doctrine the poet prevaileth, yet that the history, in his saying such a thing was done, doth warrant a man more in that he shall follow,—the answer is manifest: that if he stand upon that *was*, as if he should argue, because it rained yesterday therefore it should rain to-day, then indeed it hath some advantage to a gross conceit. But if he know an example only informs a conjectured likelihood, and /19/ so go by reason, the poet doth so far exceed him as he is to frame his example to that which is most reasonable, be it in warlike, politic, or private matters; where the historian in his bare *was* hath many times that which we call fortune to overrule the best wisdom. Many times he must tell events whereof he can yield no cause; or if he do, it must be poetically.

For, that a feigned example hath as much force to teach as a true example—for as for to move, it is clear, since the feigned may be tuned to the highest key of passion—let us take one example wherein a poet and a historian do concur. Herodotus and Justin do both testify that Zopyrus, king Darius' faithful servant, seeing his master long resisted by the rebellious Babylonians, feigned himself in extreme disgrace of his king; for verifying of which he caused his own nose and ears to be cut off, and so flying to the Babylonians, was received, and for his known valor so far credited, that he did find means to deliver them over to Darius. Much-like matter doth Livy record of Tarquinius and his son. Xenophon excellently feigneth such another stratagem, performed by Abradatas in Cyrus' behalf. Now would I fain know, if occasion be presented unto you to serve your prince by such an honest dissimulation, why do you not as well learn it of Xenophon's fiction as of the other's verity? and, truly, so much the better, as you shall save your nose by the bargain; for Abradatas did not counterfeit so far.

So, then, the best of the historian is subject to the poet; for whatsoever action or faction, whatsoever counsel, policy, or war-stratagem the historian is bound to recite, that may the poet, if he list, with his imitation make his own, beautifying it both for further teaching and more delighting, as it pleaseth him; having all, from Dante's Heaven to his Hell, under the authority of his pen. /20/ Which if I be asked what poets have done? so as I might well name some, yet say I, and say again, I speak of the art, and not of the artificer.

Now, to that which commonly is attributed to the praise of history, in respect of the notable learning is gotten by marking the success, as though therein a man should see virtue exalted and vice punished,—truly that commendation is peculiar to poetry and far off from history. For, indeed, poetry ever setteth virtue so out in her best colors, making Fortune her well-waiting handmaid, that one must needs be enamored of her. Well may you see Ulysses in a storm, and in other hard plights; but they are but exercises of patience and magnanimity, to make them shine the more in the near following prosperity. And, of the contrary part, if evil men come to the stage, they ever go out—as the tragedy writer answered to one that misliked the show of such persons—so manacled as they little animate folks to follow them. But the historian, being captived to the truth of a foolish world, is many times a terror from well-doing, and an encouragement to unbridled wickedness. For see we not valiant Miltiades rot in his fetters? The just Phocion and the accomplished Socrates put to death like traitors? The cruel Severus live prosperously? The excellent Severus miserably murdered? Sylla and Marius dying in their beds? Pompey and Cicero slain then, when they would have thought exile a happiness? See we not virtuous Cato driven to kill himself, and rebel Cæsar so advanced that his name yet, after sixteen hundred years, lasteth in the highest honor? And mark but even Cæsar's own words of the forenamed Sylla—who in that only did honestly, to put down his dishonest tyranny—*literas nescivit* [he was without learning]: as if want of learning caused him to do well. He meant it not by poetry, which, not content with earthly plagues, deviseth new punishments /21/ in hell for tyrants; nor yet by philosophy, which teacheth *occidendos esse* [that they are to be slain]; but, no doubt, by skill in history, for that indeed can afford you Cypselus, Periander, Phalaris, Dionysius, and I know not how many more of the same kennel, that speed well enough in their abominable injustice or usurpation.

I conclude, therefore, that he excelleth history, not only in furnishing the mind with knowledge, but in setting it forward to that which deserveth to be called and accounted good; which setting forward, and moving to well-doing, indeed setteth the laurel crown upon the poet as victorious, not only of the historian, but over the philosopher, howsoever in teaching it may be questionable. For suppose it be granted—that which I suppose with great reason may be denied—that the philosopher, in respect of his methodical proceeding, teach more perfectly than the poet, yet do I think that no man is so much φιλοφιλόσοφος [a friend to the philosopher] as to compare the philosopher in moving with the poet. And that moving is of a higher degree than teaching, it may by this appear, that it is well nigh both the cause and the effect of teaching; for who will be taught, if he be not moved with desire to be taught? And what so much good doth that teaching bring forth—I speak still of moral doctrine—as that it moveth one to do that which it doth teach? For,

as Aristotle saith, it is not γνῶσις [knowledge] but πρᾶξις [practice] must be the fruit; and how πρᾶξις cannot be, without being moved to practise, it is no hard matter to consider. The philosopher showeth you the way, he informeth you of the particularities, as well of the tediousness of the way, as of the pleasant lodging you shall have when your journey is ended, as of the many by-turnings that may divert you from your way; but this is to no man but to him that will read him, and read him with attentive, studious painfulness; which constant desire whosoever hath in him, /22/ hath already passed half the hardness of the way, and therefore is beholding to the philosopher but for the other half. Nay, truly, learned men have learnedly thought, that where once reason hath so much overmastered passion as that the mind hath a free desire to do well, the inward light each mind hath in itself is as good as a philosopher's book; since in nature we know it is well to do well, and what is well and what is evil, although not in the words of art which philosophers bestow upon us; for out of natural conceit the philosophers drew it. But to be moved to do that which we know, or to be moved with desire to know, *hoc opus, hic labor est* [this is the task, this the struggle].

Now therein of all sciences—I speak still of human, and according to the human conceit—is our poet the monarch. For he doth not only show the way, but giveth so sweet a prospect into the way as will entice any man to enter into it. Nay, he doth, as if your journey should lie through a fair vineyard, at the very first give you a cluster of grapes, that full of that taste you may long to pass further. He beginneth not with obscure definitions, which must blur the margent with interpretations, and load the memory with doubtfulness. But he cometh to you with words set in delightful proportion, either accompanied with, or prepared for, the well-enchanting skill of music; and with a tale, forsooth, he cometh unto you, with a tale which holdeth children from play, and old men from the chimney-corner, and, pretending no more, doth intend the winning of the mind from wickedness to virtue; even as the child is often brought to take most wholesome things, by hiding them in such other as have a pleasant taste,—which, if one should begin to tell them the nature of the aloes or rhubarb they should receive, would sooner take their physic at their ears than at their mouth. So is it in men, most of which are childish in the best things, till they /23/ be cradled in their graves,—glad they will be to hear the tales of Hercules, Achilles, Cyrus, Æneas; and, hearing them, must needs hear the right description of wisdom, valor, and justice; which, if they had been barely, that is to say philosophically, set out, they would swear they be brought to school again. . . . /24/

[Sidney now turns to a consideration of the objections that have been brought against poetry by its detractors.]

But that which giveth greatest scope to their scorning humor is riming and versing. It is already said, and as I think truly said, it is not riming and versing that maketh poesy. One may be a poet without versing, and a versifier without poetry. But yet presuppose it were inseparable—as indeed it seemeth Scaliger judgeth—truly it were an inseparable commendation. For if *oratio* next to *ratio,* speech next to reason, be the greatest gift bestowed upon mortality, that cannot be praiseless which doth most polish that blessing of speech; which considereth each word, not only as a man may say by his forcible quality, but by his best-measured quantity; carrying even in themselves a harmony,—without, perchance, number, measure, order, proportion be in our time grown odious.

But lay aside the just praise it hath by being the only fit speech for music—music, I say, the most divine striker of the senses—thus much is undoubtedly true, that if reading be foolish without remembering, memory being the only treasurer of knowledge, those words which are fittest for memory are likewise most convenient for knowledge. Now that verse far exceedeth prose in the knitting up of the memory, the reason is manifest; the words, besides their delight, which hath a great affinity to memory, being so set, as one cannot be lost but the whole work fails; which, accusing itself, calleth the /33/ remembrance back to itself, and so most strongly confirmeth it. Besides, one word so, as it were, begetting another, as, be it in rime or measured verse, by the former a man shall have a near guess to

the follower. Lastly, even they that have taught the art of memory have showed nothing so apt for it as a certain room divided into many places, well and throughly known; now that hath the verse in effect perfectly, every word having his natural seat, which seat must needs make the word remembered. But what needeth more in a thing so known to all men? Who is it that ever was a scholar that doth not carry away some verses of Virgil, Horace, or Cato, which in his youth he learned, and even to his old age serve him for hourly lessons? as:

Percontatorem fugito, nam garrulus idem est.
[Avoid a curious man; he is sure to be a gossip.]

Dum sibi quisque placet, credula turba sumus.
[While each one is satisfying himself, we are ever a credulous set.]

But the fitness it hath for memory is notably proved by all delivery of arts, wherein, for the most part, from grammar to logic, mathematic, physic, and the rest, the rules chiefly necessary to be borne away are compiled in verses. So that verse being in itself sweet and orderly, and being best for memory, the only handle of knowledge, it must be in jest that any man can speak against it.

Now then go we to the most important imputations laid to the poor poets; for aught I can yet learn they are these.

First, that there being many other more fruitful knowledges, a man might better spend his time in them than in this.

Secondly, that it is the mother of lies.

Thirdly, that it is the nurse of abuse, infecting us with many pestilent desires, with a siren's sweetness drawing the mind to the serpent's tail of sinful fancies,—and herein especially comedies give the largest field to ear, /34/ as Chaucer saith; how, both in other nations and in ours, before poets did soften us, we were full of courage, given to martial exercises, the pillars of manlike liberty, and not lulled asleep in shady idleness with poets' pastimes.

And, lastly and chiefly, they cry out with an open mouth, as if they had overshot Robin Hood, that Plato banished them out of his Commonwealth. Truly this is much, if there be much truth in it.

First, to the first, that a man might better

spend his time is a reason indeed; but it doth, as they say, but *petere principium* [beg the question]. For if it be, as I affirm, that no learning is so good as that which teacheth and moveth to virtue, and that none can both teach and move thereto so much as poesy, then is the conclusion manifest that ink and paper cannot be to a more profitable purpose employed. And certainly, though a man should grant their first assumption, it should follow, me thinks, very unwillingly, that good is not good because better is better. But I still and utterly deny that there is sprung out of earth a more fruitful knowledge.

To the second, therefore, that they should be the principal liars, I answer paradoxically, but truly, I think truly, that of all writers under the sun the poet is the least liar; and though he would, as a poet can scarcely be a liar. The astronomer, with his cousin the geometrician, can hardly escape when they take upon them to measure the height of the stars. How often, think you, do the physicians lie, when they aver things good for sicknesses, which afterwards send Charon a great number of souls drowned in a potion before they come to his ferry? And no less of the rest which take upon them to affirm. Now for the poet, he nothing affirmeth, and therefore never lieth. For, as I take it, to lie is to affirm that to be true which is false; so as the other artists, and especially the historian, affirming many things, can, in /35/ the cloudy knowledge of mankind, hardly escape from many lies. But the poet, as I said before, never affirmeth. The poet never maketh any circles about your imagination, to conjure you to believe for true what he writeth. He citeth not authorities of other histories, but even for his entry calleth the sweet Muses to inspire into him a good invention; in troth, not laboring to tell you what is or is not, but what should or should not be. And therefore though he recount things not true, yet because he telleth them not for true he lieth not; without we will say that Nathan lied in his speech, before alleged, to David; which, as a wicked man durst scarce say, so think I none so simple would say that Æsop lied in the tales of his beasts; for who thinketh that Æsop wrote it for actually true, were well worthy to have his name chronicled among the beasts he writeth

of. What child is there that, coming to a play, and seeing Thebes written in great letters upon an old door, doth believe that it is Thebes? If then a man can arrive at that child's-age, to know that the poet's persons and doings are but pictures what should be, and not stories what have been, they will never give the lie to things not affirmatively but allegorically and figuratively written. And therefore, as in history looking for truth, they may go away full-fraught with falsehood, so in poesy looking but for fiction, they shall use the narration but as an imaginative ground-plot of a profitable invention. But hereto is replied that the poets give names to men they write of, which argueth a conceit of an actual truth, and so, not being true, proveth a falsehood. And doth the lawyer lie then, when, under the names of John of the Stile, and John of the Nokes, he putteth his case? But that is easily answered: their naming of men is but to make their picture the more lively, and not to build any history. Painting men, they cannot leave men nameless. We see /36/ we cannot play at chess but that we must give names to our chess-men; and yet, me thinks, he were a very partial champion of truth that would say we lied for giving a piece of wood the reverend title of a bishop. The poet nameth Cyrus and Æneas no other way than to show what men of their fames, fortunes, and estates should do.

Their third is, how much it abuseth men's wit, training it to wanton sinfulness and lustful love. For indeed that is the principal, if not the only, abuse I can hear alleged. They say the comedies rather teach than reprehend amorous conceits. They say the lyric is larded with passionate sonnets, the elegiac weeps the want of his mistress, and that even to the heroical Cupid hath ambitiously climbed. Alas! Love, I would thou couldst as well defend thyself as thou canst offend others! I would those on whom thou dost attend could either put thee away, or yield good reason why they keep thee! But grant love of beauty to be a beastly fault, although it be very hard, since only man, and no beast, hath that gift to discern beauty; grant that lovely name of Love to deserve all hateful reproaches, although even some of my masters the philosophers spent a good deal of their lamp-oil in setting forth the excellency of it; grant, I say, whatsoever they will have granted,—that not only love, but lust, but vanity, but, if they list, scurrility, possesseth many leaves of the poets' books; yet think I when this is granted, they will find their sentence may with good manners put the last words foremost, and not say that poetry abuseth man's wit, but that man's wit abuseth poetry. For I will not deny, but that man's wit may make poesy, which should be ἐ'καστική, which some learned have defined, figuring forth good things, to be φανταστική, which doth contrariwise infect the fancy with unworthy objects; as the painter that should give to /37/ the eye either some excellent perspective, or some fine picture fit for building or fortification, or containing in it some notable example, as Abraham sacrificing his son Isaac, Judith killing Holofernes, David fighting with Goliath, may leave those, and please an ill-pleased eye with wanton shows of better-hidden matters. But what! shall the abuse of a thing make the right use odious? Nay, truly, though I yield that poesy may not only be abused, but that being abused, by the reason of his sweet charming force, it can do more hurt than any other army of words, yet shall it be so far from concluding that the abuse should give reproach to the abused, that contrariwise it is a good reason, that whatsoever, being abused, doth most harm, being rightly used—and upon the right use each thing receiveth his title—doth most good. Do we not see the skill of physic, the best rampire to our often-assaulted bodies, being abused, teach poison, the most violent destroyer? Doth not knowledge of law, whose end is to even and right all things, being abused, grow the crooked fosterer of horrible injuries? Doth not, to go in the highest, God's word abused breed heresy, and his name abused become blasphemy? Truly a needle cannot do much hurt, and as truly—with leave of ladies be it spoken—it cannot do much good. With a sword thou mayst kill thy father, and with a sword thou mayst defend thy prince and country. So that, as in their calling poets the fathers of lies they say nothing, so in this their argument of abuse they prove the commendation. . . . /38/

ALEXANDER POPE

An Essay on Criticism, Part I

[Alexander Pope (1688–1744), the chief poet of the eighteenth century in England, was born in London and lived all his life not far from that great city. A Roman Catholic, he was privately educated, and very early began writing verse. His chief works, *An Essay on Criticism, The Rape of the Lock, An Essay on Man,* and *The Dunciad,* are didactic or satirical; he is also famous for his verse translations of the *Iliad* and *Odyssey.* The good friend of Jonathan Swift and John Gay, Pope dominated the literary world of his time. *An Essay on Criticism,* written in 1709 and first published in 1711, is in a tradition of verse essays on poetry that began with Horace's *Ars Poetica* (first century B.C.). Though Pope addresses himself to would-be critics rather than poets, he is concerned with the art of poetry as well as the art of judgment. The selection below is the first of three parts, and is reprinted from *The Complete Poetical Works of Alexander Pope* (Boston and New York, 1903), pp. 67–69. Since it is customary to refer to poems such as this by part and line number (e.g., *Essay on Criticism,* I, 9–10), pagination has been omitted.]

'T is hard to say if greater want of skill
Appear in writing or in judging ill;
But of the two less dangerous is th' offence
To tire our patience than mislead our sense:
Some few in that, but numbers err in this;
Ten censure wrong for one who writes amiss;
A fool might once himself alone expose;
Now one in verse makes many more in prose.
  'Tis with our judgments as our watches, none
Go just alike, yet each believes his own.   10
In Poets as true Genius is but rare,
True Taste as seldom is the Critic's share;
Both must alike from Heav'n derive their light,
These born to judge, as well as those to write.
Let such teach others who themselves excel,
And censure freely who have written well;
Authors are partial to their wit, 't is true,
But are not Critics to their judgment too?
  Yet if we look more closely, we shall find
Most have the seeds of judgment in their mind: 20

Nature affords at least a glimm'ring light;
The lines, tho' touch'd but faintly, are drawn right:
But as the slightest sketch, if justly traced,
Is by ill col'ring but the more disgraced,
So by false learning is good sense defaced:
Some are bewilder'd in the maze of schools,
And some made coxcombs Nature meant but fools:
In search of wit these lose their common sense,
And then turn Critics in their own defence:
Each burns alike, who can or cannot write,
Or with a rival's or an eunuch's spite.   31
All fools have still an itching to deride,
And fain would be upon the laughing side.
If Mævius scribble in Apollo's spite,
There are who judge still worse than he can write.
  Some have at first for Wits, then Poets pass'd;
Turn'd Critics next, and prov'd plain Fools at last.
Some neither can for Wits nor Critics pass,
As heavy mules are neither horse nor ass.
Those half-learn'd witlings, numerous in our isle,   40
As half-form'd insects on the banks of Nile;
Unfinish'd things, one knows not what to call,
Their generation's so equivocal;
To tell them would a hundred tongues require,
Or one vain Wit's, that might a hundred tire.
  But you who seek to give and merit fame,
And justly bear a Critic's noble name,
Be sure yourself and your own reach to know,
How far your Genius, Taste, and Learning go,
Launch not beyond your depth, but be discreet,   50
And mark that point where Sense and Dulness meet.
  Nature to all things fix'd the limits fit,
And wisely curb'd proud man's pretending wit.
As on the land while here the ocean gains,

In other parts it leaves wide sandy plains;
Thus in the soul while Memory prevails,
The solid power of Understanding fails;
Where beams of warm Imagination play,
The Memory's soft figures melt away.
One Science only will one genius fit;   60
So vast is Art, so narrow human wit:
Not only bounded to peculiar arts,
But oft in those confin'd to single parts.
Like Kings we lose the conquests gain'd before,
By vain ambition still to make them more:
Each might his sev'ral province well command,
Would all but stoop to what they understand.
   First follow Nature, and your judgment frame
By her just standard, which is still the same;
Unerring Nature, still divinely bright,   70
One clear, unchanged, and universal light,
Life, force, and beauty must to all impart,
At once the source, and end, and test of Art.
Art from that fund each just supply provides,
Works without show, and without pomp presides.
In some fair body thus th' informing soul
With spirits feeds, with vigour fills the whole;
Each motion guides, and every nerve sustains,
Itself unseen, but in th' effects remains.
Some, to whom Heav'n in wit has been profuse,   80
Want as much more to turn it to its use;
For Wit and Judgment often are at strife,
Tho' meant each other's aid, like man and wife.
'T is more to guide than spur the Muse's steed,
Restrain his fury than provoke his speed:
The winged courser, like a gen'rous horse,
Shows most true mettle when you check his course.
   Those rules of old, discover'd, not devised,
Are Nature still, but Nature methodized;
Nature, like Liberty, is but restrain'd   90
By the same laws which first herself ordain'd.
   Hear how learn'd Greece her useful rules indites
When to repress and when indulge our flights:
High on Parnassus' top her sons she show'd,
And pointed out those arduous paths they trod;

Held from afar, aloft, th' immortal prize,
And urged the rest by equal steps to rise.
Just precepts thus from great examples giv'n,
She drew from them what they derived from Heav'n.
The gen'rous Critic fann'd the poet's fire,
And taught the world with reason to admire.   101
Then Criticism the Muse's handmaid prov'd,
To dress her charms, and make her more belov'd:
But following Wits from that intention stray'd:
Who could not win the mistress woo'd the maid;
Against the Poets their own arms they turn'd,
Sure to hate most the men from whom they learn'd.
So modern 'pothecaries, taught the art
By doctors' bills to play the doctor's part,
Bold in the practice of mistaken rules,   110
Prescribe, apply, and call their masters fools.
Some on the leaves of ancient authors prey;
Nor time nor moths e'er spoil'd so much as they;
Some drily plain, without invention's aid,
Write dull receipts how poems may be made;
These leave the sense their learning to display,
And those explain the meaning quite away.
   You then whose judgment the right course would steer,
Know well each ancient's proper character;
His fable, subject, scope in every page;   120
Religion, country, genius of his age:
Without all these at once before your eyes,
Cavil you may, but never criticise.
Be Homer's works your study and delight,
Read them by day, and meditate by night;
Thence form your judgment, thence your maxims bring,
And trace the Muses upward to their spring.
Still with itself compared, his text peruse;
And let your comment be the Mantuan Muse.
   When first young Maro in his boundless mind   130
A work t' outlast immortal Rome design'd,
Perhaps he seem'd above the critic's law,
And but from Nature's fountains scorn'd to draw;
But when t' examine ev'ry part he came,

Nature and Homer were, he found, the same.
Convinced, amazed, he checks the bold de-
    sign,
And rules as strict his labour'd work confine
As if the Stagyrite o'erlook'd each line.
Learn hence for ancient rules a just esteem;
To copy Nature is to copy them.   140
    Some beauties yet no precepts can declare,
For there's a happiness as well as care.
Music resembles poetry; in each
Are nameless graces which no methods teach,
And which a master-hand alone can reach.
If, where the rules not far enough extend,
(Since rules were made but to promote their
    end)
Some lucky license answer to the full
Th' intent proposed, that license is a rule.
Thus Pegasus, a nearer way to take,   150
May boldly deviate from the common track.
Great Wits sometimes may gloriously offend,
And rise to faults true Critics dare not mend;
From vulgar bounds with brave disorder part,
And snatch a grace beyond the reach of Art,
Which, without passing thro' the judgment,
    gains
The heart, and all its end at once attains.
In prospects thus some objects please our eyes,
Which out of Nature's common order rise,
The shapeless rock, or hanging precipice.
But tho' the ancients thus their rules in-
    vade,   161
(As Kings dispense with laws themselves have
    made)
Moderns, beware! or if you must offend
Against the precept, ne'er transgress its end;
Let it be seldom, and compell'd by need;
And have at least their precedent to plead;
The Critic else proceeds without remorse,
Seizes your fame, and puts his laws in force.
    I know there are to whose presumptuous
        thoughts

Those freer beauties, ev'n in them, seem
    faults.   170
Some figures monstrous and misshaped ap-
    pear,
Consider'd singly, or beheld too near,
Which, but proportion'd to their light or
    place,
Due distance reconciles to form and grace.
A prudent chief not always must display
His powers in equal ranks and fair array,
But with th' occasion and the place comply,
Conceal his force, nay, seem sometimes to fly.
Those oft are stratagems which errors seem,
Nor is it Homer nods, but we that dream.
    Still green with bays each ancient altar
        stands   181
Above the reach of sacrilegious hands,
Secure from flames, from Envy's fiercer rage,
Destructive war, and all-involving Age.
See from each clime the learn'd their incense
    bring!
Hear in all tongues consenting pæans ring!
In praise so just let ev'ry voice be join'd,
And fill the gen'ral chorus of mankind.
Hail, Bards triumphant! born in happier
    days,
Immortal heirs of universal praise!   190
Whose honours with increase of ages grow,
As streams roll down, enlarging as they flow;
Nations unborn your mighty names shall
    sound,
And worlds applaud that must not yet be
    found!
O may some spark of your celestial fire
The last, the meanest of your sons inspire,
(That on weak wings, from far, pursues your
    flights,
Glows while he reads, but trembles as he
    writes)
To teach vain Wits a science little known,
T' admire superior sense, and doubt their
    own.   200

WILLIAM WORDSWORTH
Preface to *Lyrical Ballads*

[William Wordsworth (1770–1850), leader of the Romantic revolution in English poetry, and poet laureate of England from 1843 until his death, was educated at Cambridge and published his first poetry in 1792. These verses, though not characteristic of Wordsworth's mature style, attracted the attention and friendship of Samuel Taylor Coleridge, with whom he collaborated in the production of *Lyrical Ballads* (1798). The publication of this famous volume, often taken to date the beginning of the Romantic period of English literature, excited so much controversy by its subject matter and its language that to its second edition (1800) Wordsworth added an explanatory preface, which in later editions of his poetry he slightly revised. The following text is his final one (1845); it is reprinted here from Volume II of *The Poetical Works of William Wordsworth*, edited by E. de Selincourt (Oxford, 1944). The full title of this later version, which was transferred by Wordsworth to the end of his volumes, is "Preface to the Second Edition of Several of the Foregoing Poems, Published, with an Additional Volume, under the Title of 'Lyrical Ballads.' "]

The first Volume of these Poems has already been submitted to general perusal. It was published, as an experiment, which, I hoped, might be of some use to ascertain, how far, by fitting to metrical arrangement a selection of the real language of men in a state of vivid sensation, that sort of pleasure and that quantity of pleasure may be imparted, which a Poet may rationally endeavour to impart.

I had formed no very inaccurate estimate of the probable effect of those Poems: I flattered myself that they who should be pleased with them would read them with more than common pleasure: and, on the other hand, I was well aware, that by those who should dislike /384/ them, they would be read with more than common dislike. The result has differed from my expectation in this only, that a greater number have been pleased than I ventured to hope I should please. . . .

Several of my Friends are anxious for the success of these Poems, from a belief, that, if the views with which they were composed were indeed realized, a class of Poetry would be produced, well adapted to interest mankind permanently, and not unimportant in the quality, and in the multiplicity of its moral relations: and on this account they have advised me to prefix a systematic defence of the theory upon which the Poems were written. But I was unwilling to undertake the task, knowing that on this occasion the Reader would look coldly upon my arguments, since I might be suspected of having been principally influenced by the selfish and foolish hope of *reasoning* him into an approbation of these particular Poems: and I was still more unwilling to undertake the task, because, adequately to display the opinions, and fully to enforce the arguments, would require a space wholly disproportionate to a preface. For, to treat the subject with the clearness and coherence of which it is susceptible, it would be necessary to give a full account of the present state of the public taste in this country, and to determine how far this taste is healthy or depraved; which, again, could not be determined, without pointing out in what manner language and the human mind act and re-act on each other, and without retracing the revolutions, not of literature alone, but likewise of society itself. I have therefore altogether declined to enter regularly upon this defence; yet I am sensible, that there would be something like impropriety in abruptly obtruding upon the Public, without a few words of introduction, Poems so materially different from those upon which general approbation is at present bestowed.

It is supposed, that by the act of writing in verse an Author makes a formal engagement that he will gratify certain known habits of association; that he not only thus apprises the Reader that certain classes of ideas and expressions will be found in his book, but that /385/ others will be carefully excluded. This exponent or symbol held forth by metrical language must in different eras of literature have excited very different expectations: for example, in the age of Catullus, Terence, and Lucretius, and that of Statius or Claudian; and in our own country, in the age of Shakespeare and Beaumont and Fletcher, and that of Donne and Cowley, or Dryden, or Pope. I will not take upon me to determine the exact import of the promise which, by the act of writing in verse, an Author in the present day makes to his reader: but it will undoubtedly appear to many persons that I have not fulfilled the terms of an engagement thus voluntarily contracted. They who have been accustomed to the gaudiness and inane phraseology of many modern writers, if they persist in reading this book to its conclusion, will, no doubt, frequently have to struggle with feelings of strangeness and awkwardness: they will look round for poetry, and will be induced to inquire by what species of courtesy these attempts can be permitted to assume that title. I hope therefore the reader will not censure me for attempting to state what I have proposed to myself to perform; and also (as far as the limits of a preface will permit) to explain some of the chief reasons which have determined me in the choice of my purpose: that at least he may be spared any unpleasant feeling of disappointment, and that I myself may be protected from one of the most dishonourable accusations which can be brought against an Author; namely, that of an indolence which prevents him from endeavouring to ascertain what is his duty, or, when his duty is ascertained, prevents him from performing it.

The principal object, then, proposed in these Poems was to choose incidents and situations from common life, and to relate or describe them, throughout, as far as was possible in a selection of language really used by men, and, at the same time, to throw over them a certain colouring of imagination, whereby ordinary things should be presented to the mind in an unusual aspect; and, further, and above all, to make these incidents and situations interesting by tracing in them, truly though not ostentatiously, the primary laws of our nature: chiefly, as far as regards the manner in which we associate ideas in a state of excitement. Humble and rustic life was generally chosen, because, in that condi-

tion, the essential passions of the heart find a better soil in which they can attain their maturity, are less under restraint, and speak a plainer and more emphatic language; because in that condition of life our elementary feelings coexist in a state of great simplicity, and, consequently, may be more /386/ accurately contemplated, and more forcibly communicated; because the manners of rural life germinate from those elementary feelings, and, from the necessary character of rural occupations, are more easily comprehended, and are more durable; and, lastly, because in that condition the passions of men are incorporated with the beautiful and permanent forms of nature. The language, too, of these men has been adopted (purified indeed from what appear to be its real defects, from all lasting and rational causes of dislike or disgust) because such men hourly communicate with the best objects from which the best part of language is originally derived; and because, from their rank in society and the sameness and narrow circle of their intercourse, being less under the influence of social vanity, they convey their feelings and notions in simple and unelaborated expressions. Accordingly, such a language, arising out of repeated experience and regular feelings, is a more permanent, and a far more philosophical language, than that which is frequently substituted for it by Poets, who think that they are conferring honour upon themselves and their art, in proportion as they separate themselves from the sympathies of men, and indulge in arbitrary and capricious habits of expression, in order to furnish food for fickle tastes, and fickle appetites, of their own creation.[1]

I cannot, however, be insensible to the present outcry against the triviality and meanness, both of thought and language, which some of my contemporaries have occasionally introduced into their metrical compositions; and I acknowledge that this defect, where it exists, is more dishonourable to the Writer's own character than false refinement or arbitrary innovation, though I should contend at the same time, that it is far less pernicious in

[1] It is worth while here to observe, that the affecting parts of Chaucer are almost always expressed in language pure and universally intelligible even to this day.

the sum of its consequences. From such verses the Poems in these volumes will be found distinguished at least by one mark of difference, that each of them has a worthy *purpose*. Not that I always began to write with a distinct purpose formally conceived; but habits of meditation have, I trust, so prompted and regulated my feelings, that my descriptions of such objects as strongly excite those feelings, will be found to carry along with them a *purpose*. If this opinion be erroneous, I can have little right to the name of a Poet. For all good poetry is the spontaneous overflow of powerful feelings: and though this be true, Poems to which any value can be attached were never produced on any variety of subjects but by a man who, being possessed of more than usual /387/ organic sensibility, had also thought long and deeply. For our continued influxes of feeling are modified and directed by our thoughts, which are indeed the representatives of all our past feelings; and, as by contemplating the relation of these general representatives to each other, we discover what is really important to men, so, by the repetition and continuance of this act, our feelings will be connected with important subjects, till at length, if we be originally possessed of much sensibility, such habits of mind will be produced, that, by obeying blindly and mechanically the impulses of those habits, we shall describe objects, and utter sentiments, of such a nature, and in such connexion with each other, that the understanding of the Reader must necessarily be in some degree enlightened, and his affections strengthened and purified.

It has been said that each of these poems has a purpose. Another circumstance must be mentioned which distinguishes these Poems from the popular Poetry of the day; it is this, that the feeling therein /388/ developed gives importance to the action and situation, and not the action and situation to the feeling.

A sense of false modesty shall not prevent me from asserting, that the Reader's attention is pointed to this mark of distinction, far less for the sake of these particular Poems than from the general importance of the subject. The subject is indeed important! For the human mind is capable of being excited without the application of gross and violent stimulants; and he must have a very faint perception of its beauty and dignity who does not know this, and who does not further know, that one being is elevated above another, in proportion as he possesses this capability. It has therefore appeared to me, that to endeavour to produce or enlarge this capability is one of the best services in which, at any period, a Writer can be engaged; but this service, excellent at all times, is especially so at the present day. For a multitude of causes, unknown to former times, are now acting with a combined force to blunt the discriminating powers of the mind, and, unfitting it for all voluntary exertion, to reduce it to a state of almost savage torpor. The most effective of these causes are the great national events which are daily taking place, and the increasing accumulation of men in cities, where the uniformity of their occupations produces a craving for extraordinary incident, which the rapid communication of intelligence hourly gratifies. To this tendency of life and manners the literature and theatrical exhibitions of the country have conformed themselves. The invaluable works of our elder writers, I had almost said the works of Shakespeare and Milton, are driven into neglect by frantic novels, sickly and stupid German Tragedies, and deluges of idle and extravagant stories in verse.—When I think upon this degrading thirst after outrageous stimulation, I am almost ashamed to have spoken of the feeble endeavour made in these volumes to counteract it; and, reflecting upon the magnitude of the general evil, I should be oppressed with no dishonourable melancholy, had I not a deep impression of certain inherent and indestructible qualities of the human mind, and likewise of certain powers in the great and permanent objects that act upon it, which are equally inherent and indestructible; and were there not added to this impression a belief, that the time is approaching when the evil will be systematically opposed, by men of greater powers, and with far more distinguished success.

Having dwelt thus long on the subjects and aim of these Poems, I shall request the Reader's permission to apprise him of a few circumstances relating to their *style,* in order, among other reasons, that he may not censure me for not having performed what I never /389/ attempted. The Reader will find that personifications of abstract ideas rarely occur in these volumes; and are utterly rejected, as an ordinary device to elevate the style, and raise it above prose. My purpose was to imitate, and, as far as possible, to adopt the very language of men; and assuredly such personifications do not make any natural or regular part of that language. They are, indeed, a figure of speech occasionally prompted by passion, and I have made use of them as such; but have endeavoured utterly to reject them as a mechanical device of style, or as a family language which Writers in metre seem to lay claim to by prescription. I have wished to keep the Reader in the company of flesh and blood, persuaded that by so doing I shall interest him. Others who pursue a different track will interest him likewise; I do not interfere with their claim, but wish to prefer a claim of my own. There will also be found in these volumes little of what is usually called poetic diction; as much pains has been taken to avoid it as is ordinarily taken to produce it; this has been done for the reason already alleged, to bring my language near to the language of men; and further, because the pleasure which I have proposed to myself to impart, is of a kind very different from that which is supposed by many persons to be the proper object of poetry. Without being culpably particular, I do not know how to give my Reader a more exact notion of the style in which it was my wish and intention to write, than by informing him that I have at all times endeavoured to look steadily at my subject; consequently, there is I hope in these Poems little falsehood of description, and my ideas are expressed in language fitted to their respective importance. Something must have been gained by this practice, as it is friendly to one property of all good poetry, namely, good sense: but it has necessarily cut me off from a large portion of phrases and figures of speech which from father to son have long been regarded as the common inheritance of Poets. I have also thought it expedient to restrict myself still further, having abstained from the use of many expressions, in themselves proper and beautiful, but which have been foolishly repeated by bad Poets, till such feelings of disgust are connected with them as it is scarcely possible by any art of association to overpower.

If in a poem there should be found a series of lines, or even a single line, in which the language, though naturally arranged, and according to the strict laws of metre, does not differ from that of prose, there is a numerous class of critics, who, when they stumble upon these /390/ prosaisms, as they call them, imagine that they have made a notable discovery, and exult over the Poet as over a man ignorant of his own profession. Now these men would establish a canon of criticism which the Reader will conclude he must utterly reject, if he wishes to be pleased with these volumes. And it would be a most easy task to prove to him, that not only the language of a large portion of every good poem, even of the most elevated character, must necessarily, except with reference to the metre, in no respect differ from that of good prose, but likewise that some of the most interesting parts of the best poems will be found to be strictly the language of prose when prose is well written. The truth of this assertion might be demonstrated by innumerable passages from almost all the poetical writings, even of Milton himself. To illustrate the subject in a general manner, I will here adduce a short composition of Gray, who was at the head of those who, by their reasonings, have attempted to widen the space of separation betwixt Prose and Metrical composition, and was more than any other man curiously elaborate in the structure of his own poetic diction.

In vain to me the smiling mornings shine,
And reddening Phœbus lifts his golden fire:
The birds in vain their amorous descant join,
Or cheerful fields resume their green attire.
These ears, alas! for other notes repine;
A different object do these eyes require;
My lonely anguish melts no heart but mine;
And in my breast the imperfect joys expire;
Yet morning smiles the busy race to cheer,
And new-born pleasure brings to happier men;
The fields to all their wonted tribute bear;
To warm their little loves the birds complain,
I fruitless mourn to him that cannot hear,
And weep the more because I weep in vain.[2]

2 ["Sonnet on the Death of Richard West," by Thomas Gray.]

It will easily be perceived, that the only part of this Sonnet which is of any value is the lines printed in Italics; it is equally obvious, that, except in the rhyme, and in the use of the single word "fruitless" for fruitlessly, which is so far a defect, the language of these lines does in no respect differ from that of prose.

By the foregoing quotation it has been shown that language of Prose may yet be well adapted to Poetry; and it was previously asserted, that a large portion of the language of every good poem can in no respect differ from that of good Prose. We will go further. /391/ It may be safely affirmed, that there neither is, nor can be, any *essential* difference between the language of prose and metrical composition. We are fond of tracing the resemblance between Poetry and Painting, and, accordingly, we call them Sisters: but where shall we find bonds of connexion sufficiently strict to typify the affinity betwixt metrical and prose composition? They both speak by and to the same organs; the bodies in which both of them are clothed may be said to be of the same substance, their affections are kindred, and almost identical, not necessarily differing even in degree; Poetry[3] sheds no tears "such as Angels weep," but natural and human tears; she can boast of no celestial ichor that distinguishes her vital juices from those of prose; the same human blood circulates through the veins of them both.

If it be affirmed that rhyme and metrical arrangement of themselves constitute a distinction which overturns what has just been said on the strict affinity of metrical language with that of prose, and paves the way for other artificial distinctions which the mind voluntarily admits, I answer that the language of such Poetry as is here recommended is, as far as possible, a selection of the language really spoken by men; that this selection,

[3] I here use the word "Poetry" (though against my own judgement) as opposed to the word Prose, and synonymous with metrical composition. But much confusion has been introduced into criticism by this contradistinction of Poetry and Prose, instead of the more philosophical one of Poetry and Matter of Fact, or Science. The only strict antithesis to Prose is Metre; nor is this, in truth, a *strict* antithesis, because lines and passages of metre so naturally occur in writing prose, that it would be scarcely possible to avoid them, even were it desirable.

wherever it is made with true taste and feeling, will of itself form a distinction far greater than would at first be imagined, and will entirely separate the composition from the vulgarity and meanness of ordinary life; and, if metre be superadded thereto, I believe that a dissimilitude will be produced altogether sufficient for the gratification of a rational mind. What other distinction would we have? Whence is it to come? And where is it to exist? Not, surely, where the Poet speaks through the mouths of his characters: it cannot be necessary here, either for elevation of style, or any of its supposed ornaments: for, if the Poet's subject be judiciously chosen, it will naturally, and upon fit occasion, lead him to passions the language of which, if selected truly and judiciously, must necessarily be dignified and variegated, and alive with metaphors and figures. I forbear to speak of an incongruity which would shock the intelligent Reader, should the Poet inter- /392/ weave any foreign splendour of his own with that which the passion naturally suggests: it is sufficient to say that such addition is unnecessary. And, surely, it is more probable that those passages, which with propriety abound with metaphors and figures, will have their due effect, if, upon other occasions where the passions are of a milder character, the style also be subdued and temperate.

But, as the pleasure which I hope to give by the Poems now presented to the Reader must depend entirely on just notions upon this subject, and, as it is in itself of high importance to our taste and moral feelings, I cannot content myself with these detached remarks. And if, in what I am about to say, it shall appear to some that my labour is unnecessary, and that I am like a man fighting a battle without enemies, such persons may be reminded, that, whatever be the language outwardly holden by men, a practical faith in the opinions which I am wishing to establish is almost unknown. If my conclusions are admitted, and carried as far as they must be carried if admitted at all, our judgements concerning the works of the greatest Poets both ancient and modern will be far different from what they are at present, both when we praise, and when we censure: and our moral feelings influencing and influenced by these judgements will, I believe, be corrected and purified.

Taking up the subject, then, upon general grounds, let me ask, what is meant by the word Poet? What is a Poet? To whom does he address himself? And what language is to be expected from him?—He is a man speaking to men: a man, it is true, endowed with more lively sensibility, more enthusiasm and tenderness, who has a greater knowledge of human nature, and a more comprehensive soul, than are supposed to be common among mankind; a man pleased with his own passions and volitions, and who rejoices more than other men in the spirit of life that is in him; delighting to contemplate similar volitions and passions as manifested in the goings-on of the Universe, and habitually impelled to create them where he does not find them. To these qualities he has added a disposition to be affected more than other men by absent things as if they were present; an ability of conjuring up in himself passions, which are indeed far from being the same as those produced by real events, yet (especially in those parts of the general sympathy which are pleasing and delightful) do more nearly resemble the passions produced by real events, than anything which, from the motions of their own minds merely, other men are accustomed to feel in themselves:—whence, and from practice, he has acquired a greater readiness and power in expressing what he thinks and feels, and especially those thoughts and feelings which, by his own choice, or from the structure of his own mind, arise in him without immediate external excitement. /393/

But whatever portion of this faculty we may suppose even the greatest Poet to possess, there cannot be a doubt that the language which it will suggest to him, must often, in liveliness and truth, fall short of that which is uttered by men in real life, under the actual pressure of those passions, certain shadows of which the Poet thus produces, or feels to be produced, in himself.

However exalted a notion we would wish to cherish of the character of a Poet, it is obvious, that while he describes and imitates passions, his employment is in some degree mechanical, compared with the freedom and power of real and substantial action and suffering. So that it will be the wish of the Poet to bring his feelings near to those of the persons whose feelings he describes, nay, for short spaces of time, perhaps, to let himself slip into an entire delusion, and even confound and identify his own feelings with theirs; modifying only the language which is thus suggested to him by a consideration that he describes for a particular purpose, that of giving pleasure. Here, then, he will apply the principle of selection which has been already insisted upon. He will depend upon this for removing what would otherwise be painful or disgusting in the passion; he will feel that there is no necessity to trick out or to elevate nature: and, the more industriously he applies this principle, the deeper will be his faith that no words, which *his* fancy or imagination can suggest, will be to be compared with those which are the emanations of reality and truth.

But it may be said by those who do not object to the general spirit of these remarks, that, as it is impossible for the Poet to produce upon all occasions language as exquisitely fitted for the passion as that which the real passion itself suggests, it is proper that he should consider himself as in the situation of a translator, who does not scruple to substitute excellencies of another kind for those which are unattainable by him; and endeavours occasionally to surpass his original, in order to make some amends for the general inferiority to which he feels that he must submit. But this would be to encourage idleness and unmanly despair. Further, it is the language of men who speak of what they do not understand; who talk of Poetry as of a matter of amusement and idle pleasure; who will converse with us as gravely about a *taste* for Poetry, as they express it, as if it were a thing as indifferent as a taste for rope-dancing, or Frontiniac or Sherry. Aristotle, I have been told, has said, that Poetry is the most philosophic of all writing: it is so: its object is truth, not individual and local, but general, and operative; not standing upon external /394/ testimony, but carried alive into the heart by passion; truth which is its own testimony, which gives competence and confidence to the tribunal to which it appeals, and receives them from the same tribunal. Poetry is the image of man and nature. The obstacles which stand in the way of the fidelity of the

Biographer and Historian, and of their consequent utility, are incalculably greater than those which are to be encountered by the Poet who comprehends the dignity of his art. The Poet writes under one restriction only, namely, the necessity of giving immediate pleasure to a human Being possessed of that information which may be expected from him, not as a lawyer, a physician, a mariner, an astronomer, or a natural philosopher, but as a Man. Except this one restriction, there is no object standing between the Poet and the image of things; between this, and the Biographer and Historian, there are a thousand.

Nor let this necessity of producing immediate pleasure be considered as a degradation of the Poet's art. It is far otherwise. It is an acknowledgement of the beauty of the universe, an acknowledgement the more sincere, because not formal, but indirect; it is a task light and easy to him who looks at the world in the spirit of love: further, it is a homage paid to the native and naked dignity of man, to the grand elementary principle of pleasure, by which he knows, and feels, and lives, and moves. We have no sympathy but what is propagated by pleasure: I would not be misunderstood; but wherever we sympathize with pain, it will be found that the sympathy is produced and carried on by subtle combinations with pleasure. We have no knowledge, that is, no general principles drawn from the contemplation of particular facts, but what has been built up by pleasure, and exists in us by pleasure alone. The Man of science, the Chemist and Mathematician, whatever difficulties and disgusts they may have had to struggle with, know and feel this. However painful may be the objects with which the Anatomist's knowledge is connected, he feels that his knowledge is pleasure; and where he has no pleasure he has no knowledge. What then does the Poet? He considers man and the objects that surround him as acting and reacting upon each other, so as to produce an infinite complexity of pain and pleasure; he considers man in his own nature and in his ordinary life as contemplating this with a certain quantity of immediate knowledge, with certain convictions, intuitions, and deductions, which from habit acquire the quality of intuitions; he considers him as looking upon this complex scene of ideas and sensations, and finding everywhere /395/ objects that immediately excite in him sympathies which, from the necessities of his nature, are accompanied by an overbalance of enjoyment.

To this knowledge which all men carry about with them, and to these sympathies in which, without any other discipline than that of our daily life, we are fitted to take delight, the Poet principally directs his attention. He considers man and nature as essentially adapted to each other, and the mind of man as naturally the mirror of the fairest and most interesting properties of nature. And thus the Poet, prompted by his feeling of pleasure, which accompanies him through the whole course of his studies, converses with general nature, with affections akin to those, which, through labour and length of time, the Man of science has raised up in himself, by conversing with those particular parts of nature which are the objects of his studies. The knowledge both of the Poet and the Man of science is pleasure; but the knowledge of the one cleaves to us as a necessary part of our existence, our natural and unalienable inheritance; the other is a personal and individual acquisition, slow to come to us, and by no habitual and direct sympathy connecting us with our fellow-beings. The Man of science seeks truth as a remote and unknown benefactor; he cherishes and loves it in his solitude: the Poet singing a song in which all human beings join with him, rejoices in the presence of truth as our visible friend and hourly companion. Poetry is the breath and finer spirit of all knowledge; it is the impassioned expression which is in the countenance of all Science. Emphatically may it be said of the Poet, as Shakespeare hath said of man, "that he looks before and after." He is the rock of defence for human nature; an upholder and preserver, carrying everywhere with him relationship and love. In spite of difference of soil and climate, of language and manners, of laws and customs: in spite of things silently gone out of mind, and things violently destroyed; the Poet binds together by passion and knowledge the vast empire of human society, as it is spread over the whole earth, and over all time. The objects of the Poet's thoughts are everywhere; though the eyes and senses of man are, it is true, his favourite guides, yet he will follow wheresoever he can find an atmosphere of sensation in which to move his wings. Poetry is the first and last of all knowledge—it is as immortal as the heart of man. If the labours of Men of science should ever create any material revolution, direct or indirect, in our condition, and in the impressions which we habitually receive, the Poet will sleep then no more than at present; he will be ready to follow the steps of the Man of science, not only in those general indirect effects, but he will be at his side, carrying sensation into the midst of the objects of the science itself. The remotest discoveries of the Chemist, the Botanist, or /396/ Mineralogist, will be as proper objects of the Poet's art as any upon which it can be employed, if the time should ever come when these things shall be familiar to us, and the relations under which they are contemplated by the followers of these respective sciences shall be manifestly and palpably material to us as enjoying and suffering beings. If the time should ever come when what is now called science, thus familiarized to men, shall be ready to put on, as it were, a form of flesh and blood, the Poet will lend his divine spirit to aid the transfiguration, and will welcome the Being thus produced, as a dear and genuine inmate of the household of man.—It is not, then, to be supposed that any one, who holds that sublime notion of Poetry which I have attempted to convey, will break in upon the sanctity and truth of his pictures by transitory and accidental ornaments, and endeavour to excite admiration of himself by arts, the necessity of which must manifestly depend upon the assumed meanness of his subject.

What has been thus far said applies to Poetry in general; but especially to those parts of composition where the Poet speaks through the mouths of his characters; and upon this point it appears to authorize the conclusion that there are few persons of good sense, who would not allow that the dramatic parts of composition are defective, in proportion as they deviate from the real language of nature, and are coloured by a diction of the Poet's own, either peculiar to him as an individual Poet or belonging simply to Poets in general; to a body of men who, from the circumstance of their compositions being in metre, it is

expected will employ a particular language.

It is not, then, in the dramatic parts of composition that we look for this distinction of language; but still it may be proper and necessary where the Poet speaks to us in his own person and character. To this I answer by referring the Reader to the description before given of a Poet. Among the qualities there enumerated as principally conducing to form a Poet, is implied nothing differing in kind from other men, but only in degree. The sum of what was said is, that the Poet is chiefly distinguished from other men by a greater promptness to think and feel without immediate external excitement, and a greater power in expressing such thoughts and feelings as are produced in him in that manner. But these passions and thoughts and feelings are the general passions and thoughts and feelings of men. And with what are they connected? Undoubtedly with our moral sentiments and animal sensations, and with the causes which excite these; with the operations of the elements, and the appearances of the visible universe; with storm and sunshine, with the revolutions of the seasons, with cold and heat, with loss of friends and kindred, with injuries and resentments, gratitude and hope, with fear and sorrow. These, and the like, are the sensations and objects which the Poet describes, as they are the sensa- /397/ tions of other men, and the objects which interest them. The Poet thinks and feels in the spirit of human passions. How, then, can his language differ in any material degree from that of all other men who feel vividly and see clearly? It might be *proved* that it is impossible. But supposing that this were not the case, the Poet might then be allowed to use a peculiar language when expressing his feelings for his own gratification, or that of men like himself. But Poets do not write for Poets alone, but for men. Unless therefore we are advocates for that admiration which subsists upon ignorance, and that pleasure which arises from hearing what we do not understand, the Poet must descend from this supposed height; and, in order to excite rational sympathy, he must express himself as other men express themselves. To this it may be added, that while he is only selecting from the real language of men, or, which amounts to the same thing, composing accurately in the spirit of such selection, he is treading upon safe ground, and we know what we are to expect from him. Our feelings are the same with respect to metre; for, as it may be proper to remind the Reader, the distinction of metre is regular and uniform, and not, like that which is produced by what is usually called POETIC DICTION, arbitrary, and subject to infinite caprices upon which no calculation whatever can be made. In the one case, the Reader is utterly at the mercy of the Poet, respecting what imagery or diction he may choose to connect with the passion; whereas, in the other, the metre obeys certain laws, to which the Poet and Reader both willingly submit because they are certain, and because no interference is made by them with the passion, but such as the concurring testimony of ages has shown to heighten and improve the pleasure which co-exists with it.

It will now be proper to answer an obvious question, namely, Why, professing these opinions, have I written in verse? To this, in addition to such answer as is included in what has been already said, I reply, in the first place, Because, however I may have restricted myself, there is still left open to me what confessedly constitutes the most valuable object of all writing, whether in prose or verse; the great and universal passions of men, the most general and interesting of their occupations, and the entire world of nature before me—to supply endless combinations of forms and imagery. Now, supposing for a moment that whatever is interesting in these objects may be as vividly described in prose, why should I be condemned for attempting to superadd to such description the charm which, by the consent of all nations, is acknowledged to exist in metrical language? To this, by such as are yet unconvinced, it may be answered that a very small part of the pleasure given by Poetry depends upon the metre, and that it is injudicious to /398/ write in metre, unless it be accompanied with the other artificial distinctions of style with which metre is usually accompanied, and that, by such deviation, more will be lost from the shock which will thereby be given to the Reader's associations than will be counterbalanced by any pleasure which he can derive from the general power of numbers. In answer to those who still contend for the necessity of accompanying metre with cer-

tain appropriate colours of style in order to the accomplishment of its appropriate end, and who also, in my opinion, greatly underrate the power of metre in itself, it might, perhaps, as far as relates to these Volumes, have been almost sufficient to observe, that poems are extant, written upon more humble subjects, and in a still more naked and simple style, which have continued to give pleasure from generation to generation. Now, if nakedness and simplicity be a defect, the fact here mentioned affords a strong presumption that poems somewhat less naked and simple are capable of affording pleasure at the present day; and, what I wished *chiefly* to attempt, at present, was to justify myself for having written under the impression of this belief.

But various causes might be pointed out why, when the style is manly and the subject of some importance, words metrically arranged will long continue to impart such a pleasure to mankind as he who proves the extent of that pleasure will be desirous to impart. The end of Poetry is to produce excitement in co-existence with an overbalance of pleasure; but, by the supposition, excitement is an unusual and irregular state of the mind; ideas and feelings do not, in that state, succeed each other in accustomed order. If the words, however, by which this excitement is produced be in themselves powerful, or the images and feelings have an undue proportion of pain connected with them, there is some danger that the excitement may be carried beyond its proper bounds. Now the co-presence of something regular, something to which the mind has been accustomed in various moods and in a less excited state, cannot but have great efficacy in tempering and restraining the passion by an inter-texture of ordinary feeling, and of feeling not strictly and necessarily connected with the passion. This is unquestionably true; and hence, though the opinion will at first appear paradoxical, from the tendency of metre to divest language, in a certain degree, of its reality, and thus to throw a sort of half-consciousness of unsubstantial existence over the whole composition, there can be little doubt but that more pathetic situations and sentiments, that is, those which have a greater proportion of pain connected with them, may be endured in metrical composition, especially in rhyme, than in prose. The metre of the old ballads is very artless; yet they contain many passages which would illustrate /399/ this opinion; and, I hope, if the following Poems be attentively perused, similar instances will be found in them. This opinion may be further illustrated by appealing to the Reader's own experience of the reluctance with which he comes to the re-perusal of the distressful parts of *Clarissa Harlowe,* or *The Gamester;* while Shakespeare's writings, in the most pathetic scenes, never act upon us, as pathetic, beyond the bounds of pleasure—an effect which, in a much greater degree than might at first be imagined, is to be ascribed to small, but continual and regular impulses of pleasurable surprise from the metrical arrangement.—On the other hand (what it must be allowed will much more frequently happen) if the Poet's words should be incommensurate with the passion, and inadequate to raise the Reader to a height of desirable excitement, then (unless the Poet's choice of his metre has been grossly injudicious), in the feelings of pleasure which the Reader has been accustomed to connect with metre in general, and in the feeling, whether cheerful or melancholy, which he has been accustomed to connect with that particular movement of metre, there will be found something which will greatly contribute to impart passion to the words, and to effect the complex end which the Poet proposes to himself.

If I had undertaken a SYSTEMATIC defence of the theory here maintained, it would have been my duty to develop the various causes upon which the pleasure received from metrical language depends. Among the chief of these causes is to be reckoned a principle which must be well known to those who have made any of the Arts the object of accurate reflection; namely, the pleasure which the mind derives from the perception of similitude in dissimilitude. This principle is the great spring of the activity of our minds, and their chief feeder. From this principle the direction of the sexual appetite, and all the passions connected with it, take their origin: it is the life of our ordinary conversation; and upon the accuracy with which similitude in dissimilitude, and dissimilitude in similitude are perceived, depend our taste and our moral

feelings. It would not be a useless employment to apply this principle to the consideration of metre, and to show that metre is hence enabled to afford much pleasure, and to point out in what manner that pleasure is produced. But my limits will not permit me to enter upon this subject, and I must content myself with a general summary.

I have said that poetry is the spontaneous overflow of powerful feelings: it takes its origin from emotion recollected in tranquillity: the emotion is contemplated till, by a species of reaction, the tranquillity gradually disappears, and an emotion, kindred to that which was /400/ before the subject of contemplation, is gradually produced, and does itself actually exist in the mind. In this mood successful composition generally begins, and in a mood similar to this it is carried on; but the emotion, of whatever kind, and in whatever degree, from various causes, is qualified by various pleasures, so that in describing any passions whatsoever, which are voluntarily described, the mind will, upon the whole, be in a state of enjoyment. If Nature be thus cautious to preserve in a state of enjoyment a being so employed, the Poet ought to profit by the lesson held forth to him, and ought especially to take care, that, whatever passions he communicates to his Reader, those passions, if his Reader's mind be sound and vigorous, should always be accompanied with an overbalance of pleasure. Now the music of harmonious metrical language, the sense of difficulty overcome, and the blind association of pleasure which has been previously received from works of rhyme or metre of the same or similar construction, an indistinct perception perpetually renewed of language closely resembling that of real life, and yet, in the circumstance of metre, differing from it so widely—all these imperceptibly make up a complex feeling of delight, which is of the most important use in tempering the painful feeling always found intermingled with powerful descriptions of the deeper passions. This effect is always produced in pathetic and impassioned poetry; while, in lighter compositions, the ease and gracefulness with which the Poet manages his numbers[4] are themselves confessedly a principal source of the gratifica-

4 [**manages his numbers:** solves his metrical problems.]

tion of the Reader. All that it is *necessary* to say, however, upon this subject, may be effected by affirming, what few persons will deny, that, of two descriptions, either of passions, manners, or characters, each of them equally well executed, the one in prose and the other in verse, the verse will be read a hundred times where the prose is read once.

Having thus explained a few of my reasons for writing in verse, and why I have chosen subjects from common life, and endeavoured to bring my language near to the real language of men, if I have been too minute in pleading my own cause, I have at the same time been treating /401/ a subject of general interest; and for this reason a few words shall be added with reference solely to these particular poems, and to some defects which will probably be found in them. I am sensible that my associations must have sometimes been particular instead of general, and that, consequently, giving to things a false importance, I may have sometimes written upon unworthy subjects; but I am less apprehensive on this account, than that my language may frequently have suffered from those arbitrary connexions of feelings and ideas with particular words and phrases, from which no man can altogether protect himself. Hence I have no doubt, that, in some instances, feelings, even of the ludicrous, may be given to my Readers by expressions which appeared to me tender and pathetic. Such faulty expressions, were I convinced they were faulty at present, and that they must necessarily continue to be so, I would willingly take all reasonable pains to correct. But it is dangerous to make these alterations on the simple authority of a few individuals, or even of certain classes of men; for where the understanding of an Author is not convinced, or his feelings altered, this cannot be done without great injury to himself: for his own feelings are his stay and support; and, if he set them aside in one instance, he may be induced to repeat this act till his mind shall lose all confidence in itself, and become utterly debilitated. To this it may be added, that the critic ought never to forget that he is himself exposed to the same errors as the Poet, and, perhaps, in a much greater degree: for there can be no presumption in saying of most readers, that it is not probable they will

be so well acquainted with the various stages of meaning through which words have passed, or with the fickleness or stability of the relations of particular ideas to each other; and, above all, since they are so much less interested in the subject, they may decide lightly and carelessly.

Long as the Reader has been detained, I hope he will permit me to caution him against a mode of false criticism which has been applied to Poetry, in which the language closely resembles that of life and nature. Such verses have been triumphed over in parodies, of which Dr. Johnson's stanza is a fair specimen:—

> I put my hat upon my head
> And walked into the Strand,
> And there I met another man
> Whose hat was in his hand.

Immediately under these lines let us place one of the most justly admired stanzas of the "Babes in the Wood."

> These pretty Babes with hand in hand
> Went wandering up and down;
> But never more they saw the Man
> Approaching from the Town. /402/

In both these stanzas the words, and the order of the words, in no respect differ from the most unimpassioned conversation. There are words in both, for example, "the Strand," and "the Town," connected with none but the most familiar ideas; yet the one stanza we admit as admirable, and the other as a fair example of the superlatively contemptible. Whence arises this difference? Not from the metre, not from the language, not from the order of the words; but the *matter* expressed in Dr. Johnson's stanza is contemptible. The proper method of treating trivial and simple verses, to which Dr. Johnson's stanza would be a fair parallelism, is not to say, this is a bad kind of poetry, or, this is not poetry; but, this wants sense; it is neither interesting in itself nor can *lead* to anything interesting; the images neither originate in that sane state of feeling which arises out of thought, nor can excite thought or feeling in the Reader. This is the only sensible manner of dealing with such verses. Why trouble yourself about the species till you have previously decided upon the genus? Why take pains to prove that an ape is not a Newton, when it is self-evident that he is not a man?

One request I must make of my reader, which is, that in judging these Poems he would decide by his own feelings genuinely, and not by reflection upon what will probably be the judgement of others. How common is it to hear a person say, I myself do not object to this style of composition, or this or that expression, but, to such and such classes of people it will appear mean or ludicrous! This mode of criticism, so destructive of all sound unadulterated judgement, is almost universal: let the Reader then abide, independently, by his own feelings, and, if he finds himself affected, let him not suffer such conjectures to interfere with his pleasure.

If an Author, by any single composition, has impressed us with respect for his talents, it is useful to consider this as affording a presumption, that on other occasions where we have been displeased, he, nevertheless, may not have written ill or absurdly; and further, to give him so much credit for this one composition as may induce us to review what has displeased us, with more care than we should otherwise have bestowed upon it. This is not only an act of justice, but, in our decisions upon poetry especially, may conduce, in a high degree, to the improvement of our own taste; for an *accurate* taste in poetry, and in all the other arts, as Sir Joshua Reynolds has observed, is an *acquired* talent, which can only be produced by thought and a long continued intercourse with the best models of composition. This is mentioned, not with so ridiculous a purpose as to prevent the most inexperienced Reader from judging for himself (I have already said that I wish him to judge for himself), but merely to temper the /403/ rashness of decision, and to suggest, that, if Poetry be a subject on which much time has not been bestowed, the judgement may be erroneous; and that, in many cases it necessarily will be so.

Nothing would, I know, have so effectually contributed to further the end which I have in view, as to have shown of what kind the pleasure is, and how that pleasure is produced, which is confessedly produced by metrical composition essentially different from that which I have here endeavoured to recommend: for the Reader will say that he has been pleased by such composition; and what more can be done for him? The power of any art is limited; and he will suspect, that, if it be proposed to furnish him with new friends, that can be only upon condition of his abandoning his old friends. Besides, as I have said, the Reader is himself conscious of the pleasure which he has received from such composition, composition to which he has peculiarly attached the endearing name of Poetry; and all men feel an habitual gratitude, and something of an honourable bigotry, for the objects which have long continued to please them: we not only wish to be pleased, but to be pleased in that particular way in which we have been accustomed to be pleased. There is in these feelings enough to resist a host of arguments; and I should be the less able to combat them successfully, as I am willing to allow, that, in order entirely to enjoy the Poetry which I am recommending, it would be necessary to give up much of what is ordinarily enjoyed. But, would my limits have permitted me to point out how this pleasure is produced, many obstacles might have been removed, and the Reader assisted in perceiving that the powers of language are not so limited as he may suppose; and that it is possible for poetry to give other enjoyments, of a purer, more lasting, and more exquisite nature. This part of the subject has not been altogether neglected, but it has not been so much my present aim to prove, that the interest excited by some other kinds of poetry is less vivid, and less worthy of the nobler powers of the mind, as to offer reasons for presuming, that if my purpose were fulfilled, a species of poetry would be produced, which is genuine poetry; in its nature well adapted to interest mankind permanently, and likewise important in the multiplicity and quality of its moral relations.

From what has been said, and from a perusal of the Poems, the Reader will be able clearly to perceive the object which I had in view: he will determine how far it has been attained; and, what is a much more important question, whether it be worth attaining: and upon the decision of these two questions will rest my claim to the approbation of the Public. /404/

SAMUEL TAYLOR COLERIDGE
Biographia Literaria, Ch. 14

[Samuel Taylor Coleridge (1772–1834) won poetic fame with "The Ancient Mariner," "Kubla Khan," and "Christobel," acquired critical prestige with his lectures on Shakespeare, and in his later years wrote seminal works on politics, philosophy, and religion. Born in Devonshire, briefly a student at Cambridge and the University of Göttingen, he became early a friend of Wordsworth, with whom he lived in the Lake district of England, visited Germany, and wrote *Lyrical Ballads*. The last eighteen years of his life he lived in London, within easy reach of admirers and disciples. *Biographia Literaria,* a combination of biography, philosophy, and criticism, was first published in 1817. The following selection is reprinted from Volume II of an edition published at Oxford in 1907.]

During the first year that Mr. Wordsworth and I were neighbours, our conversations turned frequently on the two cardinal points of poetry, the power of exciting the sympathy of the reader by a faithful adherence to the truth of nature, and the power of giving the interest of novelty by the modifying colors of imagination. The sudden charm, which accidents of light and shade, which moon-light or sun-set diffused over a known and familiar landscape, appeared to represent the practicability of combining both. These are the poetry of nature. The thought suggested itself (to which of us I do not recollect) that a series of poems might be composed of two sorts. In the one, the incidents and agents were to be, in part at least, supernatural; and the excellence aimed at was to consist in the interesting of the affections by the dramatic truth of such emotions, as would naturally accompany such situations, supposing them real. And real in *this* sense they have been to every human being who, from whatever source of delusion, has at any time believed himself under supernatural agency. For the second class, subjects were to be chosen from ordinary life; the characters and incidents were to be such, as will be found in every village and its vicinity, where there is a meditative and feeling mind to seek after them, or to notice them, when they present themselves.

In this idea originated the plan of the "Lyrical Ballads"; /5/ in which it was agreed, that my endeavours should be directed to persons and characters supernatural, or at least romantic; yet so as to transfer from our inward nature a human interest and a semblance of truth sufficient to procure for these shadows of imagination that willing suspension of disbelief for the moment, which constitutes poetic faith. Mr. Wordsworth, on the other hand, was to propose to himself as his object, to give the charm of novelty to things of every day, and to excite a feeling analogous to the supernatural, by awakening the mind's attention to the lethargy of custom, and directing it to the loveliness and the wonders of the world before us; an inexhaustible treasure, but for which, in consequence of the film of familiarity and selfish solicitude, we have eyes, yet see not, ears that hear not, and hearts that neither feel nor understand.

With this view I wrote "The Ancient Mariner," and was preparing among other poems, "The Dark Ladie," and the "Christabel," in which I should have more nearly realized my ideal, than I had done in my first attempt. But Mr. Wordsworth's industry had proved so much more successful, and the number of his poems so much greater, that my compositions, instead of forming a balance, appeared rather an interpolation of heterogeneous matter. Mr. Wordsworth added two or three poems written in his own character, in the impassioned, lofty, and sustained diction, which is characteristic of his genius. In this form the "Lyrical Ballads" were published; and were presented by him, as an *experiment,* whether subjects, which from their nature rejected the usual ornaments and extra-colloquial style of poems in general, might not be so managed in the language of ordinary life as to produce the pleasurable interest, which it is the peculiar business of poetry to impart. To the second edition he added a preface of considerable length; in which, notwithstanding some passages of apparently a contrary import, he was understood to contend for the extension of /6/ this style to poetry of all kinds, and to reject as vicious and indefensible all phrases and forms of style that were not included in what he (unfortunately, I think, adopting an equivocal expression) called the language of *real* life. From this preface, prefixed to poems in which it was impossible to deny the presence of original genius, however mistaken its direction might be deemed, arose the whole long-continued controversy. For from the conjunction of perceived power with supposed heresy I explain the inveteracy and in some instances, I grieve to say, the acrimonious passions, with which the controversy has been conducted by the assailants.

Had Mr. Wordsworth's poems been the silly, the childish things, which they were for a long time described as being: had they been really distinguished from the compositions of other poets merely by meanness of language and inanity of thought; had they indeed contained nothing more than what is found in the parodies and pretended imitations of them; they must have sunk at once, a dead weight, into the slough of oblivion, and have dragged the preface along with them. But year after year increased the number of Mr. Wordsworth's admirers. They were found too not in the lower classes of the reading public, but chiefly among young men of strong sensibility and meditative minds; and their admiration (inflamed perhaps in some degree by opposition) was distinguished by its intensity, I might almost say, by its *religious* fervour. These facts, and the intellectual energy of the author, which was more or less consciously felt, where it was outwardly and even boisterously denied, meeting with sentiments of aversion to his opinions, and of alarm at their consequences, produced an eddy of criticism, which would of itself have borne up the poems by the violence, with which it whirled them round and round. With many parts of this preface, in the sense attributed to them, and which the words undoubtedly seem to authorize, /7/ I never concurred; but on the contrary objected to them as erroneous in

principle, and as contradictory (in appearance at least) both to other parts of the same preface, and to the author's own practice in the greater number of the poems themselves. Mr. Wordsworth in his recent collection has, I find, degraded this prefatory disquisition to the end of his second volume, to be read or not at the reader's choice. But he has not, as far as I can discover, announced any change in his poetic creed. At all events, considering it as the source of a controversy, in which I have been honoured more than I deserve by the frequent conjunction of my name with his, I think it expedient to declare once for all, in what points I coincide with his opinions, and in what points I altogether differ. But in order to render myself intelligible I must previously, in as few words as possible, explain my views, first, of a POEM; and secondly, of POETRY itself, in *kind,* and in *essence*.

The office of philosophical *disquisition* consists in just *distinction;* while it is the privilege of the philosopher to preserve himself constantly aware, that distinction is not division. In order to obtain adequate notions of any truth, we must intellectually separate its distinguishable parts; and this is the technical *process* of philosophy. But having so done, we must then restore them in our conceptions to the unity, in which they actually co-exist; and this is the *result* of philosophy. A poem contains the same elements as a prose composition; the difference therefore must consist in a different combination of them, in consequence of a different object being proposed. According to the difference of the object will be the difference of the combination. It is possible, that the object may be merely to facilitate the recollection of any given facts or observations by artificial arrangement; and the composition will be a poem, merely because it is distinguished from prose by metre, or by rhyme, or by both conjointly. In this, the lowest sense, /8/ a man might attribute the name of a poem to the well-known enumeration of the days in the several months:

> Thirty days hath September,
> April, June, and November, &c.

and others of the same class and purpose. And as a particular pleasure is found in anticipating the recurrence of sounds and quantities, all compositions that have this charm super-added, whatever be their contents, *may* be entitled poems.

So much for the superficial *form*. A difference of object and contents supplies an additional ground of distinction. The immediate purpose may be the communication of truths; either of truth absolute and demonstrable, as in works of science; or of facts experienced and recorded, as in history. Pleasure, and that of the highest and most permanent kind, may *result* from the *attainment* of the end; but it is not itself the immediate end. In other works the communication of pleasure may be the immediate purpose; and though truth, either moral or intellectual, ought to be the *ultimate* end, yet this will distinguish the character of the author, not the class to which the work belongs. Blest indeed is that state of society, in which the immediate purpose would be baffled by the perversion of the proper ultimate end; in which no charm of diction or imagery could exempt the Bathyllus even of an Anacreon, or the Alexis of Virgil, from disgust and aversion!

But the communication of pleasure may be the immediate object of a work not metrically composed and that object may have been in a high degree attained, as in novels and romances. Would then the mere superaddition of metre, with or without rhyme, entitle *these* to the name of poems? The answer is, that nothing can permanently please which does not contain in itself the reason why it is so, and not otherwise. If metre be superadded, all other parts must /9/ be made consonant with it. They must be such, as to justify the perpetual and distinct attention to each part, which an exact correspondent recurrence of accent and sound are calculated to excite. The final definition then, so deduced, may be thus worded. A poem is that species of composition, which is opposed to works of science, by proposing for its *immediate* object pleasure, not truth; and from all other species (having *this* object in common with it) it is discriminated by proposing to itself such delight from the *whole*, as is compatible with a distinct gratification from each component *part*.

Controversy is not seldom excited in consequence of the disputants attaching each a different meaning to the same word; and in few instances has this been more striking, than in disputes concerning the present subject. If a man chooses to call every composition a poem, which is rhyme, or measure, or both, I must leave his opinion uncontroverted. The distinction is at least competent to characterize the writer's intention. If it were subjoined, that the whole is likewise entertaining or affecting, as a tale, or as a series of interesting reflections, I of course admit this as another fit ingredient of a poem, and an additional merit. But if the definition sought for be that of a *legitimate* poem, I answer, it must be one, the parts of which mutually support and explain each other; all in their proportion harmonizing with, and supporting the purpose and known influences of metrical arrangement. The philosophic critics of all ages coincide with the ultimate judgement of all countries, in equally denying the praises of a just poem, on the one hand, to a series of striking lines or distiches, each of which, absorbing the whole attention of the reader to itself, disjoins it from its context, and makes it a separate whole, instead of an harmonizing part; and on the other hand, to an unsustained composition, from which the reader collects rapidly the general result, unattracted by the component /10/ parts. The reader should be carried forward, not merely or chiefly by the mechanical impulse of curiosity, or by a restless desire to arrive at the final solution; but by the pleasurable activity of mind excited by the attractions of the journey itself. Like the motion of a serpent, which the Egyptians made the emblem of intellectual power; or like the path of sound through the air; at every step he pauses and half recedes, and from the retrogressive movement collects the force which again carries him onward. "Praecipitandus est *liber* spiritus [a free spirit ought to be hurled along]," says Petronius Arbiter most happily. The epithet, *liber*, here balances the preceding verb; and it is not easy to conceive more meaning condensed in fewer words.

But if this should be admitted as a satisfactory character of a poem, we have still to seek for a definition of poetry. The writings of PLATO, and Bishop TAYLOR, and the "Theoria Sacra" of BURNET, furnish undeniable proofs that poetry of the highest kind may exist without metre, and even without the contradistinguishing objects of a poem. The first chapter of Isaiah (indeed a very large portion of the whole book) is poetry in the most emphatic sense; yet it would be not less irrational than strange to assert, that pleasure, and not truth, was the immediate object of the prophet. In short, whatever *specific* import we attach to the word, poetry, there will be found involved in it, as a necessary consequence, that a poem of any length neither can be, or ought to be, all poetry. Yet if an harmonious whole is to be produced, the remaining parts must be preserved *in keeping* with the poetry; and this can be no otherwise effected than by such a studied selection and artificial arrangement, as will partake of *one,* though not a *peculiar* property of poetry. And this again can be no other than the property of exciting a more continuous and equal attention than the language of prose aims at, whether colloquial or written. /11/

My own conclusions on the nature of poetry, in the strictest use of the word, have been in part anticipated in the preceding disquisition on the fancy and imagination. What is poetry? is so nearly the same question with, what is a poet? that the answer to the one is involved in the solution of the other. For it is a distinction resulting from the poetic genius itself, which sustains and modifies the images, thoughts, and emotions of the poet's own mind.

The poet, described in *ideal* perfection, brings the whole soul of man into activity, with the subordination of its faculties to each other, according to their relative worth and dignity. He diffuses a tone and spirit of unity, that blends, and (as it were) *fuses,* each into each, by that synthetic and magical power, to which I would exclusively appropriate the name of imagination. This power, first put in

action by the will and understanding, and retained under their irremissive, though gentle and unnoticed, controul (*laxis effertur habenis*),[1] reveals itself in the balance or reconciliation of opposite or discordant qualities: of sameness, with difference; of the general, with the concrete; the idea, with the image; the individual, with the representative; the sense of novelty and freshness, with old and familiar objects; a more than usual state of emotion, with more than usual order; judgement ever awake and steady self-possession, with enthusiasm and feeling profound or vehement; and while it blends and harmonizes the natural and the artificial, still subordinates art to nature; the manner to the matter; and our admiration of the poet to our sympathy with the poetry. Doubtless, as Sir John Davies observes of the soul (and his words may with slight alteration be applied, and even more appropriately, to the poetic IMAGINATION)

Doubtless this could not be, but that she turns
  Bodies to spirit by sublimation strange,
As fire converts to fire the things it burns,
  As we our food into our nature change. /12/

From their gross matter she abstracts their forms,
  And draws a kind of quintessence from things;
Which to her proper nature she transforms
  To bear them light on her celestial wings.

Thus does she, when from individual states
  She doth abstract the universal kinds;
Which then re-clothed in divers names and fates
  Steal access through our senses to our minds.

Finally, GOOD SENSE is the BODY of poetic genius, FANCY its DRAPERY, MOTION its LIFE, and IMAGINATION the SOUL that is everywhere, and in each; and forms all into one graceful and intelligent whole. /13/

1 [*laxis effertur habenis:* is born onward with loose reins.]

PERCY BYSSHE SHELLEY
from *A Defence of Poetry*

[Percy Bysshe Shelley (1792–1822), idealist and Romantic poet, is famous as author of *Prometheus Unbound, Adonais, The Cenci,* and such shorter lyrics as "Ode to the West Wind" and "Ozymandias." Heir to a baronetcy, Shelley was expelled in his first year from Oxford for having written a pamphlet misleadingly entitled *The Necessity of Atheism.* After three years of youthful marriage to Harriet Westbrook, he eloped with Mary Wollstonecraft Godwin, later the author of *Frankenstein,* whom he married after his wife's death. The last four years of his life he spent in Italy, a close friend of Lord Byron. His death came by drowning at the age of thirty. The original draft of *A Defence of Poetry* was written in 1821 as a reply to "The Four Ages of Poetry" by his friend Thomas Love Peacock. Because two journals for which it was intended failed, it was not published until 1840. In revision for intended journal publication the allusions to Peacock's work were omitted, so that the essay now stands as "a defence without an attack." The following extracts are reprinted from Volume III of *The Complete Works of Percy Bysshe Shelley,* edited by Roger Ingpen and Walter E. Peck (London and New York, 1930).]

According to one mode of regarding those two classes of mental action, which are called reason and imagination, the former may be considered as mind contemplating the relations borne by one thought to another, however produced, and the latter, as mind acting upon those thoughts so as to colour them with its own light, and composing from them, as from elements, other thoughts, each containing within itself the principle of its own integrity. The one is the τὸ ποιεῖν, or the principle of synthesis, and has for its objects those forms which are common to universal nature and existence itself; the other is the τὸ λογίζειν, or principle of analysis, and its action regards the relations of things simply as relations; considering thoughts, not in their integral unity, but as the algebraical representations which conduct to certain general results. Reason is the enumeration of quantities already known; imagination is the perception of the value of those quantities, both separately and as a whole. Reason respects the differences, and imagination the similitudes of things. Reason is to imagination as the instrument to the agent, as the body to the spirit, as the shadow to the substance.

Poetry, in a general sense, may be defined to be "the expression of the imagination"; and poetry is connate with the origin of man. Man is an instrument over which a series of external and internal impressions are driven, like the alternations of an ever-changing wind over an Æolian lyre, which move it by their motion to ever-changing melody. But there is a principle within the human being, and perhaps within all sentient beings, which acts otherwise than in the lyre, and produces not melody alone, but harmony, by an internal adjustment of the sounds or motions thus excited to the impressions which excite them. It is as if the lyre could accommodate its chords to the motions of that which strikes them, in a determined proportion of sound; even as the /109/ musician can accommodate his voice to the sound of the lyre. A child at play by itself will express its delight by its voice and motions: and every inflexion of tone and every gesture will bear exact relation to a corresponding antitype in the pleasurable impressions which awakened it; it will be the reflected image of that impression; and as the lyre trembles and sounds after the wind has died away, so the child seeks, by prolonging in its voice and motions the duration of the effect, to prolong also a consciousness of the cause. In relation to the objects which delight a child, these expressions are, what poetry is to higher objects. The savage (for the savage is to ages what the child is to years) expresses the emotions produced in him by surrounding objects in a similar manner; and language and gesture, together with plastic or pictorial imitation, become the image of the combined effect of those objects, and of his apprehension of them. Man in society, with all his passions and his pleasures, next becomes the object of the passions and pleasures of man; an additional class of emotions produces an augmented treasure of expressions; and language, gesture, and the imitative arts, become at once the representation and the medium, the pencil and the picture, the chisel and the statue, the chord and the harmony. The social sympathies, or those laws from which, as from its elements, society results, begin to develop themselves from the moment that two human beings co-exist; the future is contained within the present, as the plant within the seed; and equality, diversity, unity, contrast, mutual dependence, become the principles alone capable of affording the motives according to which the will of a social being is determined to action, inasmuch as he is social; and constitute pleasure in sensation, virtue in sentiment, beauty in art, truth in reasoning, and love in the intercourse of kind. Hence men, even in the infancy of society, observe a certain order in their words and actions, distinct from that of the objects and the impressions represented by them, all expression being subject to the laws of that from which it proceeds. But let us dismiss those more general considerations which might involve an inquiry into the principles of society itself, and restrict our view to the manner in which the imagination is expressed upon its forms. /110/

In the youth of the world, men dance and sing and imitate natural objects, observing in these actions, as in all others, a certain rhythm or order. And, although all men observe a similar, they observe not the same order, in the motions of the dance, in the melody of the song, in the combinations of language, in the series of their imitations of natural objects. For there is a certain order or rhythm belonging to each of these classes of mimetic representation, from which the hearer and the spectator receive an intenser and purer pleasure than from any other: the sense of an approximation to this order has been called taste by modern writers. Every man in the infancy of art, observes an order which approximates more or less closely to that from which this highest delight results; but the diversity is not sufficiently marked, as that its gradations should be sensible, except in those instances where the predominance of

this faculty of approximation to the beautiful (for so we may be permitted to name the relation between this highest pleasure and its cause) is very great. Those in whom it exists in excess are poets, in the most universal sense of the word; and the pleasure resulting from the manner in which they express the influence of society or nature upon their own minds, communicates itself to others, and gathers a sort of reduplication from that community. Their language is vitally metaphorical; that is, it marks the before unapprehended relations of things and perpetuates their apprehension, until the words which represent them, become, through time, signs for portions or classes of thoughts instead of pictures of integral thoughts; and then if no new poets should arise to create afresh the associations which have been thus disorganized, language will be dead to all the nobler purposes of human intercourse. These similitudes or relations are finely said by Lord Bacon to be "the same footsteps of nature impressed upon the various subjects of the world"—and he considers the faculty which perceives them as the storehouse of axioms common to all knowledge. In the infancy of society every author is necessarily a poet, because language itself is poetry; and to be a poet is to apprehend the true and the beautiful, in a word, the good which exists in the /111/ relation, subsisting, first between existence and perception, and secondly between perception and expression. Every original language near to its source is in itself the chaos of a cyclic poem: the copiousness of lexicography and the distinctions of grammar are the works of a later age, and are merely the catalogue and the form of the creations of poetry.

But poets, or those who imagine and express this indestructible order, are not only the authors of language and of music, of the dance, and architecture, and statuary, and painting: they are the institutors of laws, and the founders of civil society, and the inventors of the arts of life, and the teachers, who draw into a certain propinquity with the beautiful and the true, that partial apprehension of the agencies of the invisible world which is called religion. Hence all original religions are allegorical, or susceptible of allegory, and, like Janus, have a double face of false and true. Poets, according to the circumstances of the age and nation in which they appeared, were called, in the earlier epochs of the world, legislators, or prophets: a poet essentially comprises and unites both these characters. For he not only beholds intensely the present as it is, and discovers those laws according to which present things ought to be ordered, but he beholds the future in the present, and his thoughts are the germs of the flower and the fruit of latest time. Not that I assert poets to be prophets in the gross sense of the word, or that they can foretell the form as surely as they foreknow the spirit of events: such is the pretence of superstition, which would make poetry an attribute of prophecy, rather than prophecy an attribute to poetry. A poet participates in the eternal, the infinite, and the one; as far as relates to his conceptions, time and place and number are not. The grammatical forms which express the moods of time, and the difference of persons, and the distinction of place, are convertible with respect to the highest poetry without injuring it as poetry; and the choruses of Æschylus, and the Book of Job, and Dante's Paradise, would afford, more than any other writings, examples of this fact, if the limits of this essay did not forbid citation. The creations of sculpture, painting, and music are illustrations still more decisive. /112/

Language, colour, form, and religious and civil habits of action, are all the instruments and materials of poetry; they may be called poetry by that figure of speech which considers the effect as a synonyme of the cause. But poetry in a more restricted sense expresses those arrangements of language, and especially metrical language, which are created by that imperial faculty, whose throne is curtained within the invisible nature of man. And this springs from the nature itself of language, which is a more direct representation of the actions and passions of our internal being, and is susceptible of more various and delicate combinations, than colour, form, or motion, and is more plastic and obedient to the control of that faculty of which it is the creation. For language is arbitrarily produced by the imagination, and has relation to thoughts alone; but all other materials, in-

struments, and conditions of art have relations among each other, which limit and interpose between conception and expression. The former is as a mirror which reflects, the latter as a cloud which enfeebles, the light of which both are mediums of communication. Hence the fame of sculptors, painters, and musicians, although the intrinsic powers of the great masters of these arts may yield in no degree to that of those who have employed language as the hieroglyphic of their thoughts, has never equalled that of poets in the restricted sense of the term; as two performers of equal skill will produce unequal effects from a guitar and a harp. The fame of legislators and founders of religions, so long as their institutions last, alone seems to exceed that of poets in the restricted sense; but it can scarcely be a question, whether, if we deduct the celebrity which their flattery of the gross opinions of the vulgar usually conciliates, together with that which belonged to them in their higher character of poets, any excess will remain.

We have thus circumscribed the word poetry within the limits of that art which is the most familiar and the most perfect expression of the faculty itself. It is necessary, however, to make the circle still narrower, and to determine the distinction between measured and unmeasured language; for the popular division into prose and verse is inadmissible in accurate philosophy. /113/

Sounds as well as thoughts have relation both between each other and towards that which they represent, and a perception of the order of those relations has always been found connected with a perception of the order of the relations of thoughts. Hence the language of poets has ever affected a certain uniform and harmonious recurrence of sound, without which it were not poetry, and which is scarcely less indispensable to the communication of its influence, than the words themselves, without reference to that peculiar order. Hence the vanity of translation; it were as wise to cast a violet into a crucible that you might discover the formal principle of its colour and odour, as seek to transfuse from one language into another the creations of a poet. The plant must spring again from its seed, or it will bear no flower—and this is the burthen of the curse of Babel.

An observation of the regular mode of the recurrence of harmony in the language of poetical minds, together with its relation to music, produced metre, or a certain system of traditional forms of harmony and language. Yet it is by no means essential that a poet should accommodate his language to this traditional form, so that the harmony, which is its spirit, be observed. The practice is indeed convenient and popular, and to be preferred, especially in such composition as includes much action: but every great poet must inevitably innovate upon the example of his predecessors in the exact structure of his peculiar versification. The distinction between poets and prose writers is a vulgar error. The distinction between philosophers and poets has been anticipated. Plato was essentially a poet—the truth and splendour of his imagery, and the melody of his language, are the most intense that it is possible to conceive. He rejected the measure of the epic, dramatic, and lyrical forms, because he sought to kindle a harmony in thoughts divested of shape and action, and he forebore to invent any regular plan of rhythm which would include, under determinate forms, the varied pauses of his style. Cicero sought to imitate the cadence of his periods, but with little success. Lord Bacon was a poet.[1] His language has a sweet and majestic rhythm, which satisfies the sense, no less than the almost superhuman /114/ wisdom of his philosophy satisfies the intellect; it is a strain which distends, and then bursts the circumference of the reader's mind, and pours itself forth together with it into the universal element with which it has perpetual sympathy. All the authors of revolutions in opinion are not only necessarily poets as they are inventors, nor even as their words unveil the permanent analogy of things by images which participate in the life of truth; but as their periods are harmonious and rhythmical, and contain in themselves the elements of verse; being the echo of the eternal music. Nor are those supreme poets, who have employed traditional forms of rhythm on account of the

form and action of their subjects, less capable of perceiving and teaching the truth of things, than those who have omitted that form. Shakespeare, Dante, and Milton (to confine ourselves to modern writers) are philosophers of the very loftiest power.

A poem is the very image of life expressed in its eternal truth. There is this difference between a story and a poem, that a story is a catalogue of detached facts, which have no other connection than time, place, circumstance, cause and effect; the other is the creation of actions according to the unchangeable forms of human nature, as existing in the mind of the Creator, which is itself the image of all other minds. The one is partial, and applies only to a definite period of time, and a certain combination of events which can never again recur; the other is universal, and contains within itself the germ of a relation to whatever motives or actions have place in the possible varieties of human nature. Time, which destroys the beauty and the use of the story of particular facts, stripped of the poetry which should invest them, augments that of poetry, and for ever develops new and wonderful applications of the eternal truth which it contains. Hence epitomes have been called the moths of just history; they eat out the poetry of it. A story of particular facts is as a mirror which obscures and distorts that which should be beautiful: poetry is a mirror which makes beautiful that which is distorted.

The parts of a composition may be poetical, without the composition as a whole being a poem. A single sentence may be considered as a whole, though it may be found in the midst of a series of unassimilated /115/ portions; a single word even may be a spark of inextinguishable thought. And thus all the great historians, Herodotus, Plutarch, Livy, were poets; and although the plan of these writers, especially that of Livy, restrained them from developing this faculty in its highest degree, they made copious and ample amends for their subjection, by filling all the interstices of their subjects with living images.

Having determined what is poetry, and who are poets, let us proceed to estimate its effects upon society.

Poetry is ever accompanied with pleasure: all spirits on which it falls open themselves

---

[1] See the *Filum Labyrinthi*, and the *Essay on Death* particularly.

to receive the wisdom which is mingled with its delight. In the infancy of the world, neither poets themselves nor their auditors are fully aware of the excellence of poetry: for it acts in a divine and unapprehended manner, beyond and above consciousness; and it is reserved for future generations to contemplate and measure the mighty cause and effect in all the strength and splendour of their union. Even in modern times, no living poet ever arrived at the fullness of his fame; the jury which sits in judgment upon a poet, belonging as he does to all time, must be composed of his peers: it must be impanelled by Time from the selectest of the wise of many generations. A poet is a nightingale, who sits in darkness and sings to cheer its own solitude with sweet sounds; his auditors are as men entranced by the melody of an unseen musician, who feel that they are moved and softened, yet know not whence or why. The poems of Homer and his contemporaries were the delight of infant Greece; they were the elements of that social system which is the column upon which all succeeding civilization has reposed. Homer embodied the ideal perfection of his age in human character; nor can we doubt that those who read his verses were awakened to an ambition of becoming like Achilles, Hector, and Ulysses: the truth and beauty of friendship, patriotism, and persevering devotion to an object, were unveiled to the depths in these immortal creations: the sentiments of the auditors must have been refined and enlarged by a sympathy with such great and lovely impersonations, until from admiring they imitated, and from imitation they identified themselves with the objects of their admiration. Nor let it be /116/ objected, that these characters are remote from moral perfection, and that they can by no means be considered as edifying patterns for general imitation. Every epoch, under names more or less specious, has deified its peculiar errors; Revenge is the naked idol of the worship of a semi-barbarous age; and Self-deceit is the veiled image of unknown evil, before which luxury and satiety lie prostrate. But a poet considers the vices of his contemporaries the temporary dress in which his creations must be arrayed, and which cover without concealing the eternal proportions of their beauty. An epic or dramatic personage is understood to wear them around his soul, as he may the ancient armour or the modern uniform around his body; whilst it is easy to conceive a dress more graceful than either. The beauty of the internal nature cannot be so far concealed by its accidental vesture, but that the spirit of its form shall communicate itself to the very disguise, and indicate the shape it hides from the manner in which it is worn. A majestic form and graceful motions will express themselves through the most barbarous and tasteless costume. Few poets of the highest class have chosen to exhibit the beauty of their conceptions in its naked truth and splendour; and it is doubtful whether the alloy of costume, habit, etc., be not necessary to temper this planetary music for mortal ears.

The whole objection, however, of the immorality of poetry rests upon a misconception of the manner in which poetry acts to produce the moral improvement of man. Ethical science arranges the elements which poetry has created, and propounds schemes and proposes examples of civil and domestic life: nor is it for want of admirable doctrines that men hate, and despise, and censure, and deceive, and subjugate one another. But poetry acts in another and diviner manner. It awakens and enlarges the mind itself by rendering it the receptacle of a thousand unapprehended combinations of thought. Poetry lifts the veil from the hidden beauty of the world, and makes familiar objects be as if they were not familiar; it reproduces all that it represents, and the impersonations clothed in its Elysian light stand thenceforward in the minds of those who have once contemplated them, as memorials of that gentle and exalted content which extends itself /117/ over all thoughts and actions with which it co-exists. The great secret of morals is love; or a going out of our nature, and an identification of ourselves with the beautiful which exists in thought, action, or person, not our own. A man, to be greatly good, must imagine intensely and comprehensively; he must put himself in the place of another and of many others; the pains and pleasures of his species must become his own. The great instrument of moral good is the imagination; and poetry administers to the effect by acting upon the cause. Poetry enlarges the circumference of the imagination by replenishing it with thoughts of ever new delight, which have the power of attracting and assimilating to their own nature all other thoughts, and which form new intervals and interstices whose void for ever craves fresh food. Poetry strengthens the faculty which is the organ of the moral nature of man, in the same manner as exercise strengthens a limb. A poet therefore would do ill to embody his own conceptions of right and wrong, which are usually those of his place and time, in his poetical creations, which participate in neither. By this assumption of the inferior office of interpreting the effect, in which perhaps after all he might acquit himself but imperfectly, he would resign a glory in a participation in the cause. There was little danger that Homer, or any of the eternal poets, should have so far misunderstood themselves as to have abdicated this throne of their widest dominion. Those in whom the poetical faculty, though great, is less intense, as Euripides, Lucan, Tasso, Spenser, have frequently affected a moral aim, and the effect of their poetry is diminished in exact proportion to the degree in which they compel us to advert to this purpose. . . . /118/

[The poetry of the bucolic writers of Sicily and Egypt] is intensely melodious; like the odour of the tuberose, it overcomes and sickens the spirit with excess of sweetness; while the poetry of the preceding age was as a meadow-gale of June, which mingles the fragrance of all the flowers of the field, and adds a quickening and harmonizing spirit of its own which endows the sense with a power of sustaining its extreme delight. The bucolic and erotic delicacy in written poetry is correlative with that softness in statuary, music, and the kindred arts, and even in manners and institutions, which distinguished the epoch to which I now refer. Nor is it the poetic faculty itself, or any mis-application of it, to which this want of harmony is to be imputed. An equal sensibility to the influence of the senses and the affections is to be found in the writings of Homer and Sophocles: the former, especially, has clothed sensual and pathetic images with irresistible attractions. Their superiority over these succeeding writers consists in the presence of those thoughts which belong to the inner faculties of our nature, not in the absence of those which are connected with the external: their incomparable perfection consists in a harmony of the union of all. It is not what the erotic poets have, but what they have not, in which their imperfection consists. It is not inasmuch as they were poets, but inasmuch as they were not poets, that they can be considered with any plausibility as connected with the corruption of their age. Had that corruption availed so as to extinguish in them the sensibility to pleasure, passion, and natural scenery, which is imputed to them as an imperfection, the last triumph of evil would have been achieved. For the end of social /123/ corruption is to destroy all sensibility to pleasure; and, therefore, it is corruption. It begins at the imagination and the intellect as at the core, and distributes itself thence as a paralysing venom, through the affections into the very appetites, until all become a torpid mass in which hardly sense survives. At the approach of such a period, poetry ever addresses itself to those faculties which are the last to be destroyed, and its voice is heard, like the footsteps of Astræa departing from the world. Poetry ever communicates all the pleasure which men are capable of receiving: it is ever still the light of life; the source of whatever of beautiful or generous or true can have place in an evil time. . . . /124/

But poets have been challenged to resign the civil crown to reasoners and mechanists on another plea. It is admitted that the exercise of the imagination is most delightful, but it is alleged that that of reason is more useful. Let us examine as the grounds of this distinction what is here meant by utility. Pleasure or /131/ good, in a general sense, is that which the consciousness of a sensitive and intelligent being seeks, and in which, when found, it acquiesces. There are two kinds of pleasure, one durable, universal, and permanent; the other transitory and particular. Utility may either express the means of producing the former or the latter. In the former sense, whatever strengthens and purifies the affections, enlarges the imagination, and adds spirit to sense, is useful. But a narrower meaning may be assigned to the word utility, confining it to express that which banishes the importunity of the wants of our animal nature, the surrounding men with security of life, the dispersing the grosser delusions of superstition, and the conciliating such a degree of mutual forbearance among men as may consist with the motives of personal advantage.

Undoubtedly the promoters of utility, in this limited sense, have their appointed office in society. They follow the footsteps of poets, and copy the sketches of their creations into the book of common life. They make space, and give time. Their exertions are of the highest value, so long as they confine their administration of the concerns of the inferior powers of our nature within the limits due to the superior ones. But whilst the sceptic destroys gross superstitions, let him spare to deface, as some of the French writers have defaced, the eternal truths charactered upon the imaginations of men. Whilst the mechanist abridges, and the political economist combines labour, let them beware that their speculations, for want of correspondence with those first principles which belong to the imagination, do not tend, as they have in modern England, to exasperate at once the extremes of luxury and want. They have exemplified the saying, "To him that hath, more shall be given; and from him that hath not, the little that he hath shall be taken away." The rich have become richer, and the poor have become poorer; and the vessel of the state is driven between the Scylla and Charybdis of anarchy and despotism. Such are the effects which must ever flow from an unmitigated exercise of the calculating faculty.

It is difficult to define pleasure in its highest sense; the definition involving a number of apparent paradoxes. For, from an in- /132/ explicable defect of harmony in the constitution of human nature, the pain of the inferior is frequently connected with the pleasures of the superior portions of our being. Sorrow, terror, anguish, despair itself, are often the chosen expressions of an approximation to the highest good. Our sympathy in tragic fiction depends on this principle; tragedy delights by affording a shadow of the pleasure which exists in pain. This is the source also of the melancholy which is inseparable from the sweetest melody. The pleasure that is in sorrow is sweeter than the pleasure of pleasure itself. And hence the saying, "It is better to go to the house of mourning, than to the house of mirth." Not that this highest species of pleasure is necessarily linked with pain. The delight of love and friendship, the ecstasy of the admiration of nature, the joy of the perception and still more of the creation of poetry, is often wholly unalloyed.

The production and assurance of pleasure in this highest sense is true utility. Those who produce and preserve this pleasure are poets or poetical philosophers.

The exertions of Locke, Hume, Gibbon, Voltaire, Rousseau,[2] and their disciples, in favour of oppressed and deluded humanity, are entitled to the gratitude of mankind. Yet it is easy to calculate the degree of moral and intellectual improvement which the world would have exhibited, had they never lived. A little more nonsense would have been talked for a century or two; and perhaps a few more men, women, and children burnt as heretics. We might not at this moment have been congratulating each other on the abolition of the Inquisition in Spain. But it exceeds all imagination to conceive what would have been the moral condition of the world if neither Dante, Petrarch, Boccaccio, Chaucer, Shakespeare, Calderon, Lord Bacon, nor Milton, had ever existed; if Raphael and Michael Angelo had never been born; if the Hebrew poetry had never been translated; if a revival of the study of Greek literature had never taken place; if no monuments of ancient sculpture had been handed down to us; and if the poetry of the religion of the ancient world had been extinguished /133/ together with its belief. The human mind could never, except by the intervention of these excitements, have been awakened to the invention of the grosser sciences, and that application of analytical reasoning to the aberrations of society, which it is now attempted to exalt over the direct expression of the inventive and creative faculty itself.

We have more moral, political, and historical wisdom than we know how to reduce into

2 I follow the classification adopted by the Author of the Four Ages of Poetry; but he was essentially a Poet. The others, even Voltaire, were mere reasoners.

practice; we have more scientific and eco-
nomical knowledge than can be accommo-
dated to the just distribution of the produce
which it multiplies. The poetry in these systems of thought is concealed by the accumulation of facts and calculating processes.
There is no want of knowledge respecting
what is wisest and best in morals, government, and political economy, or at least, what
is wiser and better than what men now practise and endure. But we let *"I dare not* wait
upon *I would,* like the poor cat in the adage."
We want the creative faculty to imagine that
which we know; we want the generous impulse to act that which we imagine; we want
the poetry of life: our calculations have out-
run conception; we have eaten more than we
can digest. The cultivation of those sciences
which have enlarged the limits of the empire
of men over the external world, has, for want
of the poetical faculty, proportionally circumscribed those of the internal world; and man,
having enslaved the elements, remains himself a slave. To what but a cultivation of the
mechanical arts in a degree disproportioned
to the presence of the creative faculty, which
is the basis of all knowledge, is to be attributed the abuse of all invention for abridg-
ing and combining labour, to the exaspera-
tion of the inequality of mankind? From what
other cause has it arisen that the discoveries
which should have lightened, have added a
weight to the curse imposed on Adam? Poetry,
and the principle of Self, of which money is
the visible incarnation, are the God and Mammon of the world.

The functions of the Poetical faculty are
two-fold; by one it creates new materials of
knowledge, and power, and pleasure; by the
other it engenders in the mind a desire to
reproduce and arrange them according to a
certain rhythm and order which /134/ may
be called the beautiful and the good. The
cultivation of poetry is never more to be desired than at periods when, from an excess of
the selfish and calculating principle, the accumulation of the materials of external life
exceed the quantity of the power of assimilating them to the internal laws of human nature. The body has then become too un-
wieldy for that which animates it.

Poetry is indeed something divine. It is at
once the centre and circumference of knowledge; it is that which comprehends all science,
and that to which all science must be referred.
It is at the same time the root and blossom
of all other systems of thought; it is that from
which all spring, and that which adorns all;
and that which, if blighted, denies the fruit
and the seed, and withholds from the barren
world the nourishment and the succession of
the scions of the tree of life. It is the perfect
and consummate surface and bloom of all
things; it is as the odour and the colour of
the rose to the texture of the elements which
compose it, as the form and splendour of un-
faded beauty to the secrets of anatomy and
corruption. What were virtue, love, patriotism, friendship—what were the scenery of
this beautiful universe which we inhabit;
what were our consolations on this side of the
grave—and what were our aspirations beyond
it, if poetry did not ascend to bring light and
fire from those eternal regions where the owl-
winged faculty of calculation dare not ever
soar? Poetry is not like reasoning, a power to
be exerted according to the determination of
the will. A man cannot say, "I will compose
poetry." The greatest poet even cannot say it;
for the mind in creation is as a fading coal,
which some invisible influence, like an inconstant wind, awakens to transitory brightness;
this power arises from within, like the colour
of a flower which fades and changes as it is
developed, and the conscious portions of our
natures are unprophetic either of its approach
or its departure. Could this influence be durable in its original purity and force, it is impossible to predict the greatness of the results;
but when composition begins, inspiration is
already on the decline, and the most glorious
poetry that has ever been communicated to
the world is probably a feeble shadow of the
original conceptions of the poet. I appeal to
the greatest poets of the present day, whether
it be not an error /135/ to assert that the
finest passages of poetry are produced by labour and study. The toil and the delay recommended by critics can be justly interpreted
to mean no more than a careful observation
of the inspired moments, and an artificial
connexion of the spaces between their suggestions by the intertexture of conventional
expressions; a necessity only imposed by the

limitedness of the poetical faculty itself: for Milton conceived the *Paradise Lost* as a whole before he executed it in portions. We have his own authority also for the muse having "dictated" to him the "unpremeditated song." And let this be an answer to those who would allege the fifty-six various readings of the first line of the *Orlando Furioso*. Compositions so produced are to poetry what mosaic is to painting. This instinct and intuition of the poetical faculty is still more observable in the plastic and pictorial arts: a great statue or picture grows under the power of the artist as a child in the mother's womb; and the very mind which directs the hands in formation is incapable of accounting to itself for the origin, the gradations, or the media of the process.

Poetry is the record of the best and happiest moments of the happiest and best minds. We are aware of evanescent visitations of thought and feeling sometimes associated with place or person, sometimes regarding our own mind alone, and always arising unforeseen and departing unbidden, but elevating and delightful beyond all expression: so that even in the desire and the regret they leave, there cannot but be pleasure, participating as it does in the nature of its object. It is as it were the interpenetration of a diviner nature through our own; but its footsteps are like those of a wind over the sea, which the coming calm erases, and whose traces remain only as on the wrinkled sands which pave it. These and corresponding conditions of being are experienced principally by those of the most delicate sensibility and the most enlarged imagination; and the state of mind produced by them is at war with every base desire. The enthusiasm of virtue, love, patriotism, and friendship is essentially linked with such emotions; and whilst they last, self appears as what it is, an atom to a universe. Poets are not only subject to these experiences as spirits of the most refined organization, but they can colour all that they com- /136/ bine with the evanescent hues of this ethereal world; a word, a trait in the representation of a scene or a passion will touch the enchanted chord, and reanimate, in those who have ever experienced these emotions, the sleeping, the cold, the buried image of the past. Poetry thus makes immortal all that is best and most beautiful in the world; it arrests the vanishing apparitions which haunt the interluminations of life, and veiling them, or in language or in form, sends them forth among mankind, bearing sweet news of kindred joy to those with whom their sisters abide—abide, because there is no portal of expression from the caverns of the spirit which they inhabit into the universe of things. Poetry redeems from decay the visitations of the divinity in man.

Poetry turns all things to loveliness; it exalts the beauty of that which is most beautiful, and it adds beauty to that which is most deformed; it marries exultation and horror, grief and pleasure, eternity and change; it subdues to union under its light yoke all irreconcilable things. It transmutes all that it touches, and every form moving within the radiance of its presence is changed by wondrous sympathy to an incarnation of the spirit which it breathes: its secret alchemy turns to potable gold the poisonous waters which flow from death through life; it strips the veil of familiarity from the world, and lays bare the naked and sleeping beauty, which is the spirit of its forms.

All things exist as they are perceived: at least in relation to the percipient. "The mind is its own place, and of itself can make a heaven of hell, a hell of heaven." But poetry defeats the curse which binds us to be subjected to the accident of surrounding impressions. And whether it spreads its own figured curtain, or withdraws life's dark veil from before the scene of things, it equally creates for us a being within our being. It makes us the inhabitants of a world to which the familiar world is a chaos. It reproduces the common universe of which we are portions and percipients, and it purges from our inward sight the film of familiarity which obscures from us the wonder of our being. It compels us to feel that which we perceive, and to imagine that which we know. It creates anew the universe, after it has been annihilated in our minds by the recurrence of impressions blunted by reiteration. It /137/ justifies the bold and true words of Tasso—*Non merita nome di creatore, se non Iddio ed il Poeta* [None merits the name of creator but God and the Poet].

A poet, as he is the author to others of the highest wisdom, pleasure, virtue, and glory, so he ought personally to be the happiest, the best, the wisest, and the most illustrious of men. As to his glory, let time be challenged to declare whether the frame of any other institutor of human life be comparable to that of a poet. That he is the wisest, the happiest, and the best, inasmuch as he is a poet, is equally incontrovertible: the greatest poets have been men of the most spotless virtue, of the most consummate prudence, and, if we would look into the interior of their lives, the most fortunate of men: and the exceptions, as they regard those who possessed the poetic faculty in a high yet inferior degree, will be found on consideration to confine rather than destroy the rule. Let us for a moment stoop to the arbitration of popular breath, and usurping and uniting in our own persons the incompatible characters of accuser, witness, judge, and executioner, let us decide without trial, testimony, or form, that certain motives of those who are "there sitting where we dare not soar," are reprehensible. Let us assume that Homer was a drunkard, that Virgil was a flatterer, that Horace was a coward, that Tasso was a madman, that Lord Bacon was a peculator, that Raphael was a libertine, that Spenser was a poet laureate. It is inconsistent with this division of our subject to cite living poets, but posterity has done ample justice to the great names now referred to. Their errors have been weighed and found to have been dust in the balance; if their sins "were as scarlet, they are now white as snow"; they have been washed in the blood of the mediator and redeemer, Time. Observe in what a ludicrous chaos the imputations of real or fictitious crime have been confused in the contemporary calumnies against poetry and poets; consider how little is, as it appears—or appears, as it is; look to your own motives, and judge not, lest ye be judged.

Poetry, as has been said, differs in this respect from logic, that it is not subject to the control of the active powers of the mind, and that its birth and recurrence have no necessary connexion with the consciousness or will. It is presumptuous to determine that /138/ these are the necessary conditions of all mental causation, when mental effects are experienced unsusceptible of being referred to them. The frequent recurrence of the poetical power, it is obvious to suppose, may produce in the mind a habit of order and harmony correlative with its own nature and with its effects upon other minds. But in the intervals of inspiration, and they may be frequent without being durable, a poet becomes a man, and is abandoned to the sudden reflux of the influences under which others habitually live. But as he is more delicately organized than other men, and sensible to pain and pleasure, both his own and that of others, in a degree unknown to them, he will avoid the one and pursue the other with an ardour proportioned to this difference. And he renders himself obnoxious to calumny, when he neglects to observe the circumstances under which these objects of universal pursuit and flight have disguised themselves in one another's garments.

But there is nothing necessarily evil in this error, and thus cruelty, envy, revenge, avarice, and the passions purely evil, have never formed any portion of the popular imputations on the lives of poets. . . . /139/

The most unfailing herald, companion, and follower of the awakening of a great people to work a beneficial change in opinion or institution, is poetry. At such periods there is an accumulation of the power of communicating and receiving intense and impassioned conceptions respecting man and nature. The persons in whom this power resides, may often, as far as regards many portions of their nature, have little apparent correspondence with that spirit of good of which they are the ministers. But even whilst they deny and abjure, they are yet compelled to serve, the power which is seated on the throne of their own soul. It is impossible to read the compositions of the most celebrated writers of the present day without being startled with the electric life which burns within their words. They measure the circumference and sound the depths of human nature with a comprehensive and all-penetrating spirit, and they are themselves perhaps the most sincerely astonished at its manifestations; for it is less their spirit than the spirit of the age. Poets are the hierophants of an unapprehended inspiration; the mirrors of the gigantic shadows which futurity casts upon the present; the words which express what they understand not; the trumpets which sing to battle, and feel not what they inspire; the influence which is moved not, but moves. Poets are the unacknowledged legislators of the world. /140/

JOHN STUART MILL

from "Thoughts on Poetry and Its Varieties"

[John Stuart Mill (1806–1873), English economist and philosopher, was educated by his father, James Mill, who started him with Greek at three and Latin at seven. In his adult life Mill became leader of the school of thought originally promulgated by Jeremy Bentham and called "utilitarianism" by Mill. His *Principles of Political Economy* (1848; 1871), *System of Logic* (1843; 1872), and *On Liberty* (1859) were all important contributions to their fields; by his writings and action he did much to further the cause of woman's suffrage and other reforms; late in his career he served a term in Parliament. The following selection, originally published under the title "What Is Poetry?" in *The Monthly Repository* for January 1833, was revised in 1859 and published by Mill as Part I of an essay entitled "Thoughts on Poetry and Its Varieties" in his *Dissertations and Discussions*. It is reprinted here from Volume I of a later edition of that book (Boston, 1868).]

I

It has often been asked, What is Poetry? And many and various are the answers which have been returned. The vulgarest of all—one with which no person possessed of the faculties to which poetry addresses itself can ever have been satisfied—is that which confounds poetry with metrical composition; yet to this wretched mockery of a definition many have been led back by the failure of all their attempts to find any other that would distinguish what they have been accustomed to call poetry from much which they have known only under other names.

That, however, the word "poetry" imports something quite peculiar in its nature; something which may exist in what is called prose as well as in verse; something which does not even require the instrument of words, but can speak through the other audible symbols called musical sounds, and even through the visible ones which are the language of sculpture, painting, and architecture,—all this, we believe, is and must be felt, though perhaps indistinctly, by all upon whom poetry in any of its shapes produces any impression beyond that of tickling the ear. The distinction be- /89/ tween poetry and what is not poetry, whether explained or not, is felt to be fundamental; and, where every one feels a difference, a difference there must be. All other appearances may be fallacious; but the appearance of a difference is a real difference. Appearances too, like other things, must have a cause; and that which can cause any thing, even an illusion, must be a reality. And hence, while a half-philosophy disdains the classifications and distinctions indicated by popular language, philosophy carried to its highest point frames new ones, but rarely sets aside the old, content with correcting and regularizing them. It cuts fresh channels for thought, but does not fill up such as it finds ready-made: it traces, on the contrary, more deeply, broadly, and distinctly, those into which the current has spontaneously flowed.

Let us then attempt, in the way of modest inquiry, not to coerce and confine Nature within the bounds of an arbitrary definition, but rather to find the boundaries which she herself has set, and erect a barrier round them; not calling mankind to account for having misapplied the word "poetry," but attempting to clear up the conception which they already attach to it, and to bring forward as a distinct principle that which, as a vague feeling, has really guided them in their employment of the term.

The object of poetry is confessedly to act upon the emotions;—and therein is poetry sufficiently distinguished from what Wordsworth affirms to be its logical opposite; namely, not prose, but matter of fact, or science. The one addresses itself to the belief; the other, to the feelings. The one does its work by con- /90/ vincing or persuading; the other, by moving. The one acts by presenting a proposition to the understanding; the other, by offering interesting objects of contemplation to the sensibilities.

This, however, leaves us very far from a definition of poetry. This distinguishes it from one thing; but we are bound to distinguish it from every thing. To bring thoughts or images before the mind, for the purpose of acting upon the emotions, does not belong to poetry alone. It is equally the province (for example) of the novelist: and yet the faculty of the poet and that of the novelist are as distinct as any other two faculties; as the faculties of the novelist and of the orator, or of the poet and the metaphysician. The two characters may be united, as characters the most disparate may; but they have no natural connection.

Many of the greatest poems are in the form of fictitious narratives; and, in almost all good serious fictions, there is true poetry. But there is a radical distinction between the interest felt in a story as such, and the interest excited by poetry; for the one is derived from incident, the other from the representation of feeling. In one, the source of the emotion excited is the exhibition of a state or states of human sensibility; in the other, of a series of states of mere outward circumstances. Now, all minds are capable of being affected more or less by representations of the latter kind, and all, or almost all, by those of the former; yet the two sources of interest correspond to two distinct and (as respects their greatest development) mutually exclusive characters of mind.

At what age is the passion for a story, for almost /91/ any kind of story, merely as a story, the most intense? In childhood. But that also is the age at which poetry, even of the simplest description, is least relished and least understood; because the feelings with which it is especially conversant are yet undeveloped, and, not having been even in the slightest degree experienced, cannot be sympathized with. In what stage of the progress of society, again, is story-telling most valued, and the story-teller in greatest request and honor? In a rude state like that of the Tartars and Arabs at this day, and of almost all nations in the earliest ages. But, in this state of society, there is little poetry except ballads, which are mostly narrative,—that is, essentially stories,—and derive their principal interest from the incidents. Considered as po-

etry, they are of the lowest and most elementary kind: the feelings depicted, or rather indicated, are the simplest our nature has; such joys and griefs as the immediate pressure of some outward event excites in rude minds, which live wholly immersed in outward things, and have never, either from choice or a force they could not resist, turned themselves to the contemplation of the world within. Passing now from childhood, and from the childhood of society, to the grown-up men and women of this most grown-up and unchild-like age, the minds and hearts of greatest depth and elevation are commonly those which take greatest delight in poetry: the shallowest and emptiest, on the contrary, are, at all events, not those least addicted to novel-reading. This accords, too, with all analogous experience of human nature. The sort of persons whom not merely in books, but in their lives, we find perpetually engaged in hunting for /92/ excitement from without, are invariably those who do not possess, either in the vigor of their intellectual powers or in the depth of their sensibilities, that which would enable them to find ample excitement nearer home. The most idle and frivolous persons take a natural delight in fictitious narrative: the excitement it affords is of the kind which comes from without. Such persons are rarely lovers of poetry, though they may fancy themselves so because they relish novels in verse. But poetry, which is the delineation of the deeper and more secret workings of human emotion, is interesting only to those to whom it recalls what they have felt, or whose imagination it stirs up to conceive what they could feel, or what they might have been able to feel, had their outward circumstances been different.

Poetry, when it is really such, is truth; and fiction also, if it is good for any thing, is truth: but they are different truths. The truth of poetry is to paint the human soul truly: the truth of fiction is to give a true picture of life. The two kinds of knowledge are different, and come by different ways,—come mostly to different persons. Great poets are often proverbially ignorant of life. What they know has come by observation of themselves: they have found within them one highly delicate and sensitive specimen of human nature, on which the laws of emotion are written in large characters, such as can be read off without much study. Other knowledge of mankind, such as comes to men of the world by outward experience, is not indispensable to them as poets: but, to the novelist, such knowledge is all in all; he has to describe outward things, not the inward man; actions and events, not /93/ feelings; and it will not do for him to be numbered among those, who, as Madame Roland said of Brissot, know man, but not *men*.

All this is no bar to the possibility of combining both elements, poetry and narrative or incident, in the same work, and calling it either a novel or a poem; but so may red and white combine on the same human features or on the same canvas. There is one order of composition which requires the union of poetry and incident, each in its highest kind,—the dramatic. Even there, the two elements are perfectly distinguishable, and may exist of unequal quality and in the most various proportion. The incidents of a dramatic poem may be scanty and ineffective, though the delineation of passion and character may be of the highest order, as in Goethe's admirable "Torquato Tasso"; or, again, the story as a mere story may be well got up for effect, as is the case with some of the most trashy productions of the Minerva press: it may even be, what those are not, a coherent and probable series of events, though there be scarcely a feeling exhibited which is not represented falsely, or in a manner absolutely commonplace. The combination of the two excellences is what renders Shakespeare so generally acceptable,—each sort of readers finding in him what is suitable to their faculties. To the many, he is great as a story-teller; to the few, as a poet.

In limiting poetry to the delineation of states of feeling, and denying the name where nothing is delineated but outward objects, we may be thought to have done what we promised to avoid,—to have not found, but made, a definition in opposition to the usage of lan- /94/ guage, since it is established by common consent that there is a poetry called descriptive. We deny the charge. Description is not poetry because there is descriptive poetry, no more than science is poetry because

there is such a thing as a didactic poem. But an object which admits of being described, or a truth which may fill a place in a scientific treatise, may also furnish an occasion for the generation of poetry, which we thereupon choose to call descriptive or didactic. The poetry is not in the object itself, nor in the scientific truth itself, but in the state of mind in which the one and the other may be contemplated. The mere delineation of the dimensions and colors of external objects is not poetry, no more than a geometrical ground-plan of St. Peter's or Westminster Abbey is painting. Descriptive poetry consists, no doubt, in description, but in description of things as they appear, not as they are; and it paints them, not in their bare and natural lineaments, but seen through the medium and arrayed in the colors of the imagination set in action by the feelings. If a poet describes a lion, he does not describe him as a naturalist would, nor even as a traveller would, who was intent upon stating the truth, the whole truth, and nothing but the truth. He describes him by imagery, that is, by suggesting the most striking likenesses and contrasts which might occur to a mind contemplating a lion, in the state of awe, wonder, or terror, which the spectacle naturally excites, or is, on the occasion, supposed to excite. Now, this is describing the lion professedly, but the state of excitement of the spectator really. The lion may be described falsely or with exaggeration, and the poetry be all the /95/ better: but, if the human emotion be not painted with scrupulous truth, the poetry is bad poetry; i.e., is not poetry at all, but a failure.

Thus far, our progress towards a clear view of the essentials of poetry has brought us very close to the last two attempts at a definition of poetry which we happen to have seen in print, both of them by poets, and men of genius. The one is by Ebenezer Elliott, the author of "Corn-law Rhymes," and other poems of still greater merit. "Poetry," says he, "is impassioned truth." The other is by a writer in "Blackwood's Magazine," and comes, we think, still nearer the mark. He defines poetry, "man's thoughts tinged by his feelings." There is in either definition a near approximation to what we are in search of. Every truth which a human being can enunciate, every thought,

even every outward impression, which can enter into his consciousness, may become poetry,
when shown through any impassioned medium; when invested with the coloring of joy,
or grief, or pity, or affection, or admiration, or
reverence, or awe, or even hatred or terror;
and, unless so colored, nothing, be it as interesting as it may, is poetry. But both these
definitions fail to discriminate between poetry
and eloquence. Eloquence, as well as poetry,
is impassioned truth; eloquence, as well as
poetry, is thoughts colored by the feelings. Yet
common apprehension and philosophic criticism alike recognize a distinction between the
two: there is much that every one would call
eloquence, which no one would think of class-
ing as poetry. A question will sometimes arise,
whether some particular author is a poet; and
those who maintain the negative /96/ commonly allow, that, though not a poet, he is a
highly eloquent writer. The distinction between poetry and eloquence appears to us to
be equally fundamental with the distinction
between poetry and narrative, or between
poetry and description, while it is still farther
from having been satisfactorily cleared up
than either of the others.

Poetry and eloquence are both alike the expression or utterance of feeling: but, if we
may be excused the antithesis, we should say
that eloquence is *heard;* poetry is *over*heard.
Eloquence supposes an audience. The peculiarity of poetry appears to us to lie in the
poet's utter unconsciousness of a listener. Poetry is feeling confessing itself to itself in moments of solitude, and embodying itself in
symbols which are the nearest possible representations of the feeling in the exact shape in
which it exists in the poet's mind. Eloquence
is feeling pouring itself out to other minds,
courting their sympathy, or endeavoring to
influence their belief, or move them to passion
or to action.

All poetry is of the nature of soliloquy. It
may be said that poetry which is printed on
hot-pressed paper, and sold at a bookseller's
shop, is a soliloquy in full dress and on the
stage. It is so; but there is nothing absurd in
the idea of such a mode of soliloquizing. What
we have said to ourselves we may tell to others
afterwards; what we have said or done in solitude we may voluntarily reproduce when we

know that other eyes are upon us. But no
trace of consciousness that any eyes are upon
us must be visible in the work itself. The ac-
tor knows that there is an audience present;
but, if he act as though he knew it, he acts ill.
A poet /97/ may write poetry, not only with
the intention of printing it, but for the express purpose of being paid for it. That it
should *be* poetry, being written under such
influences, is less probable, not, however, impossible; but no otherwise possible than if
he can succeed in excluding from his work
every vestige of such lookings-forth into the
outward and every-day world, and can express
his emotions exactly as he has felt them in
solitude, or as he is conscious that he should
feel them, though they were to remain for
ever unuttered, or (at the lowest) as he knows
that others feel them in similar circumstances
of solitude. But when he turns round, and addresses himself to another person; when the
act of utterance is not itself the end, but a
means to an end,—viz., by the feelings he himself expresses, to work upon the feelings, or
upon the belief or the will of another; when
the expression of his emotions, or of his
thoughts tinged by his emotions, is tinged also
by that purpose, by that desire of making an
impression upon another mind,—then it ceases
to be poetry, and becomes eloquence.

Poetry, accordingly, is the natural fruit of
solitude and meditation; eloquence, of intercourse with the world. The persons who have
most feeling of their own, if intellectual culture has given them a language in which to
express it, have the highest faculty of poetry:
those who best understand the feelings of
others are the most eloquent. The persons
and the nations who commonly excel in poetry are those whose character and tastes render them least dependent upon the applause
or sympathy or concurrence of the world in
general. Those to whom that applause, that
sympathy, /98/ that concurrence, are most
necessary, generally excel most in eloquence.
And hence, perhaps, the French, who are the
least poetical of all great and intellectual nations, are among the most eloquent; the
French also being the most sociable, the vain-
est, and the least self-dependent.

If the above be, as we believe, the true
theory of the distinction commonly admitted

between eloquence and poetry, or even though it be not so, yet if, as we cannot doubt, the distinction above stated be a real *bonâ-fide* distinction, it will be found to hold, not merely in the language of words, but in all other language, and to intersect the whole domain of art.

Take, for example, music. We shall find in that art, so peculiarly the expression of passion, two perfectly distinct styles,—one of which may be called the poetry, the other the oratory, of music. This difference, being seized, would put an end to much musical sectarianism. There has been much contention whether the music of the modern Italian school, that of Rossini and his successors, be impassioned or not. Without doubt, the passion it expresses is not the musing, meditative tenderness or pathos or grief of Mozart or Beethoven; yet it is passion, but garrulous passion,—the passion which pours itself into other ears, and therein the better calculated for dramatic effect, having a natural adaptation for dialogue. Mozart also is great in musical oratory; but his most touching compositions are in the opposite style,—that of soliloquy. Who can imagine "Dove sono" *heard*? We imagine it *over*heard.

Purely pathetic music commonly partakes of solilo- /99/ quy. The soul is absorbed in its distress; and, though there may be bystanders, it is not thinking of them. When the mind is looking within, and not without, its state does not often or rapidly vary; and hence the even, uninterrupted flow, approaching almost to monotony, which a good reader or a good singer will give to words or music of a pensive or melancholy cast. But grief, taking the form of a prayer or of a complaint, becomes oratorical: no longer low and even and subdued, it assumes a more emphatic rhythm, a more rapidly returning accent; instead of a few slow, equal notes, following one after another at regular intervals, it crowds note upon note, and often assumes a hurry and bustle like joy. Those who are familiar with some of the best of Rossini's serious compositions, such as the air "Tu che i miseri conforti," in the opera of "Tancredi," or the duet "Ebben per mia memoria," in "La Grazza Ladra," will at once understand and feel our meaning. Both are highly tragic and passionate: the passion

of both is that of oratory, not poetry. The like may be said of that most moving invocation in Beethoven's "Fidelio,"—

"Komm, Hoffnung, lass das letzte Stern
Der Müde nicht erbleichen,"—
[Come, Hope, let not the last star of
sorrow turn pale.]

in which Madame Schröder Devrient exhibited such consummate powers of pathetic expression. How different from Winter's beautiful "Paga fui," the very soul of melancholy exhaling itself in solitude! fuller of meaning, and therefore more profoundly poetical, than the words for which it was composed; for it seems to express, not simple melancholy, but the melancholy of remorse. /100/

If from vocal music we now pass to instrumental, we may have a specimen of musical oratory in any fine military symphony or march; while the poetry of music seems to have attained its consummation in Beethoven's "Overture to Egmont," so wonderful in its mixed expression of grandeur and melancholy.

In the arts which speak to the eye, the same distinctions will be found to hold, not only between poetry and oratory, but between poetry, oratory, narrative, and simple imitation or description.

Pure description is exemplified in a mere portrait or a mere landscape,—productions of art, it is true, but of the mechanical rather than of the fine arts; being works of simple imitation, not creation. We say, a mere portrait or a mere landscape; because it is possible for a portrait or a landscape, without ceasing to be such, to be also a picture, like Turner's landscapes, and the great portraits by Titian or Vandyke.

Whatever in painting or sculpture expresses human feeling,—or character, which is only a certain state of feeling grown habitual,—may be called, according to circumstances, the poetry or the eloquence of the painter's or the sculptor's art: the poetry, if the feeling declares itself by such signs as escape from us when we are unconscious of being seen; the oratory, if the signs are those we use for the purpose of voluntary communication.

The narrative style answers to what is called historical painting, which it is the fashion among connoisseurs to treat as the climax of the pictorial art. That it is the most difficult branch of the art, we do not doubt, because, in its perfection, it includes the perfection of /101/ all the other branches; as, in like manner, an epic poem, though, in so far as it is epic (i.e., narrative), it is not poetry at all, is yet esteemed the greatest effort of poetic genius, because there is no kind whatever of poetry which may not appropriately find a place in it. But an historical picture as such, that is, as the representation of an incident, must necessarily, as it seems to us, be poor and ineffective. The narrative powers of painting are extremely limited. Scarcely any picture, scarcely even any series of pictures, tells its own story without the aid of an interpreter. But it is the single figures, which, to us, are the great charm even of an historical picture. It is in these that the power of the art is really seen. In the attempt to narrate, visible and permanent signs are too far behind the fugitive audible ones, which follow so fast one after another; while the faces and figures in a narrative picture, even though they be Titian's, stand still. Who would not prefer one "Virgin and Child" of Raphael to all the pictures which Rubens, with his fat, frouzy Dutch Venuses, ever painted?—though Rubens, besides excelling almost every one in his mastery over the mechanical parts of his art, often shows real genius in *grouping* his figures, the peculiar problem of historical painting. But then, who, except a mere student of drawing and coloring, ever cared to look twice at any of the figures themselves? The power of painting lies in poetry, of which Rubens had not the slightest tincture,—not in narrative, wherein he might have excelled.

The single figures, however, in an historical picture, are rather the eloquence of painting than the poetry. /102/ They mostly (unless they are quite out of place in the picture) express the feelings of one person as modified by the presence of others. Accordingly, the minds whose bent leads them rather to eloquence than to poetry rush to historical painting. The French painters, for instance, seldom attempt, because they could make nothing of, single heads, like those glorious ones of the Italian masters with which they might feed themselves day after day in their own Louvre. They must all be historical; and they are, almost to a man, attitudinizers. If we wished to give any young artist the most impressive warning our imagination could devise against that kind of vice in the pictorial which corresponds to rant in the histrionic art, we would advise him to walk once up and once down the gallery of the Luxembourg. Every figure in French painting or statuary seems to be showing itself off before spectators. They are not poetical, but in the worst style of corrupted eloquence. /103/

EDGAR ALLAN POE
from "The Poetic Principle"

[Edgar Allan Poe (1809–1849), poet, critic, and short story writer, was born in Boston, lived with foster parents for six years in London, spent one year at the University of Virginia and over two years in the United States Army and at West Point, and lived during his adult life in Richmond, Baltimore, Philadelphia, and New York. While serving brilliantly but erratically as editor of several magazines, he acquired fame with *Tales of the Grotesque and Arabesque* (1840) and *The Raven and Other Poems* (1845). The last years of his life were saddened by the death of his young wife, by illness, and by opium. "The Poetic Principle," first published in *Sartain's Union Magazine* in 1850, is excerpted here from Volume VI of *The Works of Edgar Allan Poe,* edited by Edmund Clarence Stedman and George Edward Woodberry (Chicago, 1895).]

In speaking of the Poetic Principle, I have no design to be either thorough or profound. While discussing, very much at random, the essentiality of what we call Poetry, my principal purpose will be to cite for consideration some few of those minor English or American poems which best suit my own taste, or which, upon my own fancy, have left the most definite impression. By "minor poems" I mean, of course, poems of little length. And here, in the beginning, permit me to say a few words in regard to a somewhat peculiar principle, which, whether rightfully or wrongfully, has always had its influence in my own critical estimate of the poem. I hold that a long poem does not exist. I maintain that the phrase, "a long poem," is simply a flat contradiction in terms.

I need scarcely observe that a poem deserves its title only inasmuch as it excites, by elevating the soul. The value of the poem is in the ratio of this elevating excitement. But all excitements are, through a psychal necessity, transient. That degree of excitement which would entitle a poem to be so called at all cannot be sustained throughout a composition of /3/ any great length. After the lapse of half an hour, at the very utmost, it flags—fails —a revulsion ensues—and then the poem is, in effect, and in fact, no longer such.

There are, no doubt, many who have found difficulty in reconciling the critical dictum that the *Paradise Lost* is to be devoutly admired throughout, with the absolute impossibility of maintaining for it, during perusal, the amount of enthusiasm which that critical dictum would demand. This great work, in fact, is to be regarded as poetical, only when, losing sight of that vital requisite in all works of Art, Unity, we view it merely as a series of minor poems. If, to preserve its Unity—its totality of effect or impression—we read it (as would be necessary) at a single sitting, the result is but a constant alternation of excitement and depression. After a passage of what we feel to be true poetry, there follows, inevitably, a passage of platitude which no critical pre-judgment can force us to admire; but if, upon completing the work, we read it again omitting the first book—that is to say, commencing with the second—we shall be surprised at now finding that admirable which we before condemned—that damnable which we had previously so much admired. It follows from all this that the ultimate, aggregate, or absolute effect of even the best epic under the sun, is a nullity:—and this is precisely the fact.

In regard to the *Iliad*, we have, if not positive proof, at least very good reason, for believing it intended as a series of lyrics; but, granting the epic intention, I can say only that the work is based in an imperfect sense of Art. The modern epic is, of the supposititious ancient model, but an inconsiderate and /4/ blindfold imitation. But the day of these artistic anomalies is over. If, at any time, any very long poem *were* popular in reality, which I doubt, it is at least clear that no very long poem will ever be popular again.

That the extent of a poetical work is, *ceteris paribus*, the measure of its merit, seems undoubtedly, when we thus state it, a proposition sufficiently absurd—yet we are indebted for it to the Quarterly Reviews. Surely there can be nothing in mere *size,* abstractly considered—there can be nothing in mere *bulk,* so far as a volume is concerned, which has so continuously elicited admiration from these saturnine pamphlets! A mountain, to be sure, by the mere sentiment of physical magnitude which it conveys, *does* impress us with a sense of the sublime—but no man is impressed after *this* fashion by the material grandeur of even *The Columbiad.* Even the Quarterlies have not instructed us to be so impressed by it. *As yet,* they have not *insisted* on our estimating Lamartine by the cubic foot, or Pollock by the pound—but what else are we to *infer* from their continued prating about "sustained effort"? If, by "sustained effort," any little gentleman has accomplished an epic, let us frankly commend him for the effort—if this indeed be a thing commendable—but let us forbear praising the epic on the effort's account. It is to be hoped that common sense, in the time to come, will prefer deciding upon a work of art, rather by the impression it makes, by the effect it produces, than by the time it took to impress the effect or by the amount of "sustained effort" which had been found necessary in effecting the impression. The fact is, that perseverance is one thing, and genius quite /5/ another—nor can all the Quarterlies in Christendom confound them. By-and-by, this proposition, with many which I have been just urging, will be received as self-evident. In the mean time, by being generally condemned as falsities, they will not be essentially damaged as truths.

On the other hand, it is clear that a poem may be improperly brief. Undue brevity degenerates into mere epigrammatism. A *very* short poem, while now and then producing a brilliant or vivid, never produces a profound or enduring effect. There must be the steady pressing down of the stamp upon the wax. Béranger has wrought innumerable things, pungent and spirit-stirring; but, in general, they have been too imponderous to stamp themselves deeply into the public attention; and thus, as so many feathers of fancy, have been blown aloft only to be whistled down the wind.

A remarkable instance of the effect of un-

due brevity in depressing a poem—in keeping it out of the popular view—is afforded by the following exquisite little serenade:

I arise from dreams of thee
  In the first sweet sleep of night,
When the winds are breathing low,
  And the stars are shining bright;
I arise from dreams of thee,
  And a spirit in my feet
Hath led me—who knows how?—
  To thy chamber-window, sweet!

The wandering airs, they faint
  On the dark, the silent stream;
The champak odors fail
  Like sweet thoughts in a dream; /6/
The nightingale's complaint,
  It dies upon her heart,
As I must die on thine,
  Oh, beloved as thou art!

Oh, lift me from the grass!
  I die! I faint! I fail!
Let thy love in kisses rain
  On my lips and eyelids pale.
My cheek is cold and white, alas!
  My heart beats loud and fast:
Oh! press it close to thine again,
  Where it will break at last![1]

Very few, perhaps, are familiar with these lines—yet no less a poet than Shelley is their author. Their warm, yet delicate and ethereal imagination will be appreciated by all—but by none so thoroughly as by him who has himself arisen from sweet dreams of one beloved to bathe in the aromatic air of a southern midsummer night. . . . /7/

While the epic mania—while the idea that, to merit in poetry, prolixity is indispensable —has, for some years past, been gradually dying out of the public mind, by mere dint of its own absurdity—we find it succeeded by a heresy too palpably false to be long tolerated, but one which, in the brief period it has already endured, may be said to have accomplished more in the corruption of our Poetical Literature than all its other enemies combined. I allude to the heresy of *The Didactic.* It has been assumed, tacitly and avowedly, directly and indirectly, that the ultimate /8/ object of all Poetry is Truth. Every poem, it is said, should inculcate a moral; and by this

1 ["Indian Serenade," by Percy Bysshe Shelley.]

moral is the poetical merit of the work to be adjudged. We Americans, especially, have patronized this happy idea; and we Bostonians, very especially, have developed it in full. We have taken it into our heads that to write a poem simply for the poem's sake, and to acknowledge such to have been our design, would be to confess ourselves radically wanting in the true Poetic dignity and force:—but the simple fact is, that, would we but permit ourselves to look into our own souls, we should immediately there discover that under the sun there neither exists nor *can* exist any work more thoroughly dignified—more supremely noble than this very poem—this poem *per se*—this poem which is a poem and nothing more—this poem written solely for the poem's sake.

With as deep a reverence for the True as ever inspired the bosom of man, I would, nevertheless, limit, in some measure, its modes of inculcation. I would limit to enforce them. I would not enfeeble them by dissipation. The demands of Truth are severe. She has no sympathy with the myrtles. All *that* which is so indispensable in Song, is precisely all *that* with which *she* has nothing whatever to do. It is but making her a flaunting paradox, to wreathe her in gems and flowers. In enforcing a truth, we need severity rather than efflorescence of language. We must be simple, precise, terse. We must be cool, calm, unimpassioned. In a word, we must be in that mood which, as nearly as possible, is the exact converse of the poetical. He must be blind, indeed, who does not perceive the radical and chasmal differences between the truthful and the poetical modes of incul- /9/ cation. He must be theory-mad beyond redemption who, in spite of these differences, shall still persist in attempting to reconcile the obstinate oils and waters of Poetry and Truth.

Dividing the world of mind into its three most obvious distinctions, we have the Pure Intellect, Taste, and the Moral Sense. I place Taste in the middle, because it is just this position which in the mind it occupies. It holds intimate relations with either extreme; but from the Moral Sense is separated by so faint a difference that Aristotle has not hesitated to place some of its operations among the virtues themselves. Nevertheless, we find the *of-*

fices of the trio marked with a sufficient distinction. Just as the Intellect concerns itself with Truth, so Taste informs us of the Beautiful, while the Moral Sense is regardful of Duty. Of this latter, while Conscience teaches the obligation, and Reason the expediency, Taste contents herself with displaying the charms:—waging war upon Vice solely on the ground of her deformity—her disproportion, her animosity to the fitting, to the appropriate, to the harmonious—in a word, to Beauty.

An immortal instinct, deep within the spirit of man, is thus, plainly, a sense of the Beautiful. This it is which administers to his delight in the manifold forms, and sounds, and odors, and sentiments amid which he exists. And just as the lily is repeated in the lake, or the eyes of Amaryllis in the mirror, so is the mere oral or written repetition of these forms, and sounds, and colors, and odors, and sentiments, a duplicate source of delight. But this mere repetition is not poetry. He who shall simply sing, with however glowing enthusiasm, or with however vivid a /10/ truth of description, of the sights, and sounds, and odors, and colors, and sentiments, which greet *him* in common with all mankind—he, I say, has yet failed to prove his divine title. There is still a something in the distance which he has been unable to attain. We have still a thirst unquenchable, to allay which he has not shown us the crystal springs. This thirst belongs to the immortality of Man. It is at once a consequence and an indication of his perennial existence. It is the desire of the moth for the star. It is no mere appreciation of the Beauty before us—but a wild effort to reach the Beauty above. Inspired by an ecstatic prescience of the glories beyond the grave, we struggle, by multiform combinations among the things and thoughts of Time, to attain a portion of that Loveliness whose very elements, perhaps, appertain to eternity alone. And thus when by Poetry—or when by Music, the most entrancing of the Poetic moods—we find ourselves melted into tears—not as the Abbaté Gravia supposes—through excess of pleasure, but through a certain petulant, impatient sorrow at our inability to grasp *now*, wholly, here on earth, at once and forever, those divine and rapturous joys, of which *through* the poem, or *through* the music, we attain to but brief and indeterminate glimpses.

The struggle to apprehend the supernal Loveliness—this struggle, on the part of souls fittingly constituted—has given to the world all *that* which it (the world) has ever been enabled at once to understand and *to feel* as poetic.

The Poetic Sentiment, of course, may develop itself in various modes—in Painting, in Sculpture, in Architecture, in the Dance—very especially in Music, /11/ —and very peculiarly, and with a wide field, in the composition of the Landscape Garden. Our present theme, however, has regard only to its manifestation in words. And here let me speak briefly on the topic of rhythm. Contenting myself with the certainty that Music, in its various modes of metre, rhythm, and rhyme, is of so vast a moment in Poetry as never to be wisely rejected—is so vitally important an adjunct, that he is simply silly who declines its assistance—I will not now pause to maintain its absolute essentiality. It is in Music, perhaps, that the soul most nearly attains the great end for which, when inspired by the Poetic Sentiment, it struggles—the creation of supernal Beauty. It *may* be, indeed, that here this sublime end is, now and then, attained *in fact*. We are often made to feel, with a shivering delight, that from an earthly harp are stricken notes which *cannot* have been unfamiliar to the angels. And thus there can be little doubt that in the union of Poetry with Music in its popular sense, we shall find the widest field for the Poetic development. The old Bards and Minnesingers had advantages which we do not possess—and Thomas Moore, singing his own songs, was, in the most legitimate manner, perfecting them as poems.

To recapitulate, then:—I would define, in brief, the Poetry of words as *The Rhythmical Creation of Beauty*. Its sole arbiter is Taste. With the Intellect or with the Conscience, it has only collateral relations. Unless incidentally, it has no concern whatever either with Duty or with Truth.

A few words, however, in explanation. *That* pleasure which is at once the most pure, the most elevating, and the most intense, is derived, I maintain, from the /12/ contemplation of the Beautiful. In the contemplation of Beauty we alone find it possible to attain that pleasurable elevation, or excitement, *of the soul,* which we recognize as the Poetic Sentiment, and which is so easily distinguished from Truth, which is the satisfaction of the Reason, or from Passion, which is the excitement of the heart. I make Beauty, therefore—using the word as inclusive of the sublime—I make Beauty the province of the poem, simply because it is an obvious rule of Art that effects should be made to spring as directly as possible from their causes:—no one as yet having been weak enough to deny that the peculiar elevation in question is at least *most readily* attainable in the poem. It by no means follows, however, that the incitements of Passion, or the precepts of Duty, or even the lessons of Truth, may not be introduced into a poem, and with advantage; for they may subserve, incidentally, in various ways, the general purposes of the work:—but the true artist will always contrive to tone them down in proper subjection to that *Beauty* which is the atmosphere and the real essence of the poem. . . . /13/

Among the minor poems of Bryant, none has so much impressed me as the one which he entitles "June." I quote only a portion of it:—

There, through the long, long summer hours,
　The golden light should lie, /15/
And thick young herbs and groups of flowers
　Stand in their beauty by.
The oriole should build and tell
His love-tale, close beside my cell;
　The idle butterfly
Should rest him there, and there be heard
The housewife-bee and humming-bird.

And what if cheerful shouts at noon
　Come, from the village sent,
Or songs of maids, beneath the moon,
　With fairy laughter blent?
And what if, in the evening light,
Betrothed lovers walk in sight
　Of my low monument?
I would the lovely scene around
Might know no sadder sight nor sound.

I know that I no more should see
　The season's glorious show,
Nor would its brightness shine for me,
　Nor its wild music flow;
But if, around my place of sleep,
The friends I love should come to weep,

They might not haste to go.
Soft airs, and song, and light, and bloom
Should keep them lingering by my tomb.

These to their softened hearts should bear
The thought of what has been,
And speak of one who cannot share
The gladness of the scene;
Whose part, in all the pomp that fills
The circuit of the summer hills,
Is—that his grave is green;
And deeply would their hearts rejoice
To hear again his living voice.

The rhythmical flow, here, is even volup-tuous—nothing could be more melodious. The poem has always affected me in a remarkable manner. The /16/ intense melancholy which seems to well up, perforce, to the surface of all the poet's cheerful sayings about his grave, we find thrilling us to the soul—while there is the truest poetic elevation in the thrill. The impression left is one of a pleasurable sadness. And if, in the remaining compositions which I shall introduce to you, there be more or less of a similar tone always apparent, let me remind you that (how or why we know not) this certain taint of sadness is inseparably connected with all the higher manifestations of true Beauty. . . . /17/

From Alfred Tennyson—although in perfect sincerity I regard him as the noblest poet that ever lived—I have left myself time to cite only a very brief specimen. I call him, and *think* him, the noblest of poets—*not* because the impressions he produces are, at *all* times, the most profound—*not* because the poetical excitement which he induces is, at *all* times, the most intense—but because it *is*, at all times, the most ethereal—in other words, the most elevating and the most pure. No poet is so little of the earth, earthy. What I am about to read is from his last long poem, "The Princess":

Tears, idle tears, I know not what they mean,
Tears from the depth of some divine despair
Rise in the heart, and gather to the eyes,
In looking on the happy autumn fields,
And thinking of the days that are no more.

Fresh as the first beam glittering on a sail
That brings our friends up from the underworld,
Sad as the last which reddens over one
That sinks with all we love below the verge;
So sad, so fresh, the days that are no more.

Ah, sad and strange as in dark summer dawns
The earliest pipe of half-awakened birds
To dying ears, when unto dying eyes
The casement slowly grows a glimmering square;
So sad, so strange, the days that are no more.

Dear as remembered kisses after death,
And sweet as those by hopeless fancy feigned
On lips that are for others; deep as love,
Deep as first love, and wild with all regret;
O Death in Life, the days that are no more! /27/

Thus, although in a very cursory and imperfect manner, I have endeavored to convey to you my conception of the Poetic Principle. It has been my purpose to suggest that, while this Principle itself is, strictly and simply, the Human Aspiration for Supernal Beauty, the manifestation of the Principle is always found in *an elevating excitement of the Soul*—quite independent of that passion which is the intoxication of the Heart—or of that truth which is the satisfaction of the Reason. For, in regard to Passion, alas! its tendency is to degrade, rather than to elevate the Soul. Love, on the contrary—Love—the true, the divine Eros—the Uranian, as distinguished from the Dionæan Venus—is unquestionably the purest and truest of all poetical themes. And in regard to Truth—if, to be sure, through the attainment of a truth, we are led to perceive a harmony where none was apparent before, we experience, at once, the true poetical effect—but this effect is referable to the harmony alone, and not in the least degree to the truth which merely served to render the harmony manifest.

We shall reach, however, more immediately a distinct conception of what the true Poetry is, by mere reference to a few of the simple elements which induce in the Poet himself the true poetical effect. He recognizes the ambrosia which nourishes his soul, in the bright orbs that shine in Heaven—in the volutes of the flower—in the clustering of low shrubberies —in the waving of the grain-fields—in the slanting of tall, Eastern trees—in the blue distance of mountains—in the grouping of clouds —in the twinkling of half-hidden brooks—in the gleaming of silver rivers—in the repose of sequestered lakes—in the star-mirroring depths /28/ of lonely wells. He perceives it in the songs of birds—in the harp of Æolus—in the sighing of the night-wind—in the repining voice of the forest—in the surf that complains to the shore—in the fresh breath of the woods —in the scent of the violet—in the voluptuous perfume of the hyacinth—in the suggestive odor that comes to him, at eventide, from far-distant, undiscovered islands, over dim oceans, illimitable and unexplored. He owns it in all noble thoughts—in all unworldly motives—in all holy impulses—in all chivalrous, generous, and self-sacrificing deeds. He feels it in the beauty of woman—in the grace of her step—in the lustre of her eye—in the melody of her voice—in her soft laughter—in her sigh—in the harmony of the rustling of her robes. He deeply feels it in her winning endearments—in her burning enthusiasms—in her gentle charities—in her meek and devotional endurances—but above all—ah, far above all—he kneels to it—he worships it in the faith, in the purity, in the strength, in the altogether divine majesty—of her *love*. . . . /29/

MATTHEW ARNOLD

from "The Study of Poetry"

[Matthew Arnold (1822–1888), English poet, critic, and essayist, was the son of Dr. Thomas Arnold, the famous headmaster of Rugby, and was himself educated at Rugby and at Oxford. For most of his adult life he served in an official capacity as inspector of schools, but he also did considerable writing, and served two terms as Professor of Poetry at Oxford. In addition to his poems (e.g., "Dover Beach," "The Forsaken Merman," "The Scholar Gipsy," "Thyrsis," "Sohrab and Rustum"), he was a major critic and continually wrote on literature, education, and religion. "The Study of Poetry" was published in 1880 as the introduction to *The English Poets*, edited by T. H. Ward, and is reprinted here from Arnold's *Essays in Criticism: Second Series* (London, 1908).]

"The future of poetry is immense, because in poetry, where it is worthy of its high destinies, our race, as time goes on, will find an ever surer and surer stay. There is not a creed which is not shaken, not an accredited dogma which is not shown to be questionable, not a received tradition which does not threaten to dissolve. Our religion has materialised itself in the fact, in the supposed fact; it has attached its emotion to the fact, and now the fact it failing it. But for poetry the idea is everything; the rest is a world of illusion, of divine illusion. Poetry attaches its emotion to /1/ the idea; the idea *is* the fact. The strongest part of our religion to-day is its unconscious poetry."

Let me be permitted to quote these words of my own, as uttering the thought which should, in my opinion, go with us and govern us in all our study of poetry. In the present work it is the course of one great contributory stream to the world-river of poetry that we are invited to follow. We are here invited to trace the stream of English poetry. But whether we set ourselves, as here, to follow only one of the several streams that make the mighty river of poetry, or whether we seek to know them all, our governing thought should be the same. We should conceive of poetry worthily, and more highly than it has been the custom to conceive of it. We should conceive of it as capable of higher uses, and called to higher destinies, than those which in general men have assigned to it hitherto. More and more mankind will discover that we have to turn to poetry to interpret life for us, to console us, to sustain us. Without poetry, our science will appear incomplete; and /2/ most of what now passes with us for religion and philosophy will be replaced by poetry. Science, I say, will appear incomplete without it. For finely and truly does Wordsworth call poetry "the impassioned expression which is in the countenance of all science"; and what is a countenance without its expression? Again, Wordsworth finely and truly calls poetry "the breath and finer spirit of all knowledge": our religion, parading evidences such as those on which the popular mind relies now; our philosophy, pluming itself on its reasonings about causation and finite and infinite being; what are they but the shadows and dreams and false shows of knowledge? The day will come when we shall wonder at ourselves for having trusted to them, for having taken them seriously; and the more we perceive their hollowness, the more we shall prize "the breath and finer spirit of knowledge" offered to us by poetry.

But if we conceive thus highly of the destinies of poetry, we must also set our standard for poetry high, since poetry, to be capable of fulfilling such /3/ high destinies, must be poetry of a high order of excellence. We must accustom ourselves to a high standard and to a strict judgment. Sainte-Beuve relates that Napoleon one day said, when somebody was spoken of in his presence as a charlatan: "Charlatan as much as you please; but where is there *not* charlatanism?"—"Yes," answers Sainte-Beuve, "in politics, in the art of governing mankind, that is perhaps true. But in the order of thought, in art, the glory, the eternal honour is that charlatanism shall find no entrance; herein lies the inviolableness of that noble portion of man's being." It is admirably said, and let us hold fast to it. In poetry, which is thought and art in one, it is the glory, the eternal honour, that charlatanism shall find no entrance; that this noble sphere be kept inviolate and inviolable. Charlatanism is for confusing or obliterating the distinctions between excellent and inferior, sound and unsound or only half-sound, true and untrue or only half-true. It is charlatanism, conscious or unconscious, whenever /4/ we confuse or obliterate these. And in poetry, more than anywhere else, it is unpermissible to confuse or obliterate them. For in poetry the distinction between excellent and inferior, sound and unsound or only half-sound, true and untrue or only half-true, is of paramount importance. It is of paramount importance because of the high destinies of poetry. In poetry, as a criticism of life under the conditions fixed for such a criticism by the laws of poetic truth and poetic beauty, the spirit of our race will find, we have said, as time goes on and as other helps fail, its consolation and stay. But the consolation and stay will be of power in proportion to the power of the criticism of life. And the criticism of life will be of power in proportion as the poetry conveying it is excellent rather than inferior, sound rather than unsound or half-sound, true rather than untrue or half-true.

The best poetry is what we want; the best poetry will be found to have a power of forming, sustaining, and delighting us, as nothing else can. A clearer, deeper sense of the best in poetry, and /5/ of the strength and joy to be drawn from it, is the most precious benefit which we can gather from a poetical collection such as the present. . . . /6/

WILLIAM BUTLER YEATS
"The Symbolism of Poetry"

[William Butler Yeats (1865–1939), considered by many the greatest British poet of the twentieth century, was born in Dublin and divided his life between Ireland and England. By his insistence that Irish writers write on Irish subjects and make use of Irish legend and mythology, he became the chief figure in the Irish literary renaissance sometimes known as the Celtic Revival. He helped to found the Abbey Theater in Dublin, and wrote many plays for it, most of them in verse. Upon formation of the Irish Free State in 1922 he was made a senator and served as such for six years. In 1923 he received the Nobel prize for literature. "The Symbolism of Poetry," written in 1900 and included in *Ideas of Good and Evil,* is reprinted here from *Essays and Introductions* (New York, 1961).]

I

Symbolism, as seen in the writers of our day, would have no value if it were not seen also, under one "disguise or another, in every great imaginative writer," writes Mr. Arthur Symons in *The Symbolist Movement in Literature,* a subtle book which I cannot praise as I would, because it has been dedicated to me; and he goes on to show how many profound writers have in the last few years sought for a philosophy of poetry in the doctrine of symbolism, and how even in countries where it is almost scandalous to seek for any philosophy of poetry, new writers are following them in their search. We do not know what the writers of ancient times talked of among themselves, and one bull is all that remains of Shakespeare's talk, who was on the edge of modern times; and the journalist is convinced, it seems, that they talked of wine and women and politics, but never about their art, or never quite seriously about their art. He is certain that no one who had a philosophy of his art, or a theory of how he should write, has ever made a work of art, that people have no imagination who do not write without forethought and afterthought as he writes his own articles. He says this with enthusiasm, because he has heard it at so many comfortable dinner-tables, where some one had mentioned through carelessness, or foolish zeal, a book whose difficulty had offended indolence, or a man who had not forgotten that beauty is an accusation. Those /153/ formulas and generalisations, in which a hidden sergeant has drilled the ideas of journalists and through them the ideas of all but all the modern world, have created in their turn a forgetfulness like that of soldiers in battle, so that journalists and their readers have forgotten, among many like events, that Wagner spent seven years arranging and explaining his ideas before he began his most characteristic music; that opera, and with it modern music, arose from certain talks at the house of one Giovanni Bardi of Florence; and that the Pléiade laid the foundations of modern French literature with a pamphlet. Goethe has said, "a poet needs all philosophy, but he must keep it out of his work," though that is not always necessary; and almost certainly no great art, outside England, where journalists are more powerful and ideas less plentiful than elsewhere, has arisen without a great criticism, for its herald or its interpreter and protector, and it may be for this reason that great art, now that vulgarity has armed itself and multiplied itself, is perhaps dead in England.

All writers, all artists of any kind, in so far as they have had any philosophical or critical power, perhaps just in so far as they have been deliberate artists at all, have had some philosophy, some criticism of their art; and it has often been this philosophy, or this criticism, that has evoked their most startling inspiration, calling into outer life some portion of the divine life, or of the buried reality, which could alone extinguish in the emotions what their philosophy or their criticism would extinguish in the intellect. They have sought for no new thing, it may be, but only to understand and to /154/ copy the pure inspiration of early times, but because the divine life wars upon our outer life, and must needs change its weapons and its movements as we change ours, inspiration has come to them in beautiful startling shapes. The scientific movement brought with it a literature which was always tending to lose itself in externalities of all kinds, in opinion, in declamation, in picturesque writing, in word-painting, or in what Mr. Symons has called an attempt "to build in brick and mortar inside the covers of a book"; and now writers have begun to dwell upon the element of evocation, of suggestion, upon what we call the symbolism in great writers.

II

In "Symbolism in Painting," I tried to describe the element of symbolism that is in pictures and sculpture, and described a little the symbolism in poetry, but did not describe at all the continuous indefinable symbolism which is the substance of all style.

There are no lines with more melancholy beauty than these by Burns:—

The white moon is setting behind the white wave,
And Time is setting with me, O!

and these lines are perfectly symbolical. Take from them the whiteness of the moon and of the waves, whose relation to the setting of Time is too subtle for the intellect, and you take from them their beauty. But, /155/ when all are together, moon and wave and whiteness and setting Time and the last melancholy cry, they evoke an emotion which cannot be evoked by any other arrangement of colours and sounds and forms. We may call this metaphorical writing, but it is better to call it symbolical writing, because metaphors are not profound enough to be moving, when they are not symbols, and when they are symbols they are the most perfect of all, because the most subtle, outside of pure sound, and through them one can best find out what symbols are. If one begins the reverie with any beautiful lines that one can remember, one finds they are like those by Burns. Begin with this line by Blake:—

The gay fishes on the wave when the moon sucks
   up the dew;

or these lines by Nash:—

Brightness falls from the air,
Queens have died young and fair,
Dust hath closed Helen's eye;[1]

or these lines by Shakespeare:—

Timon hath made his everlasting mansion
Upon the beached verge of the salt flood;
Who once a day with his embossed froth
 The turbulent surge shall cover;

or take some line that is quite simple, that gets its beauty from its place in a story, and see how it flickers with the light of the many symbols that have given the story its beauty, as a sword-blade may flicker with the light of burning towers.

All sounds, all colours, all forms, either because of their preordained energies or because of long associa- /156/ tion, evoke indefinable and yet precise emotions, or, as I prefer to think, call down among us certain disembodied powers, whose footsteps over our hearts we call emotions; and when sound, and colour, and form are in a musical relation, a beautiful relation to one another, they become, as it were, one sound, one colour, one form, and evoke an emotion that is made out of their distinct evocations and yet is one emotion. The same relation exists between all portions of every work of art, whether it be an epic or a song, and the more perfect it is, and the more various and numerous the elements that have flowed into its perfection, the more powerful will be the emotion, the power, the god it calls among us. Because an emotion does not exist, or does not become perceptible and active among us, till it has found its expression, in colour or in sound or in form, or in all of these, and because no two modulations or arrangements of these evoke the same emotion, poets and painters and musicians, and in a less degree because their effects are momentary, day and night and cloud and shadow, are continually making and unmaking mankind. It is indeed only those things which seem useless or very feeble that have any power, and all those things that seem useful or strong, armies, moving wheels, modes of architecture, modes of government, speculations of the reason, would have been a little different if some mind long ago had not given

1 [For complete poem, see p. 188.]

itself to some emotion, as a woman gives herself to her lover, and shaped sounds or colours or forms, or all of these, into a musical relation, that their emotion might live in other minds. A little lyric evokes an emotion, and /157/ this emotion gathers others about it and melts into their being in the making of some great epic; and at last, needing an always less delicate body, or symbol, as it grows more powerful, it flows out, with all it has gathered, among the blind instincts of daily life, where it moves a power within powers, as one sees ring within ring in the stem of an old tree. This is maybe what Arthur O'Shaughnessy meant when he made his poets say they had built Nineveh with their sighing;[2] and I am certainly never sure, when I hear of some war, or of some religious excitement, or of some new manufacture, or of anything else that fills the ear of the world, that it has not all happened because of something that a boy piped in Thessaly. I remember once telling a seeress to ask one among the gods who, as she believed, were standing about her in their symbolic bodies, what would come of a charming but seeming trivial labour of a friend, and the form answering, "the devastation of peoples and the overwhelming of cities." I doubt indeed if the crude circumstance of the world, which seems to create all our emotions, does more than reflect, as in multiplying mirrors, the emotions that have come to solitary men in moments of poetical contemplation; or that love itself would be more than an animal hunger but for the poet and his shadow the priest, for unless we believe that outer things are the reality, we must believe that the gross is the shadow of the subtle, that things are wise before they become foolish, and secret before they cry out in the market-place. Solitary men in moments of contemplation receive, as I think, the creative impulse from the lowest of the Nine Hier- /158/ archies, and so make and unmake mankind, and even the world itself, for does not "the eye altering alter all"?

Our towns are copied fragments from our breast;
And all man's Babylons strive but to impart
The grandeurs of his Babylonian heart.

2 [See p. 212.]

III

The purpose of rhythm, it has always seemed to me, is to prolong the moment of contemplation, the moment when we are both asleep and awake, which is the one moment of creation, by hushing us with an alluring monotony, while it holds us waking by variety, to keep us in that state of perhaps real trance, in which the mind liberated from the pressure of the will is unfolded in symbols. If certain sensitive persons listen persistently to the ticking of a watch, or gaze persistently on the monotonous flashing of a light, they fall into the hypnotic trance; and rhythm is but the ticking of a watch made softer, that one must needs listen, and various, that one may not be swept beyond memory or grow weary of listening; while the patterns of the artist are but the monotonous flash woven to take the eyes in a subtler enchantment. I have heard in meditation voices that were forgotten the moment they had spoken; and I have been swept, when in more profound meditation, beyond all memory but of those things that came from beyond the threshold of waking life. I was writing once at a very symbolical and abstract poem, when my pen fell on the ground; and as I stooped to pick it up, I remembered some fantastic adventure that yet did not seem fantastic, and then another like adventure, and /159/ when I asked myself when these things had happened, I found that I was remembering my dreams for many nights. I tried to remember what I had done the day before, and then what I had done that morning; but all my waking life had perished from me, and it was only after a struggle that I came to remember it again, and as I did so that more powerful and startling life perished in its turn. Had my pen not fallen on the ground and so made me turn from the images that I was weaving into verse, I would never have known that meditation had become trance, for I would have been like one who does not know that he is passing through a wood because his eyes are on the pathway. So I think that in the making and in the understanding of a work of art, and the more easily if it is full of patterns and symbols and music, we are lured to the threshold of sleep, and it may be far beyond it, without knowing that we have ever set our feet upon the steps of horn or of ivory.

IV

Besides emotional symbols, symbols that evoke emotions alone,—and in this sense all alluring or hateful things are symbols, although their relations with one another are too subtle to delight us fully, away from rhythm and pattern,—there are intellectual symbols, symbols that evoke ideas alone, or ideas mingled with emotions; and outside the very definite traditions of mysticism and the less definite criticism of certain modern poets, these alone are called symbols. Most things belong to one or another kind, according to the /160/ way we speak of them and the companions we give them, for symbols, associated with ideas that are more than fragments of the shadows thrown upon the intellect by the emotions they evoke, are the playthings of the allegorist or the pedant, and soon pass away. If I say "white" or "purple" in an ordinary line of poetry, they evoke emotions so exclusively that I cannot say why they move me; but if I bring them into the same sentence with such obvious intellectual symbols as a cross or a crown of thorns, I think of purity and sovereignty. Furthermore, innumerable meanings, which are held to "white" or to "purple" by bonds of subtle suggestion, and alike in the emotions and in the intellect, move visibly through my mind, and move invisibly beyond the threshold of sleep, casting lights and shadows of an indefinable wisdom on what had seemed before, it may be, but sterility and noisy violence. It is the intellect that decides where the reader shall ponder over the procession of the symbols, and if the symbols are merely emotional, he gazes from amid the accidents and destinies of the world; but if the symbols are intellectual too, he becomes himself a part of pure intellect, and he is himself mingled with the procession. If I watch a rushy pool in the moonlight, my emotion at its beauty is mixed with memories of the man that I have seen ploughing by its margin, or of the lovers I saw there a night ago; but if I look at the moon herself and remember any of her ancient names and meanings, I move among divine people, and things that have shaken off our mortality, the

tower of ivory, the queen of waters, the shining stag among enchanted woods, /161/ the white hare sitting upon the hilltop, the fool of Faery with his shining cup full of dreams, and it may be "make a friend of one of these images of wonder," and "meet the Lord in the air." So, too, if one is moved by Shakespeare, who is content with emotional symbols that he may come the nearer to our sympathy, one is mixed with the whole spectacle of the world; while if one is moved by Dante, or by the myth of Demeter, one is mixed into the shadow of God or of a goddess. So, too, one is furthest from symbols when one is busy doing this or that, but the soul moves among symbols and unfolds in symbols when trance, or madness, or deep meditation has withdrawn it from every impulse but its own. "I then saw," wrote Gérard de Nerval of his madness, "vaguely drifting into form, plastic images of antiquity, which outlined themselves, became definite, and seemed to represent symbols of which I only seized the idea with difficulty." In an earlier time he would have been of that multitude whose souls austerity withdrew, even more perfectly than madness could withdraw his soul, from hope and memory, from desire and regret, that they might reveal those processions of symbols that men bow to before altars, and woo with incense and offerings. But being of our time, he has been like Maeterlinck, like Villiers de l'Isle-Adam in *Axël*, like all who are preoccupied with intellectual symbols in our time, a foreshadower of the new sacred book, of which all the arts, as somebody has said, are beginning to dream. How can the arts overcome the slow dying of men's hearts that we call the progress of the world, and lay their hands upon men's heart- /162/ strings again, without becoming the garment of religion as in old times?

V

If people were to accept the theory that poetry moves us because of its symbolism, what change should one look for in the manner of our poetry? A return to the way of our fathers, a casting out of descriptions of nature for the sake of nature, of the moral law for the sake of the moral law, a casting out of all anecdotes and of that brooding over scientific opinion that so often extinguished the central flame in Tennyson, and of that vehemence that would make us do or not do certain things; or, in other words, we should come to understand that the beryl stone was enchanted by our fathers that it might unfold the pictures in its heart, and not to mirror our own excited faces, or the boughs waving outside the window. With this change of substance, this return to imagination, this understanding that the laws of art, which are the hidden laws of the world, can alone bind the imagination, would come a change of style, and we would cast out of serious poetry those energetic rhythms, as of a man running, which are the invention of the will with its eyes always on something to be done or undone; and we would seek out those wavering, meditative, organic rhythms, which are the embodiment of the imagination, that neither desires nor hates, because it has done with time, and only wishes to gaze upon some reality, some beauty; nor would it be any longer possible for anybody to deny the importance of form, in all its kinds, for although /163/ you can expound an opinion, or describe a thing, when your words are not quite well chosen, you cannot give a body to something that moves beyond the senses, unless your words are as subtle, as complex, as full of mysterious life, as the body of a flower or of a woman. The form of sincere poetry, unlike the form of the "popular poetry," may indeed be sometimes obscure, or ungrammatical as in some of the best of the *Songs of Innocence and Experience,* but it must have the perfections that escape analysis, the subtleties that have a new meaning every day, and it must have all this whether it be but a little song made out of a moment of dreamy indolence, or some great epic made out of the dreams of one poet and of a hundred generations whose hands were never weary of the sword. /164/

A. C. BRADLEY
"Poetry for Poetry's Sake"

[A. C. Bradley (1851–1935), English university professor, was educated at Oxford and later became Professor of Poetry there. He lived the life of a teacher and scholar and won academic attention with *A Commentary on Tennyson's "In Memoriam"* (1901) and *Shakespearean Tragedy* (1904). "Poetry for Poetry's Sake" was his inaugural lecture as Oxford Professor of Poetry, delivered and originally published in 1901, reprinted here from the second edition of his *Oxford Lectures on Poetry* (London, 1950).]

The words "Poetry for poetry's sake" recall the famous phrase "Art for Art." It is far from my purpose to examine the possible meanings of that phrase, or all the questions it involves. I propose to state briefly what I understand by "Poetry for poetry's sake," and then, after guarding against one or two misapprehensions of the formula, to consider more fully a single problem connected with it. And I must premise, without attempting to justify them, certain explanations. We are to consider poetry in its essence, and apart from the flaws which in most poems accompany their poetry. We are to include in the idea of poetry the metrical form, and not to regard this as a mere accident or a mere vehicle. And, finally, poetry being poems, we are to think of a poem as it actually exists; and, without aiming here at accuracy, we may say that an actual poem is the succession of experiences—sounds, images, thoughts, emotions—through which we pass when we are reading as poetically as we can. Of course this imaginative experience—if I may use the phrase for brevity—differs with every reader and every time of reading: a poem exists in innumerable degrees. But that insurmountable fact lies in the nature of things and does not concern us now.

What then does the formula "Poetry for poetry's sake" tell us about this experience? It says, as I understand it, these things. First, this experience is an end in itself, is worth having on its own account, has an intrinsic value. Next, its *poetic* value is this intrinsic worth alone. Poetry may have also an ulterior value as a means to culture or /4/ religion; because it conveys instruction, or softens the passions, or furthers a good cause; because it brings the poet fame or money or a quiet conscience. So much the better: let it be valued for these reasons too. But its ulterior worth neither is nor can directly determine its poetic worth as a satisfying imaginative experience; and this is to be judged entirely from within. And to these two positions the formula would add, though not of necessity, a third. The consideration of ulterior ends, whether by the poet in the act of composing or by the reader in the act of experiencing, tends to lower poetic value. It does so because it tends to change the nature of poetry by taking it out of its own atmosphere. For its nature is to be not a part, nor yet a copy, of the real world (as we commonly understand that phrase), but to be a world by itself, independent, complete, autonomous; and to possess it fully you must enter that world, conform to its laws, and ignore for the time the beliefs, aims, and particular conditions which belong to you in the other world of reality.

Of the more serious misapprehensions to which these statements may give rise I will glance only at one or two. The offensive consequences often drawn from the formula "Art for Art" will be found to attach not to the doctrine that Art is an end in itself, but to the doctrine that Art is the whole or supreme end of human life. And as this latter doctrine, which seems to me absurd, is in any case quite different from the former, its consequences fall outside my subject. The formula "Poetry is an end in itself" has nothing to say on the various questions of moral judgment which arise from the fact that poetry has its place in a many-sided life. For anything it says, the intrinsic value of poetry might be so small, and its ulterior effects so mischievous, that it had better not exist. The formula only tells us that we must not place in antithesis poetry and /5/ human good, for poetry is one kind of human good; and that we must not determine the intrinsic value of this kind of good by direct reference to another. If we do, we shall find ourselves maintaining what we did not expect. If poetic value lies in the stimulation of religious feelings, *Lead, kindly Light* is no better a poem than many a tasteless version of a Psalm: if in the excitement of patriotism, why is *Scots, wha hae* superior to *We don't want to fight*? if in the mitigation of the passions, the Odes of Sappho will win but little praise: if in instruction, Armstrong's *Art of preserving Health* should win much.

Again, our formula may be accused of cutting poetry away from its connection with life. And this accusation raises so huge a problem that I must ask leave to be dogmatic as well as brief. There is plenty of connection between life and poetry, but it is, so to say, a connection underground. The two may be called different forms of the same thing: one of them having (in the usual sense) reality, but seldom fully satisfying imagination; while the other offers something which satisfies imagination but has not full "reality." They are parallel developments which nowhere meet, or, if I may use loosely a word which will be serviceable later, they are analogues. Hence we understand one by help of the other, and even, in a sense, care for one because of the other; but hence also, poetry neither is life, nor, strictly speaking, a copy of it. They differ not only because one has more mass and the other a more perfect shape, but because they have different *kinds* of existence. The one touches us as beings occupying a given position in space and time, and having feelings, desires, and purposes due to that position: it appeals to imagination, but appeals to much besides. What meets us in poetry has not a position in the same series of time and space, or, if it has or had such a position, it is taken apart from much /6/ that belonged to it there; and therefore it makes no direct appeal to those feelings, desires, and purposes, but speaks only to contemplative imagination— imagination the reverse of empty or emotionless, imagination saturated with the results of "real" experience, but still contemplative.

Thus, no doubt, one main reason why poetry has poetic value for us is that it presents to us in its own way something which we meet in another form in nature or life; and yet the test of its poetic value for us lies simply in the question whether it satisfies our imagination; the rest of us, our knowledge or conscience, for example, judging it only so far as they appear transmuted in our imagination. So also Shakespeare's knowledge or his moral insight, Milton's greatness of soul, Shelley's "hate of hate" and "love of love," and that desire to help men or make them happier which may have influenced a poet in hours of meditation—all these have, as such, no poetical worth: they have that worth only when, passing through the unity of the poet's being, they reappear as qualities of imagination, and then are indeed mighty powers in the world of poetry.

I come to a third misapprehension, and so to my main subject. This formula, it is said, empties poetry of its meaning: it is really a doctrine of form for form's sake. "It is of no consequence what a poet says, so long as he says the thing well. The *what* is poetically indifferent: it is the *how* that counts. Matter, subject, content, substance, determines nothing; there is no subject with which poetry may not deal: the form, the treatment, is everything. Nay, more: not only is the matter indifferent, but it is the secret of Art to 'eradicate the matter by means of the form,'"— phrases and statements like these meet us everywhere in current criticism of literature and the other arts. They /7/ are the stock-in-trade of writers who understand of them little more than the fact that somehow or other they are not "bourgeois." But we find them also seriously used by writers whom we must respect, whether they are anonymous or not; something like one or another of them might be quoted, for example, from Professor Saintsbury, the late R. A. M. Stevenson, Schiller, Goethe himself; and they are the watchwords of a school in the one country where Aesthetics has flourished. They come, as a rule, from men who either practise one of the arts, or, from study of it, are interested in its methods. The general reader—a being so general that I may say what I will of him—is outraged by them. He feels that he is being robbed of almost all that he cares for in a work of art. "You are asking me," he says, "to look at the Dresden Madonna as if it were a Persian rug. You are telling me that the poetic value of *Hamlet* lies solely in its style and versification, and that my interest in the man and his fate is only an intellectual or moral interest. You allege that, if I want to enjoy the poetry of *Crossing the Bar,* I must not mind what Tennyson says there, but must consider solely his way of saying it. But in that case I can care no more for a poem than I do for a set of nonsense verses; and I do not believe that the authors of *Hamlet* and *Crossing the Bar* regarded their poems thus."

These antitheses of subject, matter, substance on the one side, form, treatment, handling on the other, are the field through which I especially want, in this lecture, to indicate a way. It is a field of battle; and the battle is waged for no trivial cause; but the cries of the combatants are terribly ambiguous. Those phrases of the so-called formalist may each mean five or six different things. Taken in one sense they seem to me chiefly true; taken as the general reader not unnaturally takes them, they seem to me false and mischievous. It would be absurd to pre- /8/ tend that I can end in a few minutes a controversy which concerns the ultimate nature of Art, and leads perhaps to problems not yet soluble; but we can at least draw some plain distinctions which, in this controversy, are too often confused.

In the first place, then, let us take "subject" in one particular sense; let us understand by it that which we have in view when, looking at the title of an un-read poem, we say that the poet has chosen this or that for his subject. The subject, in this sense, so far as I can discover, is generally something, real or imaginary, as it exists in the minds of fairly cultivated people. The subject of *Paradise Lost* would be the story of the Fall as that story exists in the general imagination of a Bible-reading people. The subject of Shelley's stanzas *To a Skylark* would be the ideas which arise in the mind of an educated person when, without knowing the poem, he hears the word "skylark." If the title of a poem conveys little or nothing to us, the "subject" appears to be either what we should gather by investigating the title in a dictionary or other book of the kind, or else such a brief suggestion as might be offered by a person who had read the poem, and who said, for example, that the subject of *The Ancient Mariner* was a sailor who killed an albatross and suffered for his deed.

Now the subject, in this sense (and I intend to use the word in no other), is not, as such, inside the poem, but outside it. The contents of the stanzas *To a Skylark* are not the ideas suggested by the work "skylark" to the average man; they belong to Shelley just as much as the language does. The subject, therefore, is not the matter *of* the poem at all; and its opposite is not the *form* of the poem, but the whole poem. The subject is one thing; the poem, matter and form alike, another thing. This being so, it is surely obvious that the poetic value cannot lie in the subject, but lies entirely in /9/ its opposite, the poem. How can the subject determine the value when on one and the same subject poems may be written of all degrees of merit and demerit; or when a perfect poem may be composed on a subject so slight as a pet sparrow, and, if Macaulay may be trusted, a nearly worthless poem on a subject so stupendous as the omnipresence of the Deity? The "formalist" is here perfectly right. Nor is he insisting on something unimportant. He is fighting against our tendency to take the work of art as a mere copy or reminder of something already in our heads, or at the best as a suggestion of some idea as little removed as possible from the familiar. The sightseer who promenades a picture-gallery, remarking that this portrait is so like his cousin, or that landscape the very image of his birthplace, or who, after satisfying himself that one picture is about Elijah, passes on rejoicing to discover the subject, and nothing but the subject, of the next—what is he but an extreme example of this tendency? Well, but the very same tendency vitiates much of our criticism, much criticism of Shakespeare, for example, which, with all its cleverness and partial truth, still shows that the critic never passed from his own mind into Shakespeare's; and it may be traced even in so fine a critic as Coleridge, as when he dwarfs the sublime struggle of

Hamlet into the image of his own unhappy weakness. Hazlitt by no means escaped its influence. Only the third of that great trio, Lamb, appears almost always to have rendered the conception of the composer.

Again, it is surely true that we cannot determine beforehand what subjects are fit for Art, or name any subject on which a good poem might not possibly be written. To divide subjects into two groups, the beautiful or elevating, and the ugly or vicious, and to judge poems according as their subjects belong to one of these groups or the other, is to fall into the same pit, to confuse with our /10/ pre-conceptions the meaning of the poet. What the thing is in the poem he is to be judged by, not by the thing as it was before he touched it; and how can we venture to say beforehand that he cannot make a true poem out of something which to us was merely alluring or dull or revolting? The question whether, having done so, he ought to publish his poem; whether the thing in the poet's work will not be still confused by the incompetent Puritan or the incompetent sensualist with the thing in *his* mind, does not touch this point: it is a further question, one of ethics, not of art. No doubt the upholders of "Art for art's sake" will generally be in favour of the courageous course, of refusing to sacrifice the better or stronger part of the public to the weaker or worse; but their maxim in no way binds them to this view. Rossetti suppressed one of the best of his sonnets, a sonnet chosen for admiration by Tennyson, himself extremely sensitive about the moral affect of poetry; suppressed it, I believe, because it was called fleshly. One may regret Rossetti's judgment and at the same time respect his scrupulousness; but in any case he judged in his capacity of citizen, not in his capacity of artist.

So far then the "formalist" appears to be right. But he goes too far, I think, if he maintains that the subject is indifferent and that all subjects are the same to poetry. And he does not prove his point by observing that a good poem might be written on a pin's head, and a bad one on the Fall of Man. That truth shows that the subject *settles* nothing, but not that it counts for nothing. The Fall of Man is really a more favourable subject than a pin's head. The Fall of Man, that is to say, offers opportunities of poetic effects wider in range and more penetrating in appeal. And the fact is that such a subject, as it exists in the general imagination, has some aesthetic value before the poet /11/ touches it. It is, as you may choose to call it, an inchoate poem or the débris of a poem. It is not an abstract idea or a bare isolated fact, but an assemblage of figures, scenes, actions, and events, which already appeal to emotional imagination; and it is already in some degree organized and formed. In spite of this a bad poet would make a bad poem on it; but then we should say he was unworthy of the subject. And we should not say this if he wrote a bad poem on a pin's head. Conversely, a good poem on a pin's head would almost certainly transform its subject far more than a good poem on the Fall of Man. It might revolutionize its subject so completely that we should say, "The subject may be a pin's head, but the substance of the poem has very little to do with it."

This brings us to another and a different antithesis. Those figures, scenes, events, that form part of the subject called the Fall of Man, are not the substance of *Paradise Lost;* but in *Paradise Lost* there are figures, scenes, and events resembling them in some degree. These, with much more of the same kind, may be described as its substance, and may then be contrasted with the measured language of the poem, which will be called its form. Subject is the opposite not of form but of the whole poem. Substance is within the poem, and its opposite, form, is also within the poem. I am not criticizing this antithesis at present, but evidently it is quite different from the other. It is practically the distinction used in the old-fashioned criticism of epic and drama, and it flows down, not unsullied, from Aristotle. Addison, for example, in examining *Paradise Lost* considers in order the fable, the characters, and the sentiments; these will be the substance: then he considers the language, that is, the style and numbers; this will be the form. In like manner, the substance or meaning of a lyric may be distinguished from the form. /12/

Now I believe it will be found that a large part of the controversy we are dealing with arises from a confusion between these two distinctions of substance and form, and of subject and poem. The extreme formalist lays his whole weight on the form because he thinks its opposite is the mere subject. The general reader is angry, but makes the same mistake, and gives to the subject praises that rightly belong to the substance.[1] I will read an example of what I mean. I can only explain the following words of a good critic by supposing that for the moment he has fallen into this confusion: "The mere matter of all poetry—to wit, the appearances of nature and the thoughts and feelings of men—being unalterable, it follows that the difference between poet and poet will depend upon the manner of each in applying language, metre, rhyme, cadence, and what not, to this invariable material." What has become here of the substance of *Paradise Lost*—the story, scenery, characters, sentiments, as they are in the poem? They have vanished clean away. Nothing is left but the form on one side, and on the other not even the subject, but a supposed invariable material, the appearances of nature and the thoughts and feelings of men. Is it surprising that the whole value should then be found in the form?

So far we have assumed that this antithesis of substance and form is valid, and that it always has one meaning. In reality it has several, but we will leave it in its present shape, and pass to the question of its validity. And this question we are compelled to raise, because we have to deal with the two contentions that the poetic value lies wholly or mainly /13/ in the substance, and that it lies wholly or mainly in the form. Now these contentions, whether false or true, may seem at least to be clear; but we shall find, I think, that they are both of them false, or both of them nonsense: false if they concern anything outside the poem, nonsense if they apply to something in it. For what do they evidently

imply? They imply that there are in a poem two parts, factors, or components, a substance and a form; and that you can conceive them distinctly and separately, so that when you are speaking of the one you are not speaking of the other. Otherwise how can you ask the question, In which of them does the value lie? But really in a poem, apart from defects, there are no such factors or components; and therefore it is strictly nonsense to ask in which of them the value lies. And on the other hand, if the substance and the form referred to are not in the poem, then both the contentions are false, for its poetic value lies in itself.

What I mean is neither new nor mysterious; and it will be clear, I believe, to any one who reads poetry poetically and who closely examines his experience. When you are reading a poem, I would ask—not analysing it, and much less criticizing it, but allowing it, as it proceeds, to make its full impression on you through the exertion of your recreating imagination—do you then apprehend and enjoy as one thing a certain meaning or substance, and as another thing certain articulate sounds, and do you somehow compound these two? Surely you do not, any more than you apprehend apart, when you see some one smile, those lines in the face which express a feeling, and the feeling that the lines express. Just as there the lines and their meaning are to you one thing, not two, so in poetry the meaning and the sounds are one: there is, if I may put it so, a resonant meaning, or a meaning resonance. If you read the line, "The sun is warm, the /14/ sky is clear," you do not experience separately the image of a warm sun and clear sky, on the one side, and certain unintelligible rhythmical sounds on the other; nor yet do you experience them together, side by side; but you experience the one *in* the other. And in like manner, when you are really reading *Hamlet*, the action and the characters are not something which you conceive apart from the words; you apprehend them from point to point *in* the words, and the words as expressions of them. Afterwards, no doubt, when you are out of the poetic experience but remember it, you may by analysis decompose this unity, and attend to a substance more or less isolated, and a form more or

---

1 What is here called "substance" is what people generally mean when they use the word "subject" and insist on the value of the subject. I am not arguing against this usage, or in favour of the usage which I have adopted for the sake of clearness. It does not matter which we employ, so long as we and others know what we mean. (I use "substance" and "content" indifferently.)

less isolated. But these are things in your analytic head, not in the poem, which is *poetic* experience. And if you want to have the poem again, you cannot find it by adding together these two products of decomposition; you can only find it by passing back into poetic experience. And then what you recover is no aggregate of factors, it is a unity in which you can no more separate a substance and a form than you can separate living blood and the life in the blood. This unity has, if you like, various "aspects" or "sides," but they are not factors or parts; if you try to examine one, you find it is also the other. Call them substance and form if you please, but these are not the reciprocally exclusive substance and form to which the two contentions *must* refer. They do not "agree" for they are not apart: they are one thing from different points of view, and in that sense identical. And this identity of content and form, you will say, is no accident; it is of the essence of poetry in so far as it is poetry, and of all art in so far as it is art. Just as there is in music not sound on one side and a meaning on the other, but expressive sound, and if you ask what is the meaning you can only answer by pointing to the sounds; just as in painting there is not a meaning /15/ *plus* paint, but a meaning *in* paint, or significant paint, and no man can really express the meaning in any other way than in paint and in *this* paint; so in a poem the true content and the true form neither exist nor can be imagined apart. When then you are asked whether the value of a poem lies in a substance got by decomposing the poem, and present, as such, only in reflective analysis, or whether the value lies in a form arrived at and existing in the same way, you will answer, "It lies neither in one, nor in the other, nor in any addition of them, but in the poem, where they are not."

We have then, first, an antithesis of subject and poem. This is clear and valid; and the question in which of them does the value lie is intelligible; and its answer is, In the poem. We have next a distinction of substance and form. If the substance means ideas, images, and the like taken alone, and the form means the measured language taken by itself, this is a possible distinction, but it is a distinction

of things not in the poem, and the value lies in neither of them. If substance and form mean anything *in* the poem, then each is involved in the other, and the question in which of them the value lies has no sense. No doubt you may say, speaking loosely, that in this poet or poem the aspect of substance is the more noticeable, and in that the aspect of form; and you may pursue interesting discussions on this basis, though no principle or ultimate question of value is touched by them. And apart from that question, of course, I am not denying the usefulness and necessity of the distinction. We cannot dispense with it. To consider separately the action or the characters of a play, and separately its style or versification, is both legitimate and valuable, so long as we remember what we are doing. But the true critic in speaking of these apart does not really think of them apart; the whole, the poetic experience, of which they are but aspects, is always in /16/ his mind; and he is always aiming at a richer, truer, more intense repetition of that experience. On the other hand, when the question of principle, of poetic value, is raised, these aspects *must* fall apart into components, separately conceivable; and then there arise two heresies, equally false, that the value lies in one of two things, both of which are outside the poem, and therefore where its value cannot lie.

On the heresy of the separable substance a few additional words will suffice. This heresy is seldom formulated, but perhaps some unconscious holder of it may object: "Surely the action and the characters of *Hamlet* are in the play; and surely I can retain these, though I have forgotten all the words. I admit that I do not possess the whole poem, but I possess a part, and the most important part." And I would answer: "If we are not concerned with any question of principle, I accept all that you say except the last words, which do raise such a question. Speaking loosely, I agree that the action and characters, as you perhaps conceive them, together with a great deal more, are in the poem. Even then, however, you must not claim to possess all of this kind that is in the poem; for in forgetting the words you must have lost innumerable details of the action and the characters. And, when the question of value is raised, I must insist that the action and characters, as you conceive them, are not in *Hamlet* at all. If they are, point them out. You cannot do it. What you find at any moment of that succession of experiences called *Hamlet* is words. In these words, to speak loosely again, the action and characters (more of them than you can conceive apart) are focussed; but your experience is not a combination of them, as ideas, on the one side, with certain sounds on the other; it is an experience of something in which the two are indissolubly fused. If you deny this, to be sure I can make no answer, or can only answer that I have /17/ reason to believe that you cannot read poetically, or else are misinterpreting your experience. But if you do not deny this, then you will admit that the action and characters of the poem, as you separately imagine them, are no part of it, but a product of it in your reflective imagination, a faint analogue of one aspect of it taken in detachment from the whole. Well, I do not dispute, I would even insist, that, in the case of so long a poem as *Hamlet,* it may be necessary from time to time to interrupt the poetic experience, in order to enrich it by forming such a product and dwelling on it. Nor, in a wide sense of 'poetic,' do I question the poetic value of this product, as you think of it apart from the poem. It resembles our recollections of the heroes of history or legend, who move about in our imaginations, 'forms more real than living man,' and are worth much to us though we do not remember anything they said. Our ideas and images of the 'substance' of a poem have this poetic value, and more, if they are at all adequate. But they cannot determine the poetic value of the poem, for (not to speak of the competing claims of the 'form') nothing that is outside the poem can do that, and they, as such, are outside it."[2]

Let us turn to the so-called form—style and versification. There is no such thing as mere form in poetry. All form is expression. Style may have indeed a certain aesthetic worth in partial abstraction from the particular matter it conveys, as in a well-built sentence you may take pleasure in the build almost apart from the meaning. Even so, style is expressive—presents to sense, for example, the order, ease, and rapidity with which ideas move in the writer's mind—but it is not expressive of the /18/ meaning of that particular sentence. And it is possible, interrupting poetic experience, to decompose it and abstract for comparatively separate consideration this nearly formal element of style. But the aesthetic value of style so taken is not considerable;[3] you could not read with pleasure for an hour a composition which had no other merit. And in poetic experience you never apprehend this value by itself; the style is here expressive also of a particular meaning, or rather is one aspect of that unity whose other aspect is meaning. So that what you apprehend may be called indifferently an expressed meaning or a significant form. Perhaps on this point I may in Oxford appeal to authority, that of Matthew Arnold and Walter Pater, the latter at any rate an authority whom the formalist will not despise. What is the gist of Pater's teaching about style, if it is not that in the end the one virtue of style is truth or adequacy; that the word, phrase, sentence, should express perfectly the writer's perception, feeling, image, or thought; so that, as we read a descriptive phrase of Keats's, we exclaim, "That is the thing itself"; so that, to quote Arnold, the words are "symbols equivalent with the thing symbolized," or, in our technical language, a form identical with its content? Hence in true poetry it is, in strictness, impossible to express the meaning in any but its own words, or to change the words without changing the meaning. A translation of such poetry is not really the old meaning in a fresh dress; it is a new product, something like the poem, though, if one chooses to say so, more like it in the aspect of meaning than in the aspect of form.

No one who understands poetry, it seems to me, would dispute this, were it not that, falling away from his experience, or misled by theory, he takes /19/ the word "meaning" in a sense almost ludicrously inapplicable to poetry. People say, for instance, "steed" and

---

[2] These remarks will hold good, *mutatis mutandis*, if by "substance" is understood the "moral" or the "idea" of a poem, although perhaps in one instance out of five thousand this may be found in so many words in the poem.

[3] On the other hand, the absence, or worse than absence, of style, in this sense, is a serious matter.

"horse" have the same meaning; and in bad poetry they have, but not in poetry that *is* poetry.

"Bring forth the horse!" The horse was brought:
In truth he was a noble steed!

says Byron in *Mazeppa*. If the two words mean the same here, transpose them:

"Bring forth the steed!" The steed was brought:
In truth he was a noble horse!

and ask again if they mean the same. Or let me take a line certainly very free from "poetic diction":

To be or not to be, that is the question.

You may say that this means the same as "What is just now occupying my attention is the comparative disadvantages of continuing to live or putting an end to myself." And for practical purposes—the purpose, for example, of a coroner—it does. But as the second version altogether misrepresents the speaker at that moment of his existence, while the first does represent him, how can they for any but a practical or logical purpose be said to have the same sense? Hamlet was well able to "unpack his heart with words," but he will not unpack it with our paraphrases.

These considerations apply equally to versification. If I take the famous line which describes how the souls of the dead stood waiting by the river, imploring a passage from Charon:

Tendebantque manus ripae ulterioris amore;

and if I translate it, "and were stretching forth their hands in longing for the further bank," the charm of the original has fled. Why has it fled? Partly (but we have dealt with that) because I have substituted for five words, and those the words of Virgil, twelve words, and those my own. In some /20/ measure because I have turned into rhythmless prose a line of verse which, as mere sound, has unusual beauty. But much more because in doing so I have also changed the *meaning* of Virgil's line. What that meaning is I cannot say: Virgil has said it. But I can see this much, that the translation conveys a far less vivid picture of the outstretched hands and of their remaining outstretched, and a far less poignant sense of the distance of the shore and the longing of the souls. And it does so partly because this picture and this sense are conveyed not only by the obvious meaning of the words, but through the long-drawn sound of "tendebantque," through the time occupied by the five syllables and therefore by the idea of "ulterioris," and through the identity of the long sound "or" in the penultimate syllables of "ulterioris amore"— all this, and much more, apprehended not in this analytical fashion, nor as *added* to the beauty of mere sound and to the obvious meaning, but in unity with them and so as expressive of the poetic meaning of the whole.

It is always so in fine poetry. The value of versification, when it is indissolubly fused with meaning, can hardly be exaggerated. The gift for feeling it, even more perhaps than the gift for feeling the value of style, is the *specific* gift for poetry, as distinguished from other arts. But versification, taken, as far as possible, all by itself, has a very different worth. Some aesthetic worth it has; how much, you may experience by reading poetry in a language of which you do not understand a syllable. The pleasure is quite appreciable, but it is not great; nor in actual poetic experience do you meet with it, as such, at all. For, I repeat, it is not *added* to the pleasure of the meaning when you read poetry that you do understand: by some mystery the music is then the music *of* the /21/ meaning, and the two are one. However fond of versification you might be, you would tire very soon of reading verses in Chinese; and before long of reading Virgil and Dante if you were ignorant of their languages. But take the music as it is *in* the poem, and there is a marvellous change. Now

It gives a very echo to the seat
Where love is throned;

or "carries far into your heart," almost like music itself, the sound

Of old, unhappy, far-off things
And battles long ago.[4]

What then is to be said of the following sentence of the critic quoted before: "But when any one who knows what poetry is reads—

Our noisy years seem moments in the being
Of the eternal silence,

4 [For complete poem, see p. 169.]

he sees that, quite independently of the meaning, . . . there is one note added to the articulate music of the world—a note that never will leave off resounding till the eternal silence itself gulfs it''? I must think that the writer is deceiving himself. For I could quite understand his enthusiasm, if it were an enthusiasm for the music of the meaning; but as for the music, "quite independently of the meaning," so far as I can hear it thus (and I doubt if any one who knows English can quite do so), I find it gives some pleasure, but only a trifling pleasure. And indeed I venture to doubt whether, considered as mere sound, the words are at all exceptionally beautiful, as Virgil's line certainly is.

When poetry answers to its idea and is purely or almost purely poetic, we find the identity of form and content; and the degree of purity attained may be tested by the degree in which we feel it hopeless to convey the effect of a poem or passage in any form but its own. Where the notion of doing so is /22/ simply ludicrous, you have quintessential poetry. But a great part even of good poetry, especially in long works, is of a mixed nature; and so we find in it no more than a partial agreement of a form and substance which remain to some extent distinct. This is so in many passages of Shakespeare (the greatest of poets when he chose, but not always a conscientious poet); passages where something was wanted for the sake of the plot, but he did not care about it or was hurried. The conception of the passage is then distinct from the execution, and neither is inspired. This is so also, I think, wherever we can truly speak of merely decorative effect. We seem to perceive that the poet had a truth or fact—philosophical, agricultural, social—distinctly before him, and then, as we say, clothed it in metrical and coloured language. Most argumentative, didactic, or satiric poems are partly of this kind; and in imaginative poems anything which is really a mere "conceit" is mere decoration. We often deceive ourselves in this matter, for what we call decoration has often a new and genuinely poetic content of its own; but wherever there is mere decoration, we judge the poetry to be not wholly poetic. And so when Wordsworth inveighed against poetic diction, though he

hurled his darts rather wildly, what he was rightly aiming at was a phraseology, not the living body of a new content, but the mere worn-out body of an old one.

In pure poetry it is otherwise. Pure poetry is not the decoration of a preconceived and clearly defined matter: it springs from the creative impulse of a vague imaginative mass pressing for development and definition. If the poet already knew exactly what he meant to say, why should he write the poem? The poem would in fact already be written. For only its completion can reveal, even to him, exactly what he wanted. When he began and /23/ while he was at work, he did not possess his meaning; it possessed him. It was not a fully formed soul asking for a body: it was an inchoate soul in the inchoate body of perhaps two or three vague ideas and a few scattered phrases. The growing of this body into its full stature and perfect shape was the same thing as the gradual self-definition of the meaning. And this is the reason why such poems strike us as creations, not manufactures, and have the magical effect which mere decoration cannot produce. This is also the reason why, if we insist on asking for the meaning of such a poem, we can only be answered "It means itself."

And so at last I may explain why I have troubled myself and you with what may seem an arid controversy about mere words. It is not so. These heresies which would make poetry a compound of two factors—a matter common to it with the merest prose, *plus* a poetic form, as the one heresy says: a poetical substance *plus* a negligible form, as the other says—are not only untrue, they are injurious to the dignity of poetry. In an age already inclined to shrink from those higher realms where poetry touches religion and philosophy, the formalist heresy encourages men to taste poetry as they would a fine wine, which has indeed an aesthetic value, but a small one. And then the natural man, finding an empty form, hurls into it the matter of cheap pathos, rancid sentiment, vulgar humour, bare lust, ravenous vanity—everything which, in Schiller's phrase,[5] the form should extirpate, but which no mere form can extirpate. And the other heresy—which is indeed rather a prac-

5 Not that to Schiller "form" meant mere style and versification.

tice than a creed—encourages us in the habit so dear to us of putting our own thoughts or fancies into the place of the poet's creation. What he meant by *Hamlet*, or the *Ode to a Nightingale*, or *Abt Vogler*, we say, is this or that which we /24/ knew already; and so we lose what he had to tell us. But he meant what he said, and said what he meant.

Poetry in this matter is not, as good critics of painting and music often affirm, different from the other arts; in all of them the content is one thing with the form. What Beethoven meant by his symphony, or Turner by his picture, was not something which you can name, but the picture and the symphony. Meaning they have, but *what* meaning can be said in no language but their own: and we know this, though some strange delusion makes us think the meaning has less worth because we cannot put it into words. Well, it is just the same with poetry. But because poetry is words, we vainly fancy that some other words than its own will express its meaning. And they will do so no more—or, if you like to speak loosely, only a trifle more—than words will express the meaning of the Dresden Madonna. Something a little like it they may indeed express. And we may find analogues of the meaning of poetry outside it, which may help us to appropriate it. The other arts, the best ideas of philosophy or religion, much that nature and life offer us or force upon us, are akin to it. But they are only akin. Nor is it the expression of them. Poetry does not present to imagination our highest knowledge or belief, and much less our dreams and opinions; but it, content and form in unity, embodies in its own irreplaceable way something which embodies itself also in other irreplaceable ways, such as philosophy or religion. And just as each of these gives a satisfaction which the other cannot possibly give, so we find in poetry, which cannot satisfy the needs they meet, that which by their natures they cannot afford us. But we shall not find it fully if we look for something else. /25/

And now, when all is said, the question will still recur, though now in quite another sense, What does poetry mean? This unique expression, which cannot be replaced by any other, still seems to be trying to express something beyond itself. And this, we feel, is also what the other arts, and religion, and philosophy are trying to express: and that is what impels us to seek in vain to translate the one into the other. About the best poetry, and not only the best, there floats an atmosphere of infinite suggestion. The poet speaks to us of one thing, but in this one thing there seems to lurk the secret of all. He said what he meant, but his meaning seems to beckon away beyond itself, or rather to expand into something boundless which is only focussed in it; something also which, we feel, would satisfy not only the imagination, but the whole of us; that something within us, and without, which everywhere

> makes us seem
> To patch up fragments of a dream,
> Part of which comes true, and part
> Beats and trembles in the heart.

Those who are susceptible to this effect of poetry find it not only, perhaps not most, in the ideals which she has sometimes described, but in a child's song by Christina Rossetti about a mere crown of wind-flowers, and in tragedies like *Lear*, where the sun seems to have set for ever. They hear this spirit murmuring its undertone through the *Aeneid*, and catch its voice in the song of Keats's nightingale, and its light upon the figures on the Urn, and it pierces them no less in Shelley's hopeless lament, *O world, O life, O time*, than in the rapturous ecstasy of her *Life of Life*. This all-embracing perfection cannot be expressed in poetic words or words of any kind, nor yet in music or in colour, but the suggestion of it is in much poetry, if not all, /26/ and poetry has in this suggestion, this "meaning," a great part of its value. We do it wrong, and we defeat our own purposes, when we try to bend it to them:

> We do it wrong, being so majestical,
> To offer it the show of violence;
> For it is as the air invulnerable,
> And our vain blows malicious mockery.

It is a spirit. It comes we know not whence. It will not speak at our bidding, nor answer in our language. It is not our servant; it is our master. /27/

A. E. HOUSMAN

from *The Name and Nature of Poetry*

[A. E. Housman (1859–1936), poet and classical scholar, was born in Worcestershire, and prepared himself at Oxford for an academic career. Surprisingly, however, he failed his examinations. During ten years while he worked at the Patent Office in London he redeemed his reputation by writing scholarly articles, and from 1892 till his death he was Professor of Latin, first at the University of London, then at Cambridge. His poetic reputation rests on *A Shropshire Lad* (1896), *Last Poems* (1922), and the posthumous *More Poems* (1936). *The Name and Nature of Poetry* was delivered as a lecture at Cambridge in 1933 and published the same year in New York and Cambridge.]

In these twenty-two years I have improved in some respects and deteriorated in others; but I have not so much improved as to become a literary critic, nor so much deteriorated as to fancy that I have become one. Therefore you are not about to be addressed in that tone of authority which is appropriate to those who are, and is assumed by some of those who conceive themselves to be, literary critics. In order to hear Jehovah thundering out of Zion, or Little Bethel, you must go elsewhere.

But all my life long the best literature of /2/ several languages has been my favourite recreation; and good literature continually read for pleasure must, let us hope, do some good to the reader: must quicken his perception though dull, and sharpen his discrimination though blunt, and mellow the rawness of his personal opinions. But personal opinions they remain, not truths to be imparted as such with the sureness of superior insight and knowledge. I hope however that for brevity's sake, and your own, you will accept the disclaimer once for all, and that when hereafter I may say that things are thus or thus, you will not insist on my saying instead that I humbly venture to conceive them so or that I diffidently offer the suggestion to your better judgment. . . . /3/

When one begins to discuss the nature of poetry, the first impediment in the way is the inherent vagueness of the name, and the number of its legitimate senses. It is not bad English to speak of "prose and poetry" in the sense of "prose and verse." But it is wasteful; it squanders a valuable word by stretching it to fit a meaning which is accurately expressed by a wider term. Verse may be, like the Tale of Sir Thopas in the judgment of Our Host of the Tabard, "rym dogerel"; and the name of poetry is gener- /5/ ally restricted to verse which can at least be called literature, though it may differ from prose only in its metrical form, and be superior to prose only in the superior comeliness of that form itself, and the superior terseness which usually goes along with it. Then further there is verse which gives a positive and lively pleasure arising from the talent and accomplishment of its author.

> Now Gilpin had a pleasant wit
>   And loved a timely joke,
> And thus unto the Callender
>   In merry guise he spoke:
>
> I came because your horse would come;
>   And, if I well forbode,
> My hat and wig will soon be here:
>   They are upon the road.

Capital: but no one, if asked for a typical example of poetry, would recite those verses in reply. A typical example need not be any less plain and simple and straightforward, but it would be a little raised.

> Come, worthy Greek, Ulysses, come,
>   Possess these shores with me: /6/
> The winds and seas are troublesome,
>   And here we may be free.
> Here may we sit and view their toil
>   That travail in the deep,
> And joy the day in mirth the while,
>   And spend the night in sleep.[1]

There we are ceasing to gallop with the Callender's horse and beginning to fly with Pegasus. Indeed a promising young poetaster

1 [For complete poem, see p. 185.]

could not do better than lay up that stanza in his memory, not necessarily as a pattern to set before him, but as a touchstone to keep at his side. Diction and movement alike, it is perfect. It is made out of the most ordinary words, yet it is pure from the least alloy of prose; and however much nearer heaven the art of poetry may have mounted, it has never flown on a surer or a lighter wing.

It is perfect, I say; and nothing more than perfection can be demanded of anything: yet poetry is capable of more than this, and more therefore is expected from it. There is a conception of poetry which is not fulfilled by pure language and liquid /7/ versification, with the simple and so to speak colourless pleasure which they afford, but involves the presence in them of something which moves and touches in a special and recognisable way. Set beside that stanza of Daniel's these lines from Bruce's or Logan's Cuckoo:

> Sweet bird, thy bower is ever green,
>   Thy sky is ever clear;
> Thou hast no sorrow in thy song,
>   No winter in thy year.

There a new element has stolen in, a tinge of emotion. And I think that to transfuse emotion—not to transmit thought but to set up in the reader's sense a vibration corresponding to what was felt by the writer—is the peculiar function of poetry. Even where the verse is not thus beautiful and engaging in its external form, as in Johnson's lines,

> His virtues walked their narrow round,
>   Nor made a pause, nor left a void;
> And sure the Eternal Master found
>   The single talent well employed, /8/

it may yet possess the same virtue and elicit a like response.

Further than this I will not now ascend the stair of poetry. I have chosen these two examples because they may almost be called humble, and contain hardly more than the promise of what poetry attains to be. Here it is not lofty or magnificent or intense; it does not transport with rapture nor overwhelm with awe; it does not stab the heart nor shake the soul nor take the breath away. But it is poetry, though not in the highest, yet in the highest definable sense.

> Duncan is in his grave;
> After life's fitful fever he sleeps well.

Even for that poetry there is no other name.

I said that the legitimate meanings of the word poetry were themselves so many as to embarrass the discussion of its nature. All the more reason why we should not confound confusion worse by wresting the term to licentious use and affixing it either to dissimilar things already provided with /9/ names of their own, or to new things for which new names should be invented.

There was a whole age of English in which the place of poetry was usurped by something very different which possessed the proper and specific name of wit: wit not in its modern sense, but as defined by Johnson, "a combination of dissimilar images, or discovery of occult resemblances in things apparently unlike." Such discoveries are no more poetical than anagrams; such pleasure as they give is purely intellectual and is intellectually frivolous; but this was the pleasure principally sought and found in poems by the intelligentsia of fifty years and more of the seventeenth century. Some of the writers who purveyed it to their contemporaries were, by accident, considerable poets; and though their verse was generally inharmonious, and apparently cut into lengths and tied into faggots by deaf mathematicians, some little of their poetry was beautiful and even superb. But it was not by this that they captivated and sought to captivate. Simile and meta- /10/ phor, things inessential to poetry, were their great engrossing pre-occupation, and were prized the more in proportion as they were further fetched. They did not mean these accessories to be helpful, to make their sense clearer or their conceptions more vivid; they hardly even meant them for ornament, or cared whether an image had any independent power to please: their object was to startle by novelty and amuse by ingenuity a public whose one wish was to be so startled and amused. The pleasure, however luxurious, of hearing St Mary Magdalene's eyes described as

> Two walking baths, two weeping motions,
> Portable and compendious oceans,

was not a poetic pleasure; and poetry, as a

label for this particular commodity, is not appropriate.

Appropriateness is even more carefully to be considered when the thing which we so much admire that we wish to give it the noblest name we can lay our tongue to is a new thing. We should beware of treating /11/ the word poetry as chemists have treated the word salt. Salt is a crystalline substance recognised by its taste; its name is as old as the English language and is the possession of the English people, who know what it means: it is not the private property of a science less than three hundred years old, which, being in want of a term to embody a new conception, "an acid having the whole or part of its hydrogen replaced by a metal," has lazily helped itself to the old and unsuitable word salt, instead of excogitating a new and therefore to that extent an apt one. The right model for imitation is that chemist who, when he encountered, or thought he had encountered, a hitherto nameless form of matter, did not purloin for it the name of something else, but invented out of his own head a name which should be proper to it, and enriched the vocabulary of modern man with the useful word *gas*. If we apply the word poetry to an object which does not resemble, either in form or content, anything which has heretofore been so called, not /12/ only are we maltreating and corrupting language, but we may be guilty of disrespect and blasphemy. Poetry may be too mean a name for the object in question: the object, being certainly something different, may possibly be something superior. When the Lord rained bread from heaven so that man did eat angels' food, and the children of Israel saw upon the face of the wilderness a small round thing, as small as the hoar frost on the ground, they did not call it quails: they rose to the occasion and said to one another "it is manna."

There is also such a thing as sham poetry, a counterfeit deliberately manufactured and offered as a substitute. In English the great historical example is certain verse produced abundantly and applauded by high and low in what for literary purposes is loosely called the eighteenth century: not a hundred years accidentally begun and ended by chronology, but a longer period which is a unity and a reality; the period lying between Samson Agonistes in 1671 and the Lyrical Ballads in 1798, and in- /13/ cluding as an integral part and indeed as its most potent influence the mature work of Dryden.

Matthew Arnold more than fifty years ago, in speaking of Wordsworth's and Coleridge's low estimate of the poetry of the eighteenth century, issued the warning "there are many signs to show that the eighteenth century and its judgments are coming into favour again." I remember thinking to myself that surely this could never be; but there you see what it is to be a literary critic. There has now for a good many years been a strong disposition to revise the verdict pronounced by the nineteenth century on the poetry of the eighteenth and to represent that its disparaging judgment was no more than an expression of distaste for a sort of poetry unlike its own. That is a misconception. It set a low value on the poetry of the eighteenth century, not because it differed in kind from its own, but because, even at its best, it differed in quality, as its own best poetry did not differ, from the poetry of all those ages, /14/ whether modern or ancient, English or foreign, which are acknowledged as the great ages of poetry. Tried by that standard the poetry of the eighteenth century, even when not vicious, even when sound and good, fell short.

The literature of the eighteenth century in England is an admirable and most enjoyable thing. It has a greater solidity of excellence than any before or after; and although the special task and characteristic achievement of the age was the invention and establishment of a healthy, workman-like, athletic prose, to supersede the cumbrous and decorated and self-admiring prose of a Milton or a Jeremy Taylor, and to become a trustworthy implement for accurate thinking and the serious pursuit of truth, yet in verse also it created masterpieces, and perhaps no English poem of greater than lyric length, not even the Nonne's Priest's Tale or the Ancient Mariner, is quite so perfect as the Rape of the Lock. But the human faculty which dominated the eighteenth century and informed /15/ its literature was the intelligence, and that involved, as Arnold says, "some repressing and silencing of poetry," "some touch of frost to the imaginative life of the soul." Man had ceased to live from the depths of his nature; he occupied himself for choice with thoughts which do not range beyond the sphere of the understanding; he lighted the candles and drew down the blind to shut out that patroness of poets, the moon. The writing of poetry proceeded, and much of the poetry written was excellent literature; but excellent literature which is also poetry is not therefore excellent poetry, and the poetry of the eighteenth century was most satisfactory when it did not try to be poetical. Eighteenth-century poetry is in fact a name for two different things, which ought to be kept distinct. There was a good sound workaday article, efficiently discharging a worthy and honourable though not an exalted duty. Satire, controversy, and burlesque, to which the eighteenth century was drawn by the character of its genius, and in which its achievement was /16/ unrivalled, are forms of art in which high poetry is not at home, and to which, unless introduced with great parsimony and tact, it would be actually injurious and disfiguring. The conclusion of the Dunciad may fairly be called sublime; but such a tone was wisely reserved for the conclusion. The modicum of the poetical element which satire can easily accommodate is rather what we find in lines like these:

Riches, like insects, when conceal'd they lie,
Wait but for wings, and in their season fly.
Who sees pale Mammon pine amidst his store
Sees but a backward steward for the poor:
This year a reservoir, to keep and spare;
The next, a fountain, spouting through his heir,
In lavish streams to quench a country's thirst,
And men and dogs shall drink him till they burst.

And what sterling stuff they are! But such writing, which was their true glory and should have been their proper pride, did not content its writers. They felt that this, after all, did not rank as equal with the po- /17/ etry of other ages, nor fulfil the conception of poetry which was obscurely present in their minds; and they aspired to something which should be less pedestrian. It was as though the ostrich should attempt to fly. The ostrich on her own element is the swiftest of created things; she scorneth the horse and his rider; and although we are also told that God hath deprived her of wisdom, neither hath he imparted to her understanding, he has at any rate given her sense enough to know that she is not a lark or an eagle. To poets of the eighteenth century high and impassioned poetry did not come spontaneously, because the feelings which foster its birth were not then abundant and urgent in the inner man; but they girt up their loins and essayed a lofty strain at the bidding of ambition. The way to write real poetry, they thought, must be to write something as little like prose as possible; they devised for the purpose what was called a "correct and splendid diction," which consisted in always using the wrong word instead of the right, /18/ and plastered it as ornament, with no thought of propriety, on whatever they desired to dignify. It commanded notice and was not easy to mistake; so the public mind soon connected it with the notion of poetry and came in course of time to regard it as alone poetical.[2]

It was in truth at once pompous and poverty-stricken. It had a very limited, be- /19/ cause supposedly choice, vocabulary, and was consequently unequal to the multitude and refinement of its duties. It could not describe natural objects with sensitive fidelity to nature; it could not express human feelings with a variety and delicacy answering to their own. A thick, stiff unaccommodating medium was interposed between the writer and his work. And this deadening of language had a conse-

[2] It is now customary to say that the nineteenth century had a similar lingo of its own. A lingo it had, or came to have, and in the seventies and eighties the minor poets and poetasters were all using the same supposedly poetic diction. It was imitative and sapless, but not preposterous: its leading characteristic was a stale and faded prettiness.

> As one that for a weary space has lain
>   Lull'd by the song of Circe and her wine
>   In gardens near the pale of Proserpine,
> Where that Æean isle forgets the main,
> And only the low lutes of love complain,
>   And only shadows of wan lovers pine—
>   As such an one were glad to know the brine
> Salt on his lips, and the large air again. . . .

The atmosphere of the eighteenth century made much better poets write much worse.

>   Lo! where the rosy-bosom'd Hours,
>   Fair Venus' train, appear,
>   Disclose the long-expecting flowers
>   And wake the purple year!
>   The Attic warbler pours her throat

and so forth.

quence beyond its own sphere: its effect worked inward, and deadened perception. That which could no longer be described was no longer noticed.

The features and formation of the style can be studied under a cruel light in Dryden's translations from Chaucer. The Knight's Tale of Palamon and Arcite is not one of Chaucer's most characteristic and successful poems: he is not perfectly at home, as in the Prologue and the tale of Chauntecleer and Pertelote, and his movement is a trifle languid. Dryden's translation shows Dryden in the maturity of his power and accomplishment, and much of /20/ it can be honestly and soberly admired. Nor was he insensible to all the peculiar excellence of Chaucer: he had the wit to keep unchanged such lines as "Up rose the sun and up rose Emily" or "The slayer of himself yet saw I there"; he understood that neither he nor anyone else could better them. But much too often in a like case he would try to improve, because he thought that he could. He believed, as he says himself, that he was "turning some of the Canterbury Tales into our language, as it is now refined"; "the words" he says again "are given up as a post not to be defended in our poet, because he wanted the modern art of fortifying"; "in some places" he tells us "I have added somewhat of my own where I thought my author was deficient, and had not given his thoughts their true lustre, for want of words in the beginning of our language."

Let us look at the consequences. Chaucer's vivid and memorable line

The smiler with the knife under the cloke /21/

becomes these three:

> Next stood Hypocrisy, with holy leer,
> Soft smiling and demurely looking down,
> But hid the dagger underneath the gown.

Again:

> Alas, quod he, that day that I was bore.

So Chaucer, for want of words in the beginning of our language. Dryden comes to his assistance and gives his thoughts their true lustre thus:

Cursed be the day when first I did appear;
Let it be blotted from the calendar,
Lest it pollute the month and poison all the year.

Or yet again:

> The queen anon for very womanhead
> Gan for to weep, and so did Emily
> And all the ladies in the company.

If Homer or Dante had the same thing to say, would he wish to say it otherwise? But to Dryden Chaucer wanted the modern art of fortifying, which he thus applies: /22/

He said; dumb sorrow seized the standers-by.
The queen, above the rest, by nature good
(The pattern formed of perfect womanhood)
For tender pity wept: when she began
Through the bright quire the infectious virtue ran.
All dropped their tears, even the contended maid.

Had there not fallen upon England the curse out of Isaiah, "make the heart of this people fat, and make their ears heavy, and shut their eyes"? That there should ever have existed an obtuseness which could mistake this impure verbiage for a correct and splendid diction is a dreadful thought. . . . /23/

The first impediment, I said, to dealing with the subject of poetry is the native am- /30/ biguity of the term. But the course of these remarks has now brought us to a point where another and perhaps greater difficulty awaits us in determining the competence or incompetence of the judge, that is the sensibility or insensibility of the percipient. Am I capable of recognising poetry if I come across it? Do I possess the organ by which poetry is perceived? The majority of civilised mankind notoriously and indisputably do not; who has certified me that I am one of the minority who do? I may know what I like and admire, I may like and admire it intensely; but what makes me think that it is poetry? Is my reason for thinking so anything more than this: that poetry is generally esteemed the highest form of literature, and that my opinion of myself forbids me to believe that what I most like and admire is anything short of the highest? Yet why be unwilling to admit that perhaps you cannot perceive poetry? Why think it necessary to your self-respect that you should? How many of the good and great, how many saints and heroes have /31/ possessed this faculty? Can you hear the shriek of the bat? Probably not; but do you think the less of yourself on that account? do you pretend to others, or even try to persuade yourself, that you can? Is it an unbearable thing, and crushing to self-conceit, to be in the majority?

If a man is insensible to poetry, it does not follow that he gets no pleasure from poems. Poems very seldom consist of poetry and nothing else; and pleasure can be derived also from their other ingredients. I am convinced that most readers, when they think that they are admiring poetry, are deceived by inability to analyse their sensations, and that they are really admiring, not the poetry of the passage before them, but something else in it, which they like better than poetry.

To begin with a very obvious instance. I have been told by devout women that to them the most beautiful poetry is Keble's. Keble is a poet; there are things in the Christian Year which can be admired by atheists; but what devout women most /32/ prize in it, as Keble himself would have wished, is not its poetry; and I much doubt whether any of them, if asked to pick out the best poem in the book, would turn at once to the Second Sunday after Easter. Good religious poetry, whether in Keble or Dante or Job, is likely to be most justly appreciated and most discriminatingly relished by the undevout.

Again, there existed in the last century a great body of Wordsworthians, as they were called. It is now much smaller; but true appreciation of Wordsworth's poetry has not diminished in proportion: I suspect that it has much increased. The Wordsworthians, as Matthew Arnold told them, were apt to praise their poet for the wrong things. They were most attracted by what may be called his philosophy; they accepted his belief in the morality of the universe and the tendency of events to good; they were even willing to entertain his conception of nature as a living and sentient and benignant being, a conception as purely mythological as the Dryads and the Naiads. /33/ To that thrilling utterance which pierces the heart and brings tears to the eyes of thousands who care nothing for his opinions and beliefs they were not noticeably sensitive; and however justly they admired the depth of his insight into human nature and the nobility of his moral ideas, these things, with which his poetry was in close and harmonious alliance, are distinct from poetry itself.

When I examine my mind and try to discern clearly in the matter, I cannot satisfy myself that there are any such things as poetical ideas. No truth, it seems to me, is too precious, no observation too profound, and no sentiment too exalted to be expressed in prose. The utmost that I could admit is that some ideas do, while others do not, lend themselves kindly to poetical expression; and that these receive from poetry an enhancement which glorifies and almost transfigures them, and which is not perceived to be a separate thing except by analysis.

"Whosoever will save his life shall lose it, /34/ and whosoever will lose his life shall find it." That is the most important truth which has ever been uttered, and the greatest discovery ever made in the moral world; but I do not find in it anything which I should call poetical. On the other hand, when Wisdom says in the Proverbs "He that sinneth against me wrongeth his own soul; all they that hate me, love death," that is to me poetry, because of the words in which the idea is clothed; and as for the seventh verse of the forty-ninth Psalm in the Book of Common Prayer, "But no man may deliver his brother, nor make agreement unto God for him," that is to me poetry so moving that I can hardly keep my voice steady in reading it. And that this is the effect of language I can ascertain by experiment: the same thought in the bible version, "None of them can by any means redeem his brother, nor give to God a ransom for him," I can read without emotion.

Poetry is not the thing said but a way of saying it. Can it then be isolated and studied by itself? for the combination of /35/ language with its intellectual content, its meaning, is as close a union as can well be imagined. Is there such a thing as pure unmingled poetry, poetry independent of meaning?

Even when poetry has a meaning, as it usually has, it may be inadvisable to draw it out. "Poetry gives most pleasure" said Coleridge "when only generally and not perfectly understood"; and perfect understanding will sometimes almost extinguish pleasure. The

Haunted Palace[3] is one of Poe's best poems so long as we are content to swim in the sensations it evokes and only vaguely to apprehend the allegory. We are roused to discomfort, at least I am, when we begin to perceive how exact in detail the allegory is; when it dawns upon us that the fair palace door is Roderick Usher's mouth, the pearl and ruby his teeth and lips, the yellow banners his hair, the ramparts plumed and pallid his forehead, and when we are reduced to hoping, for it is no more than a hope, that the wingèd odours have no connexion with hair-oil. /36/

Meaning is of the intellect, poetry is not. If it were, the eighteenth century would have been able to write it better. As matters actually stand, who are the English poets of that age in whom pre-eminently one can hear and recognize the true poetic accent emerging clearly from the contemporary dialect? These four: Collins, Christopher Smart, Cowper, and Blake. And what other characteristic had these four in common? They were mad. Remember Plato: "He who without the Muses' madness in his soul comes knocking at the door of poesy and thinks that art will make him anything fit to be called a poet, finds that the poetry which he indites in his sober senses is beaten hollow by the poetry of madmen."

That the intellect is not the fount of poetry, that it may actually hinder its production, and that it cannot even be trusted to recognise poetry when produced, is best seen in the case of Smart. Neither the prize founded in this University by the Rev. Thomas Seaton nor the successive contem- /37/ plation of five several attributes of the Supreme Being could incite him to good poetry while he was sane. The only poem by which he is remembered, a poem which came to its own in the kinder climate of the nineteenth century and has inspired one of the best poems of the twentieth, was written, if not, as tradition says, in actual confinement, at any rate very soon after release; and when the eighteenth century, the age of sanity and intelligence, collected his poetical works, it excluded this piece as "bearing melancholy proofs of the recent estrangement of his mind."

Collins and Cowper, though they saw the inside of madhouses, are not supposed to have written any of their poetry there; and Blake was never mad enough to be locked up. But elements of their nature were more or less insurgent against the centralised tyranny of the intellect, and their brains were not thrones on which the great usurper could sit secure. And so it strangely came to pass that in the eighteenth century, the age of prose and of unsound or /38/ unsatisfying poetry, there sprang up one well of the purest inspiration. For me the most poetical of all poets is Blake. I find his lyrical note as beautiful as Shakespeare's and more beautiful than anyone else's; and I call him more poetical than Shakespeare, even though Shakespeare has so much more poetry, because poetry in him preponderates more than in Shakespeare over everything else, and instead of being confounded in a great river can be drunk pure from a slender channel of its own. Shakespeare is rich in thought, and his meaning has power of itself to move us, even if the poetry were not there: Blake's meaning is often unimportant or virtually non-existent, so that we can listen with all our hearing to his celestial tune.

Even Shakespeare, who had so much to say, would sometimes pour out his loveliest poetry in saying nothing.

> Take O take those lips away
>   That so sweetly were forsworn,
> And those eyes, the break of day,
>   Lights that do mislead the morn; /39/
> But my kisses bring again,
>   bring again,
> Seals of love, but seal'd in vain,
>   seal'd in vain.

That is nonsense; but it is ravishing poetry. When Shakespeare fills such poetry with thought, and thought which is worthy of it, as in *Fear no more the heat o' the sun* or *O mistress mine, where art thou roaming?* those songs, the very summits of lyrical achievement, are indeed greater and more moving poems, but I hardly know how to call them more poetical.

Now Blake again and again, as Shakespeare now and then, gives us poetry neat, or adulterated with so little meaning that nothing except poetic emotion is perceived and matters.

3 [See p. 204.]

Hear the voice of the Bard,
　Who present, past, and future sees;
Whose ears have heard
The Holy Word
　That walk'd among the ancient trees,

Calling the lapsèd soul
　And weeping in the evening dew; /40/
That might control
The starry pole,
　And fallen, fallen light renew.

"O Earth, O Earth, return!
　Arise from out the dewy grass;
Night is worn,
And the morn
　Rises from the slumberous mass.

"Turn away no more;
　Why wilt thou turn away?
The starry floor,
The watery shore
　Is giv'n thee till the break of day."⁴

That mysterious grandeur would be less grand
if it were less mysterious; if the embryo ideas
which are all that it contains should endue
form and outline, and suggestion condense
itself into thought.

　　Memory, hither come
　　　And tune your merry notes;
　　And while upon the wind
　　　Your music floats

　　I'll pore upon the stream
　　Where sighing lovers dream,
　　And fish for fancies as they pass
　　Within the watery glass. /41/

That answers to nothing real; memory's merry
notes and the rest are empty phrases, not
things to be imagined; the stanza does but en-
tangle the reader in a net of thoughtless delight. . . . /42/

In most poets, as I said, poetry is less often
found thus disengaged from its usual con-
comitants, from certain things with which it
naturally unites itself and seems to blend in-
distinguishably. For instance:

Sorrow, that is not sorrow, but delight;
And miserable love, that is not pain
To hear of, for the glory that redounds
Therefrom to human kind, and what we are.

The feeling with which those lines are read
is composite, for one constituent is supplied

⁴ [Introduction to *Songs of Experience*, by William
Blake.]

by the depth and penetrating truth of the
thought. Again: /44/

　　Though love repine and reason chafe,
　　　There came a voice without reply,—
　　" 'Tis man's perdition to be safe,
　　　When for the truth he ought to die."

Much of the emotion kindled by that verse
can be referred to the nobility of the sentiment. But in these six simple words of Milton—

　　Nymphs and shepherds, dance no more—

what is it that can draw tears, as I know it
can, to the eyes of more readers than one?
What in the world is there to cry about? Why
have the mere words the physical effect of
pathos when the sense of the passage is blithe
and gay? I can only say, because they are poetry, and find their way to something in man
which is obscure and latent, something older
than the present organisation of his nature,
like the patches of fen which still linger here
and there in the drained lands of Cambridge-
shire.

Poetry indeed seems to me more physical
than intellectual. A year or two ago, in common with others, I received from /45/ America a request that I would define poetry. I replied that I could no more define poetry than
a terrier can define a rat, but that I thought
we both recognised the object by the symptoms which it provokes in us. One of these
symptoms was described in connexion with
another object by Eliphaz the Temanite: "A
spirit passed before my face: the hair of my
flesh stood up." Experience has taught me,
when I am shaving of a morning, to keep
watch over my thoughts, because, if a line of
poetry strays into my memory, my skin bristles
so that the razor ceases to act. This particular
symptom is accompanied by a shiver down
the spine; there is another which consists in
a constriction of the throat and a precipitation of water to the eyes; and there is a third
which I can only describe by borrowing a
phrase from one of Keats's last letters, where
he says, speaking of Fanny Brawne, "everything that reminds me of her goes through
me like a spear." The seat of this sensation is
the pit of the stomach.

My opinions on poetry are necessarily /46/

tinged, perhaps I should say tainted, by the circumstance that I have come into contact with it on two sides. We were saying a while ago that poetry is a very wide term, and inconveniently comprehensive: so comprehensive is it that it embraces two books, fortunately not large ones, of my own. I know how this stuff came into existence; and though I have no right to assume that any other poetry came into existence in the same way, yet I find reason to believe that some poetry, and quite good poetry, did. Wordsworth for instance says that poetry is the spontaneous overflow of powerful feelings, and Burns has left us this confession, "I have two or three times in my life composed from the wish rather than the impulse, but I never succeeded to any purpose." In short I think that the production of poetry, in its first stage, is less an active than a passive and involuntary process; and if I were obliged, not to define poetry, but to name the class of things to which it belongs, I should call it a secretion; whether a natural secretion, like tur- /47/ pentine in the fir, or a morbid secretion, like the pearl in the oyster. I think that my own case, though I may not deal with the material so cleverly as the oyster does, is the latter; because I have seldom written poetry unless I was rather out of health, and the experience, though pleasurable, was generally agitating and exhausting. If only that you may know what to avoid, I will give some account of the process.

Having drunk a pint of beer at luncheon —beer is a sedative to the brain, and my afternoons are the least intellectual portion of my life—I would go out for a walk of two or three hours. As I went along, thinking of nothing in particular, only looking at things around me and following the progress of the seasons, there would flow into my mind, with sudden and unaccountable emotion, sometimes a line

or two of verse, sometimes a whole stanza at once, accompanied, not preceded, by a vague notion of the poem which they were destined to form part of. Then there would usually be a lull of an hour or so, then perhaps the /48/ spring would bubble up again. I say bubble up, because, so far as I could make out, the source of the suggestions thus proffered to the brain was an abyss which I have already had occasion to mention, the pit of the stomach. When I got home I wrote them down, leaving gaps, and hoping that further inspiration might be forthcoming another day. Sometimes it was, if I took my walks in a receptive and expectant frame of mind; but sometimes the poem had to be taken in hand and completed by the brain, which was apt to be a matter of trouble and anxiety, involving trial and disappointment, and sometimes ending in failure. I happen to remember distinctly the genesis of the piece which stands last in my first volume. Two of the stanzas, I do not say which, came into my head, just as they are printed, while I was crossing the corner of Hampstead Heath between the Spaniard's Inn and the footpath to Temple Fortune. A third stanza came with a little coaxing after tea. One more was needed, but it did not come: I had to turn to and compose it /49/ myself, and that was a laborious business. I wrote it thirteen times, and it was more than a twelvemonth before I got it right.

By this time you must be sated with anatomy, pathology, and autobiography, and willing to let me retire from my incursion into the foreign territory of literary criticism. Farewell for ever. I will not say with Coleridge that I recentre my immortal mind in the deep sabbath of meek self-content; but I shall go back with relief and thankfulness to my proper job. /50/

JOHN CROWE RANSOM
"Forms and Citizens"

[John Crowe Ransom (1888–   ), poet, critic, and teacher, was born in Tennessee, educated at Vanderbilt and Oxford (where he was a Rhodes Scholar), and has been a professor of literature at Vanderbilt and Kenyon. His *Selected Poems,* published in 1945, contained his choice of the best from several previous volumes, and in 1951 he received the Bollingen prize in poetry. He helped found the magazine *Fugitives,* from which the Fugitive group of poets received its name, and was later for many years editor of *The Kenyon Review.* The following essay was originally published in *The American Review* in 1933 as the second part of a two-part article on Milton's "Lycidas"; it is reprinted here (except for an omitted fifth section) from Ransom's book of critical essays *The World's Body* (New York, 1938).]

A first-rate poet performs in *Lycidas,*[1] it is plain. And this is plain too: he performs because the decencies of an occasion require it of him, but the occasion catches him at a moment when his faith in the tradition of his art is not too strong, and in the performance rebellion is mixed up with loyalty. The study of the poem leads into a very broad field of discussion, and the topic is the general relation of the poet to his formal tradition.

By formal we are not to mean the metre only; but also, and it is probably even more important, the literary type, with its fictitious point of view from which the poet approaches his object, and its prescription of style and tone. And by tradition we should mean simply the source from which the form most easily comes. Tradition is the handing down of a thing by society, and the thing handed down is just a formula, a form.

Society hands down many forms which the individual is well advised to appropriate, but we are concerned here with those which may be called the æsthetic ones. They contrast themselves with the other and more common forms in the remarkable fact that they do not serve the principle of utility. This point has not been sufficiently remarked, so far as my

1 [See p. 191.]

reading indicates. There are economic forms; /29/ there are also æsthetic forms, which are not the same thing. Or, there are work-forms and there are play-forms.

First, the economic forms. We inherit the traditional forms of such objects as plough, table, book, biscuit, machine, and of such processes as shepherding the flock, building, baking, making war. These forms are of intense practicality, and it is a good thing that they exist for the instruction of the successive generations, whose makeshifts, if they had to tutor themselves, would be blundering and ineffectual. Such forms write their own valuations, and very clearly. They are the recipes of maximum efficiency, short routes to "success," to welfare, to the attainments of natural satisfactions and comforts. They are the stock services which society confers upon its members, and the celebrated ones; doubtless in themselves alone a sufficient justification for constituted societies; sometimes, and especially where it is the modern temper which passes on it, the one usefulness which we can imagine attaching to societies, and the whole purpose of the social contract. But that is almost demonstrably an error, proceeding from a blind spot on the organ of insight which we are scarcely in a position to detect. Men absorbed in business and affairs may be excused for making that error, but it would be an egregious one for those who spend of their time and love upon æsthetic effects. It is in the æsthetic effects, if secured in those experiences that record themselves publicly as "art," or for that matter /30/ as manners and religion, that the given forms are both more and less than they seem, and not, on the whole, of any conceivable economic advantage.

Chiefly the error is an eidolon of period, a matter of the age and generation. Societies of the old order seemed better aware of the extent of their responsibilities. Along with the work-forms went the play-forms, which were elaborate in detail, and great in number, fastening upon so many of the common and otherwise practical occasions of life and making them occasions of joy and reflection, even festivals and celebrations; yet at the same time by no means a help but if anything a hindrance to direct action. The æsthetic forms are a technique of restraint, not of efficiency. They do not butter our bread, and they delay the eating of it. They stand between the individual and his natural object and impose a check upon his action; the reason must have been known well to the governors of old societies, for they honored the forms with unanimity; it must even yet be recoverable, for the argument shapes itself readily. To the concept of direct action the old society—the directed and hierarchical one—opposed the concept of æsthetic experience, as a true opposite, and checked the one in order to induce the other. Perhaps, since a social psychology is subtle, they fancied that the indissolubility of societies might depend as much on the definition they gave to play as on the definition they gave to labor. If so, modern societies, with their horror of "empty" forms and ceremonies, and /31/ their invitation to men to be themselves, and to handle their objects as quickly and rudely as they please, are not only destroying old arts and customs, which they might not mind doing, but exposing incidentally their own solidarity to the anarchy of too much greed. But that is an incident. The formal tradition in art has a validity more than political, and the latter I am content to waive. What I have in mind is an argument from æsthetics which will justify any formal art, even a formal literature.

II

When a consensus of taste lays down the ordinance that the artist shall express himself formally, the purpose is evidently to deter him from expressing himself immediately. Or, the formal tradition intends to preserve the artist from the direct approach to his object. Behind the tradition is probably the sense that the direct approach is perilous to the artist, and may be fatal. It is feared that the artist who disregards the instruction may discover at length that he has only been artless; or, what is worse, that he will not make this important discovery, which will have to be made

for him by the horrid way of autopsy. I suggest, therefore, that an art is usually, and probably of necessity, a kind of obliquity; that its fixed form proposes to guarantee the round-about of the artistic process, and the "æsthetic distance."

A code of manners also is capable of being taken in this fashion; it confers the same benefit, or the /32/ same handicap if we prefer, upon its adherent. Let us represent graphically, as in the figure I have entered below, the conduct of a man toward the woman he desires.

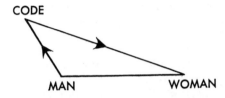

The event consists in his approach to the object. He may approach directly, and then his behavior is to seize her as quickly as possible. No inhibitions are supposed to have kept the cave-man or pirate, or any other of the admired figures of a great age when life was "in the raw," from taking this severely logical course. If our hero, however, does not propose for himself the character of the savage, or of animal, but the quaint one of "gentleman," then he has the fixed code of his *gens* to remember, and then he is estopped from seizing her, he must approach her with ceremony, and pay her a fastidious courtship. We conclude not that the desire is abandoned, but that it will take a circuitous road and become a romance. The form actually denies him the privilege of going the straight line between two points, even though this line has an axiomatic logic in its favor and is the shortest possible line. But the woman, contemplated in this manner under restraint, becomes a person and an æsthetic object; therefore a richer object. /33/

In fact the woman becomes nothing less than an individual object; for we stumble here upon a fruitful paradox. The natural man, who today sometimes seems to be becoming always a greater man in our midst, asserting his rights so insistently, causing us to hear so much about "individualism," is a predatory creature to whom every object is an object of prey and the real or individual object cannot occur; while the social man, who submits to the restraint of convention, comes to respect the object and to see it unfold at last its individuality; which, if we must define it, is its capacity to furnish us with an infinite variety of innocent experience; that is, it is a source, from which so many charming experiences have already flowed, and a promise, a possibility of future experiences beyond all prediction. There must then, really, be two kinds of individualism: one is greedy and bogus, amounting only to egoism; the other is contemplative, genuine, and philosophical. The function of a code of manners is to make us capable of something better than the stupidity of an appetitive or economic life. High comedy, for example, is technically art, but substantially it is manners, and it has the agreeable function of displaying our familiar life relieved of its fundamental animality, filled, and dignified, through a technique which has in it nothing more esoteric than ceremonious intercourse.

To return to the figure, and to change the denotation slightly. Let us have a parallel now from the /34/ field of religion. The man is bereaved, and this time the object of his attention is the dead body of his friend. Instead of having a code of manners for this case, let him owe allegiance to a religious society, one which is possessed preferably of an ancient standing, and at all events of a ritual. The new terms for our graph become: Man and Corpse at the base, and Rite at the top and back. The religious society exists in order to serve the man in this crisis. Freed from his desolation by its virtue, he is not obliged now to run and throw himself upon the body in an ecstasy of grief, nor to go apart and brood upon the riddle of mortality, which may be the way of madness. His action is through the form of a pageant of grief, which is lovingly staged and attended by the religious community. His own grief expands, is lightened, no longer has to be explosive or obsessive. A sort of by-product of this formal occasion, we need not deny, is his grateful sense that his community supports him in a dreadful hour. But what interests us rather is the fact that his preoccupation with the deadness of the body is broken by his participation in the pageantry, and his bleak situation elaborated with such rich detail that it becomes massive, substantial, and sufficient.

We may of course eliminate the pageantry of death from our public life, but only if we expect the widow and orphan not really to feel their loss; and to this end we may inform them that they will not find it an economic loss, since they shall be main- /35/ tained in their usual standards of living by the State. It is unfortunate for the economic calculus that they are likely to feel it anyway, since probably their relation to the one dead was not more economic than it was sentimental. Sentiments, those irrational psychic formations, do not consist very well with the indifference, machine-like, with which some modern social workers would have men fitting into the perfect economic organization. It is not as good animals that we are complicated with sentimental weakness. The fierce drives of the animals, whether human or otherwise, are only towards a *kind* of thing, the indifferent instance of a universal, and not some private and irreplaceable thing. All the nouns at this stage are common nouns. But we, for our curse or our pride, have sentiments; they are directed towards persons and things; and a sentiment is the totality of love and knowledge which we have of an object that is private and unique. This object might have been a simple economic object, yet we have elected to graft upon the economic relation a vast increment of diffuse and irrelevant sensibilia, and to keep it there forever, obstructing science and action. Sometimes we attach the major weight of our being, unreasonably, and to the point of absurdity, to a precious object. The adventitious interest, the sensibility that complicates and sometimes submerges the economic interest, does not seem to ask any odds of it, nor to think it necessary to theorize on behalf of its own existence. We may resent it, but even- /36/ tually we have to accept it, as, simply, an "æsthetic" requirement, a piece of foolishness, which human nature will not forego. Wise societies legalize it and make much of it; for its sake they define the forms of manners, religions, arts; conferring a public right upon the sensibilia, especially when they organize themselves, or pile up notably, as they do, into the great fixed sentiments.

In Russia[2] we gather that there is a society bent seriously on "perfecting" the human constitution, that is, rationalizing or economizing it completely. The code of manners and the religious ritual are suspended, while the arts lead a half-privileged, censored, and furtive existence. Already a recent observer notes one result of the disappearance of the sex taboos: there is less sex-consciousness in Russia than anywhere in the Western world. That is to say, I suppose, that the loyal Russians approach the perfect state of animals, with sex reduced to its pure biological business. The above observer wonders painfully whether "love," of the sort that has been celebrated by so much history and so much literature, will vanish from Russia. It will vanish, if this society succeeds in assessing it by the standard of economic efficiency. The Russian leaders are repeating, at this late stage of history, with a people whose spirit is scored by all the traditional complications of human nature, the experiment of the Garden of /37/ Eden; when the original experiment should be conclusive, and was recorded, we may imagine, with that purpose in view. The original human family was instructed not to take the life of the beast-couples as its model; and did not, exactly, mean to do so; occupied itself with a certain pretty project having to do with a Tree of Rationalization; and made the mortal discovery that it came to the very same thing. The question is whether the ideal of efficient animality is good enough for human beings; and whether the economic law, by taking precedence at every point over the imperative of manners, of religion, and of the arts, will not lead to perfect misery.

III

And now, specifically, as to art, and its form. The analogy of the above occasions to the occasion called art is strict. Our terms now are Artist, Object, and Form. Confronting his object, the artist is tempted to react at once by registering just that aspect of the object in which he is practically "interested." For he is originally, and at any moment may revert to, a natural man, having a predatory and acquisitive interest in the object, or at best looking at it with a "scientific" curiosity to see if

[2] I am not sure at this time of second publication just how true of Russia this representation may be.

he cannot discover one somewhere in it. Art has a canon to restrain this natural man. It puts the object out of his reach; or more accurately, removes him to where he cannot hurt the object, nor disrespect it by taking his practical attitude towards it, exchanging his actual station, /38/ where he is too determined by proximity to the object, and contemporaneity with it, for the more ideal station furnished by the literary form. For example: there is the position, seemingly the silly and ineffectual one, of the man who is required by some quixotic rule of art to think of his object in pentameter couplets, therefore with a good deal of lost motion; and there is the far-fetched "point of view," which will require him to adapt all his thought to the rule of drama. The motion is well lost, if that is what it costs to frustrate the natural man and induce the æsthetic one. Society may not after all be too mistaken in asking the artist to deal with his object somewhat artificially. There will be plenty of others glad to deal with it immediately. It is perfectly true that art, a priori, looks dubious; a project in which the artist has a splendid chance for being a fool. The bad artists in the world are cruelly judged, they are the good journeymen gone wrong; and the good artists may be humorously regarded, as persons strangely possessed. But the intention of art is one that is peculiarly hard to pursue steadily, because it goes against the grain of our dominant and carefully instructed instincts; it wants us to enjoy life, to taste and reflect as we drink; when we are always tending as abstract appetites to gulp it down; or as abstract intelligences to proceed, by a milder analogue, to the cold fury of "disinterested" science. A technique of art must, then, be unprepossessing, and look vain and affected, and in fact look just like the technique of /39/ fine manners, or of ritual. Heroic intentions call for heroic measures.

We should not be taken in for a moment when we hear critics talking as if the form were in no sense a discipline but a direct help to the "expressiveness"—meaning the forthrightness—of the poem. This view reflects upon the holders credit for a reach of piety which is prepared to claim everything for the true works of art, and also a suspicion of ingenuousness for their peculiar under-standing of the art-process. Given an object, and a poet burning to utter himself upon it, he must take into account a third item, the form into which he must cast his utterance. (If we like, we may call it the *body* which he must give to his passion.) It delays and hinders him. In the process of "composition" the burning passion is submitted to cool and scarcely relevant considerations. When it appears finally it may be said to have been treated with an application of sensibility. The thing expressed there is not the hundred-per cent passion at all.

If the passion burns too hot in the poet to endure the damping of the form, he might be advised that poetry can exercise no undue compulsion upon his spirit since, after all, there is prose. Milton may not always have let the form have its full effect upon the passion; some modern poets whom I admire do not; neither of which facts, however, disposes one to conclude that poetry is worse for the formal tradition. The formal tradition, as I have said, lays /40/ upon the poet evidently a double requirement. One is metrical or mechanical; but the measured speech is part of the logical identity of the poem; it goes into that "character" which it possesses as an ideal creation, out of the order of the actual. The other requirement is the basic one of the make-believe, the drama, the specific anonymity or pseudonymity, which defines the poem as poem; when that goes we may also say that the poem goes; so that there would seem to be taking place in the act of poetry a rather unprofitable labor if this anonymity is not clearly conceived when a poet is starting upon his poem, and a labor lost if the poet, who has once conceived it and established it, forgets to maintain it.

IV

We accept or refuse the arts, with their complex intention, according as we like or dislike the fruits, or it may be the flowers, they bring to us; but these arts, and their techniques, may be always reinforced by the example of manners, and the example of religion; the three institutions do not rest on three foundations but on one foundation. A natural affiliation binds together the gentle-man, the religious man, and the artist—punctilious characters, all of them, in their formalism. We have seen one distinguished figure in our times pronouncing on behalf of all three in one breath. In politics, royalism; in religion, Anglo-Catholic; in literature, classical. I am astonished upon discovering how comprehensively this /41/ formula covers the kingdom of the æsthetic life as it is organized by the social tradition. I am so grateful that it is with hesitation I pick a little quarrel with the terms. I would covet a program going something like this: In manners, aristocratic; in religion, ritualistic; in art, traditional. But I imagine the intent of Mr. Eliot's formula is about what I am representing; and on the other hand might be only the more effective to fight with for being so concrete. (Unfortunately its terms are not suited to Americans; but possibly this is so of mine too.) The word for our generation in these matters is "formal," and it might even bear the pointed qualification, "and reactionary." The phrase would carry the sense of our need to make a return to amenities which the European communities labored to evolve, and defined as their "civilization." For the intention of none of those societies can have been simply to confirm the natural man as a natural man, or to improve him in cunning and effectiveness by furnishing him with its tried economic forms. It wanted to humanize him; which means, so far as his natural economy permitted, to complicate his natural functions with sensibility, and make them æsthetic. The object of a proper society is to instruct its members how to transform instinctive experience into æsthetic experience.

Manners, rites, and arts are so close to each other that often their occasions must be confused, and it does not matter much if they are. The rule of manners is directed to those occasions when natural appe- /42/ tites and urges are concerned; when we hunger, or lust, or go into a rage, or encounter strange or possibly dangerous persons. The rites take place upon religious occasions; but I suppose this is tautology. It is my idea that religion is an institution existing for the sake of its ritual, rather than, as I have heard, for the sake of its doctrines, to which there attaches no cogency of magic, and for that matter a very precarious cogency of logic. The issues upon which the doctrines pronounce are really insoluble for human logic, and the higher religionists are aware of it. The only solution that is possible, since the economic solution is not possible, is the æsthetic one. When these issues press upon us, there is little that one man, with whatever benefit of doctrines, can do toward the understanding of the event which another man cannot do; and he had better not try too hard to understand the precise event, but enlarge its terms, and assimilate it into the form of an ornate public ritual through which the whole mind can discharge itself. This is a subtle technique, it has been a successful technique; in insisting upon it as the one thing I do not mean to subtract dignity from the world's great religions—which I revere. And what are the specific occasions for ritual? Those which are startling in our biological and economic history, and provoke reflection, and also, for fear we may forget to be startled when we are living for a long interval upon a dead level of routine, some arbitrary occasions, frequent and intercalated; therefore birth, marriage, /43/ death; war, peace, the undertaking of great enterprises, famine, storm; the seasons of the year, the Sabbath, the holidays. But as for the artistic process, what are its occasions? What prompts the artist? For we remark at once that many works of art embody ritual, and art is often apparently content to be the handmaiden to religion, as Hegel desired, and as she conceivably is in a painting by Michelangelo, or a poem on the order of *Lycidas*. We know also that works of art have been dedicated to the ceremonious life of society, commemorating chivalry, or some much easier code; art serving manners.

The occasions of art are innumerable; very probably its "future is immense." Its field is wider than that of manners, or than that of religion; the field of literary art alone is that. In fact it is about as wide as the field of science itself; and there I think lies the hint for a definition. What is the occasion which will do for the artist and the scientist indiffer-

ently? It is the occasion when we propose to "study" our object; that is, when we are more than usually undesirous and free, and find the time to become curious about the object as, actually, something "objective" and independent. Out of the surplus of our energy—thanks to the efficiency of our modern economic forms we have that increasingly—we contemplate object as object, and are not forced by an instinctive necessity to take it and devour it immediately. This contemplation may take one of two routes; and first, that of science. I study the object to see how I may /44/ wring out of it my physical satisfaction the next time; or even how I may discover for the sake of a next time the physical satisfaction which it contains, but not too transparently; analyzing and classifying, "experimenting," bringing it under the system of control which I intend as a scientist to have over the world of objects. It is superfluous to observe that I, the modern scientist, am in this case spiritually just as poor as was my ancestor the cave-man. My intention is simply to have bigger and quicker satisfactions than he had, my head still runs on satisfactions. But I may contemplate also, under another form entirely, the form of art. And that is when I am impelled neither to lay hands on the object immediately, nor to ticket it for tomorrow's outrage, but am in such a marvellous state of innocence that I would know it for its own sake, and conceive it as having its own existence; this is the knowledge, or it ought to be, which Schopenhauer praised as "knowledge without desire." The features which the object discloses then are not those which have their meaning for a science, for a set of practical values. They are those which render the body of the object, and constitute a knowledge so radical that the scientist as a scientist can scarcely understand it, and puzzles to see it rendered, richly and wastefully, in the poem, or the painting. The knowledge attained there, and recorded, is a new kind of knowledge, the world in which it is set is a new world. /45/

E. M. W. TILLYARD

from *Poetry: Direct and Oblique*

[E. M. W. Tillyard (1889–) retired in 1959 after a long and distinguished career as Professor of English Literature and Master of Jesus College at Cambridge University. He is the author of many scholarly and critical works, especially on Milton and Shakespeare. The following selection is from the introductory chapter of *Poetry: Direct and Oblique,* first published in 1934, revised in 1948. The more recent version (London, 1948) is that reprinted here.]

1. PRELIMINARY

Johnson in attacking *Lycidas*[1] provided a classic example of criticism that errs through a false assumption. *Lycidas* is an elegy; an elegy professes to lament the death of a revered or beloved person; and Johnson assumes that an elegy should be judged by the standards it professes. He found that *Lycidas* did not fulfil its professions:

> It is not to be considered as the effusion of real passion; for passion runs not after remote allusions and obscure opinions. . . . Where there is leisure for fiction, there is little grief.

Johnson assumed that *Lycidas* is what I shall call "direct" poetry or the poetry of "statement," and by such a standard he found it wanting. Actually the poem is far other than what it professes to be. Its main concern embraces vastly more than grief at the death of Edward King. It expresses a personal mental experience and a general moral truth. And it does so not by direct statement but obliquely by implication. This distinction between "direct" and "oblique" poetry will be elaborated in the next section. It suffices here to say that Johnson's attack is invalidated from the start because he has put the poem in the wrong category.

Critics today are not likely to make Johnson's specific error, but they are not always clear in their minds what degree of directness or obliquity they assume the poems they are judging to possess. They run the risk of

[1] [See p. 191.]

going astray initially, just as Johnson did. And the danger of being deceived today by a specious obliquity may not be less than the converse one of being deceived by a specious directness. The distinction between "direct" and "oblique" /9/ poetry is not new, and must be familiar enough in some form or another, but as an important initial criterion I doubt if it has been clearly formulated or consciously applied to critical practice. This book suggests a scale ranging from the greatest possible directness to the greatest possible obliquity in poetry. Between the two extremes the gradations are of course innumerable; and the scale is only of the roughest. But still it should help to eliminate the mistake of judging poems by standards to which they have no reference.

But when you have fixed your poem in the scale, you have not begun seriously to criticise it. All you have done is to put it in a position where you can see it without a certain preliminary distortion. Now if you conclude that a poem is oblique, you are not likely to get very far with it until you discover what it is that has been given oblique expression. In writing a book on Milton I was confronted with this problem when I came to *Lycidas,* and flattered myself that I had got a little way behind that poem's façade. At any rate I was attempting a kind of criticism of which there is too little and whose possibilities are large. One object of this book is to exploit this kind of criticism through a series of practical demonstrations.

The relations of direct and oblique poetry have their bearing on the general poetic health of a given epoch; including that of our own day; and I have inserted some historical comment and drawn contemporary morals.

The terms "direct" and "oblique" poetry are a false contrast. All poetry is more or less oblique: there is no direct poetry. But the terms "less oblique" and "more oblique" would sound ridiculous; and the only way to be emphatic or even generally intelligible is by exaggeration to force a hypothetical but convenient contrast.

I use the words *direct, oblique, statement,* etc., in ways that are convenient rather than quite consistent. I make *direct statement,* or merely *statement,* or *directness,* stand for the same notion; as I make *oblique statement,* or *obliquity,* stand for the opposed notion. /10/

2. THE TWO VILLAGE-GREENS

A familiar contrast, directed usually to illustrating some differences between Augustan and Romantic styles of poetry, is that between Goldsmith's picture of Auburn in *The Deserted Village* and Blake's *Echoing Green* in *Songs of Innocence.* And these two pieces will serve neatly enough as text for the quite different contrast I have to explain. Here is Goldsmith's village-green with the pleasures that enlivened it:

How often have I loitered o'er the green,
Where humble happiness endeared each scene!
How often have I paused on every charm,
The sheltered cot, the cultivated farm,
The never-failing brook, the busy mill,
The decent church that topt the neighbouring hill,
The hawthorn bush, with seats beneath the shade,
For talking age and whispering lovers made!
How often have I blest the coming day,
When toil remitting lent its turn to play,
And all the village train from labour free
Led up their sports beneath the spreading tree,
While many a pastime circled in the shade,
The young contending as the old surveyed;
And many a gambol frolicked o'er the ground,
And slights of art and feats of strength went round;
And still as each repeated pleasure tired,
Succeeding sports the mirthful band inspired.

This is a fair example of the poetry of direct statement: it is to some degree concerned with what the words state as well as with what they imply. Had Goldsmith been describing one actual village, were it certain that he were describing an actual remembered scene at Lissoy, the element of statement would be solider than it is; and in that he is imagining his village on the analogy of a number of villages he has known, he is the less direct. But at least he wants the reader to think primarily of villages /11/ when he talks of Auburn; not of the Social Contract or of heavenly beatitude. We believe this because the formal parts of the poetry reinforce the statement rather than suggest thoughts alien to it. The couplets evolve in a simple explicatory sequence; they unfold the scene with no hint of ulterior meaning; their freshness and unobstructedness are those of the clear sunny day they describe. The vocabulary is as close to simple statement as Goldsmith's epoch allowed to anyone but a rebel; and when he is not simple, it is for convention's sake and not with any view to obliquity. Thus by "humble happiness" he probably means "humble, happy people," and by "talking age" he certainly means "garrulous old folk": but these phrases are no more than the poetic idiom of his day.

True, some obliquity cannot be denied. Goldsmith wants to say that he likes villagers to be hard-working and sober and to enjoy simple pleasures, and in that he says so, not by a general statement but through describing an imagined single occasion when the villagers enjoy these pleasures, he is being slightly oblique. And there is another, much more important example of obliquity. Goldsmith idealises his Auburn not only because this is how he would like villages to be, but because, feeling homesick for some place other than the one he is in, he must imagine his perfect refuge. Thus, when he says,

And still as each repeated pleasure tired,
Succeeding sports the mirthful band inspired,

he reveals himself day-dreaming of perpetually unexhausted pleasure, forgetful of the cruel actual law of diminishing returns.

For all this, Goldsmith's lines mainly concern their professed subject, village-life, and therefore exemplify the poetry of statement. Here is Blake's village-green:

The Sun does arise,
And make happy the skies; /12/
The merry bells ring
To welcome the Spring;
The skylark and thrush,
The birds of the bush,
Sing louder around
To the bells' chearful sound,
While our sports shall be seen
On the Echoing Green.

Old John, with white hair,
Does laugh away care,
Sitting under the oak,
Among the old folk.
They laugh at our play,
And soon they all say:
"Such, such were the joys
When we all, girls and boys,
In our youth time were seen
On the Echoing Green."

Till the little ones, weary,
No more can be merry;
The sun does descend,
And our sports have an end.
Round the laps of their mothers
Many sisters and brothers,
Like birds in their nest,
Are ready for rest,
And sport no more seen
On the darkening Green.

It is very easy to allow to Blake's lines just about the same amount of directness and obliquity as to Goldsmith's. Blake's is the greater mind, and of course he uses a different language; but he has every appearance of describing as real a village as Goldsmith's and of knowing quite as much about village games. The sunshine has got into Blake's verse no less than into Goldsmith's. Blake, too, is using his village to express approval of a way of life. He /13/ finds in the traditional village sports and pieties a type of his world of innocence, a wider notion perhaps than Goldsmith's more didactic approval. All this is true as far as it goes, and did it respond to our feelings about *The Echoing Green* we might be content with criticising the poem by standards of no profounder obliquity than satisfied *The Deserted Village*.

Now the statements that confront us in *The Echoing Green* have so solid an appearance, present so winningly confident a front, that it seems initially ridiculous not to take them as the poem's major concern. It is the structure that should first put us on our guard. Blake's three verses contrast emphatically with the leisurely roll-out of Goldsmith's couplets. Dawn in the first stanza. Why in the second does Old John sit under the oak? To keep off the noonday sun. Evening in the third. The form is a stylised day-cycle; and if we heed this form, some element of abstraction is set up against the concrete activities of the villagers. There is a careful balance of idea between opening and close: the echoing green becomes the darkening green to balance (though not for this reason only) the rising sun of the first line; the awakening birds in the first stanza are balanced by the simile "like birds in their nest" in the last. Congruently with the full noonday heat and light the old unfreeze and join their mirth to make up a full chorus with the children. Why all this ingenuity? Does it merely add a pleasing regularity to the statement, or is it a symptom of something else? The truth is that Blake is expressing an idea, an idea that has nothing in itself to do with birds, old and young folk, or village-greens, and one of those most common in Blake's poetical works. It is the idea that there is a virtue in desire satisfied. Though desire is not mentioned, yet the keynote of the poem is fruition. Nature fulfils itself in the cycle of a perfect day. Old John gets a perfect vicarious satisfaction, the little ones are utterly played out and ready for rest. And at the end of the "echoing green" is the "darkening green" because its function is fulfilled. The very complete- /14/ ness of formal balance points the same way. The poem gives the sense of the perfectly grown apple that comes off at a touch of the hand. It expresses the profound peace of utterly gratified desire.

Thus explained, *The Echoing Green* is as nearly perfect an example of poetical obliquity as can be found. The main sense is stated in no particular whatever, but is diffused through every part of the poem and can be apprehended as a whole only through the synthesis of all those parts. The abstract idea, far from being stated, has been translated into completely concrete form; it has disappeared into apparently alien facts. Through its major obliquity *The Echoing Green* is in a different category from Goldsmith's lines and must be judged by different standards. . . . /15/

EDMUND WILSON
"Is Verse a Dying Technique?"

[Edmund Wilson (1895–), though he has written fiction, drama, and poetry, has won his considerable reputation mainly as a literary and social critic. Born in New Jersey and educated at Princeton, he has been editorially associated with *Vanity Fair, The New Republic,* and *The New Yorker,* and is the author of numerous volumes of critical essays. The following selection appeared in *The Triple Thinkers* in 1938 but is reprinted here from the revised and enlarged edition (New York, 1948).]

The more one reads the current criticism of poetry by poets and their reviewers, the more one becomes convinced that the discussion is proceeding on false assumptions. The writers may belong to different schools, but they all seem to share a basic confusion.

This confusion is the result of a failure to think clearly about what is meant by the words "prose," "verse," and "poetry"—a question which is sometimes debated but which never gets straightened out. Yet are not the obvious facts as follows?

What we mean by the words "prose" and "verse" are simply two different techniques of literary expression. Verse is written in lines with a certain number of metrical feet each; prose is written in paragraphs and has what we call rhythm. But what is "poetry," then? What I want to suggest is that "poetry" formerly meant one kind of thing but that it now means something different, and that one ought not to generalize about "poetry" by taking all the writers of verse, ancient, medieval and modern, away from their various periods and throwing them together in one's mind, but to consider both verse and prose in relation to their functions at different times.

The important thing to recognize, it seems to me, is that the literary technique of verse was once made to serve many purposes for which we now, as a rule, use prose. Solon, the Athenian statesman, expounded his political ideas in verse; the *Works and Days* of Hesiod are a shepherd's calendar in verse; his *Theogony* is versified mythology; and almost everything that in contempo- /15/ rary writing would be put into prose plays and novels was versified by the Greeks in epics or plays.

It is true that Aristotle tried to discriminate. "We have no common name," he wrote, "for a mime of Sophron or Xenarchus and a Socratic conversation; and we should still be without one even if the imitation in the two instances were in trimeters or elegiacs or some other kind of verse—though it is the way with people to tack on 'poet' to the name of a meter, and talk of elegiac-poets and epic-poets, thinking that they call them poets not by reason of the imitative nature of their work, but indiscriminately by reason of the meter they write in. Even if a theory of medicine or physical philosophy be put forth in a metrical form, it is usual to describe the writer in this way; Homer and Empedocles, however, have really nothing in common apart from their meter; so that, if the one is to be called a poet, the other should be termed a physicist rather than a poet."

But he admitted that there was no accepted name for the creative—what he calls the "imitative"—art which had for its mediums both prose and verse; and his posterity followed the custom of which he had pointed out the impropriety by calling anything in a meter a "poem." The Romans wrote treatises in verse on philosophy and astronomy and farming. The "poetic" of Horace's *Ars Poetica* applies to the whole range of ancient verse—though Horace did think it just as well to mingle the "agreeable" with the "useful"—and this essay in literary criticism is itself written in meter. "Poetry" remained identified with verse; and since for centuries both dramas and narratives continued largely to be written in verse, the term of which Aristotle had noticed the need—a term for imaginative literature itself, irrespective of literary techniques—never came into common use.

But when we arrive at the nineteenth century, a new conception of "poetry" appears. The change is seen very clearly in the doubts which began to be felt as to whether Pope were really a poet. Now, it is true that a critic like Johnson would hardly have assigned to Pope the position of pre-eminence he does at any other period than Johnson's own; but it is *not* true that only a critic of the latter part of the eighteenth century, a critic of an "age of prose," would have considered Pope a poet. Would not /16/ Pope have been considered a poet in any age before the age of Coleridge?

But the romantics were to redefine "poetry." Coleridge, in the *Biographia Literaria,* denies that any excellent work in meter may be properly called a "poem." "The final definition . . ." he says, "may be thus worded. A poem is that species of composition which is opposed to works of science by proposing for its *immediate* object pleasure, not truth; and from all other species—(having *this* object in common with it)—it is discriminated by proposing to itself such delight from the *whole* as is compatible with a distinct gratification from each component part." This would evidently exclude the *Ars Poetica* and the *De Rerum Natura,* whose immediate objects are as much truth as pleasure. What is really happening here is that for Coleridge the function of "poetry" is becoming more specialized. Why? Coleridge answers this question in formulating an objection which may be brought against the first part of his definition: "But the communication of pleasure may be the immediate object of a work not metrically composed; and that object may have been in a high degree attained, as in novels and romances." Precisely; and the novels and romances were formerly written in verse, whereas they are now usually written in prose. In Coleridge's time, tales in verse were more and more giving place to prose novels. Before long, novels in verse such as *Aurora Leigh* and *The Ring and the Book* were to seem more or less literary oddities. "Poetry," then, for Coleridge, has become something which, unless he amends his definition, may equally well be written in prose: Isaiah and Plato and Jeremy Taylor will, as he admits, be describable as "poetry." Thereafter, he seems to become somewhat muddled;

but he finally arrives at the conclusion that the "peculiar property of poetry" is "the property of exciting a more continuous and equal attention than the language of prose aims at, whether colloquial or written."

The truth is that Coleridge is having difficulties in attempting to derive his new conception of poetry from the literature of the past, which has been based on the old conception. Poe, writing thirty years later, was able to get a good deal further. Coleridge had said—and it seems to have been really what he was principally trying to say—that "a poem of any length neither can be, /17/ nor ought to be, all poetry." (Yet are not the *Divine Comedy* and Shakespeare's tragedies "all poetry"? Or rather, in the case of these masterpieces, is not the work as a whole really a "poem" maintained, as it is, at a consistently high level of intensity and style and with the effects of the different parts dependent on one another?) Poe predicted that "no very long poem would ever be popular again," and made "poetry" mean something even more special by insisting that it should approach the indefiniteness of music. The reason why no very long poem was ever to be popular again was simply that verse as a technique was then passing out of fashion in every department of literature except those of lyric poetry and the short idyl. The long poems of the past—Shakespeare's plays, the *Divine Comedy,* the Greek dramatists and Homer—were going to continue to be popular; but writers of that caliber in the immediate future were not going to write in verse.

Matthew Arnold was to keep on in Coleridge's direction, though by a route somewhat different from Poe's. He said, as we have heard so repeatedly, that poetry was at bottom a criticism of life; but, though one of the characteristics which true poetry might possess was "moral profundity," another was "natural magic," and "eminent manifestations of this magical power of poetry" were "very rare and very precious." "Poetry" is thus, it will be seen, steadily becoming rarer. Arnold loved quoting passages of natural magic and he suggested that the lover of literature should carry around in his mind as touchstones a handful of such topnotch passages to test any new verse he encountered. His method of presenting the poets makes poetry seem fleeting and quintessential. Arnold was not happy till he had edited Byron and Wordsworth in such a way as to make it appear that their "poetry" was a kind of elixir which had to be distilled from the mass of their work—rather difficult in Byron's case: a production like *Don Juan* does not really give up its essence in the sequences excerpted by Arnold.

There was, to be sure, some point in what Arnold was trying to do for these writers: Wordsworth and Byron both often wrote badly and flatly. But they would not have lent themselves at all to this high-handed kind of anthologizing if it had not been that, by this time, it had finally become almost impossible to handle /18/ large subjects successfully in verse. Matthew Arnold could have done nothing for Dante by reducing him to a little book of extracts—nor, with all Shakespeare's carelessness, for Shakespeare. The new specialized idea of poetry appears very plainly and oddly when Arnold writes about Homer: the *Iliad* and the *Odyssey,* which had been for the Greeks fiction and scripture, have come to appear to this critic long stretches of ancient legend from which we may pick out little crystals of moral profundity and natural magic.

And in the meantime the ideas of Poe, developed by the Symbolists in France, had given rise to the *Art poétique* of Verlaine, so different from that of Horace: "Music first of all . . . no Color only the *nuance!* . . . Shun Point, the murderer, cruel Wit and Laughter the impure . . . Take eloquence and wring its neck! . . . Let your verse be the luck of adventure flung to the crisp morning wing that brings us a fragrance of thyme and mint—and all the rest is literature."

Eliot and Valéry followed. Paul Valéry, still in the tradition of Poe, regarded a poem as a specialized machine for producing a certain kind of "state." Eliot called poetry a "superior amusement," and he anthologized, in both his poems and his essays, even more fastidiously than Arnold. He, too, has his favorite collection of magical and quintessential passages; and he possesses an uncanny gift for transmitting to them a personal accent and imbuing them with a personal

significance. And as even those passages of Eliot's poems which have not been imitated or quoted often seemed to have been pieced together out of separate lines and fragments, so his imitators came to work in broken mosaics and "pinches of glory"—to use E. M. Forster's phrase about Eliot—rather than with conventional stanzas.

The result has been an optical illusion. The critic, when he read the classic, epic, eclogue, tale or play, may have grasped it and enjoyed it as a whole; yet when the reader reads the comment of the critic, he gets the impression, looking back on the poem, that the *Divine Comedy,* say, so extraordinarily sustained and so beautifully integrated, is remarkable mainly for Eliot-like fragments. Once we know Matthew Arnold's essay, we find that the ἀνήριθμον γέλαομα [many-twinkling smile of Ocean] of Aeschylus and the "daffodils that come /19/ before the swallow dares" of Shakespeare tend to stick out from their contexts in a way that they hardly deserve to. Matthew Arnold, unintentionally and unconsciously, has had the effect of making the poet's "poetry" seem to be concentrated in the phrase or the line.

Finally, Mr. A. E. Housman, in his lecture on *The Name and Nature of Poetry,* has declared that he cannot define poetry. He can only become aware of its presence by the symptoms he finds it producing: "Experience has taught me, when I am shaving of a morning, to keep watch over my thought, because if a line of poetry strays into my memory, my skin bristles so that the razor ceases to act. This particular symptom is accompanied by a shiver down the spine; there is another which consists in a constriction of the throat and a precipitation of water to the eyes; and there is a third which I can only describe by borrowing a phrase from one of Keats's last letters, where he says, speaking of Fanny Brawne, 'everything that reminds me of her goes through me like a spear.' The seat of this sensation is the pit of the stomach."

One recognizes these symptoms; but there are other things, too, which produce these peculiar sensations: scenes from prose plays, for example (the final curtain of *The Playboy of the Western World* could make one's hair stand on end when it was first done by the Abbey Theater), passages from prose novels (Stephen Daedalus' broodings over his mother's death in the opening episode of *Ulysses* and the end of Mrs. Bloom's soliloquy), even scenes from certain historians, such as Mirabeau's arrival in Aix at the end of Michelet's *Louis XVI*, even passages in a philosophical dialogue: the conclusion of Plato's *Symposium*. Though Housman does praise a few long poems, he has the effect, like these other critics, of creating the impression that "poetry" means primarily lyric verse, and this only at its most poignant or most musical moments.

Now all that has been said here is, of course, not intended to belittle the value of what such people as Coleridge and Poe, Arnold and Eliot have written on the subject of poetry. These men are all themselves first-class poets; and their criticism is very important because it constitutes an attempt to explain what they /20/ have aimed at in their own verse, of what they have conceived, in their age, to be possible or impossible for their medium.

Yet one feels that in the minds of all of them a certain confusion persists between the new idea of poetry and the old—between Coleridge's conception, on the one hand, and Horace's, on the other; that the technique of prose is inevitably tending more and more to take over the material which had formerly provided the subjects for compositions in verse, and that, as the two techniques of writing are beginning to appear, side by side or combined, in a single work, it is becoming more and more impossible to conduct any comparative discussion of literature on a basis of this misleading division of it into the department of "poetry" and of "prose."

One result of discussion on this basis, especially if carried on by verse-writers, is the creation of an illusion that contemporary "poets" of relatively small stature (though of however authentic gifts) are the true inheritors of the genius and carriers-on of the tradition of Aeschylus, Sophocles and Virgil, Dante, Shakespeare and Milton. Is it not time to discard the word "poetry" or to define it in such a way as to take account of the fact that the most intense, the most profound, the most beautifully composed and the most com-

prehensive of the great works of literary art (which for these reasons are also the most thrilling and give us most prickly sensations while shaving) have been written sometimes in verse technique, sometimes in prose technique, depending partly on the taste of the author, partly on the mere current fashion. It is only when we argue these matters that we become involved in absurdities. When we are reading, we appraise correctly. Matthew Arnold cites examples of that "natural magic" which he regards as one of the properties of "poetry" from Chateaubriand and Maurice de Guérin, who did not write verse but prose, as well as from Shakespeare and Keats; and he rashly includes Molière among the "larger and more splendid luminaries in the poetical heaven," though Molière was scarcely more "poetic" in any sense except perhaps that of "moral profundity" when he wrote verse than when he wrote prose and would certainly not have versified at all if the conventions of his time had not demanded it. One who has first come to Flaubert at a sensitive age when he is also /21/ reading Dante may have the experience of finding that the paragraphs of the former remain in his mind and continue to sing just as the lines of the latter do. He has got the prose by heart unconsciously just as he has done with favorite passages of verse; he repeats them, admiring the form, studying the choice of words, seeing more and more significance in them. He realizes that, though Dante may be greater than Flaubert, Flaubert belongs in Dante's class. It is simply that by Flaubert's time the Dantes present their visions in terms of prose drama or fiction rather than of epics in verse. At any other period, certainly, *La Tentation de Saint Antoine* would have been written in verse instead of prose.

And if one happens to read Virgil's *Georgics* not long after having read Flaubert, the shift from verse to prose technique gets the plainest demonstration possible. If you think of Virgil with Tennyson, you have the illusion that the Virgilian poets are shrinking; but if you think of Virgil with Flaubert, you can see how a great modern prose-writer has grown out of the great classical poets. Flaubert somewhere—I think, in the Goncourt journal—expresses his admiration for Virgil; and, in method as well as in mood, the two writers are often akin. Flaubert is no less accomplished in his use of words and rhythms than Virgil; and the poet is as successful as the novelist in conveying emotion through objective statement. The *Georgics* were seven years in the writing, as *Madame Bovary* was six. And the fact that—in *Madame Bovary* especially—Flaubert's elegiac feeling as well as his rural settings run so close to the characteristic vein of Virgil makes the comparison particularly interesting. Put the bees of the *Georgics,* for example, whose swarming Virgil thus describes:

> *aethere in alto*
> *Fit sonitus, magnum mixtae glomerantur in orbem*
> *Praecipitesque cadunt*
> [High in air the din arises, they gather confusedly into a great ball, and drop headlong down]

beside the bees seen and heard by Emma Bovary on an April afternoon: "quelquefois les abeilles, tournoyant dans la lumière, frappaient contre les carreaux commes des balles d'or rebondissantes [sometimes the bees, turning in the light, struck against the glass panes like rebounding golden balls]." Put

> *Et iam summa procul villarum culmina fumant,*
> *Maioresque cadunt altis de montibus umbrae* /22/
> [and now the tall roofs of the farms smoke in the distance, and larger shadows fall from the high mountains]

beside: "La tendresse des anciens jours leur revenait au coeur, abondante et silencieuse comme la rivière qui coulait, avec autant de mollesse qu'en apportait le parfum des seringas, et projetait dans leurs souvenirs des ombres plus démesurées et plus mélancoliques que celles des saules immobiles qui s'allongeaient sur l'herbe [The tenderness of the old days reawoke in their hearts, full and silent as the flowing river, soft as the aroma of the syringas, and cast on their memories shadows longer and more melancholy than those of the motionless willows which lengthened on the grass]." And compare Virgil's sadness and wistfulness with the sadness and nostalgia of Flaubert: the melancholy of the mountainous pastures laid waste by the cattle plague:

> *desertaque regna*
> *Pastorum, et longe saltus lateque vacantes*
> [the realms of the shepherds deserted, and the lawns left desolate far and wide]

with the modern desolations of Paris in *L'Education sentimentale:* "Les rues étaient désertes. Quelquefois une charrette lourde passait, en ébranlant les pavés [The streets were deserted. Sometimes a heavy cart passed, shaking the paving stones]," etc.; or Palinurus, fallen into the sea, swimming with effort to the coast of Italy, but only to be murdered and left there "naked on the unknown sand," while his soul, since his corpse lies unburied, must forever be excluded from Hades, or Orpheus still calling Eurydice when his head has been torn from his body, till his tongue has grown cold and the echo of his love has been lost among the river banks—compare these with Charles Bovary, a schoolboy, looking out on fine summer evenings at the sordid streets of Rouen and sniffing for the good country odors, "qui ne vanaient pas jusqu'à lui [which never came to him]"—("tendebantque manus ripae ulterioris amore") [and were stretching forth their hands in longing for the opposite bank]—or with the scene in which Emma Bovary receives her father's letter and remembers the summers of her girlhood, with the galloping colts and the bees, and knows that she has spent all her illusions in maidenhood, in marriage, in adultery, as a traveler leaves something of his money at each of the inns of the road.

We find, in this connection, in Flaubert's letters the most explicit statements. "To desire to give verse-rhythm to prose, yet to leave it prose and very much prose," he wrote to Louise Colet (March 27, 1853), "and to write about ordinary life as histories and epics are written, yet without falsifying the subject, is perhaps an absurd idea. Sometimes I almost think it is. But it may also be a great experiment and very original." The truth is that Flaubert is a crucial figure. He is the first great writer in prose deliberately to try to take over for the treatment of am- /23/ bitious subjects the delicacy, the precision and the intensity that have hitherto been identified with verse. Henrik Ibsen, for the poetic drama, played a role hardly less important. Ibsen began as a writer of verse and composed many short and non-dramatic poems as well as *Peer Gynt* and *Brand* and his other plays in verse, but eventually changed over to prose for the concentrated Sophoclean tragedies that affected the whole dramatic tradition. Thereafter the dramatic "poets"—the Chekhovs, the Synges and the Shaws (Hauptmann had occasional relapses)—wrote almost invariably in prose. It was by such that the soul of the time was given its dramatic expression: there was nothing left for Rostand's alexandrines but fireworks and declamation.

In the later generation, James Joyce, who had studied Flaubert and Ibsen as well as the great classical verse-masters, set out to merge the two techniques. Dickens and Herman Melville had occasionally resorted to blank verse for passages which they meant to be elevated, but these flights had not matched their context, and the effect had not been happy. Joyce, however, now, in *Ulysses,* has worked out a new medium of his own which enables him to exploit verse metrics in a texture which is basically prose; and he has created in *Finnegans Wake* a work of which we cannot say whether it ought, in the old-fashioned phraseology, to be described as prose or verse. A good deal of *Finnegans Wake* is written in regular meter and might perfectly well be printed as verse, but, except for the interpolated songs, the whole thing is printed as prose. As one reads it, one wonders, in any case, how anything could be demanded of "poetry" by Coleridge with his "sense of novelty and freshness with old and familiar objects," by Poe with his indefiniteness of music, by Arnold with his natural magic, by Verlaine with his nuance, by Eliot with his unearthliness, or by Housman with his bristling of the beard, which the *Anna Livia Plurabelle* chapter (or canto) does not fully supply.

If, then, we take literature as a whole for our field, we put an end to many futile controversies—the controversies, for example, as to whether or not Pope is a poet, as to whether or not Whitman is a poet. If you are prepared to admit that Pope is one of the great English writers, it is less interesting to compare him with /24/ Shakespeare—which will tell you something about the develop-

ment of English verse but not bring out Pope's peculiar excellence—than to compare him with Thackeray, say, with whom he has his principal theme—the vanity of the world—in common and who throws into relief the more passionate pulse and the solider art of Pope. And so the effort to apply to Whitman the ordinary standards of verse has hindered the appreciation of his careful and exquisite art.

If, in writing about "poetry," one limits oneself to "poets" who compose in verse, one excludes too much of modern literature, and with it too much of life. The best modern work in verse has been mostly in the shorter forms, and it may be that our lyric poets are comparable to any who have ever lived, but we have had no imaginations of the stature of Shakespeare or Dante, who have done their major work in verse. The horizon and even the ambition of the contemporary writer of verse has narrowed with the specialization of the function of verse itself. (Though the novelists Proust and Joyce are both masters of what used to be called "numbers," the verses of the first are negligible and those of the second minor.)

Would not D. H. Lawrence, for example, if he had lived a century earlier, probably have told his tales, as Byron and Crabbe did: in verse? Is it not just as correct to consider him the last of the great English romantic poets as one of the most original of modern English novelists? Must we not, to appreciate Virginia Woolf, be aware that she is trying to do what Jane Austen or George Eliot were doing?

Recently the techniques of prose and verse have been getting mixed up at a bewildering rate—with the prose technique steadily gaining. You have had the verse technique of Ezra Pound gradually changing into prose technique. You have had William Faulkner, who began by writing verse, doing his major work in prose fiction without ever quite mastering prose, so that he may at any moment upset us by interpolating a patch of verse. You have had Robinson Jeffers, in narrative "poems" which are as much novels as some of Lawrence's, reeling out yards of what are really prose dithyrambs with a loose hexametric base; and you have /25/ had Carl Sandburg, of *The People, Yes,* producing a queer kind of literature which oscillates between something like verse and something like the paragraphs of a newspaper "column."

Sandburg and Pound have, of course, come out of the old *vers libre*, which, though prose-like, was either epigrammatic or had the rhythms of the Whitmanesque chant. But since the Sandburg-Pound generation, a new development in verse has taken place. The sharpness and the energy disappear; the beat gives way to demoralized weariness. Here the "sprung-rhythm" of Gerard Manley Hopkins has sometimes set the example. But the difference is that Hopkins' rhythms convey agitation and tension, whereas the rhythms of MacNeice and Auden let down the taut traditions of lyric verse with an effect that is often comic and probably intended to be so—these poets are not far at moments from the humorous rhymed prose of Ogden Nash. And finally—what is very strange to see—Miss Edna St. Vincent Millay in *Conversation at Midnight*, slackening her old urgent pace, dimming the ring of her numbers, has given us a curious example of metrics in full dissolution, with the stress almost entirely neglected, the lines running on for paragraphs and even the rhymes sometimes fading out. In some specimens of this recent work, the beat of verse has been so slurred and muted that it might almost as well have been abandoned. We have at last lived to see the day when the ballads of Gilbert and Hood, written without meter for comic effect in long lines that look and sound like paragraphs, have actually become the type of a certain amount of serious poetry.

You have also the paradox of Eliot attempting to revive the verse-drama with rhythms which, adapting themselves to the rhythms of colloquial speech, run sometimes closer to prose. And you have Mr. Maxwell Anderson trying to renovate the modern theater by bringing back blank verse again—with the result that, once a writer of prose dialogue distinguished by some color and wit, he has become, as a dramatic poet, banal and insipid beyond belief. The trouble is that no verse technique is more obsolete today than blank verse. The old iambic pentameters have no longer any relation whatever to the tempo and language of our lives. Yeats was the last

who could write them, and he only because he inhabited, in Ireland and in imagination, a grandiose anachronis- /26/ tic world. You cannot deal with contemporary events in an idiom which was already growing trite in Tennyson's and Arnold's day; and if you try to combine the rhythm of blank verse with the idiom of ordinary talk, you get something—as in Anderson's *Winterset*—which lacks the merits of either. Nor can you try to exploit the worked-out rhythm without also finding yourself let in for the antiquated point of view. The comments on the action in *Winterset* are never the expression of sentiments which we ourselves could conceivably feel in connection with the events depicted: they are the echoes of Greek choruses and Elizabethan soliloquies reflecting upon happenings of a different kind.

Thus if the poets of the Auden-MacNeice school find verse turning to prose in their hands, like the neck of the flamingo in Lewis Carroll with which Alice tried to play croquet, Mr. Anderson, returning to blank verse, finds himself in the more awkward predicament of the girl in the fairy tale who could never open her mouth without having a toad jump out.

But what has happened? What, then, is the cause of this disuse into which verse technique has been falling for at least the last two hundred years? And what are we to expect in the future? Is verse to be limited now to increasingly specialized functions and finally to go out altogether? Or will it recover the domains it has lost?

To find out, if it is possible to do so, we should be forced to approach this change from the anthropological and sociological points of view. Is verse a more primitive technique than prose? Are its fixed rules like the syntax of languages, which are found to have been stiffer and more complicated the further back one goes? Aside from the question of the requirements of taste and the self-imposed difficulties of form which have always, in any period, been involved in the production of great works of art, does the easy flexibility, say, of modern English prose bear to the versification of Horace the same relation that English syntax bears to Horace's syntax, or that Horace's bears to that of the Eskimos?

It seems obvious that one of the important factors in the history of the development of verse must have been its relations with music. Greek verse grew up in fusion with music: verse and /27/ music were learned together. It was not till after Alexander the Great that prosody was detached from harmony. The Greek name for "prose" was "bare words"— that is, words divorced from music. But what the Romans took over and developed was a prosody that was purely literary. This, I believe, accounts for the fact that we seem to find in Greek poetry, if we compare it with Latin poetry, so little exact visual observation. Greek poetry is mainly for the ear. Compare a landscape in one of the choruses of Sophocles or Aristophanes with a landscape of Virgil or Horace: the Greeks are *singing* about the landscape, the Romans are fixing it for the eye of the mind; and it is Virgil and Horace who lead the way to all the later picture poetry down to our own Imagists. Again, in the Elizabethan age, the English were extremely musical: the lyrics of Campion could hardly have been composed apart from their musical settings; and Shakespeare is permeated with music. When Shakespeare wants to make us see something, he is always compelling and brilliant; but the effect has been liquefied by music so that it sometimes gives a little the impression of objects seen under water. The main stream of English poetry continues to keep fairly close to music through Milton, the musician's son, and even through the less organ-voiced Dryden. What has really happened with Pope is that the musical background is no longer there and that the ocular sense has grown sharp again. After this, the real music of verse is largely confined to lyrics—songs—and it becomes more and more of a trick to write them so that they seem authentic—that is, so that they sound like something sung. It was the aim of the late-nineteenth-century Symbolists, who derived their theory from Poe, to bring verse closer to music again, in opposition to the school of the Parnassians, who cultivated an opaque objectivity. And the excellence of Miss Millay's lyrics is obviously connected with her musical training, as the metrical parts of Joyce—such as the Sirens episode in *Ulysses,* which attempts to render music, the response to a song of its hearer—are obviously associated with his vocal gifts. (There is of course a kind of poetry which produces plastic effects not merely by picture-making through explicit descriptions or images, but by giving the language itself—as Allen Tate is able to do—a plastic quality rather than a musical one.) /28/

We might perhaps see a revival of verse in a period and in a society in which music played a leading role. It has long played a great role in Russia; and in the Soviet Union at the present time you find people declaiming poetry at drinking parties or while traveling on boats and trains almost as readily as they burst into song to the accordion or the balalaika, and flocking to poetry-readings just as they do to concerts. It is possible that the Russians at the present time show more of an appetite for "poetry," if not always for the best grade of literature, than any of the Western peoples. Their language, half-chanted and strongly stressed, in many ways extremely primitive, provides by itself, as Italian does, a constant stimulus to the writing of verse.

Here in the United States, we have produced some of our truest poetry in the folksongs that are inseparable from their tunes. One is surprised, in going through the collections of American popular songs (of Abbé Niles and W. C. Handy, of Carl Sandburg, of the various students trained by Professor Kittredge), which have appeared during the last ten or fifteen years, to discover that the peopling of the continent has had as a by-product a body of folk-verse not unworthy of comparison with the similar material that went to make Percy's *Reliques.* The air of the popular song will no doubt be carrying the words that go with it into the "poetry" anthologies of the future when many of the set-pieces of "poetry," which strain to catch a music gone with Shakespeare, will have come to seem words on the page, incapable of reverberation or of flight from between the covers.

Another pressure that has helped to discourage verse has undoubtedly been the increased demand for reading matter which has been stimulated by the invention of the printing press and which, because ordinary prose is easier to write than verse, has been largely supplied by prose. Modern journalism has brought forth new art-forms; and you have had not only the masterpieces of fiction of such novelists as Flaubert and Joyce, who are also consummate artists in the sense that the great classical poets were, but also the work of men like Balzac and Dickens which lacks the tight organization and the careful attention to detail of the classical epic or drama, and which has to be read rapidly in bulk. The novels of such writers are the epics of societies: they /29/ have neither the concision of the folk-song nor the elegance of the forms of the court; they sprawl and swarm over enormous areas like the city populations they deal with. Their authors, no longer schooled in the literary tradition of the Renaissance, speak the practical everyday language of the dominant middle class, which has destroyed the Renaissance world. Even a writer like Dostoevsky rises out of this weltering literature. You cannot say that his insight is less deep, that his vision is less noble or narrower, or that his mastery of his art is less complete than that of the great poets of the past. You can say only that what he achieves he achieves by somewhat different methods.

The technique of prose today seems thus to be absorbing the technique of verse; but it is showing itself quite equal to that work of the imagination which caused men to call Homer "divine": that re-creation, in the harmony and logic of words, of the cruel confusion of life. Not, of course, that we shall have Dante and Shakespeare redone in some prose form any more than we shall have Homer in prose. In art, the same things are not done again or not done again except as copies. The point is that literary techniques are tools, which the masters of the craft have to alter in adapting them to fresh uses. To be too much attached to the traditional tools may be sometimes to ignore the new masters. /30/

ROBERT FROST

"The Figure a Poem Makes"

[Robert Frost (1874–   ) was born in San Francisco but moved to New England when he was ten and is most often associated with that region. His first two books of poetry, *A Boy's Will* (1913) and *North of Boston* (1914), were published during a two-year stay in England. Though he wrote poetry for over twenty years before attaining publication in book form, he has since won the Pulitzer prize for poetry four times and now enjoys the rare distinction of being both widely beloved and critically respected. Such poems as "Stopping by Woods on a Snowy Evening," "The Road Not Taken," "Mending Wall," "Birches," and "The Death of the Hired Man" have become standard anthology selections. The following essay was first published as preface to the 1939 edition of Frost's poems and is reprinted here from *Complete Poems of Robert Frost 1949* (New York, 1949).]

Abstraction is an old story with the philosophers, but it has been like a new toy in the hands of the artists of our day. Why can't we have any one quality of poetry we choose by itself? We can have in thought. Then it will go hard if we can't in practice. Our lives for it.

Granted no one but a humanist much cares how sound a poem is if it is only *a* sound. The sound is the gold in the ore. Then we will have the sound out alone and dispense with the inessential. We do till we make the discovery that the object in writing poetry is to make all poems sound as different as possible from each other, and the resources for that of vowels, consonants, punctuation, syntax, words, sentences, meter are not enough. We need the help of context—meaning—subject matter. That is the greatest help towards variety. All that can be done with words is soon told. So also with meters—particularly in our language where there are virtually but two, strict iambic and loose iambic. The ancients with many were still poor if they depended on meters for all tune. It is painful to watch our sprung-rhythmists straining at the point of omitting one short from a foot for relief from monotony. The possibilities for tune from the dramatic tones of meaning struck across the rigidity of a limited meter are endless. And we are back in poetry as merely one more art of having something to say, sound or unsound. Probably better if sound, because deeper and from wider experience.

Then there is this wildness whereof it is spoken. Granted again that it has an equal claim with sound to being a poem's better half. If it is a wild tune, it is a poem. Our problem then is, as modern abstractionists, to have the wildness pure; to be wild with nothing to be wild about. We bring up as /v/ aberrationists, giving way to undirected associations and kicking ourselves from one chance suggestion to another in all directions as of a hot afternoon in the life of a grasshopper. Theme alone can steady us down. Just as the first mystery was how a poem could have a tune in such a straightness as meter, so the second mystery is how a poem can have wildness and at the same time a subject that shall be fulfilled.

It should be of the pleasure of a poem itself to tell how it can. The figure a poem makes. It begins in delight and ends in wisdom. The figure is the same as for love. No one can really hold that the ecstasy should be static and stand still in one place. It begins in delight, it inclines to the impulse, it assumes direction with the first line laid down, it runs a course of lucky events, and ends in a clarification of life—not necessarily a great clarification, such as sects and cults are founded on, but in a momentary stay against confusion. It has denouement. It has an outcome that though unforeseen was predestined from the first image of the original mood—and indeed from the very mood. It is but a trick poem and no poem at all if the best of it was thought of first and saved for the last. It finds its own name as it goes and discovers the best waiting for it in some final phrase at once wise and sad—the happy-sad blend of the drinking song.

No tears in the writer, no tears in the reader. No surprise for the writer, no surprise for the reader. For me the initial delight is in the surprise of remembering something I didn't know I knew. I am in a place, in a situation, as if I had materialized from cloud or risen out of the ground. There is a glad recognition of the long lost and the rest follows. Step by step the wonder of unexpected supply keeps growing. /vi/ The impressions most useful to my purpose seem always those I was unaware of and so made no note of at the time when taken, and the conclusion is come to that like giants we are always hurling experience ahead of us to pave the future with against the day when we may want to strike a line of purpose across it for somewhere. The line will have the more charm for not being mechanically straight. We enjoy the straight crookedness of a good walking stick. Modern instruments of precision are being used to make things crooked as if by eye and hand in the old days.

I tell how there may be a better wildness of logic than of inconsequence. But the logic is backward, in retrospect, after the act. It must be more felt than seen ahead like prophecy. It must be a revelation; or a series of revelations, as much for the poet as for the reader. For it to be that there must have been the greatest freedom of the material to move about in it and to establish relations in it regardless of time and space, previous relation, and everything but affinity. We prate of freedom. We call our schools free because we are not free to stay away from them till we are sixteen years of age. I have given up my democratic prejudices and now willingly set the lower classes free to be completely taken care of by the upper classes. Political freedom is nothing to me. I bestow it right and left.

All I would keep for myself is the freedom of my material—the condition of body and mind now and then to summons aptly from the vast chaos of all I have lived through.

Scholars and artists thrown together are often annoyed at the puzzle of where they differ. Both work from knowledge; but I suspect they differ most importantly in the way their knowledge is come by. Scholars get theirs with conscientious thoroughness along projected lines of logic; poets theirs /vii/ cavalierly and as it happens in and out of books. They stick to nothing deliberately, but let what will stick to them like burrs where they walk in the fields. No acquirement is on assignment, or even self-assignment. Knowledge of the second kind is much more available in the wild free ways of wit and art. A schoolboy may be defined as one who can tell you what he knows in the order in which he learned it. The artist must value himself as he snatches a thing from some previous order in time and space into a new order with not so much as a ligature clinging to it of the old place where it was organic.

More than once I should have lost my soul to radicalism if it had been the originality it was mistaken for by its young converts. Originality and initiative are what I ask for my country. For myself the originality need be no more than the freshness of a poem run in the way I have described: from delight to wisdom. The figure is the same as for love. Like a piece of ice on a hot stove the poem must ride on its own melting. A poem may be worked over once it is in being, but may not be worried into being. Its most precious quality will remain its having run itself and carried away the poet with it. Read it a hundred times: it will forever keep its freshness as a metal keeps its fragrance. It can never lose its sense of a meaning that once unfolded by surprise as it went. /viii/

ROBERT PENN WARREN

"Pure and Impure Poetry"

[Robert Penn Warren (1905–), poet, novelist, and critic, is probably best known for his Pulitzer prize-winning *All the King's Men* (1946), a political novel whose protagonist was modeled on the Louisiana demagogue Huey Long. Born in Kentucky, he studied under Donald Davidson and John Crowe Ransom at Vanderbilt, where he became one of the poets in the Fugitive group. He then went on for further study at California and Yale and later at Oxford, where he was a Rhodes Scholar. He has taught at various universities and is coauthor with Cleanth Brooks of *Understanding Poetry* (1938) and other college textbooks, as well as sole author of novels and volumes of poetry. "Pure and Impure Poetry" was delivered as a lecture at Princeton in 1942. It is here reprinted from *The Kenyon Review*, V (Spring, 1943).]

Critics are rarely faithful to their labels and their special strategies. Usually the critic will confess that no one strategy—the psychological, the moralistic, the formalistic, the historical—or combination of strategies, will quite work the defeat of the poem. For the poem is like the monstrous Orillo in Boiardo's *Orlando Innamorato*. When the sword lops off any member of the monster, that member is immediately rejoined to the body, and the monster is as formidable as ever. But the poem is even more formidable than the monster, for Orillo's adversary finally gained a victory by an astonishing feat of dexterity: he slashed off both the monster's arms and quick as a wink seized them and flung them into the river. The critic who vaingloriously trusts his method to account for the poem, to exhaust the poem, is trying to emulate this dexterity: he thinks that he, too, can win by throwing the lopped-off arms into the river. But he is doomed to failure. Neither fire nor water will suffice to prevent the rejoining of the mutilated members to the monstrous torso. There is only one way to conquer the monster: you must eat it, bones, blood, skin, pelt, and gristle. And even then the monster is not dead, for it lives in you, is assimilated into you, and you are different, and somewhat monstrous yourself, for having eaten it.

So the monster will always win, and the critic knows this. He does not want to win. He knows that he must always play stooge to the monster. All he wants to do is to give the monster a chance to exhibit again its miraculous power. /228/

With this fable, I shall begin by observing that poetry wants to be pure. And it always succeeds in this ambition. In so far as we have poetry at all, it is always pure poetry; that is, it is not non-poetry. The poetry of Shakespeare, the poetry of Pope, the poetry of Herrick, is pure, in so far as it is poetry at all. We call the poetry "higher" or "lower," we say "more powerful" or "less powerful" about it, and we are, no doubt, quite right in doing so. The souls that form the great rose of Paradise are seated in banks and tiers of ascending blessedness, but they are all saved, they are all perfectly happy; they are all "pure," for they have all been purged of mortal taint. This is not to say, however, that if we get poetry from one source, such a single source, say Shakespeare, should suffice us in as much as we can always appeal to it, or that, since all poetry is equally pure, we engage in a superfluous labor in trying to explore or create new sources of poetry. No, for we can remember that every soul in the great rose is precious in the eyes of God. No soul is the substitute for another.

Poetry wants to be pure, but poems do not. At least, most of them do not want to be too pure. The poems want to give us poetry, which is pure, and the elements of a poem, in so far as it is a good poem, will work together toward that end, but many of the elements, taken in themselves, may actually seem to contradict that end, or be neutral toward the achieving of that end. Are we then to conclude that, because neutral or recalcitrant elements appear in poems, even in poems called great, these elements are simply an index to human frailty, that in a perfect world there would be no dross in poems which would, then, be perfectly pure? No, it does not seem to be merely the fault of our world, for the poems include, deliberately, more of the so-called dross than would appear necessary. They are not even as pure as they might be in this imperfect world. They mar themselves with cacophonies, jagged rhythms, ugly words and ugly thoughts, colloquialisms, clichés, sterile technical terms, head work and argument, self-contradictions, cleverness, irony, realism—all things which call us /229/ back to the world of prose and imperfection.

Sometimes a poet will reflect on this state of affairs, and grieve. He will decide that he, at least, will try to make one poem as pure as possible. So he writes:

> Now sleeps the crimson petal, now the white;
> Nor waves the cypress in the palace walk;
> Nor winks the gold fin in the porphyry font:
> The firefly wakens: waken thou with me.[1]

We know the famous garden. We know how all nature conspires here to express the purity of the moment: how the milk-white peacock glimmers like a ghost, and how like a ghost the unnamed "she" glimmers on to her tryst; how earth lies "all Danaé to the stars," as the beloved's heart lies open to the lover; and how, in the end, the lily folds up her sweetness, "and slips into the bosom of the lake," as the lovers are lost in the sweet dissolution of love.

And we know another poet and another garden. Or perhaps it is the same garden, after all:

> I arise from dreams of thee
> In the first sweet sleep of night,
> When the winds are breathing low
> And the stars are shining bright.
> I arise from dreams of thee,
> And a spirit in my feet
> Hath led me—who knows how?
> To thy chamber window, Sweet![2]

We remember how, again, all nature conspires, how the wandering airs "faint," how the Champak's odors "pine," how the nightingale's complaint "dies upon her heart," as the lover will die upon the beloved's heart.

1 [For complete poem, see p. 205.]
2 [For complete poem, see p. 67.]

Nature here strains out of nature, it wants to be called by another name, it wants to spiritualize itself by calling itself another name. How does the lover get to the chamber window? He refuses to say how, in his semi-somnambulistic daze, he got there. He blames, he says, "a spirit in my feet," and hastens to disavow any knowledge of how that spirit operates. In any case, he arrives at the chamber window. Subsequent events /230/ and the lover's reaction toward them are somewhat hazy. We only know that the lover, who faints and fails at the opening of the last stanza, and who asks to be lifted from the grass by a more enterprising beloved, is in a condition of delectable passivity, in which distinctions blur out in the "purity" of the moment.

Let us turn to another garden: the place, Verona; the time, a summer night, with full moon. The lover speaks:

> But soft! what light through yonder window breaks?
> It is the east. . . .

But we know the rest, and know that this garden, in which nature for the moment conspires again with the lover, is the most famous of them all, for the scene is justly admired for its purity of effect, for giving us the very essence of young, untarnished love. Nature conspires beneficently here, but we may chance to remember that beyond the garden wall strolls Mercutio, who can celebrate Queen Mab, but who is always aware that nature has other names as well as the names the pure poets and pure lovers put upon her. And we remember that Mercutio outside the wall, has just said:

> . . . 'twould anger him
> To raise a spirit in his mistress's circle
> Of some strange nature, letting it there stand
> Till she had laid it and conjured it down.

Mercutio has made a joke, a bawdy joke. That is bad enough, but worse, he has made his joke witty and, worst of all, intellectually complicated in its form. Realism, wit, intellectual complication—these are the enemies of the garden purity.

But the poet has not only let us see Mercutio outside the garden wall. Within the garden itself, when the lover invokes nature,

when he spiritualizes and innocently trusts
her, and says,

>Lady, by yonder blessed moon I swear,

the lady herself replies,

O, swear not by the moon, the inconstant moon,
That monthly changes in her circled orb. /231/

The lady distrusts "pure" poems, nature spiritualized into forgetfulness. She has, as it were,
a rigorous taste in metaphor, too; she brings
a logical criticism to bear on the metaphor
which is too easy; the metaphor must prove
itself to her, must be willing to subject itself
to scrutiny beyond the moment's enthusiasm.
She injects the impurity of an intellectual
style into the lover's pure poem.

And we must not forget the voice of the
nurse, who calls from within, a voice which,
we discover, is the voice of expediency, of
half-measures, of the view that circumstances
alter cases—the voice of prose and imperfection.

It is time to ask ourselves if the celebrated
poetry of this scene, which as poetry is pure,
exists despite the impurities of the total composition, if the effect would be more purely
poetic were the nurse and Mercutio absent
and the lady a more sympathetic critic of pure
poems. I do not think so. The effect might
even be more vulnerable poetically if the impurities were purged away. Mercutio, the
lady, and the nurse are critics of the lover,
who believes in pure poems, but perhaps they
are necessary. Perhaps the lover can only be
accepted in their context. The poet seems to
say: "I know the worst that can be said on
this subject, and I am giving fair warning.
Read at your own risk." So the poetry arises
from a recalcitrant and contradictory context;
and finally involves that context.

Let us return to one of the other gardens,
in which there is no Mercutio or nurse, and
in which the lady is more sympathetic. Let us
mar its purity by installing Mercutio in the
shrubbery, from which the poet was so careful to banish him. You can hear his comment
when the lover says:

>And a spirit in my feet
>Hath led me—who knows how?
>To thy chamber window, Sweet!

And we can guess what the wicked tongue
would have to say in response to the last
stanza. /232/

It may be that the poet should have made
his peace early with Mercutio, and have appealed to his better nature. For Mercutio
seems to be glad to cooperate with a poet.
But he must be invited; otherwise, he is apt to
show a streak of merry vindictiveness about
the finished product. Poems are vulnerable
enough at best. Bright reason mocks them like
sun from a wintry sky. They are easily left
naked to laughter when leaves fall in the
garden and the cold winds come. Therefore,
they need all the friends they can get, and
Mercutio, who is an ally of reason and who
himself is given to mocking laughter, is a good
friend for a poem to have.

On what terms does a poet make his peace
with Mercutio? There are about as many sets
of terms as there are good poets. I know that
I have loaded the answer with the word *good*
here, that I have implied a scale of excellence
based, in part at least, on degree of complication. I shall return to this question. For the
moment, however, let us examine a poem
whose apparent innocence and simple lyric
cry should earn it a place in any anthology
of "pure poetry."

>Western wind, when wilt thou blow
>   That the small rain down can rain?
>Christ, that my love were in my arms
>   And I in my bed again![3]

The lover, grieving for the absent beloved,
cries out for relief. Several kinds of relief are
involved in the appeal to the wind. First,
there is the relief that would be had from
the sympathetic manifestation of nature. The
lover, in his perturbation of spirit, invokes
the perturbations of nature. He exclaims,

>Western wind, when wilt thou blow

and Lear exclaims,

Blow, winds, and crack your cheeks! rage! blow!

Second, there is the relief that would be had
by the fulfillment of grief—the frost of grief,
the drought of grief broken, the full anguish
expressed, then the violence allayed in the
peace of tears. /233/ Third, there is the re-

[3] [An anonymous sixteenth-century poem, quoted
entire.]

lief that would be had in the excitement and fulfillment of love itself. There seems to be a contrast between the first two types of relief and the third type; speaking loosely, we may say that the first two types are romantic and general, the third type realistic and specific. So much for the first two lines.

In the last two lines, the lover cries out for the specific solace of his case: reunion with his beloved. But there is a difference between the two lines. The first is general, and romantic. The phrase "in my arms" does not seem to mean exactly what it says. True, it has a literal meaning, if we can look close at the words, but it is hard to look close because of the romantic aura—the spiritualized mist about them.[4] But with the last line the perfectly literal meaning suddenly comes into sharp focus. The mist is rifted and we can look straight at the words, which, we discover with a slight shock of surprise, do mean exactly what they say. The last line is realistic and specific. It is not even content to say,

> And I in bed again!

It is, rather, more scrupulously specific, and says,

> And I in *my* bed again![5]

All of this does not go to say that the realistic elements here are to be taken as cancelling, or negating, the romantic elements. There is no ironical leer. The poem is not a celebration of carnality. It is a faithful lover who speaks. He is faithful to the absent beloved, and he is also faithful to the full experience of love. That is, he does not ab-

[4] It may be objected here that I am reading the phrase "in my arms" as a twentieth century reader. I confess the fact. Certainly, several centuries have passed since the composition of the little poem, and those centuries have thickened the romantic mist about the words, but it is scarcely to be believed that the sixteenth century was the clear, literal Eden dawn of poetry when words walked without the fig leaf.

[5] In connection with the word *my* in this line, we may also feel that it helps to set over the comfort and satisfaction there specified against the bad weather of the first two lines. We may also glance at the word *small* in the second line. It is the scrupulous word, the word that, realistically, makes us believe in the rain. But, too, it is broader in its function. The storm which the lover invokes will not rend the firmament, it will not end the world; it will simply bring down the "small" rain, a credible rain.

stract one aspect of the experience and call it the whole experience. He does not strain nature out of nature; /234/ he does not over-spiritualize nature. This nameless poet would never have said, in the happier days of his love, that he had been led to his Sweet's chamber window by "a spirit in my feet"; and he certainly would not have added the coy disavowal, "who knows how?" But because the nameless poet refused to over-spiritualize nature, we can accept the spirituality of the poem.

Another poem gives us another problem.

> Ah, what avails the sceptered race,
>   Ah, what the form divine!
> What every virtue, every grace!
>   Rose Aylmer, all were thine.
>
> Rose Aylmer, whom these wakeful eyes
>   May weep, but never see,
> A night of memories and of sighs
>   I consecrate to thee.[6]

This is another poem about lost love: a "soft" subject. Now to one kind of poet the soft subject presents a sore temptation. Because it is soft in its natural state, he is inclined to feel that to get at its poetic essence he must make it softer still, that he must insist on its softness, that he must render it as "pure" as possible. At first glance, it may seem that Landor is trying to do just that. What he says seems to be emphatic, unqualified, and open. Not every power, grace, and virtue could avail to preserve his love. That statement insists on the pathetic contrast. And in the next stanza, wakefulness and tearfulness are mentioned quite unashamedly, along with memories and sighs. It is all blurted out, as pure as possible.

But only in the paraphrase is it "blurted." The actual quality of the first stanza is hard, not soft. It is a chiseled stanza, in which formality is insisted upon. We may observe the balance of the first and second lines; the balance of the first half with the second half of the third line, which recapitulates the structure of the first two lines: the balance of the two parts of the last line, though here the balance is merely a rhythmical and not a sense balance as in /235/ the preceding instances; the binders of discreet alliteration,

[6] [Walter Savage Landor's "Rose Aylmer."]

repetition, and assonance. The stanza is built up, as it were, of units which are firmly defined and sharply separated, phrase by phrase, line by line. We have the formal control of the soft subject, ritual and not surrender.

But in the second stanza the rigor of this formality is somewhat abated, as the more general, speculative emphasis (why cannot pomp, virtue, and grace avail?) gives way to the personal emphasis, as though the repetition of the beloved's name had, momentarily, released the flood of feeling. The first line of the second stanza spills over into the second; the "wakeful eyes" as subject find their verb in the next line, "weep," and the *wake-weep* alliteration, along with the rest after *weep*, points up the disintegration of the line, just as it emphasizes the situation. Then with the phrase "but never see" falling away from the long thrust of the rhetorical structure to the pause after *weep*, the poem seems to go completely soft, the frame is broken. But, even as the poet insists on "memories and sighs," in the last two lines he restores the balance. Notice the understatement of "A night." It says: "I know that life is a fairly complicated affair, and that I am committed to it and to its complications. I intend to stand by my commitment, as a man of integrity, that is, to live despite the grief. Since life is complicated, I cannot, if I am to live, spare too much time for indulging grief. I can give *a* night, but not all nights." The lover, like the hero of Frost's poem "Stopping by Woods on a Winter Evening,"[7] tears himself from the temptation of staring into the treacherous, delicious blackness, for he, too, has "promises to keep." Or he resembles the Homeric heroes who, after the perilous passage is made, after their energy has saved their lives, and after they have beached their craft and eaten their meal, can then set aside an hour before sleep to mourn the comrades lost by the way—the heroes who, as Aldous Huxley says, understand realistically a whole truth as contrasted with a half-truth.

Is this a denial of the depth and sincerity of the grief? The /236/ soft reader, who wants the poem pure, may be inclined to say so. But let us look at the last line to see what it gives us in answer to this question. The answer

seems to lie in the word *consecrate*. The meter thrusts this word at us; we observe that two of the three metrical accents in the line fall on syllables of this word forcing it beyond its prose emphasis. The word is important and the importance is justified, for the word tells us that the single night is not merely a lapse into weakness, a trivial event to be forgotten when the weakness is overcome. It is, rather, an event of the most extreme and focal importance, an event formally dedicated, "set apart for sacred uses," an event by which other events are to be measured. So the word *consecrate* formalizes, philosophizes, ritualizes the grief; it specifies what style in the first stanza has implied.

But here is another poem of grief, grief at the death of a child:

There was such speed in her little body,
And such lightness in her footfall,
It is no wonder that her brown study
Astonishes us all.

Her wars were bruited in our high window.
We looked among orchard trees and beyond
Where she took arms against her shadow,
Or harried unto the pond

The lazy geese, like a snow cloud
Dripping their snow on the green grass,
Tricking and stopping, sleepy and proud,
Who cried in goose, Alas,

For the tireless heart within the little
Lady with rod that made them rise
From their noon apple dreams, and scuttle
Goose-fashion under the skies!

But now go the bells, and we are ready;
In one house we are sternly stopped
To say we are vexed at her brown study,
Lying so primly propped.[8] /237/

Another soft subject, softer, if anything, than the subject of "Rose Aylmer," and it presents the same problem. But the problem is solved in a different way.

The first stanza is based on two time-honored clichés: first, "Heaven, won't that child ever be still, she is driving me distracted"; and second, "She was such an active, healthy-looking child, would you've ever thought she would just up and die?" In fact, the whole poem develops these clichés, and

7 [See p. 214.]

8 ["Bells for John Whiteside's Daughter," by John Crowe Ransom.]

exploits, in a backhand fashion, the ironies implicit in their inter-relation. And in this connection, we may note that the fact of the clichés, rather than more original or profound observations, at the root of the poem is important; there is in the poem the contrast between the staleness of the clichés and the shock of the reality. Further we may note that the second cliché is an answer, savagely ironical in itself, to the first: the child you wished would be still *is* still, despite all that activity which your adult occupations deplored.

But such a savage irony is not the game here. It is too desperate, too naked, in a word, too pure. And ultimately, it is, in a sense, a meaningless irony if left in its pure state, because it depends on a mechanical, accidental contrast in nature, void of moral content. The poem is concerned with modifications and modulations of this brute, basic irony, modulations and modifications contingent upon an attitude taken toward it by a responsible human being, the speaker of the poem. The savagery is masked, or ameliorated.

In this connection, we may observe, first, the phrase "brown study." It is not the "frosted flower," the "marmoreal immobility," or any one of a thousand such phrases which would aim for the pure effect. It is merely the brown study which astonishes—a phrase which denies, as it were, the finality of the situation, underplays the pathos, and merely reminds one of those moments of childish pensiveness into which the grown-up cannot penetrate. And the phrase itself is a cliché— the common now echoed in the uncommon. /238/

Next, we may observe that stanzas two, three, and four simply document, with a busy yet wavering rhythm (one sentence runs through the three stanzas) the tireless naughtiness which was once the cause of rebuke, the naughtiness which disturbed the mature going-on in the room with the "high window." But the naughtiness has been transmuted, by events just transpired, into a kind of fanciful story-book dream-world, in which geese are whiter than nature, and the grass greener, in which geese speak in goose language, saying "Alas," and have apple dreams. It is a drowsy, delicious world, in which the geese are bigger than life, and more important. It is an unreal (now unreal because lost), stylized world. Notice how the phrase "the little lady with rod" works: the detached, grown-up primness of "little lady"; the formal, stiff effect gained by the omission of the article before *rod;* the slightly unnatural use of the word *rod* itself, which sets some distance between us and the scene (perhaps with the hint of the fairy story, a magic wand, or a magic rod—not a common, everyday stick). But the stanzas tie back into the premises of the poem in other ways. The little girl, in her naughtiness, warred against her shadow. Is it crowding matters too hard to surmise that the shadow here achieves a sort of covert symbolic significance? The little girl lost her war against her "shadow," which was always with her. Certainly the phrase "tireless heart" has some rich connotations. And the geese which say "Alas!" conspire with the family to deplore the excessive activity of the child. (They do not conspire to express the present grief, only the past vexation—an inversion of the method of the pastoral elegy, or of the method of the first two garden poems.)

The business of the three stanzas, then, may be said to be twofold. First, they make us believe more fully in the child and therefore in the fact of the grief itself. They "prove" the grief, and they show the deliciousness of the lost world which will never look the same from the high window. Second, and contrary-wise, they "transcend" the grief, or at least give a hint of a means for /239/ transcending the immediate anguish: the lost world is, in one sense, redeemed out of time, it enters the pages of the picture book where geese speak, where the untrue is true, where the fleeting is fixed. What was had cannot, after all, be lost. (By way of comparison—a comparison which, because extreme, may be helpful—I cite the transcendence in *La Recherche du Temps Perdu.*) The three stanzas, then, to state it in another way, have validated the first stanza and have prepared for the last.

The three stanzas have made it possible for us to say, when the bell tolls, "we are ready." Some kind of terms, perhaps not the best terms possible but some kind, have been made with the savage underlying irony. But the terms arrived at do not prevent the occasion from being a "stern" one. The transcendence is not absolute, and in the end is possible only because of an exercise of will and self-control. Because we control ourselves, we can say "vexed" and not some big word. And the word itself picks up the first of the domestic clichés on which the poem is based—the outburst of impatience at the naughty child who, by dying, has performed her most serious piece of naughtiness. But now the word comes to us charged with the burden of the poem, and further, as re-echoed here by the phrase "brown study," charged by the sentence in which it occurs: we are gathered formally, ritualistically, sternly together to say the word *vexed*.[9] *Vexed* becomes the ritualistic, the summarizing word.

I have used the words *pure* and *impure* often in the foregoing pages, and I confess that I have used them rather loosely. But /240/ perhaps it has been evident that I have meant something like this: the pure poem tries to be pure by excluding, more or less rigidly, certain elements which might qualify or contradict its original impulse. In other words the pure poems want to be, and desperately, all of a piece. It has also been evident, no doubt, that the kinds of impurity which are admitted or excluded by the various little anthology pieces which have been analyzed, are different in the different poems. This is only to be expected, for there is not one doctrine of "pure poetry"—not one definition of what constitutes impurity in poems—but many. And not all of the doctrines are recent. When,

for example, one cites Poe as the father of *the* doctrine of pure poetry, one is in error; Poe simply fathered *a* particular doctrine of pure poetry. One can find other doctrines of purity long antedating Poe. When Sir Philip Sidney, for example, legislated against tragicomedy, he was repeating a current doctrine of purity. When Ben Johnson told William Drummond that Donne, for not keeping of accent, deserved hanging, he was defending another kind of purity, and when Dryden spoke to save the ear of the fair sex from metaphysical perplexities in amorous poems, he was defending another kind of purity, just as he was defending another when he defined the nature of the heroic drama. The 18th Century had a doctrine of pure poetry, which may be summed up under the word *sublimity*, but which involved two corollary doctrines, one concerning diction and the other concerning imagery. But at the same time that this century, by means of these corollary doctrines, was tidying up and purifying, as Mr. Monk and Mr. Henn have indicated, the doctrine derived from Longinus, it was admitting into the drama certain impurities which the theorists of the heroic drama would not have admitted.[10]

But when we think of the modern doctrine of pure poetry, we usually think of Poe, as critic and poet, perhaps of Shelley, of the Symbolists, of the Abbé Brémond, perhaps of Pater, and certainly /241/ of George Moore and the Imagists. We know Poe's position: the long poem is "a flat contradiction in terms," because intense excitement, which is essential in poetry, cannot be long maintained; the moral sense and the intellect function more satisfactorily in prose than in poetry, and, in fact, "Truth" and the "Passions," which are for Poe associated with intellect and the moral sense, may actually be inimical to poetry; vagueness, suggestiveness, are central virtues, for poetry has for "its object an *indefinite* instead of a *definite* pleasure"; poetry is not supposed to undergo close inspection, only a cursory glance, for it, "above all things, is a beautiful painting whose tints, to minute inspection, are confusion worse confounded,

---

[9] It might be profitable, in contrast with this poem, to analyze "After the Burial," by James Russell Lowell, a poem which is identical in situation. But in Lowell's poem the savagery of the irony is unqualified. In fact, the whole poem insists, quite literally, that qualification is impossible: the scheme of the poem is to set up the brute fact of death against possible consolations. It insists on "tears," the "thin-worn locket," the "anguish of deathless hair," "the smallness of the child's grave," the "little shoe in the corner." It is a poem which, we might say, does not progress, but ends where it begins, resting in the savage irony from which it stems; or we might say that it is a poem without any "insides" for the hero of the poem is not attempting to do anything about the problem which confronts him—it is a poem without issue, without conflict, a poem of unconditional surrender. In other words, it tries to be a pure poem, pure grief, absolutely inconsolable. It is a strident poem, and strident in its rhythms. The fact that we know this poem to be an expression of a bereavement historically real makes it an embarrassing poem, as well. It is a naked poem.

[10] Samuel Holt Monk: *The Sublime: a Study of Critical Theories in XVIII-Century England*, and T. R. Henn: *Longinus and English Criticism*.

but start out boldly to the cursory glance of the connoisseur''; poetry aspires toward music, since it is concerned with "indefinite sensations, to which music is an *essential*, since the comprehension of sweet sound is our most indefinite conception''; melancholy is the most poetical effect and enters into all the higher manifestations of beauty. We know, too, the Abbé Brémond's mystical interpretation, and the preface to George Moore's anthology, and the Imagist manifesto.

But these views are not identical. Shelley, for instance, delights in the imprecision praised and practiced by Poe, but he has an enormous appetite for "Truth" and the "Passions," which are, except for purposes of contrast, excluded by Poe. The Imagist manifesto, while excluding ideas, endorses precision rather than vagueness in rendering the image, and admits diction and objects which would have seemed impure to Poe and to many poets of the nineteenth century, and does not take much stock in the importance of verbal music. George Moore emphasizes the objective aspect of his pure poetry, which he describes as "something which the poet creates outside his own personality," and this is opposed to the subjective emphasis in Poe and Shelley; but he shares with both an emphasis on verbal music, and with the former a distaste for ideas.

But more recently, the notion of poetic purity has emerged in /242/ other contexts, contexts which sometimes obscure the connection of the new theories with the older theories. For instance Max Eastman has a theory. "Pure poetry," he says in *The Literary Mind*, "is the pure effort to heighten consciousness." Mr. Eastman, we discover elsewhere in his book, would ban idea from poetry, but his motive is different from, say, the motive of Poe, and the difference is important: Poe would kick out the ideas because the ideas hurt the poetry, and Mr. Eastman would kick out the ideas because the poetry hurts the ideas. Only the scientist, he tells us, is entitled to have ideas on any subject, and the rest of the citizenry must wait to be told what attitude to take toward the ideas which they are not permitted to have except at second-hand. Literary truth, he says, is truth which is "uncertain or comparatively unimportant." But

he assigns the poet a function—to heighten consciousness. But in the light of this context we would have to rewrite his original definition: pure poetry is the pure effort to heighten consciousness, but the consciousness which is heightened must not have any connection with ideas, must involve no attitude toward any ideas.

Furthermore, to assist the poet in fulfilling the assigned function, Mr. Eastman gives him a somewhat sketchy doctrine of "pure" poetic diction. For instance, the word *bloated* is not admissible into a poem because it is, as he testifies, "sacred to the memory of dead fish," and the word *tangy* is, though he knows not exactly how, "intrinsically poetic." The notion of a vocabulary which is intrinsically poetic seems, with Mr. Eastman, to mean a vocabulary which indicates agreeable or beautiful objects. So we might rewrite the original definition to read: pure poetry is the pure effort to heighten consciousness, but the consciousness which is heightened must be a consciousness exclusively of agreeable or beautiful objects—certainly not a consciousness of any ideas.

In a recent book, *The Idiom of Poetry*, Frederick Pottle has discussed the question of pure poetry. He distinguishes another type of pure poetry in addition to the types already mentioned. /243/ He calls it the "Elliptical," and would include in it symbolist and metaphysical poetry (old and new) and some work by poets such as Collins, Blake, and Browning. He observes—without any pejorative implication, for he is a critical relativist and scarcely permits himself the luxury of evaluative judgments—that the contemporary product differs from older examples of the elliptical type in that "the modern poet goes much further in employing private experiences or ideas than would formerly have been thought legitimate." To the common reader, he says, "the prime characteristic of this kind of poetry is not the nature of its imagery but its obscurity: its urgent suggestion that you add something to the poem without telling you what that something is." This omitted "something" he interprets as the prose "frame," to use his word, the statement of the occasion, the logical or narrative transitions, the generalized application derived from the poem, etc. In other words, this type of pure poetry contends that "the effect would be more powerful if we could somehow manage to feel the images fully and accurately without having the effect diluted by any words put in to give us a 'meaning'—that is, if we could expel all the talk *about* the imaginative realization and have the pure realization itself."[11]

For the moment I shall pass the question of the accuracy of Mr. Pottle's description of the impulse of Elliptical Poetry and present the question which ultimately concerns him. How pure does poetry need to be in practice? That is the question which Mr. Pottle asks. He answers by saying that a great degree of impurity *may* be admitted, and cites our famous didactic poems, *The /244/ Faerie Queene, The Essay on Man, The Vanity of Human Wishes, The Excursion.* That is the only answer which the relativist, and nominalist, can give. Then he turns to what he calls the hardest question in the theory of poetry: what kind of prosaism is acceptable and what is not? His answer, which he advances very modestly, is this:

> . . . the element of prose is innocent and even salutary when it appears as—take your choice of three metaphors—a background on which the images are projected, or a frame in which they are shown, or a thread on which they are strung. In short, when it serves a *structural* purpose. Prose in a poem seems offensive to me when . . . the prosaisms are sharp, obvious, individual, and ranked coordinately with the images.

At first glance this looks plausible, and the critic has used the sanctified word *structural.*

11 F. W. Bateson, in *English Poetry and the English Language,* discusses the impulse in contemporary poetry. Tennyson, he points out in connection with *The Sailor Boy,* dilutes his poetry by telling a story as well as writing a poem, and "a shorter poem would have spoilt his story." The claims of prose conquer the claims of poetry. Of the Victorians in general: "The dramatic and narrative framework of their poems, by circumventing the disconcerting plunges into *medias res* which are the essence of poetry, brings it down to a level of prose. The reader knows where he is; it serves the purpose of introduction and note." Such introduction and notes in the body of the poem itself are exactly what Mr. Pottle says is missing in Elliptical Poetry. Mr. Bateson agrees with Poe in accepting intensity as the criterion of the poetic effect, and in accepting the corollary that a poem should be short. But he, contradicting Poe, seems to admire precise and complicated incidental effects.

But at second glance we may begin to wonder what the sanctified word means to the critic. It means something rather mechanical—background, frame, thread. The structure is a showcase, say a jeweler's showcase, in which the little jewels of poetry are exhibited, the images. The showcase shouldn't be ornamental itself ("sharp, obvious, individual," Mr. Pottle says), for it would then distract us from the jewels; it should be chastely designed, and the jewels should repose on black velvet and not on flowered chintz. But Mr. Pottle doesn't ask what the relation among the bright jewels should be. Apparently, not only does the showcase bear no relation to the jewels, but the jewels bear no relation to each other. Each one is a shining little focus of heightened consciousness, or pure realization, existing for itself alone. Or perhaps he should desire that they be arranged in some mechanical pattern, such a pattern, perhaps, as would make it easier for the eye to travel from one little jewel to the next when the time comes to move on. Structure becomes here simply a device of salesmanship, a well arranged showcase.

It is all mechanical. And this means that Mr. Pottle, after all, is himself an exponent of pure poetry. He locates the poetry simply in the images, the nodes of "pure realization." This means /245/ that what he calls the "element of prose" includes definition of situation, movement of narrative, logical transition, factual description, generalization, ideas. Such things, for him, do not participate in the poetic effect of the poem; in fact, they work against the poetic effect, and so, though necessary as a frame, should be kept from being "sharp, obvious, individual."[12]

12 Several other difficulties concerning Mr. Pottle's statement may suggest themselves. First, since he seems to infer that the poetic essence resides in the image, what view would he take of meter and rhythm? His statement, strictly construed, would mean that these factors do not participate in the poetic effect, but are simply part of the frame. Second, what view of dramatic poetry is implied? It seems again that a strict interpretation would mean that the story and the images bear no essential relation to each other, that the story is simply part of the frame. That is, the story, characters, rhythms, and ideas, are on one level and the images, in which the poetry inheres, are on another. But Miss Spurgeon, Mr. Knight, and other critics have given us some reason for holding that the images do bear some relation to the business of the

I have referred to *The Idiom of Poetry*, first, because it is such an admirable and provocative book, sane, lucid, generous-spirited, and second, because, to my mind, it illustrates the insidiousness with which a doctrine of pure poetry can penetrate into the theory of a critic who is suspicious of such a doctrine. Furthermore, I have felt that Mr. Pottle's analysis might help me to define the common denominator of the various doctrines of pure poetry.

That common denominator seems to be the belief that poetry is an essence that is to be located at some particular place in a poem, or in some particular element. The exponent of pure poetry persuades himself that he has determined the particular something in which the poetry inheres, and then proceeds to decree that poems shall be composed, as nearly as possible, of that element and of nothing else. If we add up the things excluded by various critics and practitioners, we get a list about like this:

1. ideas, truths, generalizations, "meaning"
2. precise, complicated, "intellectual" images
3. unbeautiful, disagreeable, or neutral materials
4. situation, narrative, logical transition
5. realistic details, exact descriptions, realism in general
6. shifts in tone or mood /246/
7. irony
8. metrical variation, dramatic adaptations of rhythm, cacophony, etc.
9. meter itself
10. subjective and personal elements

No one theory of pure poetry excludes all of these items, and, as a matter of fact, the items listed are not on the same level of importance. Nor do the items always bear the same interpretation. For example, if one item seems to be central to discussions of pure poetry, it is the first: "ideas," it is said, "are not involved in the poetic effect, and may even be inimical to it." But this view can be interpreted in a variety of ways. If it is interpreted as simply meaning that the paraphrase of a poem is not equivalent to the poem, that the poetic gist is not to be defined as the statement embodied in the poem with the sugar-coating as bait, then the view can be held by opponents as well as exponents of any theory of pure poetry. We might scale down from this interpretation to the other extreme interpretation that the poem should merely give the sharp image in isolation. But there are many complicated and confused variations possible between the two extremes. There is, for example, the interpretation that "ideas," though they are not involved in the poetic effect, must appear in poems to provide, as Mr. Pottle's prosaisms do, a kind of frame, or thread, for the poetry—a spine to support the poetic flesh or a Christmas tree on which the baubles of poetry are hung.[13] T. S. Eliot has said something of this sort:

> The chief use of the "meaning" of a poem, in the ordinary sense, may be (for here again I am speaking of some kinds of poetry and not all) to satisfy one habit of the reader, to keep his mind diverted and quiet, while the poem does its work upon him: much as the imaginary burglar is always provided with a bit of nice meat for the house-dog. /247/

Here, it would seem, Mr. Eliot has simply inverted the old sugar-coated pill theory: the idea becomes the sugar-coating and the "poetry" becomes the medicine. This seems to say that the idea in a poem does not participate in the poetic effect, and seems to commit Mr. Eliot to a theory of pure poetry. But to do justice to the quotation, we should first observe that the parenthesis indicates that the writer is referring to some sort of provisional and superficial distinction and not to a fundamental one, and second observe that the passage is out of its context. In the context, Mr. Eliot goes on to say that some poets "become impatient of this 'meaning' [explicit statement of ideas in logical order][14] which seems superfluous, and perceive possibilities of intensity through its elimination." This may

other items. In fact, all of the items, as M. Maritain has said, "feelings, ideas, representations, are for the artist merely materials and means, still symbols." That is, they are all elements in a single expressive structure.

13 Such an interpretation seems to find a parallel in E. M. Forster's treatment of plot in fiction. Plot in his theory becomes a mere spine and does not really participate, except in a narrow, formal sense, in the fictional effect. By his inversion of the Aristotelian principle, the plot becomes merely a necessary evil.

14 [Mr. Warren's brackets.]

mean either of two things. It may mean that ideas do not participate in the poetic effect, or it may mean, though they do participate in the poetic effect, they need not appear in the poem in an explicit and argued form. And this second reading would scarcely be a doctrine of pure poetry at all, for it would involve poetic casuistry and not poetic principle.

We might, however, illustrate the second interpretation by glancing at Marvell's "Horatian Ode" on Cromwell. Marvell does not give us narrative; he does not give us an account of the issues behind the Civil War; he does not state the two competing ideas which are dramatized in the poem, the idea of "sanction" and the idea of "efficiency." But the effect of the poem does involve these two factors; the special reserved, scarcely resolved, irony, which is realized in the historical situation, is an irony derived from unstated materials and ideas. It is, to use Mr. Pottle's term again, a pure poem in so far as it is elliptical in method, but it is anything but a pure poem if by purity we mean the exclusion of idea from participation in the poetic effect. And Mr. Eliot's own practice implies that he believes that ideas do participate in the poetic effect. Otherwise, why did he put the clues to his ideas in the notes at the end of "The Waste Land" after so carefully excluding any explicit statement of them from the body of the /248/ poem? If he is regarding those ideas as mere bait—the "bit of nice meat for the house-dog"—he has put the ideas in a peculiar place, in the back of the book—like giving the dog the meat on the way out of the house with the swag or giving the mouse the cheese after he is in the trap. All this would lead one to the speculation that Marvell and Mr. Eliot have purged away statement of ideas from their poems, not because they wanted the ideas to participate less in the poetry, but because they wanted them to participate more fully, intensely, and immediately. This impulse, then, would account for the characteristic types of image, types in which precision, complication, and complicated intellectual relation to the theme are exploited; in other words, they are trying—whatever may be their final success—to carry the movement of mind to the center of the process. On these grounds they are the exact opposite of poets who, presumably on grounds of purity, exclude the movement of mind from the center of the poetic process—from the internal structure of the poem—but pay their respect to it as a kind of footnote, or gloss, or application coming at the end. Marvell and Eliot, by their cutting away of frame, are trying to emphasize the participation of ideas in the poetic process. Then Elliptical Poetry is not, as Mr. Pottle says it is, a pure poetry at all if we regard intention; the elliptical poet is elliptical for purposes of inclusion, not exclusion.

But waiving the question of Elliptical Poetry, no one of the other theories does—or could—exclude all the items on the list above. And that fact may instruct us. If all of these items were excluded, we might not have any poem at all. For instance, we know how some critics have pointed out that even in the strictest imagist poetry idea creeps in—when the image leaves its natural habitat and enters a poem it begins to "mean" something. The attempt to read ideas out of the poetic party violates the unity of our being and the unity of our experience. "For this reason," as Santayana puts it, "philosophy, when a poet is not mindless, enters inevitably into his poetry, since it has entered into his life; or /249/ rather, the detail of things and the detail of ideas pass equally into his verse, when both alike lie in the path that has led him to his ideal. To object to theory in poetry would be like objecting to words there; for words, too, are symbols without the sensuous character of the things they stand for; and yet it is only by the net of new connections which words throw over things, in recalling them, that poetry arises at all. Poetry is an attenuation, a rehandling, an echo of crude experience; it is itself a theoretic vision of things at arm's length." Does this not lead us to the conclusion that poetry does not inhere in any particular element but depends upon the set of relationships, the structure, which we call the poem?

Then the question arises: what elements cannot be used in such a structure? I should answer that nothing that is available in human experience is to be legislated out of poetry. This does not mean that anything can be used in *any* poem, or that some materials or elements may not prove more recalcitrant than others, or that it might not be easy to have too much of some things. But it does mean that, granted certain contexts, any sort of material, a chemical formula for instance, might appear functionally in a poem. It also may mean that, other things being equal, the greatness of a poet depends upon the extent of the area of experience which he can master poetically.

Can we make any generalizations about the nature of the poetic structure? First, it involves resistances, at various levels. There is the tension between the rhythm of the poem and the rhythm of speech (a tension which is very low at the extreme of free verse and at the extreme of verse such as that of "Ulalume," which verges toward a walloping doggerel); between the formality of the rhythm and the informality of the language; between the particular and the general, the concrete and the abstract; between the elements of even the simplest metaphor; between the beautiful and the ugly; between ideas (as in Marvell's poem); between the elements involved in irony (as in "Bells for John Whiteside's Daughter" or "Rose Aylmer"); between prosaisms and poeticisms /250/ (as in "Western Wind"). This list is not intended to be exhaustive; it is intended to be merely suggestive. But it may be taken to imply that the poet is like the jiujitsu expert; he wins by utilizing the resistance of his opponent—the materials of the poem. In other words, a poem, to be good, must earn itself. It is a motion toward a point of rest, but if it is not a resisted motion, it is motion of no consequence. For example, a poem which depends upon stock materials and stock responses is simply a toboggan slide, or a fall through space. And the good poem must, in some way, involve the resistances; it must carry something of the context of its own creation; it must come to terms with Mercutio. This is another way of saying that a good poem involves the participation of the reader; it must, as Coleridge puts it, make the reader into "an active creative being." Perhaps we can see this most readily in the case of tragedy: the definition of good or evil is not a "given" in tragedy, it is something to be earned in the process, and even the tragic villain must be "loved." We must kill him, as Brutus killed Caesar, not as butchers but as sacrificers. And all of this adds up to the fact that the struc-

ture is a dramatic structure, a movement through action toward rest, through complication toward simplicity of effect.

In the foregoing discussion, I have deliberately omitted reference to another type of pure poetry, a type which, in the context of the present war, may well become dominant. Perhaps the most sensible description of this type can be found in an essay by Herbert Muller:

> If it is not the primary business of the poet to be eloquent about these matters [faith and ideals],[15] it still does not follow that he has more dignity or wisdom than those who are, or that he should have more sophistication. At any rate the fact is that almost all poets of the past did freely make large, simple statements, and not in their prosy or lax moments.

Mr. Muller then goes on to illustrate by quoting three famous large, simple statements: /251/

> In la sua voluntade e nostra pace
> [In His will is our peace]

and

> We are such stuff
> As dreams are made on; and our little lives
> Are rounded with a sleep.

and

> The mind is its own place, and in itself
> Can make a heaven of hell, a hell of heaven.

Mr. Muller is here attacking the critical emphasis on ironic tension in poetry. His attack really involves two lines of argument. First, the poet is not wiser than the statesman, philosopher, or saint, people who are eloquent about faith and ideals and who say what they mean, without benefit of irony. This Platonic (or pseudo-Platonic) line of argument is, I think, off the point in the present context. Second, the poets of the past have made large, simple affirmations, have said what they meant. This line of argument is very much on the point.

Poets *have* tried very hard, for thousands of years, to say what they mean. But they have not only tried to say what they mean, they have tried to prove what they mean. The saint proves his vision by stepping cheerfully into the fires. The poet, somewhat less spec-

15 [Mr. Warren's brackets.]

tacularly, proves his vision by submitting it to the fires of irony—to the drama of his structure—in the hope that the first will refine it. In other words, the poet wishes to indicate that his vision has been earned, that it can survive reference to the complexities and contradictions of experience. And irony is one such device of reference.

In this connection let us look at the first of Mr. Muller's exhibits. The famous line occurs in Canto III of the *Paradiso*. It is spoken by Piccarda Donati, in answer to Dante's question as to why she does not desire to rise higher than her present sphere, the sphere of the moon. But it expresses, in unequivocal terms, a central theme of the *Commedia,* as of Christian experience. On /252/ the one hand, it may be a pious truism, fit for sampler work, and on the other hand, it may be a burning conviction, tested and earned. Dante, in his poem, sets out to show how it has been earned and tested. One set of ironic tensions, for instance, which centers about this theme concerns the opposition between the notion of human justice and the notion of divine justice. The story of Paolo and Francesca is so warm, appealing, and pathetic in its human terms and their punishment so savage and unrelenting, so incommensurable, it seems, with the fault, that Dante, torn by the conflict, falls down as a dead body falls. Or Farinata, the enemy of Dante's house, is presented by the poet in terms of his human grandeur, which now, in Hell, is transmuted into a superhuman grandeur,

> com' avesse l'inferno in gran dispitto.
> [as though he had hell in great scorn.]

Ulysses remains a hero, a hero who should draw special applause from Dante, who defined the temporal end of man as the conquest of knowledge. But Ulysses is damned, as the great Brutus is damned, who hangs from the jaws of the fiend in the lowest pit of traitors. So divine justice is set over against human pathos, human dignity, human grandeur, human intellect, human justice. And we recall how Virgil, more than once, reminds Dante that he must not apply human standards to the sights he sees. It is this long conflict, which appears in many forms, this ironic tension, which finally gives body to the simple elo-

quence of the line in question; the statement is meaningful, not for what it says, but for what has gone before. It is earned. It has been earned by the entire poem.

I do not want to misrepresent Mr. Muller. He does follow his quotations by the sentence: "If they are properly qualified in the work as a whole, they may still be taken straight, they *are* [he italicizes the word][16] taken so in recollection as in their immediate impact." But can this line be taken so in recollection, and was it taken so in its "immediate impact"? And if one does take it so, /253/ is he not violating, very definitely, the poet's meaning, for the poet means the *poem,* he doesn't mean the line.

It would be interesting to try to develop the contexts of the other passages which Mr. Muller quotes. But in any case, he was simply trying, in his essay, to guard against what he considered to be, rightly or wrongly, a too narrow description of poetry; he was not trying to legislate all poetry into the type of simple eloquence, the unqualified statement of "faith and ideas." But we have already witnessed certain, probably preliminary, attempts to legislate literature into becoming a simple, unqualified, "pure" statement of faith and ideal. We have seen the writers of the 1920's called the "irresponsibles." We have seen writers such as Proust, Eliot, Dreiser, and Faulkner, called writers of the "death drive." Why are these writers condemned? Because they have tried, within the limits of their gifts, to remain faithful to the complexities of the problems with which they were dealing, because they refused to take the easy statement as solution, because they tried to define the context in which, and the terms by which, faith and ideals could be earned. But this method will scarcely satisfy the mind which is hot for certainties; to that mind it will seem merely an index to lukewarmness, indecision, disunity, treason. The new theory of purity would purge out all complexities and all ironies and all self-criticism. And this theory will forget that the hand-me-down faith, the hand-me-down ideals, no matter what the professed content, is in the end not only meaningless but vicious. It is vicious because, as parody, it is the enemy of all faith. /254/

16 [Mr. Warren's brackets.]

T. S. ELIOT
"The Social Function of Poetry"

[T. S. Eliot (1888–   ), Nobel prize-winning poet and distinguished critic, was born in St. Louis, and educated at Harvard, the Sorbonne, and Oxford. He took up residence in England in 1915 and in 1927 became a British subject. He is the celebrated author of such poetry as *Prufrock* (1917), *The Waste Land* (1922), and *Four Quartets* (1943) and of such poetic drama as *Murder in the Cathedral* (1935) and *The Cocktail Party* (1950). Through his poetry, his editorship of *The Egoist* (1917-19) and *The Criterion* (1922-39), and by numerous critical essays, he has exercised a profound influence on modern literary opinion. The following selection was first delivered in 1943 as an address; in its present form it is taken from *On Poetry and Poets* (New York, 1957).]

The title of this essay is so likely to suggest different things to different people, that I may be excused for explaining first what I do not mean by it before going on to try to explain what I do mean. When we speak of the "function" of anything we are likely to be thinking of what that thing *ought* to do rather than of what it does do or has done. That is an important distinction, because I do not intend to talk about what I think poetry *ought* to do. People who tell us what poetry ought to do, especially if they are poets themselves, usually have in mind the particular kind of poetry that they would like to write. It is always possible, of course, that poetry may have a different task in the future from what it has had in the past; but even if that is so, it is worth while to decide first what function it has had in the past, both at one time or another in one language or another, and universally. I could easily write about what I do with poetry myself, or what I should like to do, and then try to persuade you that this is exactly what all good poets have tried to do, or ought to have done, in the past—only they have not succeeded completely, but perhaps that is not their fault. But it seems to me probable that if poetry—and I mean *all* great poetry—has had no social function in the past, it is not likely to have any in the future.

When I say *all* great poetry I mean to avoid another way in /3/ which I might treat the subject. One might take up the various kinds of poetry, one after another, and discuss the social function of each kind in turn without reaching the general question of what is the function of poetry as poetry. I want to distinguish between the general and particular functions, so that we shall know what we are not talking about. Poetry may have a deliberate, conscious social purpose. In its more primitive forms this purpose is often quite clear. There are, for example, early runes and chants, some of which had very practical magical purposes—to avert the evil eye, to cure some disease, or to propitiate some demon. Poetry is early used in religious ritual, and when we sing a hymn we are still using poetry for a particular social purpose. The early forms of epic and saga may have transmitted what was held to be history before surviving for communal entertainment only; and before the use of written language a regular verse form must have been extremely helpful to the memory—and the memory of primitive bards, story-tellers and scholars must have been prodigious. In more advanced societies, such as that of ancient Greece, the recognized social functions of poetry are also very conspicuous. The Greek drama develops out of religious rites, and remains a formal public ceremony associated with traditional religious celebrations; the pindaric ode develops in relation to a particular social occasion. Certainly, these definite uses of poetry gave poetry a framework which made possible the attainment of perfection in particular kinds.

In more modern poetry some of these forms remain, such as that of the religious hymn which I have mentioned. The meaning of the term *didactic* poetry has undergone some change. *Didactic* may mean "conveying information", or it may mean "giving moral instruction", or it may mean something which comprehends both. Virgil's *Georgics*, for instance, are very beautiful poetry, and contain some very sound information about good farming. But it would seem impossible, at the present day, to write an up-to-date book about farming which /4/ should also be fine poetry: for one thing the subject itself has become much more complicated and scientific; and for another, it can be handled more readily in prose. Nor should we, as the Romans did, write astronomical and cosmological treatises in verse. The poem, the ostensible aim of which is to convey information, has been superseded by prose. Didactic poetry has gradually become limited to poetry of moral exhortation, or poetry which aims to *persuade* the reader to the author's point of view about something. It therefore includes a great deal of what can be called *satire,* though satire overlaps with burlesque and parody, the purpose of which is primarily to cause mirth. Some of Dryden's poems, in the seventeenth century, are satires in the sense that they aim to ridicule the objects against which they are directed, and also didactic in the aim to persuade the reader to a particular political or religious point of view; and in doing this they also make use of the allegorical method of disguising reality as fiction: *The Hind and the Panther,* which aims to persuade the reader that right was on the side of the Church of Rome against the Church of England, is his most remarkable poem in this kind. In the nineteenth century a good deal of the poetry of Shelley is inspired by a zeal for social and political reforms.

As for *dramatic* poetry, that has a social function of a kind now peculiar to itself. For whereas most poetry to-day is written to be read in solitude, or to be read aloud in a small company, dramatic verse alone has as its function the making an immediate, collective impression upon a large number of people gathered together to look at an imaginary episode acted upon a stage. Dramatic poetry is different from any other, but as its special laws are those of the drama its function is merged into that of the drama in general, and I am not here concerned with the special social function of the drama.

As for the special function of philosophical poetry, that would involve an analysis and an historical account of some length. I have, I think, already mentioned enough kinds of /5/ poetry to make clear that the special function of each is related to some other function: of dramatic poetry to drama, of didactic poetry of information to the function of its subject-matter, of didactic poetry of philosophy or religion or politics or morals to the function of these subjects. We might consider the function of any of these kinds of poetry and still leave untouched the question of the function of *poetry*. For all these things can be dealt with in prose.

But before proceeding I want to dismiss one objection that may be raised. People sometimes are suspicious of any poetry that has a particular purpose: poetry in which the poet is advocating social, moral, political or religious views. And they are much more inclined to say that it isn't poetry when they dislike the particular views; just as other people often think that something is real poetry because it happens to express a point of view which they like. I should say that the question of whether the poet is using his poetry to advocate or attack a social attitude does not matter. Bad verse may have a transient vogue when the poet is reflecting a popular attitude of the moment; but real poetry survives not only a change of popular opinion but the complete extinction of interest in the issues with which the poet was passionately concerned. Lucretius' poem remains a great poem, though his notions of physics and astronomy are discredited; Dryden's, though the political quarrels of the seventeenth century no longer concern us; just as a great poem of the past may still give great pleasure, though its subject-matter is one which we should now treat in prose.

Now if we are to find the essential social function of poetry we must look first at its more obvious functions, those which it must perform if it is to perform any. The first, I think, that we can be sure about is that poetry has to give pleasure. If you ask what kind of pleasure then I can only answer, the kind of pleasure that poetry gives: simply because any other answer would take us far afield into aesthetics, and the general question of the nature of art. /6/

I suppose it will be agreed that every good poet, whether he be a great poet or not, has something to give us besides pleasure: for if it were only pleasure, the pleasure itself could not be of the highest kind. Beyond any specific intention which poetry may have, such as I have already instanced in the various kinds of poetry, there is always the communication of some new experience, or some fresh understanding of the familiar, or the expression of something we have experienced but have no words for, which enlarges our consciousness or refines our sensibility. But it is not with such individual benefit from poetry, any more than it is with the quality of individual pleasure, that this paper is concerned. We all understand, I think, both the kind of pleasure which poetry can give, and the kind of difference, beyond the pleasure, which it makes to our lives. Without producing these two effects it simply is not poetry. We may acknowledge this, but at the same time overlook something which it does for us collectively, as a society. And I mean that in the widest sense. For I think it is important that every people should have its own poetry, not simply for those who enjoy poetry—such people could always learn other languages and enjoy their poetry—but because it actually makes a difference to the society as a whole, and that means to people who do not enjoy poetry. I include even those who do not know the names of their own national poets. That is the real subject of this paper.

We observe that poetry differs from every other art in having a value for the people of the poet's race and language, which it can have for no other. It is true that even music and painting have a local and racial character: but certainly the difficulties of appreciation in these arts, for a foreigner, are much less. It is true on the other hand that prose writings have significance in their own language which is lost in translation; but we all feel that we lose much less in reading a novel in translation than in reading a poem; and in a translation of some kinds of scientific work the loss may be virtually nil. That /7/ poetry is much more local than prose can be seen in the history of European languages. Through the Middle Ages to within a few hundred years ago Latin remained the language for philosophy, theology, and science. The impulse towards the literary use of the languages of the peoples began with poetry. And this appears perfectly natural when we realize that poetry has primarily to do with the expression of feeling and emotion; and that feeling and emotion are particular, whereas thought is general. It is easier to think in a foreign language than it is to feel in it. Therefore no art is more stubbornly national than poetry. A people may have its language taken away from it, suppressed, and another language compelled upon the schools; but unless you teach that people to *feel* in a new language, you have not eradicated the old one, and it will reappear in poetry, which is the vehicle of feeling. I have just said "feel in a new language", and I mean something more than merely "express their feelings in a new language". A thought expressed in a different language may be practically the same thought, but a feeling or emotion expressed in a different language is not the same feeling or emotion. One of the reasons for learning at least one foreign language well is that we acquire a kind of supplementary personality; one of the reasons for not acquiring a new language *instead* of our own is that most of us do not want to become a different person. A superior language can seldom be exterminated except by the extermination of the people who speak it. When one language supersedes another it is usually because that language has advantages which commend it, and which offer not merely a difference but a wider and more refined range, not only for thinking but for feeling, than the more primitive language.

Emotion and feeling, then, are best expressed in the common language of the people —that is, in the language common to all classes: the structure, the rhythm, the sound, the idiom of a language, express the personality of the people /8/ which speaks it. When I say that it is poetry rather than prose that is concerned with the expression of emotion and feeling, I do not mean that poetry need have no intellectual content or meaning, or that great poetry does not contain more of such meaning than lesser poetry. But to develop this investigation would take me away from my immediate purpose. I will take it as agreed that people find the most conscious expression of their deepest feelings in the poetry of their own language rather than in any other art or in the poetry of other languages. This does not mean, of course, that true poetry is limited to feelings which everyone can recognize and understand; we must not limit poetry to *popular* poetry. It is enough that in a homogeneous people the feelings of the most refined and complex have something in common with those of the most crude and simple, which they have not in common with those of people of their own level speaking another language. And, when a civilization is healthy, the great poet will have something to say to his fellow countrymen at every level of education.

We may say that the duty of the poet, as poet, is only indirectly to his people: his direct duty is to his *language,* first to preserve, and second to extend and improve. In expressing what other people feel he is also changing the feeling by making it more conscious; he is making people more aware of what they feel already, and therefore teaching them something about themselves. But he is not merely a more conscious person than the others; he is also individually different from other people, and from other poets too, and can make his readers share consciously in new feelings which they had not experienced before. That is the difference between the writer who is merely eccentric or mad and the genuine poet. The former may have feelings which are unique but which cannot be shared, and are therefore useless; the latter discovers new variations of sensibility which can be appropriated by others. And in ex- /9/ pressing them he is developing and enriching the language which he speaks.

I have said quite enough about the impalpable differences of feeling between one people and another, differences which are affirmed in, and developed by, their different languages. But people do not only experience the world differently in different places, they experience it differently at different times. In fact, our sensibility is constantly changing, as the world about us changes: ours is not the same as that of the Chinese or the Hindu, but also it is not the same as that of our ancestors several hundreds years ago. It is not the same as that of our fathers; and finally, we ourselves are not quite the same persons that we were a year ago. This is obvious; but

what is not so obvious is that this is the reason why we cannot afford to *stop* writing poetry. Most educated people take a certain pride in the great authors of their language, though they may never read them, just as they are proud of any other distinction of their country: a few authors even become celebrated enough to be mentioned occasionally in political speeches. But most people do not realize that this is not enough; that unless they go on producing great authors, and especially great poets, their language will deteriorate, their culture will deteriorate and perhaps become absorbed in a stronger one.

One point is, of course, that if we have no living literature we shall become more and more alienated from the literature of the past; unless we keep up continuity, our literature of the past will become more and more remote from us until it is as strange to us as the literature of a foreign people. For our language goes on changing; our way of life changes, under the pressure of material changes in our environment in all sorts of ways; and unless we have those few men who combine an exceptional sensibility with an exceptional power over words, our own ability, not merely to express, but even to feel any but the crudest emotions, will degenerate.

It matters little whether a poet had a large audience in his /10/ own time. What matters is that there should always be at least a small audience for him in every generation. Yet what I have just said suggests that his importance is for his own time, or that dead poets cease to be of any use to us unless we have living poets as well. I would even press my first point and say that if a poet gets a large audience very quickly, that is a rather suspicious circumstance: for it leads us to fear that he is not really doing anything new, that he is only giving people what they are already used to, and therefore what they have already had from the poets of the previous generation. But that a poet should have the right, small audience in his own time *is* important. There should always be a small vanguard of people, appreciative of poetry, who are independent and somewhat in advance of their time or ready to assimilate novelty more quickly. The development of culture does not mean bringing everybody up to the front, which amounts to no more than making everyone keep step: it means the maintenance of such an *élite,* with the main, and more passive body of readers not lagging more than a generation or so behind. The changes and developments of sensibility which appear first in a few will work themselves into the language gradually, through their influence on other, and more readily popular authors; and by the time they have become well established, a new advance will be called for. It is, moreover, through the living authors that the dead remain alive. A poet like Shakespeare has influenced the English language very deeply, not only by his influence on his immediate successors. For the greatest poets have aspects which do not come to light at once; and by exercising a direct influence on other poets centuries later, they continue to affect the living language. Indeed, if an English poet is to learn how to use words in our time, he must devote close study to those who have used them best in *their* time; to those who, in their own day, have made the language new.

So far I have only suggested the final point to which I think the influence of poetry may be said to extend; and that can be /11/ put best by the assertion that, in the long run, it makes a difference to the speech, to the sensibility, to the lives of all the members of a society, to all the members of the community, to the whole people, whether they read and enjoy poetry or not: even, in fact, whether they know the names of their greatest poets or not. The influence of poetry, at the furthest periphery, is of course very diffused, very indirect, and very difficult to prove. It is like following the course of a bird or an aeroplane in a clear sky: if you have seen it when it was quite near, and kept your eye on it as it flew farther and farther away, you can still see it at a great distance, a distance at which the eye of another person, to whom you try to point it out, will be unable to find it. So, if you follow the influence of poetry, through those readers who are most affected by it, to those people who never read at all, you will find it present everywhere. At least you will find it if the national culture is living and healthy, for in a healthy society there is a continuous reciprocal influence and interaction of each part upon the others. And this is

what I mean by the social function of poetry in its largest sense: that it does, in proportion to its excellence and vigour, affect the speech and the sensibility of the whole nation.

You must not imagine me to be saying that the language which we speak is determined exclusively by our poets. The structure of culture is much more complex than that. Indeed it will equally be true that the quality of our poetry is dependent upon the way in which the people use their language: for a poet must take as his material his own language as it is actually spoken around him. If it is improving, he will profit; if it is deteriorating, he must make the best of it. Poetry can to some extent preserve, and even restore, the beauty of a language; it can and should also help it to develop, to be just as subtle and precise in the more complicated conditions and for the changing purposes of modern life, as it was in and for a simpler age. But poetry, like every other single element in that /12/ mysterious social personality which we call our "culture", must be dependent upon a great many circumstances which are beyond its control.

This leads me to a few after-thoughts of a more general nature. My emphasis to this point has been upon the national and local function of poetry; and this must be qualified. I do not wish to leave the impression that the function of poetry is to divide people from people, for I do not believe that the cultures of the several of Europe can flourish in isolation from each other. There have been, no doubt, in the past, high civilizations producing great art, thought and literature, which have developed in isolation. Of that I cannot speak with assurance, for some of them may not have been so isolated as at first appears. But in the history of Europe this has not been so. Even Ancient Greece owed much to Egypt, and something to the Asiatic frontiers; and in the relations of the Greek states to each other, with their different dialects and different manners, we may find a reciprocal influence and stimulus analogous to that of the countries of Europe upon each other. But the history of European literature will not show that any has been independent of the others; rather that there has been a constant give and take, and that each has in turn, from time to time, been revitalized by stimulation from outside. A general *autarky* in culture simply will not work: the hope of perpetuating the culture of any country lies in communication with others. But if separation of cultures within the unity of Europe is a danger, so also would be a unification which led to uniformity. The variety is as essential as the unity. For instance, there is much to be said, for certain limited purposes, for a universal *lingua franca* such as Esperanto or Basic English. But supposing that all communication between nations was carried on in such an artificial language, how imperfect it would be! Or rather, it would be wholly adequate in some respects, and there would be a complete lack of communication in others. Poetry is a constant reminder of all the things that can only be said in /13/ one language, and are untranslatable. The *spiritual* communication between people and people cannot be carried on without the individuals who take the trouble to learn at least one foreign language as well as one can learn any language but one's own, and who consequently are able, to a greater or less degree, to *feel* in another language as well as in their own. And one's understanding of another people, in this way, needs to be supplemented by the understanding of those individuals among that people who have gone to the pains to learn one's own language.

Incidentally, the study of another people's poetry is peculiarly instructive. I have said that there are qualities of the poetry of every language, which only those to whom the language is native can understand. But there is another side to this too. I have sometimes found, in trying to read a language which I did not know very well, that I did not understand a piece of prose until I understood it according to the standards of the school teacher: that is, I had to be sure of the meaning of every word, grasp the grammar and syntax, and then I could think the passage out in English. But I have also found sometimes that a piece of poetry, which I could not translate, containing many words unfamiliar to me, and sentences which I could not construe, conveyed something immediate and vivid, which was unique, different from anything in English—something which I could

not put into words and yet felt that I understood. And on learning that language better I found that this impression was not an illusion, not something which I had imagined to be in the poetry, but something that was really there. So in poetry you can, now and then, penetrate into another country, so to speak, before your passport has been issued or your ticket taken.

The whole question of the relation of countries of different language but related culture, within the ambit of Europe, is therefore one into which we are led, perhaps unexpectedly, by inquiring into the social function of poetry. I certainly do not /14/ intend to pass from this point into purely political questions; but I could wish that those who are concerned with political questions would more often cross the frontier into these which I have been considering. For these give the spiritual aspect of problems the material aspect of which is the concern of politics. On my side of the line one is concerned with living things which have their own laws of growth, which are not always reasonable, but must just be accepted by the reason: things which cannot be neatly planned and put into order any more than the winds and the rains and the seasons can be disciplined.

If, finally, I am right in believing that poetry has a "social function" for the whole of the people of the poet's language, whether they are aware of his existence or not, it follows that it matters to each people of Europe that the others should continue to have poetry. I cannot read Norwegian poetry, but if I were told that no more poetry was being written in the Norwegian language I should feel an alarm which would be much more than generous sympathy. I should regard it as a spot of malady which was likely to spread over the whole Continent; the beginning of a decline which would mean that people everywhere would cease to be able to express, and consequently be able to feel, the emotions of civilized beings. This of course might happen. Much has been said everywhere about the decline of religious belief; not so much notice has been taken of the decline of religious sensibility. The trouble of the modern age is not merely the inability to believe certain things about God and man which our fore-fathers believed, but the inability to *feel* towards God and man as they did. A belief in which you no longer believe is something which to some extent you can still under-stand; but when religious feeling disappears, the words in which men have struggled to ex-press it become meaningless. It is true that re-ligious feeling varies naturally from country to country, and from age to age, just as poetic feeling does; the feeling varies, even when the belief, /15/ the doctrine, remains the same. But this is a condition of human life, and what I am apprehensive of is death. It is equally possible that the feeling for poetry, and the feelings which are the material of po-etry, may disappear everywhere: which might perhaps help to facilitate that unification of the world which some people consider de-sirable for its own sake. /16/

STEPHEN SPENDER
"The Making of a Poem"

[Stephen Spender (1909–), poet and critic, was born in London and educated at Oxford, where he was the friend of W. H. Auden, C. Day Lewis, Christopher Isherwood, and Louis MacNeice, later associated in the public mind as leaders of a new school of English poetry. Like others of his generation Spender was deeply interested in social causes, took an active part in left-wing political movements, and proclaimed himself a Communist, a cause which he has since disavowed, publishing his disillusionment in *The God that Failed* (1950), a volume to which five other prominent figures also contributed. In addition to his poetry he has published fiction and criticism, has been an associate editor of *Horizon*, and has written a sensitive autobiography, *World Within World* (1951). The following essay is taken from the *Partisan Review*, XIII (Summer, 1946).]

APOLOGY

It would be inexcusable to discuss my own way of writing poetry unless I were able to relate this to a wider view of the problems which poets attempt to solve when they sit down at a desk or table to write, or walk around composing their poems in their heads. There is a danger of my appearing to put across my own experiences as the general rule, when every poet's way of going about his work and his experience of being a poet are different, and when my own poetry may not be good enough to lend my example any authority.

Yet the writing of poetry is an activity which makes certain demands of attention on the poet and which requires that he should have certain qualifications of ear, vision, imagination, memory and so on. He should be able to think in images; he should have as great a mastery of language as a painter has over his palette, even if the range of his language be very limited. All this means that, in ordinary society, a poet has to adapt himself, more or less consciously, to the demands of his vocation, and hence the peculiarities of poets and the condition of inspiration which many

people have said is near to madness. One poet's example is only his adaptation of his personality to the demands of poetry, but if it is clearly stated it may help us to understand other poets, and even something of poetry.

Today we lack very much a whole view of poetry, and have instead many one-sided views of certain aspects of poetry which have been advertised as the only aims which poets should attempt. Movements such as free verse, imagism, surrealism, expressionism, personalism and so on, tend to make people think that poetry is simply a matter of not writing in metre or rhyme, or of free association, or of thinking in images, or of a kind of drawing room madness (surrealism) which corresponds to drawing room communism. Here is a string of ideas: Night, dark, stars, immensity, blue, voluptuous, clinging, columns, clouds, moon, sickle, harvest, vast camp fire, hell. Is this poetry? A lot of strings of words almost as simple as this are set down on /294/ the backs of envelopes and posted off to editors or to poets by the vast army of amateurs who think that to be illogical is to be poetic, with that fond question. Thus I hope that this discussion of how poets work will imply a wider and completer view of poets.

CONCENTRATION

The problem of creative writing is essentially one of concentration, and the supposed eccentricities of poets are usually due to mechanical habits or rituals developed in order to concentrate. Concentration, of course, for the purpose of writing poetry, is different from the kind of concentration required for working out a sum. It is a focussing of the attention in a special way, so that the poet is aware of all the implications and possible developments of his idea, just as one might say that a plant was not concentrating on developing mechanically in one direction, but in many directions, towards the warmth and light with its leaves, and towards the water with its roots, all at the same time.

Schiller liked to have a smell of rotten apples, concealed beneath the lid of his desk, under his nose when he was composing poetry. Walter de la Mare has told me that he must smoke when writing. Auden drinks endless cups of tea. Coffee is my own addiction, besides smoking a great deal, which I hardly ever do except when I am writing. I notice also that as I attain a greater concentration, this tends to make me forget the taste of the cigarette in my mouth, and then I have a desire to smoke two or even three cigarettes at a time, in order that the sensation from the outside may penetrate through the wall of concentration which I have built round myself.

For goodness' sake, though, do not think that rotten apples or cigarettes or tea have anything to do with the quality of the work of a Schiller, a de la Mare, or an Auden. They are a part of a concentration which has already been attained rather than the causes of concentration. De la Mare once said to me that he thought the desire to smoke when writing poetry arose from a need, not of a stimulus, but to canalize a distracting leak of his attention away from his writing towards the distraction which is always present in one's environment. Concentration may be disturbed by someone whistling in the street or the ticking of a clock. There is always a slight tendency of the body to sabotage the attention of the mind by providing some distraction. If this need for distraction can be directed into one chan- /295/ nel—such as the odor of rotten apples or the taste of tobacco or tea—then other distractions outside oneself are put out of competition.

Another possible explanation is that the concentrated effort of writing poetry is a spiritual activity which makes one completely forget, for the time being, that one has a body. It is a disturbance of the balance of body and mind and for this reason one needs a kind of anchor of sensation with the physical world. Hence the craving for a scent or taste or even, sometimes, for sexual activity. Poets speak of the necessity of writing poetry rather than of a liking for doing it. It is spiritual compulsion, a straining of the mind to attain heights surrounded by abysses and it cannot be entirely happy, for in the most important sense, the only reward worth having is absolutely denied: for, however confident a poet may be, he is never quite sure that all his energy is not misdirected nor that what he is writing is great poetry. At the moment when art attains its highest attainment it reaches beyond its medium of words or paints or music, and the artist finds himself realizing that these instruments are inadequate to the spirit of what he is trying to say.

Different poets concentrate in different ways. In my own mind I make a sharp distinction between two types of concentration: one is immediate and complete, the other is plodding and only completed by stages. Some poets write immediately works which, when they are written, scarcely need revision. Others write their poems by stages, feeling their way from rough draft to rough draft, until finally, after many revisions, they have produced a result which may seem to have very little connection with their early sketches.

These two opposite processes are vividly illustrated in two examples drawn from music: Mozart and Beethoven. Mozart thought out symphonies, quartets, even scenes from operas, entirely in his head—often on a journey or perhaps while dealing with pressing problems —and then he transcribed them, in their completeness, onto paper. Beethoven wrote fragments of themes in note books which he kept beside him, working on and developing them over years. Often his first ideas were of a clumsiness which makes scholars marvel how he could, at the end, have developed from them such miraculous results.

Thus genius works in different ways to achieve its ends. But although the Mozartian type of genius is the more brilliant and dazzling, genius, unlike virtuosity, is judged by greatness of results, not by brilliance of performance. The result must be the fullest development in a created aesthetic form of an original moment of insight, and it /296/ does not matter whether genius devotes a lifetime to producing a small result if that result be immortal. The difference between two types of genius is that one type (the Mozartian) is able to plunge the greatest depths of his own experience by the tremendous effort of a moment, the other (the Beethovenian) must dig deeper and deeper into his consciousness, layer by layer. What counts in either case is the vision which sees and pursues and attains the end; the logic of the artistic purpose.

A poet may be divinely gifted with a lucid and intense and purposive intellect; he may be clumsy and slow; that does not matter, what matters is integrity of purpose and the ability to maintain the purpose without losing oneself. Myself, I am scarcely capable of immediate concentration in poetry. My mind is not clear, my will is weak, I suffer from an excess of ideas and a weak sense of form. For every poem that I begin to write, I think of at least ten which I do not write down at all. For every poem which I do write down, there are seven or eight which I never complete.

The method which I adopt therefore is to write down as many ideas as possible, in however rough a form, in note books (I have at least twenty of these, on a shelf beside my desk, going back over fifteen years). I then make use of some of the sketches and discard others.

The best way of explaining how I develop the rough ideas which I use, is to take an example. Here is a Notebook begun in 1944. About a hundred pages of it are covered with writing, and from this have emerged about six poems. Each idea, when it first occurs, is given a number. Sometimes the ideas do not get beyond one line. For example, No. 3 (never developed) is the one line:—

> *A language of flesh and roses.*

I shall return to this line in a few pages, when I speak of inspiration. For the moment, I turn to No. 13, because here is an idea which has been developed to its conclusion. The first sketch begins thus:—

a) *There are some days when the sea lies like a*
  harp
  Stretched flat beneath the cliffs. The waves
  Like wires burn with the sun's copper glow
  [all the murmuring blue
          every silent][1]
  Between whose spaces every image
  Of sky [field and] *hedge and field and boat*
  /297/
  Dwells like the huge face of the afternoon.
  [Lies]

[1][This and the following four bracketed phrases and words were introduced by Mr. Spender.]

When the heat grows tired, the afternoon
Out of the land may breathe a sigh
[Across these wires like a hand. They vibrate
With]
Which moves across those wires like a soft hand
[Then the vibration]
Between those spaces the vibration holds
Every bird-cry, dog's bark, man-shout
And creak of rollock from the land and sky
With all the music of the afternoon.

Obviously these lines are attempts to sketch out an idea which exists clearly enough on some level of the mind where it yet eludes the attempt to state it. At this stage, a poem is like a face which one seems to be able to visualize clearly in the eye of memory, but when one examines it mentally or tries to think it out, feature by feature, it seems to fade.

The idea of this poem is a vision of the sea. The faith of the poet is that if this vision is clearly stated it will be significant. The vision is of the sea stretched under a cliff. On top of the cliff there are fields, hedges, houses. Horses draw carts along lanes, dogs bark far inland, bells ring in the distance. The shore seems laden with hedges, roses, horses and men, all high above the sea, on a very fine summer day when the ocean seems to reflect and absorb the shore. Then the small strung-out glittering waves of the sea lying under the shore are like the strings of a harp which catch the sunlight. Between these strings lies the reflection of the shore. Butterflies are wafted out over the waves, which they mistake for the fields of the chalky landscape, searching them for flowers. On a day such as this, the land, reflected in the sea, appears to enter into the sea, as though it lies under it, like Atlantis. The wires of the harp are like a seen music fusing seascape and landscape.

Looking at this vision in another way, it obviously has symbolic value. The sea represents death and eternity, the land represents the brief life of the summer and of one human generation which passes into the sea of eternity. But let me here say at once that although the poet may be conscious of this aspect of his vision, it is exactly what /298/ he wants to avoid stating, or even being too concerned with. His job is to recreate his vision, and let it speak its moral for itself. The poet must distinguish clearly in his own mind between that which most definitely must be said and that which must not be said. The unsaid inner meaning is revealed in the music and the tonality of the poem, and the poet is conscious of it in his knowledge that a certain tone of voice, a certain rhythm, are necessary.

In the next twenty versions of the poem I felt my way towards the clarification of the seen picture, the music and the inner feeling. In the first version quoted above, there is the phrase in the second and third lines:—

> *The waves*
> *Like wires burn with the sun's copper glow.*

This phrase fuses the image of the sea with the idea of music, and it is therefore a key-phrase, because the theme of the poem is the fusion of the land with the sea. Here, then are several versions of these one and a quarter lines, in the order in which they were written:—

b) *The waves are wires*
   Burning as with the secret song of fires

c) *The day burns in the trembling wires*
   With a vast music golden in the eyes

d) *The day glows on its trembling wires*
   Singing a golden music in the eyes

e) *The day glows on its burning wires*
   Like waves of music golden to the eyes.

f) *Afternoon burns upon its wires*
   Lines of music dazzling the eyes

g) *Afternoon gilds its tingling wires*
   To a visual silent music of the eyes

In the final version, these two lines appear as in the following stanza:—

h) *There are some days the happy ocean lies*
   Like an unfingered harp, below the land.
   /299/

> *Afternoon gilds all the silent wires*
> *Into a burning music of the eyes.*

> *On mirroring paths between those fine-strung fires*
> *The shore, laden with roses, horses, spires,*
> *Wanders in water, imaged above ribbed sand.*

INSPIRATION

The hard work evinced in these examples, which are only a fraction of the work put into the whole poem, may cause the reader to wonder whether there is no such thing as inspiration, or whether it is merely Stephen Spender who is uninspired. The answer is that everything in poetry is work except inspiration, whether this work is achieved at one swift stroke, as Mozart wrote his music, or whether it is a slow process of evolution from stage to stage. Here again, I have to qualify the word "work," as I qualified the word "concentration": the work on a line of poetry may take the form of putting a version aside for a few days, weeks or years, and then taking it up again, when it may be found that the line has, in the interval of time, almost rewritten itself.

Inspiration is the beginning of a poem and it is also its final goal. It is the first idea which drops into the poet's mind and it is the final idea which he at last achieves in words. In between this start and this winning post there is the hard race, the sweat and toil.

Paul Valéry speaks of the *"une ligne donnée"* of a poem. One line is given to the poet by God or by nature, the rest he has to discover for himself.

My own experience of inspiration is certainly that of a line or a phrase or a word or sometimes something still vague, a dim cloud of an idea which I feel must be condensed into a shower of words. The peculiarity of the key word or line is that it does not merely attract, as, say, the word "braggadocio" attracts. It occurs in what seems to be an active, male, germinal form as though it were the centre of a statement requiring a beginning and an end, and as though it had an impulse in a certain direction. Here are examples:—

> *A language of flesh and roses*

This phrase (not very satisfactory in itself) brings to my mind a whole series of experiences and the idea of a poem which I shall perhaps write some years hence. I was standing in the corridor of a /300/ train passing through the Black Country. I saw a landscape of pits and pitheads, artificial mountains, jagged yellow wounds in the earth, everything transformed as though by the toil of an enormous animal or giant tearing up the earth in search of prey or treasure. Oddly enough, a stranger next to me in the corridor echoed my inmost thought. He said: "Everything there is man-made." At this moment the line flashed into my head:—

A language of flesh and roses.

The sequence of my thought was as follows: the industrial landscape which seems by now a routine and act of God which enslaves both employers and workers who serve and profit by it, is actually the expression of man's will. Men willed it to be so, and the pitheads, slag-heaps and the ghastly disregard of anything but the pursuit of wealth, are a symbol of modern man's mind. In other words, the world which we create—the world of slums and telegrams and newspapers—is a kind of language of our inner wishes and thoughts. Although this is so, it is obviously a language which has got outside our control. It is a con-fused language, an irresponsible senile gib-berish. This thought greatly distressed me, and I started thinking that if the phenomena created by humanity are really like words in a language, what kind of language do we really aspire to? All this sequence of thought flashed into my mind with the answer which came before the question: *A language of flesh and roses.*

I hope this example will give the reader some idea of what I mean by inspiration. Now the line, which I shall not repeat again, is a way of thinking imaginatively. If the line embodies some of the ideas which I have re-lated above, these ideas must be further made clear in other lines. That is the terrifying challenge of poetry. Can I think out the logic of images? How easy it is to explain here the poem that I would have liked to write! How difficult it would be to write it. For writing it would imply living my way through the imaged experience of all these ideas, which here are mere abstractions, and such an effort of imaginative experience requires a lifetime of patience and watching.

Here is an example of a cloudy form of thought germinated by the word *cross,* which is the key word of the poem which exists formlessly in my mind. Recently my wife had a son. On the first day that I visited her after the boy's birth, I went by bus to the hospital. Passing through the streets on the top of the bus, they all seemed very clean, and the thought occurred to me that everything was prepared for our /301/ child. Past genera-tions have toiled so that any child born today inherits, with his generation, cities, streets, organization, the most elaborate machinery for living. Everything has been provided for him by people dead long before he was born. Then, naturally enough, sadder thoughts colored this picture for me, and I reflected how he also inherited vast maladjustments, vast human wrongs. Then I thought of the child as like a pin-point of present existence, the moment incarnate, in whom the whole of the past, and all possible futures *cross.* This word *cross* somehow suggested the whole situation to me of a child born into the world and also of the form of a poem about his situation. When the word *cross* appeared in the poem, the idea of the past should give place to the idea of the future and it should be apparent that the *cross* in which present and future meet is the secret of an individual human existence. And here again, the un-spoken secret which lies beyond the poem, the moral significance of other meanings of the word "cross" begins to glow with its virtue that should never be said and yet should shine through every image in the poem.

This account of inspiration is probably weak beside the accounts that other poets might give. I am writing of my own ex-perience, and my own inspiration seems to me like the faintest flash of insight into the nature of reality beside that of other poets whom I can think of. However, it is possible that I describe here a kind of experience which, however slight it may be, is far truer to the real poetic experience than Aldous Huxley's account of how a young poet writes poetry in his novel *Time Must Have a Stop.* It is hard to imagine anything more self-con-scious and unpoetic than Mr. Huxley's ac-count.

MEMORY

If the art of concentrating in a particular way is the discipline necessary for poetry to reveal itself, memory exercised in a particular way is the natural gift of poetic genius. The poet, above all else, is a person who never forgets certain sense-impressions which he has experienced and which he can re-live again and again as though with all their original freshness.

All poets have this highly developed sensitive apparatus of memory, and they are usually aware of experiences which happened to them at the earliest age and which retain their pristine significance throughout life. The meeting of Dante and Beatrice when the poet was only nine years of age is the experience which became a symbol in Dante's mind around which the *Divine Comedy* crystallized. The /302/ experience of nature which forms the subject of Wordsworth's poetry was an extension of a childhood vision of "natural presences" which surrounded the boy Wordsworth. And his decision in later life to live in the Lake District was a decision to return to the scene of these childhood memories which were the most important experiences in his poetry. There is evidence for the importance of this kind of memory in all the creative arts, and the argument certainly applies to prose which is creative. Sir Osbert Sitwell has told me that his book *Before the Bombardment,* which contains an extremely civilized and satiric account of the social life of Scarborough before and during the last war, was based on his observations of life in that resort before he had reached the age of twelve.

It therefore is not surprising that although I have no memory for telephone numbers, addresses, faces and where I have put this morning's correspondence, I have a perfect memory for the sensation of certain experiences which are crystallized for me around certain associations. I could demonstrate this from my own life by the overwhelming nature of associations which, suddenly aroused, have carried me back so completely into the past, particularly into my childhood, that I have lost all sense of the present time and place. But the best proofs of this power of memory are found in the odd lines of poems written in note books fifteen years ago. A few fragments of unfinished poems enable me to enter immediately into the experiences from which they were derived, the circumstances in which they were written, and unwritten feelings in the poem that were projected but never put into words.

> *. . . Knowledge of a full sun*
> *That runs up his big sky, above*
> *The hill, then in those trees and throws*
> *His smiling on the turf.*

That is an incomplete idea of fifteen years ago, and I remember exactly a balcony of a house facing a road, and, on the other side of the road, pine trees, beyond which lay the sea. Every morning the sun sprang up, first of all above the horizon of the sea, then it climbed to the tops of the trees and shone on my window. And this memory connects with the sun that shines through my window in London now in spring and early summer. So that the memory is not exactly a memory. It is more like one prong upon which a whole calendar of similar experiences happening throughout years, collect. A memory once clearly stated ceases to be a memory, it becomes perpetually present, because /303/ every time we experience something which recalls it, the clear and lucid original experience imposes its formal beauty on the new experiences. It is thus no longer a memory but an experience lived through again and again.

Turning over these old note books my eye catches some lines, in a projected long poem, which immediately reshape themselves into the following short portrait of a woman's face:—

> *Her eyes are gleaming fish*
> *Caught in her nervous face, as if in a net.*
> *Her hair is wild and fair, haloing her cheeks*
> *Like a fantastic flare of Southern sun.*
> *There is madness in her cherishing her children.*
> *Sometimes, perhaps a single time in years,*
> *Her wandering fingers stoop to arrange some*
> *   flowers—*
> *Then in her hands her whole life stops and*
> *   weeps.*

It is perhaps true to say that memory is the faculty of poetry, because the imagination itself is an exercise of memory. There is nothing we imagine which we do not already know. And our ability to imagine is our ability to remember what we have already once experienced and to apply it to some different situation. Thus the greatest poets are those with memories so great that they extend beyond their strongest experiences to their minutest observations of people and things far outside their own self-centredness (the weakness of memory is its self-centredness: hence the narcissistic nature of most poetry).

Here I can detect my own greatest weakness. My memory is defective and self-centred. I lack the confidence in using it to create situations outside myself, although I believe that, in theory, there are very few situations in life which a poet should not be able to imagine, because it is a fact that most poets have experienced almost every situation in life. I do not mean by this that a poet who writes about a Polar Expedition has actually been to the North Pole. I mean, though, that he has been cold, hungry, etc., so that it is possible for him by remembering imaginatively his own felt experiences to know what it is like to explore the North Pole. That is where I fail. I cannot write about going to the North Pole.

FAITH

It is evident that a faith in their vocation, mystical in intensity, sustains poets. There are many illustrations from the lives of poets to /304/ show this, and Shakespeare's sonnets are full of expressions of his faith in the immortality of his lines.

From my experience I can clarify the nature of this faith. When I was nine, we went to the Lake District, and there my parents read me some of the poems of Wordsworth. My sense of the sacredness of the task of poetry began then, and I have always felt that a poet's was a sacred vocation, like a saint's. Since I was nine, I have wanted to be various things, for example, Prime Minister (when I was twelve). Like some other poets I am attracted by the life of power and the life of action, but I am still more repelled by them. Power involves forcing oneself upon the attention of historians by doing things and occupying offices which are, in themselves, important, so that what is truly powerful is not the soul of a so-called powerful and prominent man but the position which he fills and the things which he does. Similarly, the life of "action" which seems so very positive is, in fact, a selective, even a negative kind of life. A man of action does one thing or several

things because he does not do something else. Usually men who do very spectacular things fail completely to do the ordinary things which fill the lives of most normal people, and which would be far more heroic and spectacular perhaps, if they did not happen to be done by many people. Thus in practice the life of action has always seemed to me an act of cutting oneself off from life.

Although it is true that poets are vain and ambitious, their vanity and ambition is of the purest kind attainable in this world, for the saint renounces ambition. They are ambitious to be accepted for what they ultimately are as revealed by their inmost experiences, their finest perceptions, their deepest feelings, their uttermost sense of truth, in their poetry. They cannot cheat about these things, because the quality of their own being is revealed not in the noble sentiments which their poetry expresses, but in sensibility, control of language, rhythm and music, things which cannot be attained by a vote of confidence from an electorate, or by the office of Poet Laureate. Of course, work is tremendously important, but, in poetry, even the greatest labor can only serve to reveal the intrinsic qualities of soul of the poet as he really is.

Since there can be no cheating, the poet, like the saint, stands in all his works before the bar of a perpetual day of judgment. His vanity of course is pleased by success, though even success may contribute to his understanding that popularity does not confer on him /305/ the favorable judgment of all the ages which he seeks. For what does it mean to be praised by one's own age, which is soaked in crimes and stupidity, except perhaps that future ages, wise where we are foolish, will see him as a typical expression of this age's crimes and stupidity? Nor is lack of success a guarantee of great poetry, though there are some who pretend that it is. Nor can the critics, at any rate beyond a certain limited point of technical judgment, be trusted.

The poet's faith is therefore, firstly, a mystique of vocation, secondly, a faith in his own truth, combined with his own devotion to a task. There can really be no greater faith than the confidence that one is doing one's utmost to fulfill one's high vocation, and it is this that has inspired all the greatest poets. At the same time this faith is coupled with a deep humility because one knows that, ultimately, judgment does not rest with oneself. All one can do is to achieve nakedness, to be what one is with all one's faculties and perceptions, strengthened by all the skill which one can acquire, and then to stand before the judgment of time.

In my Notebooks, I find the following Prose Poem, which expresses these thoughts:

Bring me peace bring me power bring me assurance. Let me reach the bright day, the high chair, the plain desk, where my hand at last controls the words, where anxiety no longer undermines me. If I don't reach these I'm thrown to the wolves, I'm a restless animal wandering from place to place, from experience to experience.

Give me the humility and the judgment to live alone with the deep and rich satisfaction of my own creating: not to be thrown into doubt by a word of spite or disapproval.

In the last analysis don't mind whether your work is good or bad so long as it has the completeness, the enormity of the whole world which you love.

SONG

Inspiration and song are the irreducible final qualities of a poet which make his vocation different from all others. Inspiration is an experience in which a line or an idea is given to one, and perhaps also a state of mind in which one writes one's best poetry. Song is far more difficult to define. It is the music which a poem as yet unthought of will assume, the empty womb of poetry for ever in the poet's consciousness, waiting for the fertilizing seed. /306/

Sometimes, when I lie in a state of half-waking half-sleeping, I am conscious of a stream of words which seem to pass through my mind, without their having a meaning, but they have a sound, a sound of passion, or a sound recalling poetry that I know. Again sometimes when I am writing, the music of the words I am trying to shape takes me far beyond the words, I am aware of a rhythm, a dance, a fury, which is as yet empty of words.

In these observations, I have said little about headaches, midnight oil, pints of beer or of claret, love affairs, and so on, which are supposed to be stations on the journeys of poets through life. There is no doubt that writing poetry, when a poem appears to succeed, results in an intense physical excitement, a sense of release and ecstasy. On the other hand, I dread writing poetry, for, I suppose, the following reasons: a poem is a terrible journey, a painful effort of concentrating the imagination; words are an extremely difficult medium to use, and sometimes when one has spent days trying to say a thing clearly one finds that one has only said it dully; above all, the writing of a poem brings one face to face with one's own personality with all its familiar and clumsy limitations. In every phase of existence, one can exercise the orthodoxy of a conventional routine: one can be polite to one's friends, one can get through the day at the office, one can pose, one can draw attention to one's position in society, one is—in a word—dealing with men. In poetry, one is wrestling with a god.

Usually, when I have completed a poem, I think "this is my best poem," and I wish to publish it at once. This is partly because I only write when I have something new to say, which seems more worth while than what I have said before, partly because optimism about my present and future makes me despise my past. A few days after I have finished a poem, I relegate it to the past of all my other wasted efforts, all the books I do not wish to open.

Perhaps the greatest pleasure I have got from poems that I have written is when I have heard some lines quoted which I have not at once recognized. And I have thought "how good and how interesting," before I have realized that they are my own.

In common with other creative writers I pretend that I am not, and I am, exceedingly affected by unsympathetic criticism, whilst praise usually makes me suspect that the reviewer does not know what he is talking about. Why are writers so sensitive to criticism? Partly, because it is their business to be sensitive, and they are sensitive /307/ about this as about other things. Partly, because every serious creative writer is really in his heart concerned with reputation and not with success (the most successful writer I have known, Sir Hugh Walpole, was far and away the most unhappy about his reputation, because the "highbrows" did not like him). Again, I suspect that every writer is secretly writing for *someone*, probably for a parent or teacher who did not believe in him in childhood. The critic who refuses to "understand" immediately becomes identified with this person, and the understanding of many admirers only adds to the writer's secret bitterness if this one refusal persists.

Gradually one realizes that there is always this someone who will not like one's work. Then, perhaps, literature becomes a humble exercise of faith in being all that one can be in one's art, of being more than oneself, expecting little, but with a faith in the mystery of poetry which gradually expands into a faith in the mysterious service of truth.

Yet what failures there are! And how much mud sticks to one; mud not thrown by other people but acquired in the course of earning one's living, answering or not answering the letters which one receives, supporting or not supporting public causes. All one can hope is that this mud is composed of little grains of sand which will produce pearls. /308/

CLEANTH BROOKS

"What Does Poetry Communicate?"

[Cleanth Brooks (1906–), scholar, critic, and teacher, was born in Kentucky and educated at Vanderbilt, Tulane, and Oxford, where he was a Rhodes Scholar. He was for many years on the faculty of Louisiana State University, and is currently a professor of English at Yale. For seven years he edited the *Southern Review* with Robert Penn Warren, with whom he has also collaborated on a number of textbooks, including *Understanding Poetry* (1938), which did much to revolutionize the teaching of poetry in America. The following essay is from his book *The Well Wrought Urn* (New York, 1947).]

[Corinna's Going a-Maying

Get up, get up for shame, the blooming morn
Upon her wings presents the god unshorn.
    See how Aurora throws her fair
    Fresh-quilted colors through the air:
    Get up, sweet slug-a-bed, and see
    The dew bespangling herb and tree.
Each flower has wept and bowed toward the east
Above an hour since: yet you not dressed;
    Nay; not so much as out of bed?
    When all the birds have matins said
    And sung their thankful hymns, 'tis sin,
    Nay, profanation, to keep in,
Whenas a thousand virgins on this day
Spring, sooner than the lark, to fetch in May.

Rise, and put on your foliage, and be seen
To come forth, like the spring-time, fresh and
    green,
    And sweet as Flora. Take no care
    For jewels for your gown or hair:
    Fear not; the leaves will strew
    Gems in abundance upon you:
Besides, the childhood of the day has kept,
Against you come, some orient pearls unwept;
    Come and receive them while the light
    Hangs on the dew-locks of the night:
    And Titan on the eastern hill
    Retires himself, or else stands still
Till you come forth. Wash, dress, be brief in
    praying:
Few beads are best when once we go a-Maying.

Come, my Corinna, come; and, coming, mark
How each field turns a street, each street a park
    Made green and trimmed with trees; see how

Devotion gives each house a bough
    Or branch; each porch, each door ere this
    An ark, a tabernacle is,
Made up of white-thorn, neatly interwove;
As if here were those cooler shades of love.
    Can such delights be in the street
    And open fields and we not see't?
    Come, we'll abroad; and let's obey
    The proclamation made for May:
And sin no more, as we have done, by staying;
But, my Corinna, come, let's go a-Maying.

There's not a budding boy or girl this day
But is got up, and gone to bring in May.
    A deal of youth, ere this, is come
    Back, and with white-thorn laden home.
    Some have dispatched their cakes and cream
    Before that we have left to dream:
And some have wept, and wooed, and plighted
    troth,
And chose their priest, ere we can cast off sloth:
    Many a green-gown has been given;
    Many a kiss, both odd and even:
    Many a glance too has been sent
    From out the eye, love's firmament;
Many a jest told of the keys betraying
This night, and locks picked, yet we're not a-
    Maying.

Come, let us go while we are in our prime;
And take the harmless folly of the time.
    We shall grow old apace, and die
    Before we know our liberty.
    Our life is short, and our days run
    As fast away as does the sun;
And, as a vapor or a drop of rain,
Once lost, can ne'er be found again,
    So when or you or I are made
    A fable, song, or fleeting shade,
    All love, all liking, all delight
    Lies drowned with us in endless night.
Then while time serves, and we are but decaying,
Come, my Corinna, come, let's go a-Maying.

ROBERT HERRICK (*1591–1674*)]

The question of what poetry communicates, if anything, has been largely forced upon us by the advent of "modern" poetry. Some of that poetry is admittedly highly difficult—a very great deal of it is bound to *appear* difficult to the reader of conventional reading habits, even in spite of the fact—actually, in many cases, *because* of the fact—that he is a professor of literature.

For this reason, the difficult moderns are often represented as untraditional and generally irresponsible. (The War, incidentally, has encouraged the tendency: critics who ought to know better lend themselves to the popular plea that we should go back to the good old days when a poet meant what he said and there was no nonsense about it.)

The question, however, allows only one honest answer: modern poetry (if it is really poetry, and, at its best, it is really poetry) communicates whatever any other poetry communicates. The fact is that the question is badly asked. What does traditional poetry communicate? What does a poem like Herrick's "Corinna's going a-Maying" communicate? The example is a fair one: the poem has been long praised, and it is not noted for its difficulty.

The textbook answer is easy: the poem is a statement of the *carpe diem* theme. So it is, of course. But what does the poem do with the theme—specifically: Does the poet accept the theme? /62/ How seriously does he accept it? Within what context? etc., etc. These are questions of the first importance, a point that becomes obvious when we come to deal with such a matter as the following: after describing the joys of the May-day celebration, the poet prefaces his final invitation to Corinna to accept these joys by referring to them as "the harmlesse follie of the time." Unless we are absent-mindedly dictating a stock answer to an indifferent freshman, we shall certainly feel constrained to go further in describing what the poem "says."

Well, let us try again. Herrick's poem says that the celebration of nature is a beautiful but harmless folly, and his invitation to Corinna, thus, is merely playful, not serious. The Anglican parson is merely pretending for the moment that he is Catullus and that his Corinna is a pagan nymph. The poem is a pretense, a masquerade.

But there are the closing lines of the poem:

> Our life is short; and our dayes run
> As fast away as do's the Sunne:

And as a vapour, or a drop of raine
Once lost, can ne'er be found againe:
    So when or you or I are made
    A fable, song, or fleeting shade;
    All love, all liking, all delight
    Lies drown'd with us in endlesse night.
Then while time serves, and we are but decaying;
Come, my *Corinna*, come, let's goe a-Maying.

Obviously, there is a sense in which the invitation is thoroughly serious.

Confronted with this apparent contradiction, we can conclude, if we like, that Herrick is confused; or, softening the censure, we can explain that he was concerned only with providing some sort of framework for a description of the Devonshire spring. But if Herrick is confused about what he is saying in the poem, he behaves very strangely for a man in that plight. /63/ Far from being unconscious of the contradictory elements in the poem, he quite obviously has them in mind. Indeed, he actually takes pains to stress the clash between the Christian and pagan world views; or, rather, while celebrating the pagan view, he refuses to suppress references to the Christian. For instance, for all the dew-besprinkled description of the morning, he makes the ominous, unpagan word "sin" run throughout the poem. While the flowers are rejoicing and the birds are singing their hymns of praise, it is a "sin" and a "profanation" for Corinna to remain within doors. In the second stanza, the clash between paganism and Christianity becomes quite explicit: Corinna is to be "briefe in praying:/ Few Beads are best" on this morning which is dedicated to the worship of the nature god. And in the third stanza, paganism becomes frankly triumphant. Corinna is to

... sin no more, as we have done, by staying. ...

Moreover, a great deal that is usually glossed over as decoration or atmosphere in this poem is actually used by the poet to point up this same conflict. Herrick persists (with a shrewdness worthy of Sir James Frazer) in seeing the May-day rites as religious rites, though, of course, those of a pagan religion. The flowers, like worshipers, bow to the east; the birds sing "Mattens" and "Hymnes"; and the village itself, bedecked with greenery, becomes a cluster of pagan temples:

> Devotion gives each House a Bough,
> Or Branch: Each Porch, each doore, ere this,
> An Arke a Tabernacle is. . . .

The religious terms—"devotion," "ark," "tabernacle"—appear insistently. Corinna is actually being reproached for being late to church —the church of nature. The village itself has become a grove, subject to the laws of nature. One remembers that the original sense of "pagan" was "country-dweller" because the worship of the old gods and goddesses persisted longest there. /64/ On this May morning, the country has come into the village to claim it, at least on this one day, for its own. Symbolically, the town has disappeared and its mores are superseded.

I cannot see how we can avoid admitting that all this is communicated by the poem. Here it is in the poem. And its repercussions on the theme (if we still want to view the poem as a communication of a theme) are important. Among other things, they qualify the theme thus: the poem is obviously not a brief for the acceptance of the pagan ethic so much as it is a statement that the claims of the pagan ethic—however much they may be overlaid—exist, and on occasion emerge, as on this day.

The description of Corinna herself supplies another important qualification of the theme. The poet suggests that she properly falls under the dominion of nature as do the flowers and birds and trees. Notice the opening of the second stanza:

> Rise; and put on your Foliage. . . .

And this suggestion that she is a part of nature, like a plant, is reinforced throughout the poem. The trees drenched in dew will shake down dew-drops on her hair, accepting her as a companion and equal. Her human companions, the boys and girls of the village, likewise are plants—

> There's not a budding Boy, or Girle, this day,
> But is got up, and gone to bring in May.

Indeed, as we go through the first three stanzas of the poem, the old relationships gradually dissolve: the street itself turns into a park, and the boys and girls returning with their arms loaded with branches of whitethorn, merge into the plants themselves. Corinna, like them, is subject to nature, and to the claims of nature; and the season of springtime cannot, and ought not, to be denied. Not to respond is to "sin" against nature itself.

All this is "communicated" by the poem, and must be taken /65/ into account when we attempt to state what the poem "says." No theory of communication can deny that this is part of what the poem communicates, however awkwardly a theory of communication may be put to it to handle the problem.

We have still not attempted to resolve the conflict between the Christian and pagan attitudes in the poem, though the qualification of each of them, as Herrick qualifies each in the poem, may make it easier to discover possible resolutions which would have appealed to Herrick the Anglican parson who lived so much of his life in Devonshire and apparently took so much interest, not only in the pagan literature of Rome and Greece, but in the native English survivals of the old fertility cults.

Something of the nature of the poet's reconcilement of the conflicting claims of paganism and Christianity—and this, again, is part of what the poem communicates—is foreshadowed in the fourth stanza. The paganism with which the poem is concerned is clearly not an abstract and doctrinaire paganism. It comes to terms with the authoritative Christian mores, casually and without undue thought about the conflict—at least the paganism in action does: the village boys and the girls with their grass-stained gowns, coming to the priest to receive the blessing of the church.

> And some have wept, and woo'd, and plighted Troth,
> And chose their Priest, ere we can cast off sloth. . . .

After the poet's teasing play between attitudes in the first three stanzas, we are apparently approaching some kind of viable relation between them in this most realistic stanza of the poem with its

> Many a jest told of the Keyes betraying
> This night, and Locks pickt. . . .

The explicit resolution, of course, is achieved, with a change of tone, in the last stanza, with its /66/

Come, let us goe, while we are in our prime;
And take the harmlesse follie of the time.
　We shall grow old apace, and die . . .

I shall not try to indicate in detail what the resolution is. Here one must refer the reader to the poem itself. Yet one can venture to suggest the tone. The tone would be something like this: All right, let's be serious. Dismiss my pagan argument as folly. Still, in a sense, we are a part of nature, and are subject to its claims, and participate in its beauty. Whatever may be true in reality of the life of the soul, the body does decay, and unless we make haste to catch some part of that joy and beauty, that beauty—whatever else may be true—is lost.

If my clumsy paraphrase possesses any part of the truth, then this is still another thing which the poem communicates, though I shall hardly be able to "prove" it. As a matter of fact, I do not care to insist upon this or any other paraphrase. Indeed it is just because I am suspicious of such necessarily abstract paraphrases that I think our initial question, "What does the poem communicate?" is badly asked. It is not that the poem communicates nothing. Precisely the contrary. The poem communicates so much and communicates it so richly and with such delicate qualifications that the thing communicated is mauled and distorted if we attempt to convey it by any vehicle less subtle than that of the poem itself.

This general point is reinforced if we consider the function of particular words and phrases within the poem. For instance, consider

Our life is short; and our dayes run
　As fast away as do's the Sunne:
And as a vapour, or a drop of raine
Once lost, can ne'er be found againe. . . .

Why does the rain-drop metaphor work so powerfully? It is hardly because the metaphor is startlingly novel. Surely one /67/ important reason for its power is the fact that the poet has filled the first two stanzas of his poem with references to the dew. And the drops of dew have come to stand as a symbol of the spring and early dawn and of the youth of the lovers themselves. The dew-drops are the free gift of nature, spangling every herb and tree; they sparkle in the early light like something precious, like gems; they are the appropriate decoration for the girl; but they will not last—Corinna must hasten to enjoy them if she is to enjoy them at all. Thus, in the context of the poem they become a symbol heavily charged with meanings which no dictionary can be expected to give. When the symbol is revived at the end of the poem, even though in somewhat different guise, the effect is powerful; for the poet has made the little globule of moisture come to stand for the brief beauty of youth. And this too is part of what the poem says, though it is said indirectly, and the dull or lazy reader will not realize that it has been said at all.

The principle of rich indirection applies even to the individual word. Consider

Then while time serves, and we are but decaying;
Come, my *Corinna*, come, let's goe a-Maying.

"While time serves" means loosely "while there is yet time," but in the full context of the poem it also means "while time serves us," while time is still servant, not master—before we are mastered by time. Again, mere recourse to the dictionary will not give us this powerful second meaning. The poet is exploiting the potentialities of language—indeed, as all poets must do, he is remaking language.

To sum up: our examination of the poem has not resulted in our locating an idea or set of ideas which the poet has communicated with certain appropriate decorations. Rather, our examination has carried us further and further into the poem itself in a process of exploration. As we have made this exploration, it has become more and more clear that the poem is not /68/ only the linguistic vehicle which conveys the thing communicated most "poetically," but that it is also the sole linguistic vehicle which conveys the things communicated accurately. In fact, if we are to speak exactly, the poem itself is the *only* medium that communicates the particular "what" that is communicated. The conventional theories of communication offer no easy solution to our problem of meanings: we emerge with nothing more enlightening than this graceless bit of tautology: the poem says what the poem says.

There is a further point that comes out of our examination: our examination tends to suggest that not only our reading of the poem is a process of exploration, but that Herrick's process of making the poem was probably a process of exploration too. To say that Herrick "communicates" certain matters to the reader tends to falsify the real situation. The old description of the poet was better and less dangerous: the poet is a maker, not a communicator. He explores, consolidates, and "forms" the total experience that is the poem. I do not mean that he fashions a replica of his particular experience of a certain May morning like a detective making a moulage of a footprint in wet clay. But rather, out of the experiences of many May mornings, and out of his experience of Catullus, and possibly out of a hundred other experiences, he fashions, probably through a process akin to exploration, the total experience which is the poem.

This experience is *communicable,* partially so, at least. If we are willing to use imaginative understanding, we can come to know the poem as an object—we can share in the experience. But the poet is most truthfully described as a *poietes* or maker, not as an expositor or communicator. I do not mean to split hairs. It is doubtless possible to elaborate a theory of communication which will adequately cover these points. I believe that I. A. Richards, if I understand him correctly, has attempted to qualify his theory in precisely this way. At any rate, the net effect of his criticism has been to emphasize the need of a more /69/ careful reading of poetry and to regard the poem as an organic thing.

But most proponents of poetry as communication have been less discerning, and have used this view of poetry to damn the modern poets. I refer to such typical critics as Max Eastman and F. L. Lucas. But perhaps the most hard-bitten and vindictive of all the adherents of the theory is a man to whom the phrase "theory of communication" may seem novel and unfamiliar: I mean the average English professor. In one form or another,

whether in a conception which makes poetry a romantic raid on the absolute, or in a conception of more didactic persuasion which makes poetry an instrument of edification, some form of the theory of communication is to be found deeply embedded in the average teacher's doctrine of poetry. In many contexts its does little or no harm; but it can emerge to becloud the issues thoroughly when one confronts poetry which is unfamiliar or difficult.

Much modern poetry is difficult. Some of it may be difficult because the poet is snobbish and definitely wants to restrict his audience, though this is a strange vanity and much rarer than Mr. Eastman would have us think. Some modern poetry is difficult because it is bad—the total experience remains chaotic and incoherent because the poet could not master his material and give it a form. Some modern poetry is difficult because of the special problems of our civilization. But a great deal of modern poetry is difficult for the reader simply because so few people, relatively speaking, are accustomed to reading *poetry as poetry.* The theory of communication throws the burden of proof upon the poet, overwhelmingly and at once. The reader says to the poet: Here I am; it's your job to "get it across" to me—when he ought to be assuming the burden of proof himself.

Now the modern poet has, for better or worse, thrown the weight of the responsibility upon the reader. The reader must be on the alert for shifts of tone, for ironic statement, for sug- /70/ gestion rather than direct statement. He must be prepared to accept a method of indirection. He is further expected to be reasonably well acquainted with the general tradition—literary, political, philosophical, for he is reading a poet who comes at the end of a long tradition and who can hardly be expected to write honestly and with full integrity and yet ignore this fact. But the difficulties are not insuperable, and most of them can be justified in principle as the natural results of the poet's employment of his characteristic methods. For example, surely there can be no objection to the poet's placing emphasis on methods characteristic of poetry—the use of symbol rather than abstraction, of suggestion rather than explicit pronouncement, of metaphor rather than direct statement.

In stressing such methods, it is true, the modern poet has not produced a poetry which easily yields manageable abstractions in the way that some of the older poetry seems to do. But this is scarcely a conclusion that is flattering to the antagonists of modern poetry. What does an "older poem" like "Corinna's going a-Maying" say? What does this poem communicate? If we are content with the answer that the poem says that we should enjoy youth before youth fades, and if we are willing to write off everything else in the poem as "decoration," then we can properly censure Eliot or Auden or Tate for not making poems so easily tagged. But in that case we are not interested in poetry; we are interested in tags. Actually, in a few years, when time has wrought its softening changes, and familiarity has subdued the modern poet's frightful mien, and when the tags have been obligingly supplied, we may even come to terms with our difficult moderns. /71/

YVOR WINTERS
Foreword to *In Defense of Reason*

[Yvor Winters (1900–), professor, poet, and critic, was born in Chicago, was educated at the University of Colorado and Stanford, and has taught in the English department at Stanford since 1928. His *Collected Poems* won the Bollingen Prize for 1960. He has acquired his widest reputation as a vigorous and provocative critic of literature, his chief books being *Primitivism and Decadence* (1937), *Maule's Curse* (1938), *The Anatomy of Nonsense* (1943), *Edwin Arlington Robinson* (1946), and *The Function of Criticism* (1957). The first three of these books were collected in *In Defense of Reason* (Denver, 1947), to which, in the third edition, the following selection served as a foreword.]

The essays now reprinted in this volume are the work of more than fifteen years. Although this collection, like any collection of essays, suffers from its miscellaneous character, there is a single theory of literature developed throughout and a single theory of the history of literature since the Renaissance. These theories are developed mainly with reference to American literature. It may be of some service to the reader if I recapitulate briefly.

There have been various ideas regarding the nature and function of literature during the twenty-five hundred years or so that literature has been seriously discussed. One might think, offhand, that the possibilities were limitless; but they are actually limited and even narrowly limited—the ideas are all classifiable under a fairly small number of headings. I shall not attempt an historical survey but shall merely attempt a brief classificatory survey. The theories in question can all be classified, I believe, under three headings: the didactic, the hedonistic, and the romantic. I am not in sympathy with any of these, but with a fourth, which for lack of a better term I call the moralistic. This concept of literature has not been adequately defined in the past so far as my limited knowledge extends, but I believe that it has been loosely implicit in the inexact theorizing which has

led to the most durable judgments in the history of criticism.

The didactic theory of literature is simple; it is this: that literature offers us useful precepts and explicit moral instruction. If the theory is sound, then literature is useful; but the question arises as to whether there may not be other fields of study, such /3/ as religion or ethics, which may accomplish the same end more efficiently. The question is usually met by the Horatian formula, which combines the didactic with the hedonistic, telling us that the function of literature is to provide instruction (or profit) in conjunction with pleasure, to make instruction palatable. Of this I shall say more later. There arises another question in connection with the didactic theory: can one say, as someone—I believe it was Kenneth Burke—has remarked, that *Hamlet* was written to prove that procrastination is the thief of time, or to prove something comparably simple? Or is there more than that to *Hamlet*? And if there is more, is it worth anything? It seems obvious to me that there is more and that it is worth a great deal, that the paraphrasable content of the work is never equal to the work, and that our theory of literature must account not only for the paraphrasable content but for the work itself. The didactic theory of literature fails to do this.

The hedonist sees pleasure as the end of life, and literature either as a heightener of pleasure or as the purveyor of a particular and more or less esoteric variety of pleasure. The term *pleasure* is applied indiscriminately to widely varying experiences: we say, for example, that we derive pleasure from a glass of good whisky and that we derive pleasure from reading *Hamlet*. The word is thus misleading, for it designates two experiences here which have little relationship to each other. There is a great range in the kinds of pleasure advocated in various hedonistic philosophies, but in general one might remark this defect which is common to nearly all, perhaps to all, such systems: pleasure is treated as an end in itself, not as a by-product of something else. If we recognize that certain feelings which are loosely classifiable as forms of pleasure result from our recognition of various kinds of truth and from the proper functioning of our natures in the process of this recognition, we then have a principle which may enable us to distinguish these pleasures from pleasures less important or less desirable, such as the pleasures or satisfactions which we derive from the gratification of physical appetites or from the excitement of stimulants, and a principle which may even enable us to evaluate relatively to each other the /4/ higher pleasures themselves. But pleasure then becomes incidental and not primary, and our system can no longer be classified as properly hedonistic. Furthermore, there is this distinction at least between hedonistic ethics and hedonistic aesthetics: hedonistic ethics, as in the philosophy of Epicurus, may take on a somewhat passive or negativistic character; that is pleasure may come to be more or less nearly identified simply with the avoidance of pain. But one cannot praise a poem or a picture merely by saying that it gives no pain: the experience of the poem or of the picture must be strongly positive. Hedonistic theories of literature tend in the main, and this is especially true in the past two hundred years, to take one of two forms.

The first might be connected with the name of Walter Pater. According to this view there is a close relation between hedonistic ethics and hedonistic aesthetics. Pleasure is the aim of life. Pleasure consists in intensity of experience; that is in the cultivation of the feelings for their own sake, as a good in themselves. And literature, or at any rate the arts in general, can provide a finer technique of such cultivation than can any other mode of activity. We meet here the first difficulty which I mentioned in connection with hedonistic doctrines; namely, that unless we have illicit relations with some non-hedonistic ethical theory, we have no way of distinguishing among the many and diverse excitements that are commonly described as pleasurable. And we shall discover, as a matter of human nature which is recorded in the history of literature and the other arts, that

this search for intensity of experience leads inevitably to an endless pursuit either of increasing degrees of violence of emotion or of increasingly elusive and more nearly meaningless nuances, and ultimately to disillusionment with art and with life. It is possible, of course, that art and life are really worthless, but on the other hand it is possible that they are valuable. And until we have made sure that our hedonistic theory offers a true description of human experience, that no better description is possible, we should be unwise to commit ourselves to it, for the ultimate consequences appear both certain and unfortunate.

The second form of hedonistic theory tends to dissociate the /5/ artistic experience sharply from all other experience. T. S. Eliot, for example, tells us that the human experience about which the poem appears to be written has been transmuted in the aesthetic process into something new which is different in kind from all other experience. The poem is not then, as it superficially appears, a statement about a human experience, but is a thing in itself. The beginnings of this notion are to be found in Poe and are developed further by the French Symbolists, notably by Mallarmé. The aim of the poem so conceived is again pleasure, pleasure conceived as intensity of emotion; but the emotion is of an absolutely special sort. Some such notion of the artistic experience is the essential concept of Santayana's aesthetics; in fact, it is essential to almost any treatment of "aesthetics" as a branch of philosophy, and one will find it everywhere in the work of the academic aestheticians of the past half-century. The nature of the "aesthetic" experience as conceived in these terms has never been clearly defined; we commonly meet here a kind of pseudo-mysticism. The chief advantage of this kind of hedonism over the Paterian variety is that one can adhere to it without adhering to a doctrine of ethical hedonism, for art and life are absolutely severed from each other. Eliot, for example, considers himself a Christian. The chief disadvantage is that it renders intelligible discussion of art impossible, and it relegates art to the position of an esoteric indulgence, possibly though not certainly harmless, but hardly of sufficient importance to merit a high position among other human activities. Art, however, has always been accorded a high position, and a true theory of art should be able to account for this fact.

Certain theorists who have been aware that art is more than moral precept on the one hand and more than a search for cultivated excitement on the other have tried to account for its complexity by combining the didactic and the hedonistic theories: this gives us the Horatian formula, that art combines profit with pleasure. When this formula occurs, as if often does, in the writing of a great poet or of some other person who takes his poetry seriously, it apparently represents a somewhat rough and ready recognition of the fact that poetry has intellectual content and /6/ something more; that its power is real and cannot be accounted for too easily. But if one regard the doctrine itself, and regard it as pure theory, it is unsatisfactory; or at any rate it relegates art to an unsatisfactory position. For the didactic element in art so conceived will be no more efficient as didacticism than we have seen it to be before: that is, the serious moralist may quite reasonably argue that he prefers to get his teaching in a more direct and compact form; and the pleasure is still in the unhappy predicament in which we found it in the purely hedonistic theory.

The Romantic theory of literature takes account more seriously than the theories which I have thus far mentioned of the power which literature seems to exert over human nature, and to that extent offers a more realistic view of literature. I am concerned with literature which may be loosely described as artistic: that is, with literature which communicates not only thought but also emotion. I do not like the expression *imaginative literature,* for in its colloquial acceptation the phrase excludes too much: it excludes the persuasive and hortatory, for example, the sermon and the political tract; and *imagination* as a term of sophisticated criticism has been used so variously and so elusively, especially during the past hundred and fifty years, that I am not quite sure what it means. But the power of artistic literature is real: if we consider such writers as Plato, Augustine, Dante, Shakespeare, Rousseau,

Voltaire, Emerson, and Hitler, to go no further, we must be aware that such literature has been directly and indirectly one of the greatest forces in human history. The Gospels gave a new direction to half the world; *Mein Kampf* very nearly reversed that direction. The influence of Rimbaud and of Mallarmé is quite as real but has operated more slowly and with less of obvious violence. It behooves us to discover the nature of artistic literature, what it does, how it does it, and how one may evaluate it. It is one of the facts of life, and quite as important a fact as atomic fission. In our universities at present, for example, one or another of the hedonistic views of literature will be found to dominate, although often colored by Romantic ideas, with the result that the professors of literature, who for /7/ the most part are genteel but mediocre men, can make but a poor defence of their profession, and the professors of science, who are frequently men of great intelligence but of limited interests and education, feel a politely disguised comtempt for it; and thus the study of one of the most pervasive and powerful influences on human life is traduced and neglected.

The Romantics, however, although they offer a relatively realistic view of the power of literature, offer a fallacious and dangerous view of the nature both of literature and of man. The Romantic theory assumes that literature is mainly or even purely an emotional experience, that man is naturally good, that man's impulses are trustworthy, that the rational faculty is unreliable to the point of being dangerous or possibly evil. The Romantic theory of human nature teaches that if man will rely upon his impulses, he will achieve the good life. When this notion is combined, as it frequently is, with a pantheistic philosophy or religion, it commonly teaches that through surrender to impulse man will not only achieve the good life but will achieve also a kind of mystical union with the Divinity: this, for example, is the doctrine of Emerson. Literature thus becomes a form of what is known popularly as self-expression. It is not the business of man to understand and improve himself, for such an effort is superfluous: he is good as he is, if he will only let himself alone, or, as we might say, let him-

self go. The poem is valuable because it enables us to share the experience of a man who
has let himself go, who has expressed his feelings, without hindrance, as he has found them
at a given moment. The ultimate ideal at
which such a theory aims is automatism.
There is nothing in the theory to provide a
check on such automatism; if the individual
man is restrained by some streak of personal
but unformulated common sense, by some
framework of habit derived from a contrary
doctrine, such as Christian doctrine, or by
something in his biological inheritance, that
is merely his good fortune—the Romantic doctrine itself will not restrain him. The Romantic doctrine itself will urge him toward
automatism. And the study of history seems
to show that if any doctrine is widely accepted
for a long period of time, it tends more and
more strongly /8/ to exact conformity from
human nature, to alter human nature. The
Romantic theory of literature and of human
nature has been the dominant theory in western civilization for about two and a half centuries. Its influence is obviously disastrous in
literature and is already dangerous in other
departments of human life.

There are certain other general notions of
human nature and of values which are related
to the notions which I have been discussing,
but which are not exactly correlative with
them. I shall refer to them rather baldly as
determinism, relativism, and absolutism.

Determinism is that theory of the universe
which holds that the whole is a single organism, pursuing a single and undeviating course
which has been predestined by God or determined by its own nature. It sees the human
being simply as a part of this organism, with
no independent force of his own. One must
distinguish sharply between a deterministic
theory and a theory which recognizes the real
existence of influences outside of the individual, whether those influences be historical,
biological, or other. One may even take a pes-
simistic view of such influences without being
a determinist. If one admits that man may
understand in some measure the conditions of
his existence, that as a result of such understanding he may choose a mode of action, that
as a result of such choice he may persevere in
the mode of action chosen, and that as a result
of his perseverance he may in some measure

alter the conditions of his existence, then one
is not a determinist. Few people who profess
deterministic doctrines are willing to envisage
clearly their implications, however. As a result, one will find all three of the views of poetry which I have mentioned held by determinists.

It is natural that deterministic and Romantic theories should coincide, for Romanticism
teaches the infinite desirability of automatism, and determinism teaches the inevita-
bility of automatism. Determinism is Romanticism in a disillusioned mood; Henry
Adams is little more than the obverse side of
Emerson, the dark side of the moon. And
since hedonism is, like determinism, an anti-
intellectualistic philosophy and is somewhat
vague in all its tenets, it is not surprising that
determinists should /9/ sometimes appear as
hedonists: since they cannot control in any
measure the courses of their lives, the determinists sometimes find solace in seeking
pleasure along the way, without stopping to
consider that such a search is a willful activity involving at least limited consideration
and choice. It is curious that the didactic view
of literature should so often be adopted by
determinists, however, for the determinist
really has no right to the didactic method. Yet
the most vigorous, one might say the most religious, of the various species of determinist,
such for example as the Calvinists of the past
and the Marxists of the present, are commonly the most didactic of men, both in their
literature and in their behavior.

The absolutist believes in the existence of
absolute truths and values. Unless he is very
foolish, he does not believe that he personally
has free access to these absolutes and that his
own judgments are final; but he does believe
that such absolutes exist and that it is the
duty of every man and of every society to endeavor as far as may be to approximate them.
The relativist, on the other hand, believes
that there are no absolute truths, that the
judgment of every man is right for himself. I
am aware that many persons believe that they
have arrived at some kind of compromise between these two positions, but actually no
compromise is possible. Any such attempt at
compromise, if closely examined, will exhibit
an ultimate allegiance to one position or the
other or else will exhibit simple confusion. It

is popular at present to profess relativism and yet in important matters to act as if we were absolutists. Our ideas of justice, which we endeavor to define by law and for which wars are often fought, can be defended only by invoking moral absolutism. Our universities, in which relativistic doctrines are widely taught, can justify their existence only in terms of a doctrine of absolute truth. The professor of English Literature, who believes that taste is relative, yet who endeavors to convince his students that *Hamlet* is more worthy of their attention than some currently popular novel, is in a serious predicament, a predicament which is moral, intellectual, and in the narrowest sense professional, though he commonly has not the wit to realize the fact. /10/

The Romantic is almost inescapably a relativist, for if all men follow their impulses there will be a wide disparity of judgments and of actions and the fact enforces recognition. The Emersonian formula is the perfect one: that is right for me which is after my constitution; that is right for you which is after yours; the common divinity will guide each of us in the way which is best for him. The hedonist is usually a relativist and should logically be one, but there is often an illicit and veiled recognition of absolutism in his attempts to classify the various pleasures as more or less valuable, not for himself alone but in general. The defender of the didactic view of literature has been traditionally an absolutist, but he is not invariably so: didacticism is a method, and when one sees literature only as didacticism one sees it as a method, and the method may be used, as Emerson used it, to disseminate relativistic doctrine.

The theory of literature which I defend in these essays is absolutist. I believe that the work of literature, in so far as it is valuable, approximates a real apprehension and communication of a particular kind of objective truth. The form of literature with which I am for the most part concerned is the poem; but since the poem exhausts more fully than any other literary form the inherent possibilities of language, what I say about poetry can be extended to include other literary forms with relatively unimportant qualifications, and in point of fact I devote considerable space to other literary forms. The poem is a statement in words about a human experience. Words are primarily conceptual, but through use and because human experience is not purely conceptual, they have acquired connotations of feeling. The poet makes his statement in such a way as to employ both concept and connotation as efficiently as possible. The poem is good in so far as it makes a defensible rational statement about a given human experience (the experience need not be real but must be in some sense possible) and at the same time communicates the emotion which ought to be motivated by that rational understanding of that experience. This notion of poetry, whatever its defects, will account both for the power of poetry and of artistic literature in general on its readers and for the seriousness /11/ with which the great poets have taken their art. Milton, for example, did not write *Paradise Lost* to give pleasure to Professor So-and-So, nor did he write to give free rein to his emotions; he wrote it in order to justify the ways of God to men, and the justification involved not merely a statement of theory but a conformity of the emotional nature of man with the theory.

Poetry, and in a less definite fashion all artistic literature, involves not only the two aspects of language which I have just mentioned, but also the rhythmic and formal. Rhythm, for reasons which I do not wholly understand, has the power of communicating emotion; and as a part of the poem it has the power of qualifying the total emotion. What we speak of loosely as the "form" of a poem is probably, at least for the most part, twofold: we have on the one hand the rational structure of the poem, the orderly arrangement and progression of thought; and we have on the other a kind of rhythm broader and less easily measurable than the rhythm of the line—the poem exists in time, the mind proceeds through it in time, and if the poet is a good one he takes advantage of this fact and makes the progression rhythmical. These aspects of the poem will be efficient in so far as the poet subordinates them to the total aim of the poem.

One criticism which has been made of me repeatedly is this: that I wish to discard every poem to which I make objections. This is not true. Probably no poem is perfect in the eye of God. So far as I am concerned, a good many poems approach so nearly to perfection that I find them satisfactory. But there are many poems which seem to me obviously imperfect and even very seriously imperfect, which I have no wish to discard. Some of these I have analyzed both in respect to their virtues and to their defects; others, because of the nature of my discussion, mainly with reference to their defects; but I have dealt with few works which do not seem to me to have discernible virtues, for to do otherwise would seem to me a waste of time. If we were all to emulate Hart Crane, the result would be disastrous to literature and to civilization; it is necessary to understand the limitations of Hart Crane, which are of the utmost seriousness; but when we understand those limitations, we are in a position to profit by his /12/ virtues with impunity, and his virtues are sometimes very great. If we are not aware of his limitations but are sufficiently sensitive to guess in some fashion at his virtues, he may easily take possession of us wholly. This difficulty indicates the function of criticism.

Certain poetry of the sixteenth and seventeenth centuries approximates most closely the qualities which seem to me the best. It seems to me, as it has seemed to many others, that there has been a general deterioration of the quality of poetry since the opening of the eighteenth century. Like many others, I have endeavored to account for this deterioration. It would surprise no one if I stated that Collins' *Ode to Evening* was an imperfect and secondary poem if judged in comparison with all English poetry; but it arouses antagonism when I give reasons, partly because there is a general dislike for reasons, and partly because my reasons are not complimentary to the orthodoxies of our time. I regret the antagonism, but since I believe my reasons to be sound and the matter in general serious, I must maintain my position and take the consequences. These essays, then, endeavor not only to defend a theory of poetry and to judge certain writers with reference to that theory, but to outline as far as this kind of writing permits certain historical tendencies and the reasons for them. I do this in the hope that my efforts may in some small measure contribute to the alteration of these tendencies; our literary culture (to mention nothing more) appears to me to be breaking up, and the rescue of it appears to me a matter of greater moment than the private feelings of some minor poet or scholar.

I should perhaps call attention to one other matter in connection with my aims. It seems to me impossible to judge the value of any idea in a vacuum. That is, the hedonistic view of literature may conceivably appear sound, or the relativistic view of literature and morals may appear sound, if the idea is circumscribed by a few words. But either idea implies a fairly complete description of a large range of human experience, and if the description does not agree with the facts as we are forced to recognize them, then something is wrong. I am acquainted, for /13/ example, with the arguments which prove that the wall is not there, but if I try to step through the wall, I find that the wall is there notwithstanding the arguments. During the past century or so, the number of poets who have endeavored to conform their practice to the ideas which seem to me unsound has been rather large, and we can judge the ideas more or less clearly in the light of these experiments. A large part of this book is devoted to the analysis of such experiments.

Finally, I am aware that my absolutism implies a theistic position, unfortunate as this admission may be. If experience appears to indicate that absolute truths exist, that we are able to work toward an approximate apprehension of them, but that they are antecedent to our apprehension and that our apprehension is seldom and perhaps never perfect, then there is only one place in which those truths may be located, and I see no way to escape this conclusion. I merely wish to point out that my critical and moral notions are derived from the observation of literature and of life, and that my theism is derived from my critical and moral notions. I did not proceed from the opposite direction.

All of the concepts outlined briefly and incompletely in this foreword, with the exception of that mentioned in the last paragraph, will be found more fully explained at various points in the present volume. These remarks are not offered as a complete statement, but are offered merely as a guide and an introduction. /14/

W. K. WIMSATT, JR.
"The Concrete Universal"

[W. K. Wimsatt, Jr. (1907–), born in Washington, D.C., and educated at Georgetown and Yale, has been a professor of English literature at Yale since 1939. He is the author of books on Samuel Johnson and on literary criticism. The following selection, originally published in *PMLA* in 1947, is reprinted here in revised form from his book *The Verbal Icon* (Lexington, Ky., 1954).]

The central argument of this essay, concerning what I shall call the "concrete universal," proceeds from the observation that literary theorists have from early times to the present persisted in making statements which in their contexts seem to mean that a work of literary art is in some peculiar sense a very individual thing or a very universal thing or both. What that paradox can mean, or what important fact behind the paradox has been discerned by such various critics as Aristotle, Plotinus, Hegel, and Ransom, it will be the purpose of the essay to inquire, and by the inquiry to discuss not only a significant feature of metaphysical poetics from Aristotle to the present day but the relation between metaphysical poetics and more practical and specific rhetorical analysis. In the brief historical survey which forms one part of this essay it will not be my purpose to suggest that any of these writers meant exactly what I shall mean in later parts where I describe the structure of poetry. Yet throughout the essay I shall proceed on the theory not only that men have at different times used the same terms and have meant differently, but that they have sometimes /69/ used different terms and have meant the same or somewhat the same. In other words, I assume that there is continuity in the problems of criticism, and that a person who studies poetry today has a legitimate interest in what Plato said about poetry.

The view of common terms and their relations to classes of things from which I shall start is roughly that which one may read in the logic of J. S. Mill, a view which is not much different from the semantic view of to-

day and for most purposes not much different from the Aristotelian and scholastic view. Mill speaks of the word and its denotation and connotation (the term, referent and reference, the sign, denotatum and designatum of more recent terminologies). The denotation is the *it*, the individual thing or the aggregate of things to which the term may refer; the connotation is the *what*, the quality or classification inferred for the it, or implicitly predicated by the application of the term or the giving of the name.[1] One main difference between all modern positivistic, nominalistic, and semantic systems and the scholastic and classical systems is that the older ones stress the similarity of the individuals denoted by the common term and hence the real universality of meaning, while the modern systems stress the differences in the individuals, the constant flux even of each individual in time and space and its kinetic structure, and hence infer only an approximate or nominal universality of meaning and a convenience rather than a truth in the use of general terms. A further difference lies in the view of how the individual is related to the various connotations of terms which may be applied to it. That is, to the question: What is it? the older writers seem to hold there is but one (essentially right) answer, while the moderns accept as many answers as there are classes to which the individual may be assigned (an indefinite number). The older writers speak of a proper essence or whatness of the individual, a quality which in some cases at least is that designated by the class name most commonly applied to the /70/ individual: a bench is a bench, essentially a bench, accidentally a heavy wooden object or something covered with green paint. "When we say *what* it is,"

[1] The terms "denotation" and "connotation" are commonly and loosely used by literary critics to distinguish the dictionary meaning of a term (denotation) from the vaguer aura of suggestion (connotation). Both these are parts of the connotation in the logical sense.

observes Aristotle, "we do not say 'white,' or 'hot,' or 'three cubits long,' but 'a man' or 'a god.'" And this view is also a habit scarcely avoidable in our own daily thinking, especially when we think of living things or of artifacts, things made by us or our fellows for a purpose. What is it? Bench, we think, is an adequate answer. An assemblage of sticks painted green, we consider freakish.

II

Whether or not one believes in universals, one may see the persistence in literary criticism of a theory that poetry presents the concrete and the universal, or the individual and the universal, or an object which in a mysterious and special way is both highly general and highly particular. The doctrine is implicit in Aristotle's two statements that poetry imitates action and that poetry tends to express the universal. It is implicit again at the end of the classic period in the mystic doctrine of Plotinus, who in his later writing on beauty reverses the Platonic objection that art does not know the ultimate reality of the forms. Plotinus arrives at the view that the artist by a kind of bypass of the inferior natural productions of the world soul reaches straight to the forms that lie behind in the divine intelligence. Another version of the classic theory, with affinities for Plotinus, lies in the scholastic phrase *resplendentia formae*.

Cicero's account of how Zeuxis painted an ideal Helen from the five most beautiful virgins of Crotona is a typical development of Aristotelian theory, in effect the familiar neoclassic theory found in Du Fresnoy's *Art of Painting,* in the writings of Johnson, especially in the tulip passage in *Rasselas,* and in the *Discourses* and *Idlers* of Reynolds. The business of the poet is not to number the streaks of the tulip; it is to give us not the individual, but the species. The same thing is stated in a more complicated way by Kant in telling how the imagination constructs the "aesthetical normal Idea": /71/

It is the image for the whole race, which floats among all the variously different intuitions of individuals, which nature takes as archetype in her productions of the same species, but which seems not to be fully reached in any individual case.

And Hegel's account is as follows:

The work of art is not only for the sensuous apprehension as sensuous object, but its position is of such a kind that as sensuous it is at the same time essentially addressed to the *mind.*

In comparison with the show or semblance of immediate sensuous existence or of historical narrative, the artistic semblance has the advantage that in itself it points beyond self, and refers us away from itself to something spiritual which it is meant to bring before the mind's eye. . . . The hard rind of nature and the common world give the mind more trouble in breaking through to the idea than do the products of art.

The excellence of Shakespeare, says Coleridge, consists in a "union and interpenetration of the universal and particular." In one terminology or another this idea of a concrete universal is found in most metaphysical aesthetic of the eighteenth and nineteenth centuries.

A modern literary critic, John Crowe Ransom, speaks of the argument of a poem (the universal) and a local texture or tissue of concrete irrelevance. Another literary critic, Allen Tate, manipulating the logical terms "extension" and "intension," has arrived at the concept of "tension" in poetry. "Extension," as logicians use the word, is the range of individuals denoted by a term (denotation); "intension" is the total of qualities connoted (connotation). In the ordinary or logical use of the terms, extension and intension are of inverse relationship—the wider the one, the shallower the other. A poem, says Tate, as I interpret him, is a verbal structure which in some peculiar way has both a wide extension and a deep intension.

Not all these theories of the concrete universal lay equal stress on the two sides of the paradox, and it seems indicative of the vitality of the theory and of the truth implicit in it that /72/ the two sides have been capable of exaggeration into antithetic schools and theories of poetry. For Du Fresnoy, Johnson, and Reynolds poetry and painting give the universal; the less said about the particulars the better. This is the neoclassic theory, the illustrations of which we seek in Pope's *Essay on Man* or in Johnson's *Ramblers,* where the ideas are moral and general and concerned with "nature," "one clear, unchanged, and universal light." The opposite theory had notable expression in England, a few years before Johnson wrote *Rasselas*, in Joseph Warton's *Essay on Pope*:

A minute and particular enumeration of circumstances judiciously selected, is what chiefly discriminates poetry from history, and renders the former, for that reason, a more close and faithful representation of nature than the latter.

And Blake's marginal criticism of Reynolds was: "THIS Man was Hired to Depress art." "To Generalize is to be an Idiot. To Particularize is the Alone Distinction of Merit. General Knowledges are those Knowledges that Idiots possess." "Sacrifice the Parts: What becomes of the whole?" The line from Warton's *Essay* to Croce's *Aesthetic* seems a straight and obvious one, from Thomson's specific descriptions of flowers to the individual act of intuition-expression which is art—its opposite and enemy being the concept or generality. The two views of art (two that can be held by different theorists about the same works of art) may be startlingly contrasted in the following passages about fictitious character—one a well known statement by Johnson, the other by the philosopher of the *élan vital* [Bergson].

[Shakespeare's] characters are not modified by the customs of particular places, unpractised by the rest of the world; by the peculiarities of studies or professions, which can operate but upon small numbers; or by the accidents of transient fashions or temporary opinions: they are the genuine progeny of common humanity, such as the world will always supply, and observation will always find. His persons act and speak by the influence of those general passions and principles by which all minds are agitated, and the whole /73/ system of life is continued in motion. In the writings of other poets a character is too often an individual; in those of Shakespeare it is commonly a species.

Hence it follows that art always aims at what is *individual*. What the artist fixes on his canvas is something he has seen at a certain spot, on a certain day, at a certain hour, with a colouring that will never be seen again. What the poet sings of is a certain mood which was his, and his alone, and which will never return. . . . Nothing could be more unique than the char-

acter of Hamlet. Though he may resemble other men in some respects, it is clearly not on that account that he interests us most.

Other critics, notably the most ancient and the most modern, have tried to hold the extremes together. Neither of the extremes gives a good account of art and each leads out of art. The theory of particularity leads to individuality and originality (Edward Young was another eighteenth century Crocean), then to the idiosyncratic and the unintelligible and to the psychology of the author, which is not in the work of art and is not a standard for judgment. The theory of universality as it appears in Johnson and Reynolds leads to platitude and to a standard of material objectivity, the average tulip, the average human form, some sort of average.

III

"Just representations of general nature," said Johnson, and it ought to be noted, though it perhaps rarely is, that two kinds of generality are involved, as indeed they are in the whole neoclassic theory of generality. There is the generality of logic or classification, of the more general as opposed to the more specific, "essential" generality, one might say. And there is the generality of literal truth to nature, "existential" generality. The assumption of neoclassic theory seems to be that these two must coincide. As a matter of fact they may and often do, but need not. Thus: "purple cow" is a more general (less specific) term and concept than "tan cow with a broken horn," yet the latter is more general or true to nature. We have, in short, realism or fantasy, and in either there may be various degrees /74/ of the specific or the general. We have *A Journal of the Plague Year* and *The Rambler, Gulliver's Travels* and *Rasselas*. The fact that there are a greater number of "vicissitudes" and "miscarriages" (favorite *Rambler* events) in human experience than plagues at London, that there are more tan cows than tan cows with broken horns, makes it true in a sense that a greater degree of essential generality involves a greater degree of existential. But in this sense the most generally reliable concept is simply that of "being."

The question is how a work of literature.

can be either more individual (unique) or more universal than other kinds of writing, or how it can combine the individual and the universal more than other kinds. Every description in words, so far as it is a direct description (The barn is red and square) is a generalization. That is the nature of words. There are no individuals conveyed in words but only more or less specific generalizations, so that Johnson is right, though we have to ask him what degree of verbal generality makes art, and whether "tulip" is a better or more important generality than "tulip with ten streaks," or whether "beauty" is not in fact a much more impressive generality than "tulip." On the other hand, one cannot deny that in some sense there are more tulips in poetry than pure abstracted beauty. So that Bergson is right too; only we shall have to ask him what degree of specificity in verbal description makes art. And he can never claim complete verbal specificity or individuality, even for Hamlet.

If he could, if a work of literary art could be looked on as an artifact or concrete physical work, the paradox for the student of universals would return from the opposite direction even more forcibly—as it does in fact for theorists of graphic art. If Reynolds' picture "The Age of Innocence" presents a species or universal, what species does it present? Not an Aristotelian essence—"man," or "humanity," nor even a more specific kind of being such as "womanhood." For then the picture would present the same universal as Reynolds' portrait of Mrs. Siddons as "The Tragic Muse," and all differences between "The Age of Innocence" and "The Tragic Muse" would be aesthetically irrelevant. Does the picture then present girlhood, /75/ or barefoot girlhood, or barefoot girlhood in a white dress against a gloomy background? All three are equally valid universals (despite the fact that makeshift phrases are required to express two of them), and all three are presented by the picture. Or is it the title which tells us what universal is presented, "The Age of Innocence," and without the title should we not know the universal? The question will be: What in the individual work of art demands that we attribute to it one universal rather than another?

We may answer that for poetry it is the generalizing power of words already mentioned, and go on to decide that what distinguishes poetry from scientific or logical discourse is a degree of irrelevant concreteness in descriptive details. This is in effect what Ransom says in his doctrine of argument and local irrelevance, but it seems doubtful if the doctrine is not a version of the theory of ornamental metaphor. The argument, says Ransom, is the prose or scientific meaning, what the poem has in common with other kinds of writing. The irrelevance is a texture of concreteness which does not contribute anything to the argument but is somehow enjoyable or valuable for its own sake, the vehicle of a metaphor which one boards heedless of where it runs, whether crosstown or downtown—just for the ride. So Ransom nurses and refines the argument, and on one page he makes the remark that the poet searches for "suitability" in his particular phrases, and by suitability Ransom means "the propriety which consists in their denoting the particularity which really belongs to the logical object." But the difference between "propriety" and relevance in such a context is not easy to see. And relevance is logic. The fact is that all concrete illustration has about it something of the irrelevant. An apple falling from a tree illustrates gravity, but apple and tree are irrelevant to the pure theory of gravity. It may be that what happens in a poem is that the apple and the tree are somehow made more than usually relevant.

Such a theory, not that of Johnson and Reynolds, not that of Warton and Bergson, not quite that of Ransom, is what I would suggest—yet less as a novelty than as something already widely /76/ implicit in recent poetical analyses and exegeses, in those of Empson, for instance, Tate, Blackmur, or Brooks. If a work of literature is not in a simple sense either more individual or more universal than other kinds of writing, it may yet be such an individual or such a complex of meaning that it has a special relation to the world of universals. Some acute remarks on this suject were made by Ruskin in a chapter of *Modern Painters* neglected today perhaps because of its distasteful ingredient of "noble emotion." Poetry, says Ruskin in criticizing

Reynolds' *Idlers,* is not distinguished from history by the omission of details, nor for that matter by the mere addition of details. "There must be something either in the nature of the details themselves, or the method of using them, which invests them with poetical power." Their nature, one may add, as assumed through their relation to one another, a relation which may also be called the method of using them. The poetic character of details consists not in what they say directly and explicitly (as if roses and moonlight were poetic) but in what by their arrangement they *show* implicitly.

IV

"One," observes Ben Jonson, thinking of literature, "is considerable two waies: either, as it is only separate, and by it self: or as being compos'd of many parts it beginnes to be one as those parts grow or are wrought together." A literary work of art is a complex of detail (an artifact, if we may be allowed that metaphor for what is only a verbal object), a composition so complicated of human values that its interpretation is dictated by the understanding of it, and so complicated as to seem in the highest degree individual—a concrete universal. We are accustomed to being told, for example, that what makes a character in fiction or drama vital is a certain fullness or rotundity: that the character has many sides. Thus E. M. Forster:

> We may divide characters into flat and round. Flat characters were called "humours" in the seventeenth century, and are sometimes called types, and sometimes caricatures. In their purest form, they /77/ are constructed round a single idea or quality: when there is more than one factor in them, we get the beginning of the curve towards the round. The really flat character can be expressed in one sentence such as "I never will desert Mr. Micawber."

It remains to be said, however, that the many traits of the round character (if indeed it is one character and not a hodgepodge) are harmonized or unified, and that if this is so, then all the traits are chosen by a principle, just as are the traits of the flat character. Yet it cannot be that the difference between the round and flat character is simply numerical; the difference cannot be merely that the presiding principle is illustrated by more examples in the round character. Something further must be supposed—a special interrelation in the traits of the round character. Bobadil is an example of the *miles gloriosus* [braggart soldier], a flat humour. He swears by "The foot of Pharaoh," takes tobacco, borrows money from his landlady, is found lying on a bench fully dressed with a hangover, brags about his feats at the siege of Strigonium, beats Cob a poor water carrier, and so on. It is possible that he has numerically as many traits as Falstaff, one of the most vital of all characters. But one of the differences between Falstaff and Bobadil is that the things Falstaff says are funny; the things Bobadil says are not. Compared to Falstaff, Bobadil is unconscious, an opaque butt. There is the vitality of consciousness in Falstaff. And further there is the crowning complexity of self-consciousness. The fact that Morgann could devote a book to arguing that Falstaff is not a coward, that lately Professor Wilson has argued that at Gadshill Falstaff may exhibit " 'all the common symptoms of the malady' of cowardice" and at the same time persuade the audience that he has " 'never once lost his self-possession,' " the fact that one can conceive that Falstaff in the Gadshill running-away scene really knows that his assailants are the Prince and Poins—all this shows that in Falstaff there is a kind of interrelation among his attributes, his cowardice, his wit, his debauchery, his presumption, that makes them in a special way an organic harmony. He is a rounded character not only in the sense that he is gross (a fact which may have tempted critics to speak of /78/ a rounded character) or in the sense that he is a bigger bundle of attributes, stuffed more full, than Bobadil or Ralph Roister Doister; but in the sense that his attributes make a circuit and connection. A kind of awareness of self (a high and human characteristic), with a pleasure in the fact, is perhaps the central principle which instead of simplifying the attributes gives each one a special function in the whole, a double or reflex value. Falstaff or such a character of self-conscious "infinite variety"[2] as Cleopatra are

---

2 I do not mean that self-consciousness is the only principle of complexity in character, yet a considerable degree of it would appear to be a requisite for poetic interest.

concrete universals because they have no class names, only their own proper ones, yet are structures of such precise variety and centrality that each demands a special interpretation in the realm of human values.

Character is one type of concrete universal; there are other types, as many perhaps as the central terms of criticism; but most can be learned I believe by examination of metaphor—the structure most characteristic of concentrated poetry. The language of poets, said Shelley, "is vitally metaphorical: that is, it marks the before unapprehended relations of things and perpetuates their apprehension." Wordsworth spoke of the abstracting and modifying powers of the imagination. Aristotle said that the greatest thing was the use of metaphor, because it meant an eye for resemblances. Even the simplest form of metaphor or simile ("My love is like a red, red rose") presents us with a special and creative, in fact a concrete, kind of abstraction different from that of science. For behind a metaphor lies a resemblance between two classes, and hence a more general third class. This class is unnamed and most likely remains unnamed and is apprehended only through the metaphor. It is a new conception for which there is no other expression. Keats discovering Homer is like a traveler in the realms of gold, like an astronomer who discovers a planet, like Cortez gazing at the Pacific. The title of the sonnet, "On First Looking into Chapman's Homer,"[3] seems to furnish not so much the subject of the poem as a fourth member of a central meta- /79/ phor, the real subject of the poem being an abstraction, a certain kind of thrill in discovering, for which there is no name and no other description, only the four members of the metaphor pointing, as to the center of their pattern. The point of the poem seems to lie outside both vehicle and tenor.

To take a more complicated instance, Wordsworth's "Solitary Reaper"[4] has the same basic metaphorical structure, the girl alone reaping and singing, and the two bird images, the nightingale in Arabian sands and the cuckoo among the Hebrides, the three figures serving the parallel or metaphorical function of bringing out the abstraction of loneliness, remoteness, mysterious charm in the singing. But there is also a kind of third-dimensional significance, in the fact that one bird is far out in the northern sea, the other far off in southern sands, a fact which is not part of the comparison between the birds and the girl. By an implication cutting across the plane of logic of the metaphor, the girl and the two birds suggest extension in space, universality, and world communion—an effect supported by other details of the poem such as the overflowing of the vale profound, the mystery of the Erse song, the bearing of the song away in the witness' heart, the past and future themes which the girl may be singing. Thus a central abstraction is created, of communion, telepathy in solitude, the prophetic soul of the wide world dreaming on things to come—an abstraction which is the effect not wholly of the metaphor elaborated logically (in a metaphysical way) but of a working on two axes, by association rather than by logic, by a three-dimensional complexity of structure.

To take yet a third instance, metaphoric structure may appear where we are less likely to realize it explicitly—in poetic narratives, for example, elliptically concealed in the more obvious narrative outlines. "I can bring you," writes Max Eastman, "examples of diction that is metrical but not metaphoric—a great part of the popular ballads, for example—and you can hardly deny that they too are poetic." But the best story poems may be analyzed, I believe, as metaphors without expressed tenors, as symbols which speak for themselves. "La /80/ Belle Dame Sans Merci," for example (if a literary ballad may be taken), is about a knight, by profession a man of action, but sensitive, like the lily and the rose, and about a faery lady with wild, wild eyes. At a more abstract level, it is about the loss of self in the mysterious lure of beauty—whether woman, poetry, or poppy. It sings the irretrievable departure from practical normality (the squirrel's granary is full), the wan isolation after ecstasy. Each reader will experience the poem at his own level of experience or at several. A good story poem is like a stone thrown into a pond, into our minds, where ever widening concentric circles of meaning

---

3 [See p. 203.]
4 [See p. 169.]

go out—and this because of the structure of the story.

"A poem should not mean but be."[5] It is an epigram worth quoting in every essay on poetry. And the poet "nothing affirmeth, and therefore never lieth." "Sit quidvis," said Horace, "simplex dumtaxat et unum" [Be the work what you will, let it be simple and uniform]. It seems almost the reverse of the truth. "Complex dumtaxat et unum" [Let it be complex and uniform] would be better. Every real poem is a complex poem, and only in virtue of its complexity does it have artistic unity. A newspaper poem by Edgar Guest[6] does not have this kind of unity, but only the unity of an abstractly stated sentiment.

The principle is expressed by Aristotle when he says that beauty is based on unity in variety, and by Coleridge when he says that "The Beautiful, contemplated in its essentials, that is, in *kind* and not in *degree,* is that in which the *many,* still seen as many becomes one," and that a work of art is "rich in proportion to the variety of parts which it holds in unity." /81/

v

It is usually easier to show how poetry works than to show why anyone should want it to work in a given way. Rhetorical analysis of poetry has always tended to separate from evaluation, technique from worth. The structure of poems as concrete and universal is the principle by which the critic can try to keep the two together. If it be granted that the "subject matter" of poetry is in a broad sense the moral realm, human actions as good or bad, with all their associated feelings, all the thought and imagination that goes with happiness and suffering (if poetry submits "the shews of things to the desires of the Mind"), then the rhetorical structure of the concrete universal, the complexity and unity of the poem, is also its maturity or sophistication or richness or depth, and hence its value. Complexity of form is sophistication of content. The unity and maturity of good poems are two sides of the same thing. The kind of unity which we look for and find in poetry is attained only through a degree of complexity in design which itself involves maturity and richness. For a visual diagram of the metaphysics of poetry one might write vertically the word complexity, a column, and give it a head with Janus faces, one looking in the rhetorical direction, unity, and the other in the axiological, maturity.

A final point to be made is that a criticism of structure and of value is an objective criticism. It rests on facts of human psychology (as that a man may love a woman so well as to give up empires), facts, which though psychological, yet are so well acknowledged as to lie in the realm of what may be called public psychology—a realm which one should distinguish from the private realm of the author's psychology and from the equally private realm of the individual reader's psychology (the vivid pictures which poetry or stories are supposed to create in the imagination, or the venerable action of catharsis—all that poetry is said to *do* rather than to *be*). Such a criticism, again, is objective and absolute, as distinguished from the relative criticism of idiom and period. I mean that this criticism will notice that Pope is different from Shakespeare, but /82/ will notice even more attentively that Shakespeare is different from Taylor the Water Poet and Pope different from Sir Richard Blackmore. Such a criticism will be interested to analyze the latter two differences and see what these differences have in common and what Shakespeare and Pope have in common, and it will not despair of describing that similarity (that formula or character of great poetry) even though the terms be abstract and difficult. Or, if we are told that there is no universal agreement about what is good—that Pope has not been

---

5 [See p. 219.]

6 A reader whose judgment I esteem tells me that such a name appears in a serious discussion of poetics anomalously and in bad taste. I have allowed it to remain (in preference to some more dignified name of mediocrity) precisely because I wish to insist on the existence of badness in poetry and so to establish an antithetic point of reference for the discussion of goodness. Relativistic argument often creates an illusion in its own favor by moving steadily in a realm of great and nearly great art. See, for example, George Boas, *A Primer for Critics* (Baltimore, 1937), where a cartoon by Daumier appears toward the end as a startling approach to the vulgar. The purpose of my essay is not judicial but theoretical, that is, not to exhibit original discoveries in taste, but to show the relationship between examples acknowledged to lie in the realms of the good and the bad.

steadily held in esteem, that Shakespeare has been considered a barbarian, the objective analyst of structures can at least say (and it seems much to say) that he is describing a class of poems, those which through a peculiar complexity possess unity and maturity and in a special way can be called both individual and universal. Among all recorded "poems," this class is of a relative rarity, and further this class will be found in an impressive way to coincide with those poems which have by some body of critics, some age of educated readers, been called great.

The function of the objective critic is by approximate descriptions of poems, or multiple restatements of their meaning, to aid other readers to come to an intuitive and full realization of poems themselves and hence to know good poems and distinguish them from bad ones. It is of course impossible to tell all about a poem in other words. Croce tells us, as we should expect him to, of the "impossibility of ever rendering in logical terms the full effect of any poetry or of other artistic work." "Criticism, nevertheless," he tells us, "performs its own office, which is to discern and to point out exactly where lies the poetical motive and to formulate the divisions which aid in distinguishing what is proper to every work." The situation is something like this: In each poem there is something (an individual intuition—or a concept) which can never be expressed in other terms. It is like the square root of two or like pi, which cannot be expressed by rational numbers, but only as their *limit*. Criticism of poetry is like 1.414 . . . or 3.1416 . . ., not all it would be, yet all that can be had and very useful. /83/

C. DAY LEWIS

The Poet's Way of Knowledge

[C. Day Lewis (1904–), English poet and (under the pseudonym of "Nicholas Blake") detective-story writer, was born in Ireland but educated in England, where he has made his home. While at Oxford he became a close friend of W. H. Auden and Stephen Spender, and as a poet he is commonly associated with these men. He has been Professor of Poetry at Oxford, and is author of *A Hope for Poetry* (1934), *The Poetic Image* (1947), and an autobiography, *The Buried Day* (1960). The following selection was delivered as a lecture at Cambridge University in 1956 and was published in book form the following year (Cambridge, 1957).]

Once upon a time poetry and science were one, and its name was Magic. Magic, for our earliest ancestors, was the most effective way of understanding nature and their fellow-men, and of gaining power over them. It was not till some three centuries ago that science finally broke away from magic: the scientific revolution of the seventeenth century withdrew from the "supernatural" as a field of study; and if science since then has led to other varieties of superstition, we must blame, not the scientists, but the layman, who finds superstition a difficult thing to live without. The course of poetry has been different. If the first great pre-scientific hypothesis was animism, and the first great pre-scientific method was imitation, then poetry, in so far as it still rests upon imitation and animism, must seem a very primitive procedure.

Nevertheless, I believe poetry to be a possible way of gaining and imparting knowledge—a son of the same father as science: the brothers may quarrel from time to time, but each in his own field they are working towards compatible ends. To define the field of poetry should make it clear in what sense we may claim that poetry is concerned with knowledge. This I shall try to do. And I shall also suggest that there are remarkable affinities between the method of the scientist and the method of the poet—between the ways their minds work, particularly at one crucial stage of their investigations. /3/

Although no one has ever succeeded in defining poetry, there have been many praiseworthy attempts to say what poetry is *for*. These have always been bounded by two extremes—the idea of poetry as an end in itself, and the idea of poetry as a means. In the 1890's, for example, reacting no doubt against the prevalent utilitarianism of their day, poets proclaimed "Art for Art's sake". Poetry should be a ritual, a mystique, detached from morality, from the factual and the topical, from any religious preaching or scientific teaching: its job was to be beautiful, and useless. The young Yeats could deplore "that brooding over scientific opinion which", he believed, had "extinguished the central flame in Tennyson". And it is noticeable that this manifestation took place at a time when science, flushed with a century of practical success, had got rather above itself and was claiming the whole world of knowledge, achieved or potential, as its own. Let me quote from a popular handbook of science first published in 1892:

> There is no short cut to truth, no way to gain a knowledge of the universe except through the gateway of scientific method. The hard and stony path of classifying facts and reasoning upon them is the only way to ascertain truth. It is the reason and not the imagination which must ultimately be appealed to. The poet may give us in sublime language an account of the origin and purport of the universe, but in the end it will not satisfy our aesthetic judgment, our idea of harmony and beauty, like the few facts which the scientist may venture to tell us in the same field. /4/

No wonder, faced with such a deluge of complacency, there was a scramble for the summit of pure poetry. To the passage I have just quoted—and it does not represent the scientific attitude today—one might reply like this: Let us suppose that, not a "few facts" but everything there is to be known about the oceans had been discovered by hydrographers, marine biologists and the rest; and let us suppose that psychologists and neurologists had arrived at a complete comprehension of the workings of the human mind; and let us suppose that some artist-scientist, some Leonardo, had incorporated all this knowledge in a lucid and commanding book: would that book "satisfy our aesthetic judgment, our idea of harmony and beauty" more fully than they are satisfied by *The Ancient Mariner?* I doubt it. Would that book supersede *The Ancient Mariner?* I am quite sure it would not.

"Well, of course it wouldn't", you may say: "the two works are not comparable: the one is a poem of pure imagination, whereas the other would be an assembly of observed facts and verified laws, of knowledge about real things." Certainly: but are you implying that poetry is not concerned with "real things"? Is not the feel of a thing as real, as much a fact, as the thing felt? Is not the conveying of the quality or value of an experience, therefore, a contribution to knowledge no less useful than the analysis of that experience in terms of physical fact and natural law? Coleridge's poem, through images of ocean travel, tells a story of guilt, retribution and expiation—a sequence of events no less /5/ actual than the sequence of events which produces coal gas. Any psychologist would agree, I think, that the mental events symbolised in the poem are true to observed facts of human behaviour. But the poem does not merely embody a complex of experiences; it *is* an experience: and thus the kind of knowing it offers is different from the knowledge we should get from a number of case-histories illustrating the same sequence of mental events.

If we reject the idea of poetry as nothing but an end in itself, we shall see it as a means towards a special kind of knowing. What is this "special kind of knowing" we claim for poetry? Poetry, they tell us, gives us a keener awareness of life. Such definitions are lamentably vague. But attempts at greater precision have not proved much more satisfactory. These can be summed up under two general headings: the idea that poetry improves us, by showing us images of perfection—"the end of

all earthly learning being virtuous action", or, as Bacon put it, "Poesy serveth and conferreth to magnanimity, morality, and to delectation"; and the idea that poetry is a way of penetrating through appearances to the heart of reality. The former leans upon Aristotle's definition of poetry as *mimesis,* imitation; the latter, towards poetry as the re-ordering and re-creation of experience: here we have, respectively, the traditions of mimetic and of symbolic magic.

The common factor is, of course, pleasure. And critics have theorised for centuries about the nature of the pleasure which poetry gives. I. A. Richards, for /6/ example, who based his critique on the profoundly romantic principle that "experience is its own justification", explained the pleasure we receive from poetry in terms of psychic balance. "We must picture . . . the stream of the poetic experience as the swinging back into equilibrium of these disturbed interests." A poem a day keeps the psychiatrist away. Richards distinguishes between the statement of science and the pseudo-statement of poetry: the latter, he says, "makes us remember how we felt"; it operates in a field which is closed to science. "Language logically and scientifically used cannot describe a landscape or a face." Mr. T. R. Henn has spoken of the moral value of art as the "sensitizing of the human mind to the living world and its complexities"; "the final justification of all poetry", he says, is "that it seeks to express a peculiar fusion of ideas and emotions which are normally on the edge of consciousness, or even beyond it."

But, for the most eloquent justification of poetry by a contemporary, I might go, not to any poet or critic, but to a great mathematician. Here is what A. N. Whitehead wrote:

The soul cries aloud for release into change. It suffers the agonies of claustrophobia. The transitions of humour, wit, irreverence, play, sleep, and—above all—of art are necessary for it. Great art is the arrangement of the environment so as to provide for the soul vivid, but transient, values.

But, he goes on,

great art is more than a transient refreshment. It is something which adds to the permanent richness of the soul's /7/ self-attainment. It justifies itself both by its immediate enjoyment, and also by its discipline of the inmost being. Its discipline is not distinct from enjoyment, but by reason of it. . . . The fertilisation of the soul is the reason for the necessity of art.

"The soul cries aloud for release into change." Set that beside Yeats's lines, "Man is in love and loves what vanishes. What more is there to say?", and you get one of the great paradoxes on which poetry is based.

Let us descend now from this rarefied atmosphere and see if, by means of a parable, or pseudo-statement, we may more sharply distinguish the poet's way of knowledge from the scientist's. I will ask you to imagine Wordsworth on a motor-tour of the Western Highlands with a young scientist called Jones—an anthropologist. I must also ask you to forget, for the time being, the actual origin of Wordsworth's *The Solitary Reaper*. Well now, driving through a remote glen, they see a girl, all by herself in a field, wielding a sickle. It is very picturesque. Jones stops the car, for a better look. He and Wordworth become aware that the girl is singing—a tune they have never heard, in an unfamiliar mode.

"I wish I knew what she's singing," says Wordsworth.

"Why not ask her?" says Jones. "No. Wait a minute." Jones, you see, is a conscientious scientist: the girl may not speak English, he thinks; she may not know the name of the song, or her evidence may be inaccurate.

"Look here, Wordsworth," he says. "I'll just run back to the hotel and fetch my tape-recorder. You hold her in conversation till I get back." /8/

Wordsworth's capacity for holding country folk in conversation is, of course, notorious. All goes well: the tape-recorder is fetched, the girl induced to repeat her song. Jones notices, while she is doing so, that Wordsworth has gone back to the car and is holding his hands over his ears: the behaviour-patterns of poets really are unpredictable.

Jones got his recording, and having submitted it to musical experts, learnt that it was a Jacobite lament, in Gaelic, previously unknown. His curiosity stimulated, he presently returned to the neighbourhood of the glen and put in several months' hard field work. He found there an isolated pocket of earlier civilisation almost untouched by modern communications. The girl, for instance, was reaping that field with a sickle, alone, in accordance with an ancient belief that to do so would ensure fertility in a young bride. The Jacobite lament had got superimposed upon this much more primitive custom as a result of the Young Pretender's having made a brief sojourn in the glen, in the course of which he begot several children. Jones set out his findings in an article contributed to a learned periodical: the article was entitled "Some Notes towards a Survey of Residual Culture-Patterns in the Western Highlands of Scotland." This article started a lively correspondence: a fellow-anthropologist, for instance, wrote to tell Jones that he had observed curiously similar fertility-rites in the Trobriand Islands. Gradually, a mass of facts was accumulated. Brooding over these, Jones one day in a flash of illumination perceived a certain thread running /9/ through them, relating them. Cautiously, perseveringly he tested it: the thread held firm. He had discovered a law. Jones' First Law, as it is called, is familiar to all anthropologists, and I need not trouble you with it.

Meantime, Wordsworth also had made his contribution to knowledge. It, too, is familiar:

Behold her, single in the field,
Yon solitary Highland Lass!
Reaping and singing by herself;
Stop here, or gently pass!
Alone she cuts and binds the grain,
And sings a melancholy strain;
O listen! for the Vale profound
Is overflowing with the sound.

No nightingale did ever chaunt
More welcome notes to weary bands
Of travellers in some shady haunt,
Among Arabian sands:
A voice so thrilling ne'er was heard
In spring-time from the Cuckoo-bird,
Breaking the silence of the seas
Among the farthest Hebrides.

Will no one tell me what she sings?—
Perhaps the plaintive numbers flow
For old, unhappy, far-off things,
And battles long ago:
Or is it some more humble lay,
Familiar matter of today?

Some natural sorrow, loss, or pain,
That has been, and may be again. /10/

Whate'er the theme, the Maiden sang
As if her song could have no ending;
I saw her singing at her work,
And o'er the sickle bending;—
I listened, motionless and still;
And, as I mounted up the hill,
The music in my heart I bore,
Long after it was heard no more.

A contribution to knowledge? Yes. "Art is concerned with uniqueness, science with generality"; and, as Yeats said, "Nothing unique is measurable". For Jones, the girl in the field became one fact in a heap of similar facts whose discovered relationships finally led to the great generalisation known as Jones's First Law. We remember Wordsworth's moral distaste for scientific ideas—for their abstraction, the way they seemed to leave out everything that was most important. Wordsworth's task was to show, not similarity, but uniqueness—the uniqueness immanent in a commonplace experience. His concern is not even with the girl as an unique individual, so much as with the state of mind she produces in him. The knowledge we get from the poem is knowledge of a certain mood; and this is the mood of "Man is in love and loves what vanishes". Each of us has experienced this sense of revelation, or at least of profound significance trembling on the edge of revelation, which some chance encounter inspires. We want the encounter prolonged until we have extracted its full meaning; but only art can stabilise the passing experience, the fleeting mood, into something both /11/ momentous and permanent. "The Maiden sang As if her song could have no ending." But every song has to end: although its life may be protracted for a while—"The music in my heart I bore, Long after it was heard no more", the unique quality of the experience it gives can survive only as a dwindling memory, unless it is fixed, developed, printed in a work of art.

We imagined Wordsworth returning to the car and holding his hands over his ears when the song was resung. The poet's trained instinct had told him that he must hear no more: the germ of a poem was already at work in his mind, and further factual knowledge might endanger it. How significant it is

that his first version of the line, "I listened, motionless and still," was "I listened, *till I had my fill*". Just as it was necessary for Jones to find out what the girl was singing, so, for Wordsworth, it was essential *not* to know. Look at the structure of the poem. Stanza 1 states the physical facts. Stanza 2, with its images of nightingale and cuckoo, enlarges those facts by giving us the tone and thrill of the experience. In stanza 3 we concentrate upon its essential meaning; and it is done, you notice, by asking questions to which the answers must remain for ever unknown—was the song about "battles long ago", or some "familiar matter of today"? Had Wordsworth followed his "Will no one tell me what she sings?" with seven lines informing us that it was a Jacobite lament, we might still have had a good poem: but it would have been quite a different poem, because it would be giving us knowledge of a different state of mind; and it would /12/ have required a resolution of the theme other than the one we get in stanza 4, where the poet returns to the physical facts, charged now with the emotional meaning that has been generated in stanzas 2 and 3.

Here is a poem, then, which offers us knowledge of a particular state of mind—one that the poet experienced originally, but that the sensitive reader may to some degree share with him through the poem.

Certain objections may now arise. The crudest would be this: "But I don't *need* knowledge about my feelings or my states of mind: they are mine: if I know anything at all, I know them." This is like a man saying, "Oh but I live in Suffolk, so I don't need to look at Constable's paintings." Next, a more serious objection: a chemist might argue,

"A chemical experiment in accordance with a given formula, provided it is correctly carried out with adequate equipment, will invariably produce the same result through the same sequence of events. That predictability is what *I* mean by knowledge. You may talk of a poem as a controlled experiment; but its results are unpredictable—no two readers respond identically to a given poem: it is wrong to give the name 'knowledge' to so variable a set of responses."

I do not think this argument is very sound. Though competent readers (and I do not mean literary critics only) might differ on the meaning of particular passages in a poem, there is unlikely to be any wide divergence between them in respect to its general tenor. Even if there were, it would not greatly matter: must uniformity /13/ of response be a condition of every kind of knowledge? Individuals, because they are each unique, will within certain limits interpret differently the unique events we call a poem: but their responses have one thing in common—the conviction of truth, a sense that the poem has enabled them to *know* more clearly, more deeply or more passionately.

But apart from this, the enlightened scientist today will *not* equate knowledge with predictability: he is more likely to say, "there is a probability amounting to a certainty that the result of a given experiment will be *x*". For instance, if you put several hundred tons of ammonium nitrate in a dump, there is a probability, amounting to a certainty, that they will stay quiet: but there have been one or two cases where dumps of pure ammonium nitrate have spontaneously blown up. It may have been, of course, that the ammonium nitrate was not, as it was believed to be, pure. But it is also possible that some *unpredictable* grouping of random micro-events occurred, to render the mass unstable. Now until recently the scientist has sought for general laws governing macro-events, and has drawn from them inferences about individual events. Whereas the poet generally seeks first for knowledge of the individual micro-event and its relation to the macrocosm: that is one thing Coleridge meant when he said that a poem is an organic growth from within outwards. But, during the last half-century, physical scientists have moved towards the study of the micro-event: this has brought them nearer to the poets, and brought them up /14/ against the realisation that there is an irreducible limit to what can be known by observation about even the smallest event in isolation from all other events. Heisenberg's Principle of Uncertainty says that there is a limit to the knowledge we can gain about a micro-event in isolation, because in order to observe it we have to do something to it, and thus to change it. Both the scientist and the poet are concerned to diminish as far as possible the area of uncertainty. Wordsworth, stopping his ears when the girl was singing her song again, did so in order to preserve intact and precise his sensations on first hearing her—in order not to widen the area of uncertainty. So, a physicist will evacuate a tube to study the behaviour of the electrons in it, unconfused by the presence of gas atoms. He and Wordsworth are both selecting from the sum total of "real" conditions.

A third objection to poetry as knowledge is based on perception. We know what we do know through our senses. Science is concerned with the perceptible world: poetry, though it uses material of the perceptible world, is concerned with the imperceptible. But the imperceptible admits of no examination, no proof; therefore no activity within the field of the imperceptible can claim to produce knowledge. This—the materialist argument—has been rendered obsolete by modern physics. Let me quote from Martin Johnson's *Art and Scientific Thought:*

> Now much of the concern of the modern physical scientist, atoms, electrons, atomic nuclei, electron-waves, etc., is essentially not of a nature to be directly known to /15/ sight, touch, or hearing. These "things" are as far from being objects of direct sense-perception as anything imagined by the most fantastic of artists. If the latter justifies himself by the coherence of the communicated ideas to which his patterns give rise, where is he resembling and where is he differing from, the physicist whose view of the universe is a deliberately woven structure of ideas which also radically diverges from sense perception?

This, coming from a scientist, puts the whole problem of scientific knowledge and poetic knowledge on a different, a much sounder basis. Elsewhere Mr. Johnson writes, "It becomes profitable to regard art and science as each attempting to communicate mental images through patterns and structures and forms, in the qualitative domain of feeling and in the quantitative domain of measurement respectively". And again, "The test of the validity of the scientist's 'pattern' of ideas is that its form must render it communicable". The distinction between qualitative and quantitative defines the separate fields of science and poetry: the emphasis on communicability shows the common interest of the two. If you still like to think of science as "knowledge", and poetry as at best some kind of "pseudo-knowledge", no one can stop you, but you will be thinking in terms unacceptable to many scientists today. Here, for instance, is what a biologist, Professor J. Z. Young, says:

> . . . in our specialized society there are many individuals who contribute to the whole by the study of the means of communication itself—artists, writers, critics, and thinkers, for example. We can describe their activities also in objective /16/ language. The creative artist is an observer whose brain works in new ways, making it possible for him to convey information to others about matters that were not a subject for communication before. It is by search for means of communication that we sharpen our powers of observation. The discoveries of the artist and scientist are exactly alike in this respect.

As I understand it, perhaps the greatest problem now facing those sciences which cannot use the language of mathematics is the problem of finding a language more efficient to communicate their ideas. It is a problem greatly complicated, even for the mathematician, by the principles of Relativity, which demand that a statement about any course of events should admit the modifications necessary if it is to be equally true for any other observer stationed anywhere or moving in any direction at any speed. In the writings of scientists we frequently come across such phrases as "Physiologists have no generally accepted way of talking about" so and so. They tell us that the exact *description* of their thoughts is part of the discipline required for discovery: if we could find the right way to describe a given process, we should know more about the process. It is here that the affinity between poetic method and modern scientific method is most striking. The poet today, like the scientist, thinks of his work as a kind of exploration. Not all poets in all their poems, but at least many poets in many of their poems, are aiming to relate and clarify their experiences, to arrive at greater self-knowledge. The poet's problem of communication is this: he wishes /17/ to communicate something to himself; if he suc-

ceeds in doing so, he will also communicate something—though not precisely the same something—to the reader. He is unlikely nowadays to think of poetry as an imitation of nature, of human actions and virtues: he sees it rather as a re-ordering of experience, or as a process by which the symbolic value of his memories is discovered.

I would not want you to forget what is often lost to sight among the ramifications of critical theory—the poet as a maker. Absorbed in the pure but not simple craft of verse, in the extreme pleasure and pain of making a poem, he will become temporarily unaware of the searcher after knowledge who stands at his elbow. The poet is still, above all, a maker: but, for good or ill, his mind does seem committed to a more insistent self-consciousness and a greater degree of complexity than many of his predecessors shared: one sign of this is the number of poems written nowadays which are in effect poems about the poetic sensibility and the poetic act.

The initial stage of making a poem is often a kind of groping in the dark. Consider the possible ways in which a poem such as *The Solitary Reaper* might be conceived. The poet may first become aware of a certain poetic form, its structure and rhythms, insistently haunting his mind—a song without words, which demands of him that he find the words for it. Or he might simply say to himself "I've been writing a great deal of blank verse this year: I need a change, what about some rhyming eight-line stanzas with four beats to the line?" Or a phrase out of a book he is reading makes him /18/ prick up his inward ear. Or a line of poetry comes to him, full-fledged, out of the blue. He may find himself arrested by a snapshot in a photograph album, or pondering some past episode which has suddenly presented itself to him with a look of singular complicity. The clue, the donnée, whatever it be, may have a self-evident bearing on what happens to be preoccupying the poet at the time; or it may seem to have none at all.

The poet fixes this clue as bait on the end of his line, casts it into the sea of his experience, and in a watchful passivity waits for whatever may attach itself to the bait. What is he fishing for? Memories, images, phrases.

Many come up; and most of them have to be thrown back into the sea, because they are misleading, or unsuitable, or irrelevant. To what? To the pattern just beginning to take shape in the poet's mind—a pattern still only hinted at, which will reveal the theme of the poem. Let us suppose that the subject of the poem is a girl cutting corn in a field, alone, singing to herself. The poet has to discover what this subject means to him: the experience, whether first-hand or second-hand, embodied in this subject could allow many interpretations: the interpretation finally offered by the poet is the theme of the poem.

We are compelled to speak of the poetic process in metaphor. At this early stage, the poet has begun to build a house with only one small part of the blue-print available to him, or while he is still drawing the blue-print, or with many alternative blue-prints at his disposal. If he has to work in this hand-to-mouth way, it is /19/ because conception and form are for him inseparable, because a poem is an organic growth in which the theme only reveals itself through the growing pattern. "How can I tell what I mean till I see what I say?" Most poems which go wrong, go wrong through the poet's failure to extract the right theme, or extract it whole, from his subject-matter. His activity during the initial stages of making a poem is equivalent to what Professor Young calls "doubt" in scientific investigation: it is rigorous questioning of data—data which include the poem's original subject, the secondary subject-matter which is attracted into the field of the poem out of the poet's whole life-experience, and the formal patterns into which he is beginning to arrange it. This questioning is, for the poet as for the scientist, an arduous intellectual exertion. He must justify himself, as Martin Johnson puts it, "by the coherence of the communicated ideas to which his patterns give rise". Coherence is achieved formally by the pattern of rhyme and metre, the correspondences of phrasing and imagery. But formal coherence is vain unless it is coherence round a well articulated theme: the latter alone can give poetic meaning to experience, and thus communicate a unique state of mind.

In this questioning, language is of supreme importance. Poets are compelled to break

away from the language of their predecessors, a poet may be compelled to alter his own style radically, because language is the instrument of poetic investigation and quickly grows blunt. If we write in the style of Herrick, say, or Browning, we shall find ourselves feebly reproducing /20/ Herrick's or Browning's state of mind. If I have perfected a language of my own, I may have to discard it because its very perfection induces facility—the poet's greatest danger: a much-used idiom, like a well-worn path, will lead the poet's steps insensibly away from the theme he should be searching for, to some familiar and exhausted one. It is a paradoxical truth that the poet needs his instrument, language, to resist him if it is to cut deep and disclose some new, living aspect of whatever themes are implicit in his experience.

I have spoken of the early stages of a poem as a kind of groping in the dark. I want you now to consider three quotations:

> (i) . . . the state of imaginative muddled suspense which precedes successful inductive generalisation.
>
> (ii) There were no particular questions that I asked myself: there were no special objects upon which I directed my mind: there was only a formless and aimless intellectual disturbance, as if I were wrestling with a fog. I know now that this is what always happens when I am in the early stages of work on a problem. Until the problem has gone a long way towards being solved, I do not know what it is.
>
> (iii) For him . . . the ultimate synthesis of a design was never revealed in a flash; rather he approached it with infinite precautions, stalking it, as it were, now from one point of view, now from another, and always in fear lest a premature definition might deprive it of something of its total complexity.

Those three quotations, which could be luminously /21/ describing the conditions at the start of a poem, are in fact from A. N. Whitehead, from the philosopher and historian R. G. Collingwood, and from an essay on Cézanne by Roger Fry. "The state of imaginative muddled suspense", the "formless and aimless intellectual disturbance, as if I were wrestling with a fog"—how gratifying it is to the poet, that a mathematician and a philosopher should start in a muddle, just as he does. "Until the problem has gone a long way towards being solved, I do not know what it is": exactly—until the poem has gone a long way towards being written, *I* do not know what *it* is. And Cézanne's careful "stalking" of his design, his fear "lest a premature definition might deprive it of something of its total complexity"—how often my own impatience has sent a poem off at half-cock, so that it missed its proper theme, or only scored an outer on it.

That "stalking" metaphor brings to mind the legend of Bellerophon and Pegasus. Bellerophon, you remember, spent a whole day, exerting all his strength and science to catch the winged horse. All day it eluded him. That night, as he slept, he dreamed that the goddess of Wisdom had given him a golden bridle. Waking, he found the bridle beside him, and Pegasus at once submitted his neck to it. So the poet must exercise all his skill if he is to capture his theme and mount upon its inspiration. But the skill and devotion are not in themselves enough: without them, he would indeed never be given the magic bridle; one may think of the bridle as a charm woven from his skilful though unavailing /22/ manœuvres to catch Pegasus. But, however devotedly he has used his resources, the bridle still may not come to him. He needs luck, too —the favour of the goddess.

Is not this legend true, not only for the discoveries of the artist, but for those of the scientist, the historian, the philosopher? They, too, must do a great deal of spade-work before the imaginative leap becomes possible; and no amount of spade-work can guarantee that a leap will be made; and when it *is* made, it is often a leap in the dark, or, if you like, *from* the dark—the mathematician Poincaré getting the solution of a problem as he stepped into a cab thinking about other matters, or Kekulé, while riding on top of a London bus, suddenly seeing the carbon and hydrogen atoms, already known to be in the hydro-carbons, join hands to form a long chain, and later seeing them in a dream dance round to join hands again and thus form the benzene ring. The poet's recognition of his theme may seem instantaneous, but it is the end of a gradual process, just as the scientist's recognition of the relationship between recurring sequences of facts has been preceded

by the amassing, the orderly classification and the severe scrutiny of those facts. And one point more; it is unwise to equate scientific activity with what we call reason, poetic activity with what we call imagination. Without the imaginative leap from facts to generalisation, no theoretic discovery in science is made.[1] The poet, on the other hand, must /23/ not only imagine but reason—that is to say, he must exercise a great deal of consciously directed thought in the selection and rejection of his data: there is a technical logic, a poetic reasoning in his choice of the words, rhythms and images by which a poem's coherence is achieved.

Similarly we must be careful to avoid thinking that, whereas poetry is a language based upon metaphor, science always gives us direct, unvarnished, prose statement. The fact is that all languages, except that of the mathematician, have frequent recourse to metaphor. The scientist speaks of electric charges "attracting" or "repelling", of matter "obeying" certain laws. He finds such animistic expressions convenient. But he will use metaphor and analogy, as the poet does, not only for expressing but for discovering. Let us compare the nervous system to a clock and see what this tells us, said Descartes. Let me compare my love to a red, red rose, and see what follows, said Burns. The modern biologist compares the human brain to an automatic pilot, a telephone-exchange, a sorting-office, a government department: he even goes to the electronic engineer and says, "Build me an automatic brain. It may teach me something about the workings of the human brain." Professor Young tells us, of such analogies, "The point is that comparing something unknown with something already known makes it possible to talk about the un- /24/ known. The value of making the analogy is that it facilitates communication."

This is equally true for the communications of science and of poetry. But of course there is a fundamental difference between their

[1] "Copernicus found that the orbits of the planets would look simpler if they were looked at from the sun and not from the earth. But he did not in the first place find this by routine calculation. His first step was a leap of imagination—to lift himself from the earth and put himself wildly, speculatively into the sun" (J. Bronowski).

attitudes towards analogy and metaphor. In a poem, metaphors cannot contradict or cancel one another: they can only blur one another. When they fail, it is because they have failed to make for coherence of pattern. If a poetic metaphor is right, it is always right. A scientific metaphor, on the other hand, like a scientific law, is valid only as long as it covers the known facts, illuminates them, and offers the most effective way of talking about them.

"Where our knowledge halts, our description will resort to metaphor", said Sir Charles Sherrington. This could be taken by the simple-minded as an argument that poetry is not knowledge—or, by the perverse, that much scientific description is a kind of poetry. I should be perverse enough myself to agree with the latter proposition, up to a point. But, at least if we substituted "knowing" for "knowledge", I do not think Sherrington would have quarrelled with my claim for poetry. "The 'I' ", he wrote, "can never come into the plane of objects of sensual perception. It *is* awareness. . . . But the mind does experience itself. Memory attaches to that experience. The self can remember and relive." Poetry, I have suggested, can be a record of the mind experiencing itself, and thus a way of knowing better, of understanding, our moods, feelings, passions. In an /25/ eloquent passage of his Gifford lectures, Sherrington wrote this:

> Mind, for anything perception can compass, goes therefore in our spatial world more ghostly than a ghost. Invisible, intangible, it is a thing not even of outline; it is not a "thing". It remains without sensual confirmation, and remains without it for ever. Stripped to nakedness there remains to it but itself. What then does that amount to? All that counts in life. Desire, zest, truth, love, knowledge, "values". . . .

I have tried to point out certain affinities between the scientific and the poetic approach. I shall now move on to still more debatable ground. What use, if any, can the poet make of scientific theory or applied science? In Wordsworth's preface to the second edition of *Lyrical Ballads*, there are two well-known passages. First, "The poet writes under one restriction only, namely, the necessity of giving immediate pleasure to a human Being possessed of that information which

may be expected from him, not as a lawyer, a physician, a mariner, an astronomer, or a natural philosopher, but as a Man". Second, "The remotest discoveries of the Chemist, the Botanist, or Mineralogist, will be as proper objects of the Poet's art as any upon which it can be employed"—this seems to conflict with what Wordsworth has just said, but he goes on—"if the time should ever come when these things shall be familiar to us, and the relations under which they are contemplated by the followers of these respective sciences shall be manifestly and palpably material to us as enjoying and suffering beings". /26/

I do not think that literary criticism or aesthetics, since Wordsworth's time, have produced any more definitive statement upon this point. Scientific knowledge must have become common knowledge before the poet can use it: for example, as a contemporary critic more boldly puts it, there needs to be a "total assimilation of Freud's discoveries of a kind which allows the writer *to be no longer aware that he is using them*". The scientist might well protest that such a use would mean oversimplification and distortion, but we must for the moment ignore his protests. We must also exclude from this discussion the mere versifying of scientific information: no one is likely nowadays to write a poem on the lines of Erasmus Darwin's *Lives of the Plants*. But most poets are stimulated by the ideas of their age, and all must respond to the climate of their times. Ours, as everyone tells us, is a scientific age; and scientific theory has relaxed the rigid mechanism which so appalled Tennyson when he tried to come to terms with science. It should be not only possible but rewarding for poets now to approach the body of material which scientists have accumulated.

In doing so, however, they are faced with two difficulties. First, the body of material is so vast, demanding ever narrower specialisation. No one could aim, as Humboldt did 150 years ago, to represent the whole of the physical aspect of the universe in one work. A thing of the past, too, is that hopeful amateurism which allowed Alan Sedgwick to get himself elected in 1818 to the Woodwardian Chair of Geology in this University, /27/ while admitting total ignorance of the subject. "Hitherto," he said, "I have never turned a stone: henceforth I will leave no stone unturned." How can the poet today derive any cosmology from science, when the scientific experts themselves are each working within a narrow and seemingly self-contained field? Yet, if the poet's field is the human mind and its values, and men's minds are so widely affected by modern scientific theory and technology, the poet must in his own explorations take account of this changing country through which he moves. He will be better able to do so, perhaps, if he shares the scientist's view of Nature as operating through inexorable laws of necessity, indifferent to Man's notion that he is a special case—the view which caused Whitehead to declare, "the pilgrim fathers of the scientific imagination as it exists today are . . . Aeschylus, Sophocles, Euripides".

The poet's second difficulty is a technical one, and was hinted in that passage from Wordsworth's preface. If, as poets did in the 1930's, he tries to use for metaphor "the remotest discoveries of the Chemist, the Botanist, or Mineralogist", he is in danger of falling into shallow conceit. Until the constructions of modern technology become naturalised objects in landscape and townscape, it is very hard to assimilate them into a poem, for they lack connotation—lack, so to speak, that depth of soil, accumulated by long periods of sensuous and emotional reference, in which poetry may strike roots. No doubt a poem drawing some analogy with the internal-combustion engine would be more likely to com- /28/ municate something to the Common Reader than a poem using metaphor of atomic fission. But poets must still walk a long way behind the technologists for their gleanings and meanings. With scientific theory, the problem is even more awkward. Poetry on the whole requires a stable foundation of ideas from which to make its flights: but today, and particularly in the all-important field of physics, there seems to be a constant modification and readjustment of scientific theory.

Nevertheless, that scientific ideas can be assimilated into poetic knowledge is shown by poems of Edwin Muir, William Empson, Kathleen Raine, and others of our day. Analogies from the sciences have proved useful, also, in literary criticism. Professor George Whalley,

for example, in his illuminating book, *Poetic Process*, proposes the analogy of "the interface" to illustrate the several attitudes towards reality of the poet, the mystic, the scientist and the common man. Sherrington had used the term "interface" to describe the surface of our planet "where phases solid, liquid and gaseous meet", and where "special opportunities for interaction occur". Professor Whalley asks us to "imagine that man and nature (or 'subject' and 'object') meet and embrace each other at an interface"; that "life, naked living, occurs at this interface . . . it is here that man meets and shapes 'nature' and is himself shaped by nature. . . . All values cluster at the interface and are not to be found elsewhere. . . . To be 'involved' at the interface is to be 'real', to engage /29/ in reality". The purpose of the poet, Professor Whalley suggests, is "to reveal 'what it is like' at the interface".

I myself find this parable, of which I have not time to give more than a cursory sketch, an extremely helpful way of talking about poetry. "Reality" is a precarious word; but sooner or later, in discussing the field and purpose of poetry, one cannot avoid it, for if poets are not concerned with the exploration of "life, naked living", at its most intense, and with giving us the feel of it, then I do not know what they *are* up to. Their task is to show the momentousness of life's most commonplace happenings; and it is a task all the more important at a time when man and his planet have dwindled into physical insignificance against the immense distances of space and time which science has revealed. As a recent writer puts it, "There is no immutable law to say that scenes which have been enacted on a puff of stardust in a moment of time should have any ultimate significance". If it is only through religion that we may be *convinced* of the ultimate significance of the human scene, poetry and the other arts can at least give some of us a *sense* of its significance, its momentousness.

It is here, perhaps, that poetry may best act nowadays as corrective and complementary to science. When science tells us that the galaxy to which our solar system belongs is so enormous that light, travelling at 186,000 miles per second, takes between 60,000 and

100,000 years to cross from one rim to the other of the galaxy, we laymen accept the statement but find it meaningless—beyond the comprehension of heart or mind. When /30/ science tells us that a human being contains "1000 billions of unit principles, each of which lives" or that "the human eye has about 137 million separate 'seeing' elements spread out in the sheet of the retina", we are no less paralysed, intellectually and emotionally. Man is appalled by the immensities and the minutenesses which science has disclosed for him. They are indeed unimaginable. But may not poetry be a possible way of mediating them to our imagination? of scaling them down to imaginative comprehension? Let us remember Perseus, who could not look directly at the nightmare Gorgon without being turned to stone, but could look at her image reflected in the shield the goddess of Wisdom lent him.

Certainly, the pictures which science shows to man of the universe he lives in, and of the universe within himself, offer the most amazing material for the poet to meditate upon. It would be a sad thing if no poets could be found to dwell upon it and give it imaginative meaning. Whether the poet is attempting these heights and depths, or is giving significance to life's commonplaces, poetry still involves some kind of animism, some projection of self into the so-called "inanimate" world. This projection will take subtler, more self-conscious forms, no doubt—

The red rose cries, "She is near, she is near":
And the white rose weeps, "She is late";

—it's a long way from that to T. S. Eliot's

> for the roses
> Had the look of flowers that are looked at. /31/

But Eliot with his sophisticated roses and Tennyson with his romantic ones are each giving us knowledge of a certain state of mind.

Early in my lecture I quoted from a handbook of popular science of 1892. Let me now quote from a book of popular science published last year: in his *A Guide to Earth History*, Richard Carrington writes: "Science, art and religion, evolving to new insight from their starting place in the mind of primitive man, are inseparable processes. They are all techniques of knowledge, operating with equal validity at different levels of awareness." If we think of poetry thus, as a technique of knowledge, we shall help break down the artificial and indefensible barriers between science and poetry which, alas, our modern educational system still tends to maintain. And we shall also answer, or rather put into the discard, that other question with which I began—poetry, means or end? Every poet knows that his poem is both an end in itself and a means to further discovery. "To treat life in the spirit of art", said Walter Pater, "is to make life a thing in which means and ends are identified." /32/

Some Definitions of Poetry

The following definitions and statements about poetry have been selected for their aptness, ineptness, historical interest, or picturesqueness. They supplement the definitions and statements included in the essays.

1. . . . the art of poetry is simply the art of electrifying language with extraordinary meaning.—Lascelles Abercrombie, *The Theory of Poetry* (New York, 1926), p. 93.

2. . . . poetry is simply the most beautiful, impressive, and widely effective mode of saying things, . . . —Matthew Arnold, "Heinrich Heine," *Essays in Criticism: First Series* (London, 1921), p. 161.

3. . . . Poetry is Transfiguration, the transfiguration of the Actual or the Real into the Ideal, at a lofty elevation, through the medium of melodious or nobly sounding verse. —Alfred Austin, "The Growing Distaste for the Higher Kinds of Poetry," *Fortnightly Review*, LXXIV N.S. (March, 1904), p. 383.

4. [Poetry] is the lava of the imagination whose eruption prevents an earthquake.— George Gordon, Lord Byron, *Letters and Journals*, III, ed. Rowland E. Prothero (London, 1922) , p. 405.

5. . . . poetry is man's rebellion against being what he is.—James Branch Cabell, *Jurgen* (New York, 1927), p. 333.

6. I wish our clever young poets would remember my homely definitions of prose and poetry; that is, prose = words in their best order; poetry = the *best* words in the best order.—Samuel Taylor Coleridge, *The Table Talk and Omniana of Samuel Taylor Coleridge*, ed. T. Ashe (London, 1896), p. 54.

7. We may . . . define poetry as the art which produces pleasure for the imagination by imitating human actions, thoughts, and passions, in metrical language.—William John Courthope, *Life in Poetry: Law in Taste* (London and New York, 1901), p. 42.

8. Poetry's unnat'ral; no man ever talked poetry 'cept a beadle on boxin' day, or Warren's blackin', or Rowland's oil, or some o' them low fellows; . . . —Mr. Sam Weller,

Senior, in Charles Dickens, *Pickwick Papers* (London and New York, 1910) , II, p. 57.

9. If I read a book [and] it makes my whole body so cold no fire ever can warm me I know *that* is poetry. If I feel physically as if the top of my head were taken off, I know *that* is poetry. These are the only way I know it. Is there any other way.—Emily Dickininson, *The Letters of Emily Dickinson,* ed. Thomas H. Johnson (Cambridge, Mass., 1958), II, pp. 473–74.

10. Poetry seems to me to be the announcement of spiritual discovery.—John Drinkwater, *William Morris* (London, 1912), p. 18.

11. [Poetry] is metaphor, saying one thing and meaning another, the pleasure of ulteriority. Poetry is simply made of metaphor.— Robert Frost, "The Constant Symbol," *Atlantic Monthly*, CLXXVIII (October, 1946), p. 50.

12. Poetry is the language in which man explores his own amazement. It is the language in which he says heaven and earth in one word. It is the language in which he speaks of himself and his predicament as though for the first time. It has the virtue of being able to say twice as much as prose in half the time, and the drawback, if you don't happen to give it your full attention, of seeming to say half as much in twice the time.— Christopher Fry, "Poetry in the Theatre," *Saturday Review*, XXXVI (March 21, 1953), p. 18.

13. Poetry is speech framed for contemplation of the mind by the way of hearing or speech framed to be heard for its own sake and interest even over and above its interest of meaning.—Gerard Manley Hopkins, *The Note-Books and Papers of Gerard Manley Hopkins,* ed. Humphry House (London and New York, 1937), p. 249.

14. . . . poetry is the breath of beauty, flowing around the spiritual world, as the winds that wake up the flowers do about the material; . . . —Leigh Hunt, "Of Statesmen Who Have Written Verses," *A Selection of*

Sketches, Essays, and Critical Memoirs (New York, 1847), I, p. 249.

15. Poetry is the art of uniting pleasure with truth, by calling imagination to the help of reason.—Samuel Johnson, "John Milton," *Lives of the English Poets* (London and New York, 1958), I, p. 100.

16. The business of words in prose is primarily to *state;* in poetry, not only to state, but also (and sometimes primarily) to *suggest.* —John Livingston Lowes, *Convention and Revolt in Poetry* (Boston and New York, 1919), p. 181.

17. Perhaps no person can be a poet, or can even enjoy poetry, without a certain unsoundness of mind, . . . By poetry we mean the art of employing words in such a manner as to produce an illusion on the imagination, the art of doing by means of words what the painter does by means of colours.—Thomas Babington Macaulay, "Milton," *Essays and Biographies* (London, 1906), I, p. 7.

18. [Poetry is] the emotion of life rhythmically remembering beauty: as pictorial art and the art of verbal romance are the vision of life seen in beauty and in beauty revealed: and as music is the echo of life heard in beauty. —Fiona MacLeod, *The Winged Destiny* (London, 1925), p. 274.

19. . . . poetry is a comforting piece of fiction set to more or less lascivious music—a slap on the back in waltz time—a grand release of longings and repressions to the tune of flute, harps, sackbuts, psalteries and the usual strings.—H. L. Mencken, *Prejudices: Third Series* (New York, 1922), p. 151.

20. Poetry comes with anger, hunger and dismay; it does not often visit groups of citizens sitting down to be literary together, and would appal them if it did.—Christopher Morley, *John Mistletoe* (Garden City, N.Y., 1931), p. 55.

21. . . . poetry is not what some have (in intention, rightly) maintained it is—namely, communication—whether of mere emotion, which would be sheer sensation, or of mere thought. It is the communication of an entire experience.—John Middleton Murry, "Pure Poetry," *Countries of the Mind: Second Series* (London, 1931), p. 25.

22. . . . the quintessence of poetry—the pure grain of it that is left when all the chaff has been winnowed away, the unalloyed gold that constitutes its substance—is little else than metaphor.—Helen Huss Parkhurst, *Beauty* (New York, 1930), p. 208.

23. Let us understand by poetry all literary production which attains the power of giving pleasure by its form, as distinct from its matter.—Walter Pater, "Winckelmann," *The Renaissance* (London, 1914), p. 230.

24. Great literature is simply language charged with meaning to the utmost possible degree. . . . The language of prose is much less highly charged, that is perhaps the only availing distinction between prose and poesy. —Ezra Pound, *Literary Essays of Ezra Pound,* ed. T. S. Eliot (Norfolk, Conn., 1954), pp. 23, 26.

25. Poetry is a language that tells us, through a more or less emotional reaction, something that cannot be said.—Edwin Arlington Robinson, as quoted in Joyce Kilmer, *Literature in the Making* (New York and London, 1917), p. 266.

26. . . . poetry is the suggestion, by the imagination, of noble grounds for the noble emotions. I mean, by the noble emotions, those four principal sacred passions—Love, Veneration, Admiration, and Joy . . . ; and their opposites—Hatred, Indignation (or Scorn), Horror, and Grief, . . . —John Ruskin, *Modern Painters* (London and New York, 1904), III, p. 28.

27. Poetry is the achievement of the synthesis of hyacinths and biscuits.—Carl Sandburg, "Poetry Considered," *Atlantic Monthly,* CXXXI (March, 1923), p. 343.

28. Touchstone: Truly, I would the gods had made thee poetical.

Audrey: I do not know what "poetical" is: is it honest in deed and word? is it a true thing?

Touchstone: No, truly; for the truest poetry is the most feigning; and lovers are given to poetry.—William Shakespeare, *As You Like It,* Act III, scene 3.

29. Poetry is a revelation in words by means of the words.—Wallace Stevens, "The Noble Rider and the Sound of Words," *The Necessary Angel* (New York, 1951), p. 33.

30. Poetry is like shot silk with many glowing colours, and every reader must find his own interpretation according to his ability,

and according to his sympathy with the poet. —Alfred, Lord Tennyson, *The Works of Tennyson,* ed. Hallam, Lord Tennyson (New York, 1939), p. 879.

31. Poetry is the rhythmic, inevitably narrative, movement from an overclothed blindness to a naked vision that depends in its intensity on the strength of the labor put into the creation of the poetry.—Dylan Thomas, "Replies to an Enquiry," *Quite Early One Morning* (New York, 1954), p. 188.

32. Poetry is the power to define the undefinable in terms of the unforgettable.— Louis Untermeyer and Carter Davidson, *Poetry: Its Appreciation and Enjoyment* (New York, 1934), p. 9.

33. Poetry is the music of the soul, and above all of great and of feeling souls. One merit of poetry few persons will deny; it says more and in fewer words than prose.—Voltaire, "Poets," *A Philosophical Dictionary,* trans. William F. Fleming (New York, 1901), p. 218.

34. . . . we can say now, at least tentatively, that poetry is the statement of a strongly personal and poignant emotion in words that sing, that it is of near kin to ecstasy, and that it quintessentializes some part of life that the poet has discovered for himself.—Cornelius Weygandt, *The Time of Tennyson* (New York and London, 1936), p. 7.

PART TWO

Poems

Sir Patrick Spens

The king sits in Dumferling toune,
　　Drinking the blude-reid wine:
"O whar will I get guid sailor,
　　To sail this schip of mine?"

Up and spak an eldern knicht,
　　Sat at the kings richt kne:
"Sir Patrick Spens is the best sailor,
　　That sails upon the se."

The king has written a braid letter,
　　And signd it wi his hand,
And sent it to Sir Patrick Spens,
　　Was walking on the sand.

The first line that Sir Patrick red,
　　A loud lauch lauched he;
The next line that Sir Patrick red,
　　The teir blinded his ee.

"O wha is this has don this deid,
　　This ill deid don to me,
To send me out this time o' the yeir,
　　To sail upon the se!

"Mak haste, mak haste, my mirry men all,
　　Our guid schip sails the morne."
"O say na sae, my master deir,
　　For I feir a deadlie storme.

"Late, late yestreen I saw the new moone,
　　Wi the auld moone in hir arme,
And I feir, I feir, my deir master,
　　That we will cum to harme."

O our Scots nobles wer richt laith
　　To weet their cork-heild schoone;°
Bot lang owre a' the play wer playd,
　　Thair hats they swam aboone.

O lang, lang may their ladies sit,
　　Wi thair fans into their hand,
Or eir they se Sir Patrick Spens
　　Cum sailing to the land.

O lang, lang may the ladies stand,
　　Wi thair gold kems in their hair,
Waiting for thair ain deir lords,
　　For they'll se thame na mair.

Haf owre, haf owre to Aberdour,
　　It's fiftie fadom deip,
And thair lies guid Sir Patrick Spens,
　　Wi the Scots lords at his feit.

ANONYMOUS

cork-heild schoone: cork-heeled shoes.

＊ ＊ ＊

Adam lay ibounden

Adam lay ibounden,
　　Bounden in a bond;
Four thousand winter
　　Thoght he not too long;
And all was for an appil,
　　An appil that he tok,
As clerkès finden
　　Wreten in here° book.
Ne hadde the appil takè ben,
　　The appil taken ben,
Ne haddè never our lady
　　A ben heavenè quene.
Blessèd be the time
　　That appil takè was.
Therefore we moun° singen
　　Deo gracias.

ANONYMOUS

here: their.　moun: may.

＊ ＊ ＊

Sumer is icumen in

Sumer is icumen in,
　　Lhudè sing cuccu;
Groweth sed and bloweth med
　　And springth the wudè nu.
　　　Sing cuccu!

Awè bleteth after lomb,
　　Lhouth after calvè cu;
Bulluc sterteth, buckè verteth,°
　　Murie sing cuccu.

Cuccu, cuccu, wel
　　Singès thu, cuccu:

Na swike° thu naver nu;
Sing cuccu, nu,
   Sing cuccu,
Sing cuccu, sing cuccu, nu.

ANONYMOUS (c. 1250)

buckè verteth: harbors in the green. swike: cease.

* * *

Forget not yet

Forget not yet the tried intent
Of such a truth, as I have meant,
My great travail, so gladly spent,
   Forget not yet.

Forget not yet when first began
The weary life ye know, since when
The suit, the service none tell can,
   Forget not yet.

Forget not yet the great assays,
The cruel wrong, the scornful ways;
The painful patience of denays,
   Forget not yet.

Forget not yet, forget not this,
How long ago hath been, and is,
The mind that never meant amiss,
   Forget not yet.

SIR THOMAS WYATT (1503?–1542)

* * *

Prothalamion

Calm was the day, and through the trembling
   air
Sweet breathing Zephyrus did softly play,
A gentle spirit, that lightly did delay
Hot Titan's beams, which then did glister
   fair;
When I (whom sullen care,
Through discontent of my long fruitless stay
In princes' court, and expectation vain
Of idle hopes, which still do fly away,
Like empty shadows, did afflict my brain)
Walked forth, to ease my pain,
Along the shore of silver streaming Thames;
Whose rutty bank, the which his river hems,
Was painted all with variable flowers,
And all the meads adorned with dainty gems,
Fit to deck maidens' bowers,
And crown their paramours,
Against the bridal day, which is not long:
   Sweet Thames! run softly, till I end my
   song.

There, in a meadow, by the river's side,
A flock of nymphs I chancèd to espy,
All lovely daughters of the flood thereby,
With goodly greenish locks, all loose untied,
As each had been a bride:
And each one had a little wicker basket,
Made of fine twigs, entrailèd curiously,
In which they gathered flowers to fill their
   flasket,
And with fine fingers cropt full feateously
The tender stalks on high.
Of every sort which in that meadow grew
They gathered some; the violet, pallid blue,
The little daisy, that at evening closes,
The virgin lily, and the primrose true,
With store of vermeil roses,
To deck their bridegroom's posies,
Against the bridal day, which was not long:
   Sweet Thames! run softly, till I end my
   song.

With that, I saw two swans of goodly hue
Come softly swimming down along the Lee;
Two fairer birds I yet did never see;
The snow which doth the top of Pindus strew
Did never whiter shew,
Nor Jove himself, when he a swan would be
For love of Leda, whiter did appear;
Yet Leda was, they say, as white as he
Yet not so white as these, nor nothing near;
So purely white they were,
That even the gentle stream, the which them
   bare,
Seemed foul to them, and bade his billows
   spare
To wet their silken feathers, lest they might
Soil their fair plumes with water not so fair,
And mar their beauties bright,
That shone as heaven's light,
Against their bridal day, which was not long:

Sweet Thames! run softly, till I end my
    song.

Eftsoons the nymphs, which now had flowers
    their fill,
Ran all in haste to see that silver brood,
As they came floating on the crystal flood;
Whom when they saw, they stood amazèd still,
    Their wondering eyes to fill;
Them seemed they never saw a sight so fair
Of fowls so lovely, that they sure did deem
Them heavenly born, or to be that same pair
Which through the sky draw Venus' silver
    team;
For sure they did not seem
To be begot of any earthly seed,
But rather angels, or of angels' breed;
Yet were they bred of summer's heat, they say,
In sweetest season, when each flower and weed
    The earth did fresh array;
So fresh they seemed as day,
Even as their bridal day, which was not long:
    Sweet Thames! run softly, till I end my
    song.

Then forth they all out of their baskets drew
Great store of flowers, the honour of the field,
That to the sense did fragrant odours yield,
All which upon those goodly birds they threw,
And all the waves did strew,
That like old Peneus' waters they did seem,
When down along by pleasant Tempe's shore,
Scattered with flowers, through Thessaly they
    stream,
That they appear, through lilies' plenteous
    store,
Like a bride's chamber floor.
Two of those nymphs, meanwhile, two gar-
    lands bound
Of freshest flowers which in that mead they
    found,
The which presenting all in trim array,
Their snowy foreheads therewithal they
    crowned,
Whilst one did sing this lay,
Prepared against that day,
Against their bridal day, which was not long:
    Sweet Thames! run softly, till I end my
    song.

"Ye gentle birds! the world's fair ornament,
And heaven's glory, whom this happy hour

Doth lead unto your lover's blissful bower,
Joy may you have, and gentle hearts' content
Of your love's couplement;
And let fair Venus, that is queen of love,
With her heart-quelling son upon you smile,
Whose smile, they say, hath virtue to remove
All love's dislike, and friendship's faulty guile
For ever to assoil;
Let endless peace your steadfast hearts accord,
And blessed plenty wait upon your board;
And let your bed with pleasures chaste
    abound,
That fruitful issue may to you afford,
Which may your foes confound,
And make your joys redound
Upon your bridal day, which is not long:
    Sweet Thames! run softly, till I end my
    song."

So ended she; and all the rest around
To her redoubled that her undersong,
Which said their bridal day should not be
    long:
And gentle Echo from the neighbour ground
Their accents did resound.
So forth those joyous birds did pass along,
Adown the Lee, that to them murmured low,
As he would speak, but that he lacked a
    tongue,
Yet did by signs his glad affection show,
Making his stream run slow.
And all the fowl which in his flood did dwell
'Gan flock about these twain, that did excel
The rest, so far as Cynthia doth shend°
The lesser stars. So they, enrangèd well,
Did on those two attend,
And their best service lend,
Against their wedding day, which was not
    long:
    Sweet Thames! run softly, till I end my
    song.

At length they all to merry London came,
To merry London, my most kindly nurse,
That to me gave this life's first native source;
Though from another place I take my name,
An house of ancient fame:
There when they came, whereas° those bricky
    towers
The which on Thames' broad, agèd back do
    ride,

       shend: shame.   **whereas:** where.

Where now the studious lawyers have their
    bowers,
There whilom wont the Templar Knights to
    bide,
Till they decayed through pride:
Next whereunto there stands a stately place,
Where oft I gainèd gifts and goodly grace
Of that great lord which therein wont to
    dwell,
Whose want too well now feels my friendless
    case;
But ah! here fits not well
Old woes, but joys, to tell,
Against the bridal day, which is not long:
    Sweet Thames! run softly, till I end my
      song.

Yet therein now doth lodge a noble peer,
Great England's glory, and the world's wide
    wonder,
Whose dreadful name late through all Spain
    did thunder,
And Hercules' two pillars standing near
Did make to quake and fear:
Fair branch of honour, flower of chivalry!
That fillest England with thy triumph's fame,
Joy have thou of thy noble victory,
And endless happiness of thine own name,
That promiseth the same;
That through thy prowess and victorious arms
Thy country may be freed from foreign
    harms;
And great Elisa's glorious name may ring
Through all the world, filled with thy wide
    alarms,
Which some brave muse may sing
To ages following,
Upon the bridal day, which is not long:
    Sweet Thames! run softly, till I end my
      song.

From those high towers this noble lord issuing,
Like radiant Hesper when his golden hair
In th' ocean billows he hath bathèd fair,
Descended to the river's open viewing,
With a great train ensuing.
Two gentle knights of lovely face and feature
Beseeming well the bower of any queen,
With gifts of wit, and ornaments of nature,
Fit for so goodly stature,
That like the twins of Jove they seemed in
    sight,

Which deck the baldrick of the heavens
    bright;
They two, forth pacing to the river's side,
Received those two fair brides, their love's
    delight;
Which, at th' appointed tide,
Each one did make his bride,
Against their bridal day, which is not long:
    Sweet Thames! run softly, till I end my
      song.

EDMUND SPENSER (1552?–1599)

* * *

Cupid and my Campaspe

Cupid and my Campaspe played
At cards for kisses; Cupid paid.
He stakes his quiver, bow, and arrows,
His mother's doves and team of sparrows,
Loses them too; then down he throws
The coral of his lip, the rose
Growing on's cheek (but none knows how),
With these the crystal of his brow,
And then the dimple of his chin:
All these did my Campaspe win.
At last he set her both his eyes;
She won, and Cupid blind did rise.
    O Love! has she done this to thee?
    What shall, alas, become of me?

JOHN LYLY (1554?–1606)

* * *

Ulysses and the Siren

Siren

Come, worthy Greek, Ulysses, come,
    Possess these shores with me;
The winds and seas are troublesome,
    And here we may be free.
Here may we sit and view their toil
    That travail on the deep,
And joy the day in mirth the while,
    And spend the night in sleep.

Ulysses

Fair nymph, if fame or honor were
  To be attained with ease,
Then would I come and rest with thee,
  And leave such toils as these.
But here it dwells, and here must I
  With danger seek it forth;
To spend the time luxuriously
  Becomes not men of worth.

Siren

Ulysses, O be not deceived
  With that unreal name;
This honor is a thing conceived,
  And rests on others' fame;
Begotten only to molest
  Our peace, and to beguile
The best thing of our life, our rest,
  And give us up to toil.

Ulysses

Delicious nymph, suppose there were
  Nor honor nor report,
Yet manliness would scorn to wear
  The time in idle sport.
For toil doth give a better touch,
  To make us feel our joy;
And ease finds tediousness, as much
  As labor, yields annoy.

Siren

Then pleasure likewise seems the shore
  Whereto tends all your toil,
Which you forgo to make it more,
  And perish oft the while,
Who may disport them diversly,
  Find never tedious day,
And ease may have variety
  As well as action may.

Ulysses

But natures of the noblest frame
  These toils and dangers please,
And they take comfort in the same
  As much as you in ease,
And with the thoughts of actions past
  Are recreated still;
When pleasure leaves a touch at last
  To show that it was ill.

Siren

That doth opinion only cause
  That's out of custom bred,
Which makes us many other laws
  Than ever nature did.
No widows wail for our delights,
  Our sports are without blood;
The world, we see, by warlike wights
  Receives more hurt than good.

Ulysses

But yet the state of things require
  These motions of unrest,
And these great spirits of high desire
  Seem born to turn them best,
To purge the mischiefs that increase
  And all good order mar;
For oft we see a wicked peace
  To be well changed for war.

Siren

Well, well, Ulysses, then I see
  I shall not have thee here,
And therefore I will come to thee,
  And take my fortunes there.
I must be won that cannot win,
  Yet lost were I not won;
For beauty hath created been
  T' undo, or be undone.

SAMUEL DANIEL (*1562–1619*)

* * *

Since there's no help

Since there's no help, come let us kiss and
    part.
Nay, I have done, you get no more of me;
And I am glad, yea, glad with all my heart,
That thus so cleanly I myself can free.
Shake hands for ever, cancel all our vows,
And when we meet at any time again,
Be it not seen in either of our brows
That we one jot of former love retain.
Now at the last gasp of Love's latest breath,
When, his pulse failing, Passion speechless
    lies,
When Faith is kneeling by his bed of death,

And Innocence is closing up his eyes,
　Now, if thou wouldst, when all have given
　　him over,
　From death to life thou mightst him yet
　　recover.

MICHAEL DRAYTON   (*1563–1631*)

* * *

Who is Silvia?

Who is Silvia? what is she,
　That all our swains commend her?
Holy, fair, and wise is she;
　The heaven such grace did lend her,
That she might admirèd be.

Is she kind as she is fair?
　For beauty lives with kindness.
Love doth to her eyes repair,
　To help him of his blindness,
And, being helped, inhabits there.

Then to Silvia let us sing,
　That Silvia is excelling;
She excels each mortal thing
　Upon the dull earth dwelling:
To her let us garlands bring.

WILLIAM SHAKESPEARE   (*1564–1616*)

* * *

SONNET 29

When in disgrace with Fortune

When in disgrace with Fortune and men's
　eyes
I all alone beweep my outcast state,
And trouble deaf heaven with my bootless
　cries,
And look upon myself, and curse my fate,
Wishing me like to one more rich in hope,
Featured like him, like him with friends
　possessed,
Desiring this man's art, and that man's scope,

With what I most enjoy contented least;
Yet in these thoughts myself almost despising,
Haply I think on thee,—and then my state,
Like to the lark at break of day arising
From sullen earth, sings hymns at heaven's
　gate;
For thy sweet love remembered such wealth
　brings
That then I scorn to change my state with
　Kings.

WILLIAM SHAKESPEARE   (*1564–1616*)

* * *

SONNET *129*

The expense of spirit

The expense of spirit in a waste of shame
Is lust in action; and till action, lust
Is perjured, murderous, bloody, full of blame,
Savage, extreme, rude, cruel, not to trust;
Enjoyed no sooner but despisèd straight;
Past reason hunted; and no sooner had,
Past reason hated, as a swallowed bait
On purpose laid to make the taker mad:
Mad in pursuit, and in possession so;
Had, having, and in quest to have, extreme;
A bliss in proof, and proved, a very woe;
Before, a joy proposed; behind, a dream.
　All this the world well knows; yet none
　　knows well
　To shun the heaven that leads men to this
　　hell.

WILLIAM SHAKESPEARE   (*1564–1616*)

* * *

Full fathom five thy father lies

Full fathom five thy father lies;
　Of his bones are coral made:
Those are pearls that were his eyes:
　Nothing of him that doth fade,
But doth suffer a sea-change
Into something rich and strange.

Sea-nymphs hourly ring his knell:
Ding-dong!
Hark! now I hear them,—Ding-dong, bell!

WILLIAM SHAKESPEARE (*1564–1616*)

* * *

Cherry-ripe

There is a garden in her face,
Where roses and white lilies grow,
A heavenly paradise is that place,
Wherein all pleasant fruits do flow.
There cherries grow, which none may buy
Till "Cherry ripe!" themselves do cry.

Those cherries fairly do enclose
Of orient pearl a double row;
Which when her lovely laughter shows,
They look like rose-buds filled with snow.
Yet them nor peer nor prince can buy,
Till "Cherry ripe!" themselves do cry.

Her eyes like angels watch them still;
Her brows like bended bows do stand,
Threatening with piercing frowns to kill
All that attempt with eye or hand
Those sacred cherries to come nigh,
Till "Cherry ripe!" themselves do cry.

THOMAS CAMPION (*1567–1620*)

* * *

Adieu, farewell earth's bliss

Adieu, farewell earth's bliss,
This world uncertain is;
Fond are life's lustful joys,
Death proves them all but toys,
None from his darts can fly.
I am sick, I must die.
Lord, have mercy on us!

Rich men, trust not in wealth,
Gold cannot buy you health;
Physic himself must fade,
All things to end are made.

The plague full swift goes by;
I am sick, I must die.
Lord, have mercy on us!

Beauty is but a flower
Which wrinkles will devour:
Brightness falls from the air,
Queens have died young and fair,
Dust has closed Helen's eye.
I am sick, I must die.
Lord, have mercy on us!

Strength stoops unto the grave,
Worms feed on Hector brave,
Swords may not fight with fate.
Earth still holds ope her gate;
Come! come! the bells do cry.
I am sick, I must die.
Lord, have mercy on us!

Wit with his wantonness
Tasteth death's bitterness;
Hell's executioner
Hath no ears for to hear
What vain art can reply.
I am sick, I must die.
Lord, have mercy on us!

Haste, therefore, each degree,
To welcome destiny.
Heaven is our heritage,
Earth but a player's stage;
Mount we unto the sky.
I am sick, I must die.
Lord, have mercy on us!

THOMAS NASH (*1567–1601*)

* * *

A Valediction: Forbidding Mourning

As virtuous men pass mildly away,
And whisper to their souls to go,
While some of their sad friends do say,
The breath goes now, and some say, no:

So let us melt, and make no noise,
No tear-floods, nor sigh-tempests move,
'Twere profanation of our joys
To tell the laity our love.

Moving of th' earth brings harms and fears,
    Men reckon what it did and meant,
But trepidation of the spheres,
    Though greater far, is innocent.

Dull sublunary lovers' love
    (Whose soul is sense) cannot admit
Absence, because it doth remove
    Those things which elemented it.

But we by a love so much refined,
    That ourselves know not what it is,
Inter-assurèd of the mind,
    Care less, eyes, lips, and hands to miss.

Our two souls therefore, which are one,
    Though I must go, endure not yet
A breach, but an expansion,
    Like gold to airy thinness beat.

If they be two, they are two so
    As stiff twin compasses are two,
Thy soul, the fixed foot, makes no show
    To move, but doth, if th' other do.

And though it in the center sit,
    Yet when the other far doth roam,
It leans, and hearkens after it,
    And grows erect, as that comes home.

Such wilt thou be to me, who must
    Like th' other foot, obliquely run;
Thy firmness makes my circle just,
    And makes me end, where I begun.

JOHN DONNE (*1572–1631*)

* * *

The Canonization

For God's sake hold your tongue, and let me
        love;
    Or chide my palsy, or my gout;
    My five gray hairs, or ruined fortune flout;
With wealth your state, your mind with arts
        improve;
    Take you a course, get you a place,
    Observe his honor, or his grace;

Or the king's real, or his stampèd face
    Contemplate; what you will, approve,
    So you will let me love.

Alas! alas! who's injured by my love?
    What merchant's ships have my sighs
        drowned?
    Who says my tears have overflowed his
        ground?
When did my colds a forward spring remove?
    When did the heats which my veins fill
    Add one more to the plaguy bill?
Soldiers find wars, and lawyers find out still
    Litigious men, which quarrels move,
    Though she and I do love.

Call us what you will, we are made such by
        love;
    Call her one, me another fly;
    We're tapers too, and at our own cost die,
And we in us find the eagle and the dove.
    The phoenix riddle hath more wit
    By us; we two being one, are it.
So, to one neutral thing both sexes fit;
    We die and rise the same, and prove
    Mysterious by this love.

We can die by it, if not live by love,
    And if unfit for tomb or hearse
    Our legend be, it will be fit for verse;
And if no piece of chronicle we prove,
    We'll build in sonnets pretty rooms;
    As well a well-wrought urn becomes
The greatest ashes, as half-acre tombs,
    And by these hymns all shall approve
    Us canonized for love;

And thus invoke us: "You, whom reverend
        love
    Made one another's hermitage;
    You, to whom love was peace, that now is
        rage;
Who did the whole world's soul contract, and
        drove
    Into the glasses of your eyes—
    So made such mirrors, and such spies,
That they did all to you epitomize,—
    Countries, towns, courts; beg from above
    A pattern of your love."

JOHN DONNE (*1572–1631*)

* * *

Queen and Huntress

Queen and Huntress, chaste and fair,
Now the sun is laid to sleep,
Seated, in thy silver chair,
State in wonted manner keep;
    Hesperus entreats thy light,
    Goddess excellently bright.

Earth, let not thy envious shade
Dare itself to interpose;
Cynthia's shining orb was made
Heaven to clear, when day did close;
    Bless us then with wishèd sight,
    Goddess excellently bright.

Lay thy bow of pearl apart,
And thy crystal-shining quiver;
Give unto the flying hart
Space to breathe, how short soever:
    Thou that mak'st a day of night,
    Goddess excellently bright.

                    BEN JONSON   (*1573?–1637*)

                        * * *

The Pulley

When God at first made man,
Having a glass of blessings standing by,
"Let us," said he, "pour on him all we can;
Let the world's riches, which dispersèd lie,
    Contract into a span."

So strength first made a way,
Then beauty flowed, then wisdom, honor,
    pleasure;
When almost all was out, God made a stay,
Perceiving that, alone of all his treasure,
    Rest in the bottom lay.

"For if I should," said he,
"Bestow this jewel also on my creature,
He would adore my gifts instead of me,
And rest in Nature, not the God of Nature;
    So both should losers be.

"Yet let him keep the rest,
But keep them with repining restlessness;
Let him be rich and weary, that at least,

If goodness lead him not, yet weariness
May toss him to my breast."

                    GEORGE HERBERT   (*1593–1633*)

                        * * *

Jordan [1]

Who says that fictions only and false hair
Become a verse? Is there in truth no beauty?
Is all good structure in a winding stair?
May no lines pass except they do their duty
    Not to a true, but painted chair?

Is it no verse except enchanted groves
And sudden arbors shadow coarse-spun lines?
Must purling streams refresh a lover's loves?
Must all be veiled, while he that reads, divines,
    Catching the sense at two removes?

Shepherds are honest people; let them sing.
Riddle who list for me, and pull for prime;
I envy no man's nightingale or spring,
Nor let them punish me with loss of rhyme,
    Who plainly say, My God, my King.

                    GEORGE HERBERT   (*1593–1633*)

                        * * *

Ask me no more

Ask me no more where Jove bestows,
When June is past, the fading rose;
For in your beauty's orient deep,
These flowers as in their causes sleep.

Ask me no more whither do stray
The golden atoms of the day;
For in pure love heaven did prepare
Those powders to enrich your hair.

Ask me no more whither doth haste
The nightingale, when May is past;
For in your sweet dividing throat
She winters, and keeps warm her note.

Ask me no more where those stars light
That downwards fall in dead of night;
For in your eyes they sit, and there
Fixèd become as in their sphere.

Ask me no more if east or west,
The phoenix builds her spicy nest;
For unto you at last she flies,
And in your fragrant bosom dies.

THOMAS CAREW   (*1595?–1639?*)

* * *

Go, lovely rose

Go, lovely rose,
Tell her that wastes her time and me,
That now she knows,
When I resemble her to thee,
How sweet and fair she seems to be.

Tell her that's young,
And shuns to have her graces spied,
That hadst thou sprung
In deserts, where no men abide,
Thou must have uncommended died.

Small is the worth
Of beauty from the light retired;
Bid her come forth,
Suffer herself to be desired,
And not blush so to be admired.

Then die, that she
The common fate of all things rare,
May read in thee;
How small a part of time they share,
That are so wondrous sweet and fair.

EDMUND WALLER   (*1606–1687*)

* * *

Lycidas

*In this Monody the Author bewails a
learned Friend, unfortunately drowned
in his passage from Chester on the Irish
Seas, 1637; and by occasion foretells the
ruin of our corrupted Clergy, then in
their height.*

Yet once more, O ye laurels, and once more,
Ye myrtles brown, with ivy never sere,
I come to pluck your berries harsh and crude,
And with forced fingers rude
Shatter your leaves before the mellowing year.
Bitter constraint and sad occasion dear
Compels me to disturb your season due;
For Lycidas is dead, dead ere his prime,
Young Lycidas, and hath not left his peer.
Who would not sing for Lycidas? he knew
Himself to sing, and build the lofty rhyme.
He must not float upon his watery bier
Unwept, and welter to the parching wind,
Without the meed of some melodious tear.
    Begin then, Sisters of the sacred well
That from beneath the seat of Jove doth
        spring;
Begin, and somewhat loudly sweep the string.
Hence with denial vain and coy excuse;
So may some gentle Muse
With lucky words favour my destined urn,
And as he passes turn,
And bid fair peace be to my sable shroud.
    For we were nursed upon the self-same hill,
Fed the same flock, by fountain, shade, and
        rill;
Together both, ere the high lawns appeared
Under the opening eyelids of the morn,
We drove a-field, and both together heard
What time the gray-fly winds her sultry horn,
Battening our flocks with the fresh dews of
        night,
Oft till the star that rose at evening, bright,
Toward heaven's descent had sloped his west-
        ering wheel.
Meanwhile the rural ditties were not mute,
Tempered to the oaten flute;
Rough Satyrs danced, and Fauns with cloven
        heel
From the glad sound would not be absent
        long;
And old Damœtas loved to hear our song.
    But O the heavy change, now thou art gone,
Now thou art gone, and never must return!
Thee, Shepherd, thee the woods and desert
        caves,
With wild thyme and the gadding vine o'er-
        grown,
And all their echoes, mourn.
The willows and the hazel copses **green**
Shall now no more be seen,
Fanning their joyous leaves to thy soft lays.

As killing as the canker to the rose,
Or taint-worm to the weanling herds that
    graze,
Or frost to flowers, that their gay wardrobe
    wear,
When first the white-thorn blows;
Such, Lycidas, thy loss to shepherd's ear.
    Where were ye, Nymphs, when the remorse-
        less deep
Closed o'er the head of your loved Lycidas?
For neither were ye playing on the steep
Where your old bards, the famous Druids, lie,
Nor on the shaggy top of Mona high,
Nor yet where Deva spreads her wizard
    stream.
Ay me, I fondly dream!
Had ye been there—for what could that have
    done?
What could the Muse herself that Orpheus
    bore,
The Muse herself, for her enchanting son,
Whom universal nature did lament,
When by the rout that made the hideous roar
His gory visage down the stream was sent,
Down the swift Hebrus to the Lesbian shore?
    Alas! what boots it with uncessant care
To tend the homely, slighted, shepherd's
    trade,
And strictly meditate the thankless Muse?
Were it not better done, as others use,
To sport with Amaryllis in the shade,
Or with the tangles of Neæra's hair?
Fame is the spur that the clear spirit doth
    raise
(That last infirmity of noble mind)
To scorn delights and live laborious days;
But the fair guerdon when we hope to find,
And think to burst out into sudden blaze,
Comes the blind Fury with the abhorrèd
    shears,
And slits the thin-spun life. "But not the
    praise,"
Phœbus replied, and touched my trembling
    ears:
"Fame is no plant that grows on mortal soil
Nor in the glistering foil
Set off to the world, nor in broad rumour lies;
But lives and spreads aloft by those pure eyes
And perfect witness of all-judging Jove;
As he pronounces lastly on each deed,
Of so much fame in heaven expect thy meed."

O fountain Arethuse, and thou honoured
    flood,
Smooth-sliding Mincius, crowned with vocal
    reeds,
That strain I heard was of a higher mood:
But now my oat proceeds,
And listens to the herald of the sea,
That came in Neptune's plea.
He asked the waves, and asked the felon
    winds,
What hard mishap hath doomed this gentle
    swain?
And questioned every gust of rugged wings
That blows from off each beakèd promontory:
They knew not of his story;
And sage Hippotades their answer brings,
That not a blast was from his dungeon
    strayed;
The air was calm, and on the level brine
Sleek Panope with all her sisters played.
It was that fatal and perfidious bark,
Built in the eclipse, and rigged with curses
    dark,
That sunk so low that sacred head of thine.
    Next Camus, reverend sire, went footing
        slow,
His mantle hairy, and his bonnet sedge,
Inwrought with figures dim, and on the edge
Like to that sanguine flower inscribed with
    woe.
"Ah! who hath reft," quoth he, "my dearest
    pledge?"
Last came, and last did go,
The pilot of the Galilean lake;
Two massy keys he bore of metals twain
(The golden opes, the iron shuts amain).
He shook his mitred locks, and stern bespake:
"How well could I have spared for thee, young
    swain,
Enough of such as for their bellies' sake,
Creep and intrude and climb into the fold!
Of other care they little reckoning make
Than how to scramble at the shearers' feast,
And shove away the worthy bidden guest.
Blind mouths! that scarce themselves know
    how to hold
A sheep-hook, or have learnt aught else the
    least
That to the faithful herdman's art belongs!
What recks it them? What need they? They
    are sped;
And when they list, their lean and flashy songs

Grate on their scrannel pipes of wretched
    straw;
The hungry sheep look up, and are not fed,
But swoln with wind and the rank mist they
    draw,
Rot inwardly, and foul contagion spread;
Besides what the grim wolf with privy paw
Daily devours apace, and nothing said.
But that two-handed engine at the door
Stands ready to smite once, and smite no
    more."
    Return, Alpheus; the dread voice is past
That shrunk thy streams; return, Sicilian
    Muse,
And call the vales, and bid them hither cast
Their bells and flowrets of a thousand hues.
Ye valleys low, where the mild whispers use
Of shades and wanton winds and gushing
    brooks,
On whose fresh lap the swart star sparely
    looks,
Throw hither all your quaint enamelled eyes,
That on the green turf suck the honeyed
    showers,
And purple all the ground with vernal flowers.
Bring the rathe primrose that forsaken dies,
The tufted crow-toe, and pale jessamine,
The white pink, and the pansy freaked with
    jet,
The glowing violet,
The musk-rose, and the well-attired woodbine,
With cowslips wan that hang the pensive
    head,
And every flower that sad embroidery wears;
Bid amaranthus all his beauty shed,
And daffodillies fill their cups with tears,
To strew the laureate hearse where Lycid lies.
For so to interpose a little ease,
Let our frail thoughts dally with false surmise,
Ay me! whilst thee the shores and sounding
    seas
Wash far away, where'er thy bones are hurled;
Whether beyond the stormy Hebrides,
Where thou perhaps under the whelming tide
Visit'st the bottom of the monstrous world;
Or whether thou, to our moist vows denied,
Sleep'st by the fable of Bellerus old,
Where the great vision of the guarded mount
Looks toward Namancos and Bayona's hold.
Look homeward, Angel, now, and melt with
    ruth;
And O ye dolphins, waft the hapless youth.

Weep no more, woeful shepherds, weep no
    more,
For Lycidas, your sorrow, is not dead,
Sunk though he be beneath the watery floor;
So sinks the day-star in the ocean bed,
And yet anon repairs his drooping head,
And tricks his beams, and with new-spangled
    ore
Flames in the forehead of the morning sky:
So Lycidas sunk low, but mounted high,
Through the dear might of him that walked
    the waves,
Where, other groves and other streams along,
With nectar pure his oozy locks he laves,
And hears the unexpressive° nuptial song,
In the blest kingdoms meek of joy and love.
There entertain him all the saints above,
In solemn troops and sweet societies,
That sing, and singing in their glory move,
And wipe the tears for ever from his eyes.
Now, Lycidas, the shepherds weep no more;
Henceforth thou art the Genius of the shore,
In thy large recompense, and shalt be good
To all that wander in that perilous flood.
    Thus sang the uncouth swain to the oaks
    and rills,
While the still morn went out with sandals
    gray;
He touched the tender stops of various quills,
With eager thought warbling his Doric lay:
And now the sun had stretched out all the
    hills,
And now was dropt into the western bay.
At last he rose, and twitched his mantle blue:
To-morrow to fresh woods and pastures new.

JOHN MILTON   *(1608–1674)*

unexpressive: inexpressible.

* * *

To His Coy Mistress

Had we but world enough, and time,
This coyness, lady, were no crime.
We would sit down and think which way
To walk, and pass our long love's day;
Thou by the Indian Ganges' side
Shouldst rubies find; I by the tide
Of Humber would complain. I would

Love you ten years before the Flood;
And you should, if you please, refuse
Till the conversion of the Jews.
My vegetable love should grow
Vaster than empires, and more slow.
An hundred years should go to praise
Thine eyes, and on thy forehead gaze;
Two hundred to adore each breast,
But thirty thousand to the rest;
An age at least to every part,
And the last age should show your heart.
For, lady, you deserve this state,
Nor would I love at lower rate.
   But at my back I always hear
Time's wingèd chariot hurrying near;
And yonder all before us lie
Deserts of vast eternity.
Thy beauty shall no more be found,
Nor in thy marble vault shall sound
My echoing song; then worms shall try
That long preserved virginity,
And your quaint honor turn to dust,
And into ashes all my lust.
The grave's a fine and private place,
But none, I think, do there embrace.
   Now therefore, while the youthful hue
Sits on thy skin like morning dew,
And while thy willing soul transpires
At every pore with instant fires,
Now let us sport us while we may;
And now, like amorous birds of prey,
Rather at once our time devour,
Than languish in his slow-chapped power.
Let us roll all our strength, and all
Our sweetness, up into one ball;
And tear our pleasures with rough strife
Through the iron gates of life.
Thus, though we cannot make our sun
Stand still, yet we will make him run.

ANDREW MARVELL *(1621–1678)*

* * *

The World

I saw Eternity the other night
Like a great ring of pure and endless light,
  All calm, as it was bright,
And round beneath it, Time in hours, days,
    years

   Driven by the spheres
Like a vast shadow moved, in which the world
  And all her train were hurled;
The doting Lover in his quaintest strain
  Did there complain,
Near him, his lute, his fancy, and his flights,
  Wit's sour delights,
With gloves, and knots the silly snares of
    pleasure
  Yet his dear treasure
All scattered lay, while he his eyes did pour
  Upon a flower.

The darksome Statesman hung with weights
   and woe
Like a thick midnight-fog moved there so
   slow
  He did nor stay, nor go;
Condemning thoughts (like sad eclipses) scowl
  Upon his soul,
And clouds of crying witnesses without
  Pursued him with one shout.
Yet digged the Mole, and lest his ways be
   found
  Worked under ground,
Where he did clutch his prey, but one did see
  That policy,
Churches and altars fed him, perjuries
  Were gnats and flies,
It rained about him blood and tears, but he
  Drank them as free.

The fearful Miser on a heap of rust
Sat pining all his life there, did scarce trust
  His own hands with the dust,
Yet would not place one piece above, but lives
  In fear of thieves.
Thousands there were as frantic as himself
  And hugged each one his pelf,
The downright Epicure placed heaven in sense
  And scorned pretense
While others slipped into a wide excess
  Said little less;
The weaker sort slight, trivial wares enslave
  Who think them brave,
And poor, despisèd Truth sat counting by
  Their victory.

Yet some, who all this while did weep and
   sing,
And sing, and weep, soared up into the ring,
  But most would use no wing.

O fools (said I), thus to prefer dark night
  Before true light,
To give in grots, and caves, and hate the day
  Because it shows the way,
The way which from this dead and dark
    abode
  Leads up to God,
A way where you might tread the sun, and be
  More bright than he.
But as I did their madness so discuss
  One whispered thus,
*This ring the Bridegroom did for none
    provide*
  But for his Bride.

HENRY VAUGHAN (*1622–1695*)

* * *

Shadwell

(from *Absalom and Achitophel*)

Now stop your noses, readers, all and some,
For here's a tun of midnight work to come,
Og, from a treason-tavern rolling home.
Round as a globe, and liquored ev'ry chink,
Goodly and great he sails behind his link;
With all this bulk there's nothing lost in Og,
For ev'ry inch that is not fool is rogue:
A monstrous mass of foul corrupted matter,
As all the devils had spewed to make the
    batter.
When wine has given him courage to blas-
    pheme,
He curses God, but God before cursed him;
And if man could have reason, none has more,
That made his paunch so rich, and him so
    poor.
With wealth he was not trusted, for Heav'n
    knew
What 'twas of old to pamper up a Jew;
To what would he on quail and pheasant
    swell,
That ev'n on tripe and carrion could rebel?
But though Heav'n made him poor, (with
    rev'rence speaking,)
He never was a poet of God's making;
The midwife laid her hand on his thick skull,
With this prophetic blessing: *Be thou dull;*

Drink, swear, and roar, forbear no lewd
    delight
Fit for thy bulk, do anything but write.
Thou art of lasting make, like thoughtless
    men,
A strong nativity—but for the pen;
Eat opium, mingle arsenic in thy drink,
Still thou mayst live, avoiding pen and ink.
I see, I see, 'tis counsel given in vain,
For treason botched in rhyme will be thy
    bane;
Rhyme is the rock on which thou art to wreck,
'Tis fatal to thy fame and to thy neck.
Why should thy metre good King David blast,
A psalm of his will surely be thy last.
Dar'st thou presume in verse to meet thy foes,
Thou whom the penny pamphlet foiled in
    prose?
Doeg, whom God for mankind's mirth has
    made,
O'ertops thy talent in thy very trade;
Doeg to thee, thy paintings are so coarse,
A poet is, though he's the poets' horse.
A double noose thou on thy neck dost pull
For writing treason, and for writing dull;
To die for faction is a common evil,
But to be hanged for nonsense is the devil.
Hadst thou the glories of thy kind expressed,
Thy praises had been satire at the best;
But thou in clumsy verse, unlicked, un-
    pointed,
Hast shamefully defied the Lord's anointed:
I will not rake the dunghill of thy crimes,
For who would read thy life that reads thy
    rhymes?
But of King David's foes, be this the doom,
May all be like the young man Absalom;
And for my foes may this their blessing be,
To talk like Doeg, and to write like thee.

JOHN DRYDEN (*1631–1700*)

* * *

Elegy Written in a Country Church-Yard

The Curfew tolls the knell of parting day,
The lowing herd winds slowly o'er the lea,
The plowman homeward plods his weary way,
And leaves the world to darkness and to me.

Now fades the glimmering landscape on the
    sight,
And all the air a solemn stillness holds,
Save where the beetle wheels his droning
    flight,
And drowsy tinklings lull the distant folds;

Save that from yonder ivy-mantled tower
The moping owl does to the moon complain
Of such, as wandering near her secret bower,
Molest her ancient solitary reign.

Beneath those rugged elms, that yew-tree's
    shade,
Where heaves the turf in many a mouldering
    heap,
Each in his narrow cell for ever laid,
The rude Forefathers of the hamlet sleep.

The breezy call of incense-breathing Morn,
The swallow twittering from the straw-built
    shed,
The cock's shrill clarion, or the echoing horn,
No more shall rouse them from their lowly
    bed.

For them no more the blazing hearth shall
    burn,
Or busy housewife ply her evening care:
No children run to lisp their sire's return,
Or climb his knees the envied kiss to share.

Oft did the harvest to their sickle yield,
Their furrow oft the stubborn glebe has
    broke;
How jocund did they drive their team afield!
How bowed the woods beneath their sturdy
    stroke!

Let no Ambition mock their useful toil,
Their homely joys, and destiny obscure;
Nor Grandeur hear with a disdainful smile,
The short and simple annals of the poor.

The boast of heraldry, the pomp of power,
And all that beauty, all that wealth e'er gave,
Awaits alike the inevitable hour.
The paths of glory lead but to the grave.

Nor you, ye Proud, impute to These the fault,
If Memory o'er their Tomb no Trophies raise,

Where through the long-drawn aisle and
    fretted vault
The pealing anthem swells the note of praise.

Can storied urn or animated bust
Back to its mansion call the fleeting breath?
Can Honor's voice provoke the silent dust,
Or Flattery sooth the dull cold ear of Death?

Perhaps in this neglected spot is laid
Some heart once pregnant with celestial fire;
Hands, that the rod of empire might have
    swayed,
Or waked to ecstasy the living lyre.

But Knowledge to their eyes her ample page
Rich with the spoils of time did ne'er unroll;
Chill Penury repressed their noble rage,
And froze the genial current of the soul.

Full many a gem of purest ray serene,
The dark unfathomed caves of ocean bear:
Full many a flower is born to blush unseen,
And waste its sweetness on the desert air.

Some village-Hampden, that with dauntless
    breast
The little Tyrant of his fields withstood;
Some mute inglorious Milton here may rest,
Some Cromwell guiltless of his country's
    blood.

The applause of listening senates to command,
The threats of pain and ruin to despise,
To scatter plenty o'er a smiling land,
And read their history in a nation's eyes,

Their lot forbade: nor circumscribed alone
Their growing virtues, but their crimes con-
    fined;
Forbade to wade through slaughter to a
    throne,
And shut the gates of mercy on mankind,

The struggling pangs of conscious truth to
    hide,
To quench the blushes of ingenuous shame,
Or heap the shrine of Luxury and Pride
With incense kindled at the Muse's flame.

Far from the madding crowd's ignoble strife,
Their sober wishes never learned to stray;

Along the cool sequestered vale of life
They kept the noiseless tenor of their way.

Yet even these bones from insult to protect,
Some frail memorial still erected nigh,
With uncouth rhymes and shapeless sculpture
    decked,
Implores the passing tribute of a sigh.

Their name, their years, spelt by the unlet-
    tered Muse,
The place of fame and elegy supply:
And many a holy text around she strews,
That teach the rustic moralist to die.

For who to dumb Forgetfulness a prey,
This pleasing anxious being e'er resigned,
Left the warm precincts of the cheerful day,
Nor cast one longing lingering look behind?

On some fond breast the parting soul relies,
Some pious drops the closing eye requires;
Even from the tomb the voice of Nature cries,
Even in our Ashes live their wonted Fires.

For thee, who mindful of the unhonored
    Dead
Dost in these lines their artless tale relate;
If chance, by lonely contemplation led,
Some kindred Spirit shall inquire thy fate,

Haply some hoary-headed Swain may say,
"Oft have we seen him at the peep of dawn
Brushing with hasty steps the dews away,
To meet the sun upon the upland lawn.

"There at the foot of yonder nodding beech
That wreathes its old fantastic roots so high,
His listless length at noontide would he
    stretch,
And pore upon the brook that babbles by.

"Hard by yon wood, now smiling as in scorn,
Muttering his wayward fancies he would rove,
Now drooping, woeful wan, like one forlorn,
Or crazed with care, or crossed in hopeless
    love.

"One morn I missed him on the customed hill,
Along the heath and near his favorite tree,
Another came; nor yet beside the rill,
Nor up the lawn, nor at the wood was he;

"The next, with dirges due in sad array
Slow through the church-way path we saw
    him borne.
Approach and read (for thou can'st read) the
    lay,
Graved on the stone beneath yon agèd thorn."

THE EPITAPH

Here rests his head upon the lap of Earth
A Youth to Fortune and to Fame unknown.
Fair Science frowned not on his humble birth,
And Melancholy marked him for her own.

Large was his bounty, and his soul sincere,
Heaven did a recompense as largely send:
He gave to Misery all he had, a tear,
He gained from Heaven ('twas all he wished)
    a friend.

No farther seek his merits to disclose,
Or draw his frailties from their dread abode,
(There they alike in trembling hope repose)
The bosom of his Father and his God.

THOMAS GRAY (*1716–1771*)

* * *

Ode to Evening

If aught of oaten stop, or pastoral song,
May hope, chaste Eve, to soothe thy modest
    ear,
    Like thy own solemn springs,
    Thy springs and dying gales,

O nymph reserved, while now the bright-
    haired sun
Sits in yon western tent, whose cloudy skirts,
    With brede ethereal wove,
    O'erhang his wavy bed:

Now air is hushed, save where the weak-eyed
    bat,
With short shrill shriek, flits by on leathern
    wing,
    Or where the beetle winds
    His small but sullen horn,

As oft he rises 'midst the twilight path,
Against the pilgrim borne in heedless hum:
    Now teach me, maid composed,
    To breathe some softened strain,

Whose numbers, stealing through thy dark-
    ening vale,
May not unseemly with its stillness suit,
    As musing slow, I hail
    Thy genial loved return!

For when thy folding-star arising shows
His pale circlet, at his warning lamp
    The fragrant Hours, and elves
    Who slept in flowers the day,

And many a nymph who wreaths her brows
    with sedge,
And sheds the freshening dew, and, lovelier
    still,
    The pensive Pleasures sweet,
    Prepare thy shadowy car.

Then lead, calm votaress, where some sheety
    lake
Cheers the lone hearth, or some time-hallowed
    pile
    Or upland fallows gray
    Reflect its last cool gleam.

But when chill blustering winds, or driving
    rain,
Forbid my willing feet, be mine the hut
    That from the mountain's side
    Views wilds, and swelling floods,

And hamlets brown, and dim-discovered spires,
And hears their simple bell, and marks o'er all
    Thy dewy fingers draw
    The gradual dusky veil.

While Spring shall pour his showers, as oft he
    wont,
And bathe thy breathing tresses, meekest Eve;
    While Summer loves to sport
    Beneath thy lingering light;

While sallow Autumn fills thy lap with leaves;
Or Winter, yelling through the troublous air,
    Affrights thy shrinking train,
    And rudely rends thy robes;

So long, sure-found beneath the sylvan shed,
Shall Fancy, Friendship, Science, rose-lipped
    Health,
    Thy gentlest influence own,
    And hymn thy favorite name!

           WILLIAM COLLINS   (*1721–1759*)

* * *

The Tiger

    Tiger! Tiger! burning bright
    In the forests of the night,
    What immortal hand or eye
    Could frame thy fearful symmetry?

    In what distant deeps or skies
    Burnt the fire of thine eyes?
    On what wings dare he aspire?
    What the hand dare seize the fire?

    And what shoulder, and what art,
    Could twist the sinews of thy heart?
    And when thy heart began to beat,
    What dread hand forged thy dread feet?

    What the hammer? what the chain?
    In what furnace was thy brain?
    What the anvil? what dread grasp
    Dare its deadly terrors clasp?

    When the stars threw down their spears,
    And watered heaven with their tears,
    Did he smile his work to see?
    Did he who made the Lamb make thee?

    Tiger! Tiger! burning bright
    In the forests of the night,
    What immortal hand or eye,
    Dare frame thy fearful symmetry?

           WILLIAM BLAKE   (*1757–1827*)

* * *

A Red, Red Rose

    O, my luve is like a red, red rose,
      That's newly sprung in June.
    O my luve is like the melodie
      That's sweetly played in tune.

As fair art thou, my bonnie lass,
   So deep in luve am I,
And I will luve thee still, my dear,
   Till a'° the seas gang° dry.

Till a' the seas gang dry, my dear,
   And the rocks melt wi' the sun!
And I will luve thee still, my dear,
   While the sands o' life shall run.

And fare thee weel, my only luve,
   And fare thee weel awhile!
And I will come again, my luve,
   Though it were ten thousand mile!

          ROBERT BURNS (*1759–1796*)

    a': all. **gang:** go.

                ❋ ❋ ❋

Resolution and Independence

There was a roaring in the wind all night;
The rain came heavily and fell in floods;
But now the sun is rising calm and bright;
The birds are singing in the distant woods;
Over his own sweet voice the Stock-dove
   broods;
The Jay makes answer as the Magpie chatters;
And all the air is filled with pleasant noise of
   waters.

All things that love the sun are out of doors;
The sky rejoices in the morning's birth;
The grass is bright with rain-drops;—on the
   moors
The hare is running races in her mirth;
And with her feet she from the plashy earth
Raises a mist; that, glittering in the sun,
Runs with her all the way, wherever she doth
   run.

I was a Traveller then upon the moor;
I saw the hare that raced about with joy;
I heard the woods and distant waters roar;
Or heard them not, as happy as a boy:
The pleasant season did my heart employ:
My old remembrances went from me wholly:
And all the ways of men, so vain and melan-
   choly.

But, as it sometimes chanceth, from the might
Of joy in minds that can no further go,
As high as we have mounted in delight
In our dejection do we sink as low;
To me that morning did it happen so;
And fears and fancies thick upon me came;
Dim sadness—and blind thoughts, I knew not,
   nor could name.

I heard the skylark warbling in the sky;
And I bethought me of the playful hare:
Even such a happy child of earth am I;
Even as these blissful creatures do I fare;
Far from the world I walk, and from all care;
But there may come another day to me—
Solitude, pain of heart, distress, and poverty.

My whole life I have lived in pleasant thought,
As if life's business were a summer mood;
As if all needful things would come un-
   sought
To genial faith, still rich in genial good;
But how can He expect that others should
Build for him, sow for him, and at his call
Love him, who for himself will take no heed
   at all?

I thought of Chatterton, the marvellous Boy,
The sleepless Soul that perished in his pride;
Of Him who walked in glory and in joy
Following his plough, along the mountain-
   side:
By our own spirits are we deified:
We Poets in our youth begin in gladness;
But thereof come in the end despondency and
   madness.

Now, whether it were by peculiar grace,
A leading from above, a something given,
Yet it befell that, in this lonely place,
When I with these untoward thoughts had
   striven,
Beside a pool bare to the eye of heaven
I saw a Man before me unawares:
The oldest man he seemed that ever wore grey
   hairs.

As a huge stone is sometimes seen to lie
Couched on the bald top of an eminence;
Wonder to all who do the same espy,
By what means it could thither come, and
   whence;

So that it seems a thing endued with sense:
Like a sea-beast crawled forth, that on a shelf
Of rock or sand reposeth, there to sun itself;

Such seemed this Man, not all alive nor dead,
Nor all asleep—in his extreme old age:
His body was bent double, feet and head
Coming together in life's pilgrimage;
As if some dire constraint of pain, or rage
Of sickness felt by him in times long past,
A more than human weight upon his frame
    had cast.

Himself he propped, limbs, body, and pale
    face,
Upon a long grey staff of shaven wood:
And, still as I drew near with gentle pace,
Upon the margin of that moorish flood
Motionless as a cloud the old Man stood,
That heareth not the loud winds when they
    call;
And moveth all together, if it move at all.

At length, himself unsettling, he the pond
Stirred with his staff, and fixedly did look
Upon the muddy water, which he conned,
As if he had been reading in a book:
And now a stranger's privilege I took;
And, drawing to his side, to him did say,
"This morning gives us promise of a glorious
    day."

A gentle answer did the old Man make,
In courteous speech which forth he slowly
    drew:
And him with further words I thus bespake,
"What occupation do you there pursue?
This is a lonesome place for one like you."
Ere he replied, a flash of mild surprise
Broke from the sable orbs of his yet-vivid
    eyes.

His words came feebly, from a feeble chest,
But each in solemn order followed each,
With something of a lofty utterance drest—
Choice word and measured phrase, above the
    reach
Of ordinary men; a stately speech;
Such as grave Livers do in Scotland use,
Religious men, who give to God and man
    their dues.

He told, that to these waters he had come
To gather leeches, being old and poor:

Employment hazardous and wearisome!
And he had many hardships to endure:
From pond to pond he roamed, from moor to
    moor;
Housing, with God's good help, by choice or
    chance;
And in this way he gained an honest mainte-
    nance.

The old Man still stood talking by my side;
But now *his* voice to me was like a stream
Scarce heard; nor word from word could I
    divide;
And the whole body of the Man did seem
Like one whom I had met with in a dream;
Or like a man from some far region sent,
To give me human strength, by apt admonish-
    ment.

My former thoughts returned: the fear that
    kills;
And hope that is unwilling to be fed;
Cold, pain, and labour, and all fleshly ills;
And mighty Poets in their misery dead.
—Perplexed, and longing to be comforted
My question eagerly did I renew,
"How is it that you live, and what is it you
    do?"

He with a smile did then his words repeat;
And said that, gathering leeches, far and wide
He travelled; stirring thus about his feet
The waters of the pools where they abide.
"Once I could meet with them on every side;
But they have dwindled long by slow decay;
Yet still I persevere, and find them where I
    may."

While he was talking thus, the lonely place,
The old Man's shape, and speech—all trou-
    bled me:
In my mind's eye I seemed to see him pace
About the weary moors continually,
Wandering about alone and silently.
While I these thoughts within myself pursued,
He, having made a pause, the same discourse
    renewed.

And soon with this he other matter blended,
Cheerfully uttered, with demeanour kind,
But stately in the main; and, when he ended,
I could have laughed myself to scorn to find
In that decrepit Man so firm a mind.

"God," said I, "be my help and stay secure;
I'll think of the Leech-gatherer on the lonely
   moor!"

WILLIAM WORDSWORTH   (*1770–1850*)

* * *

Kubla Khan

In Xanadu did Kubla Khan
A stately pleasure-dome decree:
Where Alph, the sacred river, ran
Through caverns measureless to man
   Down to a sunless sea.
So twice five miles of fertile ground
With walls and towers were girdled round:
And there were gardens bright with sinuous
   rills,
Where blossomed many an incense-bearing
   tree;
And here were forests ancient as the hills,
Enfolding sunny spots of greenery.

But oh! that deep romantic chasm which
   slanted
Down the green hill athwart a cedarn cover!
A savage place! as holy and enchanted
As e'er beneath a waning moon was haunted
By woman wailing for her demon-lover!
And from this chasm, with ceaseless turmoil
   seething,
As if this earth in fast thick pants were breath-
   ing,
A mighty fountain momently was forced:
Amid whose swift half-intermitted burst
Huge fragments vaulted like rebounding hail,
Or chaffy grain beneath the thresher's flail:
And 'mid these dancing rocks at once and
   ever
It flung up momently the sacred river.
Five miles meandering with a mazy motion
Through wood and dale the sacred river ran,
Then reached the caverns measureless to man,
And sank in tumult to a lifeless ocean:
And 'mid this tumult Kubla heard from far
Ancestral voices prophesying war!
   The shadow of the dome of pleasure
   Floated midway on the waves;
   Where was heard the mingled measure
   From the fountain and the caves.
It was a miracle of rare device,
A sunny pleasure-dome with caves of ice!

A damsel with a dulcimer
In a vision once I saw:
It was an Abyssinian maid,
And on her dulcimer she played,
Singing of Mount Abora.
Could I revive within me
Her symphony and song,
To such a deep delight 'twould win me,
That with music loud and long,
I would build that dome in air,
That sunny dome! those caves of ice!
And all who heard should see them there,
And all should cry, Beware! Beware!
His flashing eyes, his floating hair!
Weave a circle round him thrice,
And close your eyes with holy dread,
For he on honey-dew hath fed,
And drunk the milk of Paradise.

SAMUEL TAYLOR COLERIDGE   (*1772–1834*)

* * *

You smiled, you spoke

You smiled, you spoke, and I believed,
By every word and smile deceived.
Another man would hope no more;
Nor hope I what I hoped before:
But let not this last wish be vain;
Deceive, deceive me once again!

WALTER SAVAGE LANDOR   (*1775–1864*)

* * *

Rose Aylmer

Ah what avails the sceptred race,
   Ah what the form divine!
What every virtue, every grace!
   Rose Aylmer, all were thine.
Rose Aylmer, whom these wakeful eyes
   May weep, but never see,
A night of memories and of sighs
   I consecrate to thee.

WALTER SAVAGE LANDOR   (*1775–1864*)

* * *

So we'll go no more a roving

So we'll go no more a roving
  So late into the night,
Though the heart be still as loving,
  And the moon be still as bright.

For the sword outwears its sheath,
  And the soul wears out the breast,
And the heart must pause to breathe,
  And Love itself have rest.

Though the night was made for loving,
  And the day returns too soon,
Yet we'll go no more a roving
  By the light of the moon.

GEORGE GORDON, LORD BYRON   (1788–1824)

✿ ✿ ✿

Ode to the West Wind

1

O wild West Wind, thou breath of Autumn's
  being,
Thou, from whose unseen presence the leaves
  dead
Are driven, like ghosts from an enchanter
  fleeing,

Yellow, and black and pale, and hectic red,
Pestilence-stricken multitudes: O thou,
Who chariotest to their dark wintry bed

The wingèd seeds, where they lie cold and
  low,
Each like a corpse within its grave, until
Thine azure sister of the Spring shall blow

Her clarion o'er the dreaming earth, and fill
(Driving sweet buds like flocks to feed in air)
With living hues and odors plain and hill:

Wild Spirit, which are moving everywhere;
Destroyer and preserver; hear, oh, hear!

2

Thou on whose stream, 'mid the steep sky's
  commotion,
Loose clouds like earth's decaying leaves are
  shed,
Shook from the tangled boughs of Heaven
  and Ocean,

Angels of rain and lightning: there are spread
On the blue surface of thine aery surge,
Like the bright hair uplifted from the head

Of some fierce Maenad, even from the dim
  verge
Of the horizon to the zenith's height,
The locks of the approaching storm. Thou
  dirge

Of the dying year, to which this closing night
Will be the dome of a vast sepulchre,
Vaulted with all thy congregated might

Of vapors, from whose solid atmosphere
Black rain, and fire, and hail will burst: oh,
  hear!

3

Thou who didst waken from his summer
  dreams
The blue Mediterranean, where he lay,
Lulled by the coil of his crystàlline streams,

Beside a pumice isle in Baiae's bay,
And saw in sleep old palaces and towers
Quivering within the wave's intenser day,

All overgrown with azure moss and flowers
So sweet, the sense faints picturing them!
  Thou
For whose path the Atlantic's level powers

Cleave themselves into chasms, while far below
The sea-blooms and the oozy woods which
  wear
The sapless foliage of the ocean, know

Thy voice, and suddenly grow gray with fear,
And tremble and despoil themselves: oh, hear!

4

If I were a dead leaf thou mightest bear;
If I were a swift cloud to fly with thee;
A wave to pant beneath thy power, and share

The impulse of thy strength, only less free
Than thou, O uncontrollable! If even
I were as in my boyhood, and could be

The comrade of thy wanderings over Heaven,
As then, when to outstrip thy skiey speed
Scarce seemed a vision; I would ne'er have
   striven

As thus with thee in prayer in my sore need.
Oh, lift me as a wave, a leaf, a cloud!
I fall upon the thorns of life! I bleed!

A heavy weight of hours has chained and
   bowed
One too like thee: tameless, and swift, and
   proud.

5

Make me thy lyre, even as the forest is:
What if my leaves are falling like its own!
The tumult of thy mighty harmonies

Will take from both a deep, autumnal tone,
Sweet though in sadness. Be thou, Spirit fierce,
My spirit! Be thou me, impetuous one!

Drive my dead thoughts over the universe
Like withered leaves to quicken a new birth!
And, by the incantation of this verse,

Scatter, as from an unextinguished hearth
Ashes and sparks, my words among mankind!
Be through my lips to unawakened earth

The trumpet of a prophecy! O, Wind,
If Winter comes, can Spring be far behind?

PERCY BYSSHE SHELLEY   (*1792–1822*)

* * *

On First Looking into Chapman's Homer

Much have I travelled in the realms of gold,
And many goodly states and kingdoms seen;
Round many western islands have I been
Which bards in fealty to Apollo hold.
Oft of one wide expanse had I been told
That deep-browed Homer ruled as his de-
   mesne;
Yet did I never breathe its pure serene
Till I heard Chapman speak out loud and
   bold:
Then felt I like some watcher of the skies
When a new planet swims into his ken;
Or like stout Cortez when with eagle eyes
He stared at the Pacific—and all his men
Looked at each other with a wild surmise—
Silent, upon a peak in Darien.

JOHN KEATS   (*1795–1821*)

* * *

Ode on a Grecian Urn

Thou still unravished bride of quietness,
   Thou foster-child of Silence and slow Time,
Sylvan historian, who canst thus express
   A flowery tale more sweetly than our
      rhyme:
What leaf-fringed legend haunts about thy
      shape
   Of deities or mortals, or of both,
      In Tempe or the dales of Arcady?
   What men or gods are these? What maid-
      ens loth?
What mad pursuit? What struggle to escape?
   What pipes and timbrels? What wild
      ecstasy?

Heard melodies are sweet, but those unheard
   Are sweeter; therefore, ye soft pipes, play
      on;
Not to the sensual ear, but, more endeared,
   Pipe to the spirit ditties of no tone:
Fair youth, beneath the trees, thou canst not
      leave
   Thy song, nor ever can those trees be bare;
   Bold Lover, never, never canst thou kiss
Though winning near the goal—yet, do not
      grieve;
   She cannot fade, though thou hast not
      thy bliss,
For ever wilt thou love, and she be fair!

Ah, happy, happy boughs! that cannot shed
  Your leaves, nor ever bid the Spring adieu;
And, happy melodist, unwearièd,
  For ever piping songs for ever new;
More happy love! more happy, happy love!
  For ever warm and still to be enjoyed,
    For ever panting, and for ever young;
All breathing human passion far above,
    That leaves a heart high-sorrowful and
      cloyed,
      A burning forehead, and a parching
      tongue.

Who are these coming to the sacrifice?
  To what green altar, O mysterious priest,
Lead'st thou that heifer lowing at the skies,
    And all her silken flanks with garlands
      dressed?
What little town by river or sea shore,
  Or mountain-built with peaceful citadel,
    Is emptied of this folk, this pious morn?
And, little town, thy streets for evermore
  Will silent be; and not a soul to tell
    Why thou art desolate, can e'er return.

O Attic shape! Fair attitude! with brede
  Of marble men and maidens overwrought,
With forest branches and the trodden weed;
  Thou, silent form, dost tease us out of
    thought
As doth eternity: Cold Pastoral!
  When old age shall this generation waste,
    Thou shalt remain, in midst of other woe
Than ours, a friend to man, to whom thou
    say'st,
"Beauty is truth, truth beauty,"—that is all
    Ye know on earth, and all ye need to
    know.

              JOHN KEATS   (1795–1821)

                                * * *

Days

Daughters of Time, the hypocritic Days,
Muffled and dumb like barefoot dervishes,
And marching single in an endless file,
Bring diadems and fagots in their hands.

To each they offer gifts after his will,
Bread, kingdoms, stars, and sky that holds
  them all.
I, in my pleachèd garden, watched the pomp,
Forgot my morning wishes, hastily
Took a few herbs and apples, and the Day
Turned and departed silent. I, too late,
Under her solemn fillet saw the scorn.

         RALPH WALDO EMERSON   (1803–1882)

                           * * *

The Haunted Palace

In the greenest of our valleys
  By good angels tenanted,
Once a fair and stately palace—
  Radiant palace—reared its head.
In the monarch Thought's dominion—
  It stood there!
Never seraph spread a pinion
  Over fabric half so fair!

Banners yellow, glorious, golden,
  On its roof did float and flow,
(This—all this—was in the olden
  Time long ago),
And every gentle air that dallied,
  In that sweet day,
Along the ramparts plumed and pallid,
  A wingèd odor went away.

Wanderers in that happy valley,
  Through two luminous windows, saw
Spirits moving musically,
  To a lute's well-tunèd law,
Round about a throne where, sitting,
  (Porphyrogene!)
In state his glory well befitting,
  The ruler of the realm was seen.

And all with pearl and ruby glowing
  Was the fair palace door,
Through which came flowing, flowing, flowing,
  And sparkling evermore,
A troop of Echoes, whose sweet duty
  Was but to sing,

In voices of surpassing beauty,
    The wit and wisdom of their king.

But evil things, in robes of sorrow,
    Assailed the monarch's high estate.
(Ah, let us mourn!—for never morrow
    Shall dawn upon him, desolate!
And round about his home the glory
    That blushed and bloomed,
Is but a dim-remembered story
    Of the old time entombed.

And travellers, now, within that valley,
    Through the red-litten windows see
Vast forms, that move fantastically
    To a discordant melody,
While, like a ghastly rapid river,
    Through the pale door
A hideous throng rush out forever
    And laugh—but smile no more.

                    EDGAR ALLAN POE   (*1809–1849*)

                                * * *

Now sleeps the crimson petal

    Now sleeps the crimson petal, now the
        white;
Nor waves the cypress in the palace walk;
Nor winks the gold fin in the porphyry font:
The fire-fly wakens: waken thou with me.

    Now droops the milkwhite peacock like a
        ghost,
And like a ghost she glimmers on to me.

    Now lies the Earth all Danaë to the stars,
And all thy heart lies open unto me.

    Now slides the silent meteor on, and leaves
A shining furrow, as thy thoughts in me.

    Now folds the lily all her sweetness up,
And slips into the bosom of the lake:
So fold thyself, my dearest, thou, and slip
Into my bosom and be lost in me.

            ALFRED, LORD TENNYSON   (*1809–1892*)

                                * * *

Mariana

        "Mariana in the moated grange."
                    —*Measure for Measure.*

With blackest moss the flower-plots
    Were thickly crusted, one and all:
The rusted nails fell from the knots
    That held the pear to the gable-wall.
The broken sheds looked sad and strange:
    Unlifted was the clinking latch;
    Weeded and worn the ancient thatch
Upon the lonely moated grange.
        She only said, "My life is dreary,
            He cometh not," she said;
        She said, "I am aweary, aweary,
            I would that I were dead!"

Her tears fell with the dews at even;
    Her tears fell ere the dews were dried;
She could not look on the sweet heaven,
    Either at morn or eventide.
After the flitting of the bats,
    When thickest dark did trance the sky,
    She drew her casement-curtain by,
And glanced athwart the glooming flats.
        She only said, "The night is dreary,
            He cometh not," she said;
        She said, "I am aweary, aweary,
            I would that I were dead!"

Upon the middle of the night,
    Waking she heard the night-fowl crow:
The cock sung out an hour ere light:
    From the dark fen the oxen's low
Came to her: without hope of change,
    In sleep she seemed to walk forlorn,
    Till cold winds woke the gray-eyed morn
About the lonely moated grange.
        She only said, "The day is dreary,
            He cometh not," she said;
        She said, "I am aweary, aweary,
            I would that I were dead!"

About a stone-cast from the wall
    A sluice with blackened waters slept,
And o'er it many, round and small,
    The clustered marish-mosses crept.
Hard by a poplar shook alway,
    All silver-green with gnarled bark:
    For leagues no other tree did mark
The level waste, the rounding gray.
        She only said, "My life is dreary,

He cometh not," she said;
   She said, "I am aweary, aweary,
     I would that I were dead!"

And ever when the moon was low,
   And the shrill winds were up and away,
In the white curtain, to and fro,
   She saw the gusty shadow sway.
But when the moon was very low,
   And wild winds bound within their cell,
   The shadow of the poplar fell
Upon her bed, across her brow.
     She only said, "The night is dreary,
      He cometh not," she said;
     She said, "I am aweary, aweary,
      I would that I were dead!"

All day within the dreamy house,
   The doors upon their hinges creaked;
The blue fly sung in the pane; the mouse
   Behind the mouldering wainscot shrieked,
Or from the crevice peered about.
   Old faces glimmered through the doors,
   Old footsteps trod the upper floors,
Old voices called her from without.
     She only said, "My life is dreary,
      He cometh not," she said;
     She said, "I am aweary, aweary,
      I would that I were dead!"

The sparrow's chirrup on the roof,
   The slow clock ticking, and the sound
Which to the wooing wind aloof
   The poplar made, did all confound
Her sense; but most she loathed the hour
   When the thick-moted sunbeam lay
   Athwart the chambers, and the day
Was sloping toward his western bower.
     Then, said she, "I am very dreary,
      He will not come," she said;
     She wept, "I am aweary, aweary,
      Oh God, that I were dead!"

    ALFRED, LORD TENNYSON (1809–1892)

                 * * *

Out of the Cradle Endlessly Rocking

Out of the cradle endlessly rocking,
Out of the mocking-bird's throat, the musical
   shuttle,
Out of the Ninth-month midnight,
Over the sterile sands and the fields beyond
   where the child leaving his bed wandered
   alone, bareheaded, barefoot,
Down from the showered halo,
Up from the mystic play of shadows twining
   and twisting as if they were alive,
Out from the patches of briers and black-
   berries,
From the memories of the bird that chanted
   to me,
From your memories sad brother, from the
   fitful risings and fallings I heard,
From under that yellow half-moon late-risen
   and swollen as if with tears,
From those beginning notes of yearning and
   love there in the mist,
From the thousand responses of my heart
   never to cease,
From the myriad thence-aroused words,
From the word stronger and more delicious
   than any,
From such as now they start the scene re-
   visiting,
As a flock, twittering, rising, or overhead
   passing,
Borne hither, ere all eludes me, hurriedly,
A man, yet by these tears a little boy again,
Throwing myself on the sand, confronting
   the waves,
I, chanter of pains and joys, uniter of here
   and hereafter,
Taking all hints to use them, but swiftly leap-
   ing beyond them,
A reminiscence sing.

Once Paumanok,
When the lilac-scent was in the air and Fifth-
   month grass was growing,
Up this seashore in some briers,
Two feathered guests from Alabama, two to-
   gether,
And their nest, and four light-green eggs
   spotted with brown,
And every day the he-bird to and fro near at
   hand,
And every day the she-bird crouched on her
   nest, silent, with bright eyes,
And every day I, a curious boy, never too
   close, never disturbing them,
Cautiously peering, absorbing, translating.

Shine! shine! shine!
Pour down your warmth, great sun!
While we bask, we two together,

Two together!
Winds blow south, or winds blow north,
Day come white, or night come black,
Home, or rivers and mountains from home,
Singing all time, minding no time,
While we two keep together.

Till of a sudden,
May-be killed, unknown to her mate,
One forenoon the she-bird crouched not on
  the nest,
Nor returned that afternoon, nor the next,
Nor ever appeared again.

And thenceforward all summer in the sound
  of the sea,
And at night under the full of the moon in
  calmer weather,
Over the hoarse surging of the sea,
Or flitting from brier to brier by day,
I saw, I heard at intervals the remaining one,
  the he-bird,
The solitary guest from Alabama.

Blow! blow! blow!
Blow up sea-winds along Paumanok's shore;
I wait and I wait till you blow my mate to me.

Yes, when the stars glistened,
All night long on the prong of a moss-scal-
  loped stake,
Down almost amid the slapping waves,
Sat the lone singer wonderful causing tears.

He called on his mate,
He poured forth the meanings which I of all
  men know.

Yes my brother I know,
The rest might not, but I have treasured
  every note,
For more than once dimly down to the beach
  gliding,
Silent, avoiding the moonbeams, blending myself with the shadows,
Recalling now the obscure shapes, the echoes,
  the sounds and sights after their sorts.

The white arms out in the breakers tirelessly
  tossing,
I, with bare feet, a child, the wind wafting my
  hair,
Listened long and long.

Listened to keep, to sing, now translating the
  notes,
Following you my brother.

Soothe! soothe! soothe!
Close on its wave soothes the wave behind,
And again another behind embracing and
  lapping, every one close,
But my love soothes not me, not me.
Low hangs the moon, it rose late,
It is lagging—O I think it is heavy with love,
  with love.

O madly the sea pushes upon the land,
With love, with love.

O night! do I not see my love fluttering out
  among the breakers?
What is that little black thing I see there in
  the white?

Loud! loud! loud!
Loud I call to you, my love!
High and clear I shoot my voice over the
  waves,
Surely you must know who is here, is here,
You must know who I am, my love.

Low-hanging moon!
What is that dusky spot in your brown
  yellow?
O it is the shape, the shape of my mate!
O moon do not keep her from me any longer.

Land! land! O land!
Whichever way I turn, O I think you could
  give me my mate back again if you only
  would,
For I am almost sure I see her dimly which-
  ever way I look.

O rising stars!
Perhaps the one I want so much will rise, will
  rise with some of you.

O throat! O trembling throat!
Sound clearer through the atmosphere!

Pierce the woods, the earth,
Somewhere listening to catch you must be
the one I want.

Shake out carols!
Solitary here, the night's carols!
Carols of lonesome love! death's carols!
Carols under that lagging, yellow, waning
moon!
O under that moon where she droops almost
down into the sea!
O reckless despairing carols.

But soft! sink low!
Soft, let me just murmur,
And do you wait a moment you husky-noised
sea,
For somewhere I believe I heard my mate
responding to me,
So faint, I must be still, be still to listen,
But not altogether still, for then she might
not come immediately to me.

Hither my love!
Here I am! Here!
With this just-sustained note I announce my-
self to you,
This gentle call is for you my love, for you.

Do not be decoyed elsewhere,
That is the whistle of the wind, it is not my
voice,
That is the fluttering, the fluttering of the
spray,
Those are the shadows of leaves.
O darkness! O in vain!
O I am very sick and sorrowful.

O brown halo in the sky near the moon,
drooping upon the sea!
O troubled reflection in the sea!
O throat! O throbbing heart!
And I singing uselessly, uselessly all the night.

O past! O happy life! O songs of joy!
In the air, in the woods, over fields,
Loved! loved! loved! loved! loved!
But my mate no more, no more with me!
We two together no more.

The aria sinking,
All else continuing, the stars shining,
The winds blowing, the notes of the bird
continuous echoing,
With angry moans the fierce old mother in-
cessantly moaning,
On the sands of Paumanok's shore gray and
rustling,
The yellow half-moon enlarged, sagging down,
drooping, the face of the sea almost
touching,
The boy ecstatic, with his bare feet the waves,
with his hair the atmosphere dallying,
The love in the heart long pent, now loose,
now at last tumultuously bursting,
The aria's meaning, the ears, the soul, swiftly
depositing,
The strange tears down the cheeks coursing,
The colloquy there, the trio, each uttering,
The undertone, the savage old mother inces-
santly crying,
To the boy's soul's questions sullenly timing,
some drowned secret hissing,
To the outsetting bard.

Demon or bird! (said the boy's soul,)
Is it indeed toward your mate you sing? or is
it really to me?
For I, that was a child, my tongue's use sleeping, now I have heard you,
Now in a moment I know what I am for, I
awake,
And already a thousand singers, a thousand
songs, clearer, louder and more sorrowful
than yours,
A thousand warbling echoes have started to
life within me, never to die.

O you singer solitary, singing by yourself, pro-
jecting me,
O solitary me listening, never more shall I
cease perpetuating you,
Never more shall I escape, never more the
reverberations,
Never more the cries of unsatisfied love be ab-
sent from me,
Never again leave me to be the peaceful child
I was before what there in the night,
By the sea under the yellow and sagging moon,
The messenger there aroused, the fire, the
sweet hell within,
The unknown want, the destiny of me.

O give me the clue! (it lurks in the night here
somewhere,)

O if I am to have so much, let me have more!

A word then, (for I will conquer it,)
The word final, superior to all,
Subtle, sent up—what is it?—I listen;
Are you whispering it, and have been all the
time, you sea-waves?
Is that it from your liquid rims and wet sands?

Whereto answering, the sea,
Delaying not, hurrying not,
Whispered me through the night, and very
plainly before daybreak,
Lisped to me the low and delicious word
death,
And again death, death, death, death,
Hissing melodious, neither like the bird nor
like my aroused child's heart,
But edging near as privately for me rustling at
my feet,
Creeping thence steadily up to my ears and
laving me softly all over,
Death, death, death, death, death.

Which I do not forget,
But fuse the song of my dusky demon and
brother,
That he sang to me in the moonlight on
Paumanok's gray beach,
With the thousand responsive songs at ran-
dom,
My own songs awaked from that hour,
And with them the key, the word up from the
waves,
The word of the sweetest song and all songs,
That strong and delicious word which, creep-
ing to my feet,
(Or like some old crone rocking the cradle,
swathed in sweet garments, bending aside,)
The sea whispered me.

WALT WHITMAN   (*1819–1892*)

* * *

When I heard the learn'd astronomer

When I heard the learn'd astronomer,
When the proofs, the figures, were ranged in
columns before me,
When I was shown the charts and diagrams,
to add, divide, and measure them,
When I sitting heard the astronomer where
he lectured with much applause in the
lecture-room,
How soon unaccountable I became tired and
sick,
Till rising and gliding out I wandered off by
myself,
In the mystical moist night-air, and from time
to time,
Looked up in perfect silence at the stars.

WALT WHITMAN   (*1819–1892*)

* * *

Soliloquy of the Spanish Cloister

Gr-r-r—there go, my heart's abhorrence!
    Water your damned flower-pots, do!
If hate killed men, Brother Lawrence,
    God's blood, would not mine kill you!
What? your myrtle-bush wants trimming?
    Oh, that rose has prior claims—
Needs its leaden vase filled brimming?
    Hell dry you up with its flames!

At the meal we sit together:
    Salve tibi! I must hear
Wise talk of the kind of weather,
    Sort of season, time of year:
Not a plenteous cork-crop: scarcely
    Dare we hope oak-galls, I doubt:
What's the Latin name for "parsley"?
    What's the Greek name for Swine's Snout?

Whew! We'll have our platter burnished,
    Laid with care on our own shelf!
With a fire-new spoon we're furnished,
    And a goblet for ourself,
Rinsed like something sacrificial
    Ere 't is fit to touch our chaps—
Marked with L for our initial!
    (He-he! There his lily snaps!)

Saint, forsooth! While brown Dolores
    Squats outside the Convent bank
With Sanchicha, telling stories,
    Steeping tresses in the tank,

Blue-black, lustrous, thick like horsehairs
—Can't I see his dead eye glow,
Bright as 't were a Barbary corsair's?
(That is, if he'd let it show!)

When he finishes refection,
Knife and fork he never lays
Cross-wise, to my recollection,
As do I, in Jesu's praise.
I the Trinity illustrate,
Drinking watered orange-pulp—
In three sips the Arian frustrate;
While he drains his at one gulp.

Oh, those melons! If he's able
We're to have a feast! so nice!
One goes to the Abbot's table,
All of us get each a slice.
How go on your flowers? None double?
Not one fruit-sort can you spy?
Strange!—And I, too, at such trouble
Keep them close-nipped on the sly!

There's a great text in Galatians,
Once you trip on it, entails
Twenty-nine distinct damnations,
One sure, if another fails:
If I trip him just a-dying,
Sure of heaven as sure can be,
Spin him round and send him flying
Off to hell, a Manichee?

Or, my scrofulous French novel
On gray paper with blunt type!
Simply glance at it, you grovel
Hand and foot in Belial's gripe:
If I double down its pages
At the woful sixteenth print,
When he gathers his greengages,
Ope a sieve and slip it in 't?

Or, there's Satan!—one might venture
Pledge one's soul to him, yet leave
Such a flaw in the indenture
As he'd miss till, past retrieve,
Blasted lay that rose-acacia
We're so proud of! *Hy, Zy, Hine* . . .
'St, there's Vespers! *Plena gratiâ,
Ave, Virgo!* Gr-r-r—you swine!

ROBERT BROWNING   (*1812–1889*)

❋ ❋ ❋

The Latest Decalogue

Thou shalt have one God only; who
Would be at the expense of two?
No graven images may be
Worshipped, except the currency.
Swear not at all; for, for thy curse
Thine enemy is none the worse.
At church on Sunday to attend
Will serve to keep the world thy friend.
Honor thy parents; that is, all
From whom advancement may befall.
Thou shalt not kill; but need'st not strive
Officiously to keep alive.
Do not adultery commit;
Advantage rarely comes of it.
Thou shalt not steal: an empty feat,
When it's so lucrative to cheat.
Bear not false witness; let the lie
Have time on its own wings to fly.
Thou shalt not covet, but tradition
Approves all forms of competition.

ARTHUR HUGH CLOUGH   (*1819–1861*)

❋ ❋ ❋

Dover Beach

The sea is calm tonight,
The tide is full, the moon lies fair
Upon the straits;—on the French coast the
    light
Gleams and is gone; the cliffs of England
    stand,
Glimmering and vast, out in the tranquil bay.
Come to the window, sweet is the night-air!
Only, from the long line of spray
Where the sea meets the moon-blanched land,
Listen! you hear the grating roar
Of pebbles which the waves draw back, and
    fling,
At their return, up the high strand,
Begin, and cease, and then again begin,
With tremulous cadence slow, and bring
The eternal note of sadness in.

Sophocles long ago
Heard it on the Ægean, and it brought
Into his mind the turbid ebb and flow

Of human misery; we
Find also in the sound a thought,
Hearing it by this distant northern sea.

The Sea of Faith
Was once, too, at the full, and round earth's
   shore
Lay like the folds of a bright girdle furled.
But now I only hear
Its melancholy, long, withdrawing roar,
Retreating, to the breath
Of the night-wind, down the vast edges drear
And naked shingles of the world.

Ah, love, let us be true
To one another! for the world, which seems
To lie before us like a land of dreams,
So various, so beautiful, so new,
Hath really neither joy, nor love, nor light,
Nor certitude, nor peace, nor help for pain;
And we are here as on a darkling plain
Swept with confused alarms of struggle and
   flight,
Where ignorant armies clash by night.

MATTHEW ARNOLD   (*1822–1888*)

* * *

A bird came down the walk

A bird came down the walk;
He did not know I saw;
He bit an angleworm in halves
And ate the fellow, raw,

And then he drank a dew
From a convenient grass,
And then hopped sidewise to the wall
To let a beetle pass.

He glanced with rapid eyes
That hurried all around;
They looked like frightened beads, I thought;
He stirred his velvet head

Like one in danger; cautious,
I offered him a crumb
And he unrolled his feathers
And he rowed him softer home

Than oars divide the ocean,
Too silver for a seam,
Or butterflies, off banks of noon
Leap, plashless, as they swim.

EMILY DICKINSON   (*1830–1886*)

* * *

After great pain

After great pain a formal feeling comes—
The nerves sit ceremonious, like tombs;
The stiff Heart questions was it He that bore?
And yesterday, or centuries before?

The feet, mechanical, go round
A wooden way
Of ground or air or ought
Regardless grown,
A quartz contentment, like a stone.

This is the hour of lead,
Remembered, if outlived,
As freezing persons recollect the snow—
First chill, then stupor, then the letting go.

EMILY DICKINSON   (*1830–1886*)

* * *

The Darkling Thrush

I leaned upon a coppice gate
   When Frost was specter-gray,
And Winter's dregs made desolate
   The weakening eye of day.
The tangled bine-stems scored the sky
   Like strings from broken lyres,
And all mankind that haunted nigh
   Had sought their household fires.

The land's sharp features seemed to be
   The Century's corpse outleant,
His crypt the cloudy canopy,
   The wind his death-lament.
The ancient pulse of germ and birth
   Was shrunken hard and dry,

And every spirit upon earth
  Seemed fervorless as I.

At once a voice burst forth among
  The bleak twigs overhead
In a full-hearted evensong
  Of joy illimited;
An aged thrush, frail, gaunt, and small,
  In blast-beruffled plume,
Had chosen thus to fling his soul
  Upon the growing gloom.

So little cause for carolings
  Of such ecstatic sound
Was written on terrestrial things
  Afar or nigh around,
That I could think there trembled through
  His happy good-night air
Some blessed Hope, whereof he knew
  And I was unaware.

THOMAS HARDY (*1840–1928*)

* * *

Ode

We are the music-makers,
  And we are the dreamers of dreams,
Wandering by lone sea-breakers,
  And sitting by desolate streams;
World-losers and world-forsakers,
  On whom the pale moon gleams:
Yet we are the movers and shakers
  Of the world for ever, it seems.

With wonderful deathless ditties
We build up the world's great cities,
  And out of a fabulous story
  We fashion an empire's glory:
One man with a dream, at pleasure,
  Shall go forth and conquer a crown;
And three with a new song's measure
  Can trample an empire down.

We, in the ages lying
  In the buried past of the earth,
Built Nineveh with our sighing,
  And Babel itself with our mirth;
And o'erthrew them with prophesying

To the old of the new world's worth;
For each age is a dream that is dying,
  Or one that is coming to birth.

ARTHUR O'SHAUGHNESSY (*1844–1881*)

* * *

The Windhover:

To Christ our Lord

I caught this morning morning's minion, kingdom of daylight's dauphin, dapple-dawn-
  drawn Falcon, in his riding
Of the rolling level underneath him steady
  air, and striding
High there, how he rung upon the rein of a
  wimpling wing
In his ecstasy! then off, off forth on swing,
  As a skate's heel sweeps smooth on a bow-
  bend: the hurl and gliding
Rebuffed the big wind. My heart in hiding
Stirred for a bird,—the achieve of, the mastery
  of the thing!

Brute beauty and valor and act, oh, air, pride,
  plume, here
  Buckle! AND the fire that breaks from thee
  then, a billion
Times told lovelier, more dangerous, O my
  chevalier!

  No wonder of it: sheer plod makes plough
  down sillion
Shine, and blue-bleak embers, ah my dear,
  Fall, gall themselves, and gash gold-
  vermilion.

GERARD MANLEY HOPKINS (*1844–1889*)

* * *

Farewell to barn and stack and tree

"Farewell to barn and stack and tree,
  Farewell to Severn shore.
Terence, look your last at me,
  For I come home no more.

"The sun burns on the half-mown hill,
   By now the blood is dried;
And Maurice among the hay lies still
   And my knife is in his side.

"My mother thinks us long away;
   'Tis time the field were mown.
She had two sons at rising day,
   To-night she'll be alone.

"And here's a bloody hand to shake,
   And oh, man, here's good-bye;
We'll sweat no more on scythe and rake,
   My bloody hands and I.

"I wish you strength to bring you pride,
   And love to keep you clean,
And I wish you luck, come Lammastide,
   At racing on the green.

"Long for me the rick will wait,
   And long will wait the fold,
And long will stand the empty plate,
   And dinner will be cold."

A. E. HOUSMAN   (1859–1936)

● ● ●

Sailing to Byzantium

That is no country for old men. The young
In one another's arms, birds in the trees
—Those dying generations—at their song,
The salmon-falls, the mackerel-crowded seas,
Fish, flesh, or fowl, commend all summer long
Whatever is begotten, born, and dies.
Caught in that sensual music all neglect
Monuments of unageing intellect.

An aged man is but a paltry thing,
A tattered coat upon a stick, unless
Soul clap its hands and sing, and louder sing
For every tatter in its mortal dress,
Nor is there singing school but studying
Monuments of its own magnificence;
And therefore I have sailed the seas and come
To the holy city of Byzantium.

O sages standing in God's holy fire
As in the gold mosaic of a wall,

Come from the holy fire, perne in a gyre,
And be the singing-masters of my soul.
Consume my heart away; sick with desire
And fastened to a dying animal
It knows not what it is; and gather me
Into the artifice of eternity.

Once out of nature I shall never take
My bodily form from any natural thing,
But such a form as Grecian goldsmiths make
Of hammered gold and gold enamelling
To keep a drowsy Emperor awake;
Or set upon a golden bough to sing
To lords and ladies of Byzantium
Of what is past, or passing, or to come.

WILLIAM BUTLER YEATS (1865–1939)

● ● ●

Eros Turannos

She fears him, and will always ask
   What fated her to choose him;
She meets in his engaging mask
   All reasons to refuse him;
But what she meets and what she fears
Are less than are the downward years,
Drawn slowly to the foamless weirs
   Of age, were she to lose him.

Between a blurred sagacity
   That once had power to sound him,
And Love, that will not let him be
   The Judas that she found him,
Her pride assuages her almost,
As if it were alone the cost.
He sees that he will not be lost,
   And waits and looks around him.

A sense of ocean and old trees
   Envelops and allures him;
Tradition, touching all he sees,
   Beguiles and reassures him;
And all her doubts of what he says
Are dimmed with what she knows of days—
Till even prejudice delays
   And fades, and she secures him.

The falling leaf inaugurates
   The reign of her confusion;

The pounding wave reverberates
  The dirge of her illusion;
And home, where passion lived and died,
Becomes a place where she can hide,
While all the town and harbor-side
  Vibrate with her seclusion.

We tell you, tapping on our brows,
  The story as it should be,
As if the story of a house
  Were told, or ever could be;
We'll have no kindly veil between
Her visions and those we have seen,—
As if we guessed what hers have been,
  Or what they are or would be.

Meanwhile we do no harm; for they
  That with a god have striven,
Not hearing much of what we say,
  Take what the god has given;
Though like waves breaking it may be,
Or like a changed familiar tree,
Or like a stairway to the sea
  Where down the blind are driven.

    EDWIN ARLINGTON ROBINSON   *(1869–1935)*

* * *

Stopping by Woods on a Snowy Evening

Whose woods these are I think I know.
His house is in the village though;
He will not see me stopping here
To watch his woods fill up with snow.

My little horse must think it queer
To stop without a farmhouse near
Between the woods and frozen lake
The darkest evening of the year.

He gives his harness bells a shake
To ask if there is some mistake.
The only other sound's the sweep
Of easy wind and downy flake.

The woods are lovely, dark and deep,
But I have promises to keep,
And miles to go before I sleep,
And miles to go before I sleep.

    ROBERT FROST   *(1874–)*

* * *

Not To Keep

They sent him back to her. The letter came
Saying . . . And she could have him. And
  before
She could be sure there was no hidden ill
Under the formal writing, he was there,
Living. They gave him back to her alive—
How else? They are not known to send the
  dead—
And not disfigured visibly. His face?
His hands? She had to look, to look and ask,
"What is it, dear?" And she had given all
And still she had all—*they* had—they the lucky!
Wasn't she glad now? Everything seemed won,
And all the rest for them permissible ease.
She had to ask, "What was it, dear?"

                 "Enough,
Yet not enough. A bullet through and
  through,
High in the breast. Nothing but what good
  care
And medicine and rest, and you a week,
Can cure me of to go again." The same
Grim giving to do over for them both.
She dared no more than ask him with her eyes
How was it with him for a second trial.
And with his eyes he asked her not to ask.
They had given him back to her, but not to
  keep.

    ROBERT FROST   *(1874–)*

* * *

Fog

The fog comes
on little cat feet.

It sits looking
over harbor and city
on silent haunches
and then moves on.

    CARL SANDBURG   *(1878–)*

* * *

Six Significant Landscapes

I

An old man sits
In the shadow of a pine tree
In China.
He sees larkspur,
Blue and white,
At the edge of the shadow,
Move in the wind.
His beard moves in the wind.
The pine tree moves in the wind.
Thus water flows
Over weeds.

II

The night is of the color
Of a woman's arm:
Night, the female,
Obscure,
Fragrant and supple,
Conceals herself.
A pool shines,
Like a bracelet
Shaken in a dance.

III

I measure myself
Against a tall tree.
I find that I am much taller,
For I reach right up to the sun,
With my eye;
And I reach to the shore of the sea
With my ear.
Nevertheless, I dislike
The way the ants crawl
In and out of my shadow.

IV

When my dream was near the moon,
The white folds of its gown
Filled with yellow light.
The soles of its feet
Grew red.
Its hair filled
With certain blue crystallizations
From stars,
Not far off.

V

Not all the knives of the lamp-posts,
Nor the chisels of the long streets,
Nor the mallets of the domes
And high towers,
Can carve
What one star can carve,
Shining through the grape-leaves.

VI

Rationalists, wearing square hats,
Think, in square rooms,
Looking at the floor,
Looking at the ceiling.
They confine themselves
To right-angled triangles.
If they tried rhomboids,
Cones, waving lines, ellipses—
As, for example, the ellipse of the half-moon—
Rationalists would wear sombreros.

WALLACE STEVENS   (*1879–1955*)

* * *

Negation

Hi! The creator too is blind,
Struggling toward his harmonious whole,
Rejecting intermediate parts,
Horrors and falsities and wrongs;
Incapable master of all force,
Too vague idealist, overwhelmed
By an afflatus that persists.
For this, then, we endure brief lives,
The evanescent symmetries
From that meticulous potter's thumb.

WALLACE STEVENS   (*1879–1955*)

* * *

In Waste Places

As a naked man I go
Through the desert, sore afraid;
Holding high my head, although
I'm as frightened as a maid.

The lion crouches there! I saw
In barren rocks his amber eye!
He parts the cactus with his paw!
He stares at me as I go by!

He would pad upon my trace
If he thought I was afraid!
If he knew my hardy face
Veils the terrors of a maid.

He rises in the night-time, and
He stretches forth! He snuffs the air!
He roars! He leaps along the sand!
He creeps! He watches everywhere!

His burning eyes, his eyes of bale
Through the darkness I can see!
He lashes fiercely with his tail!
He makes again to spring at me!

I am the lion, and his lair!
I am the fear that frightens me!
I am the desert of despair!
And the night of agony!

Night or day, whate'er befall,
I must walk that desert land,
Until I dare my fear and call
The lion out to lick my hand.

JAMES STEPHENS   (*1882–1950*)

❖ ❖ ❖

Poetry

I, too, dislike it: there are things that are im-
         portant beyond all this fiddle.
     Reading it, however, with a perfect con-
         tempt for it, one discovers in
it, after all, a place for the genuine.
     Hands that can grasp, eyes
     that can dilate, hair that can rise
         if it must, these things are important
         not because a

high-sounding interpretation can be put upon
         them but because they are
     useful. When they become so derivative as
         to become unintelligible,
     the same thing may be said for all of us,
         that we
     do not admire what
     we cannot understand: the bat
         holding on upside down or in quest of
         something to

eat, elephants pushing, a wild horse taking a
         roll, a tireless wolf under
     a tree, the immovable critic twitching his
         skin like a horse that feels a flea, the
         base-
     ball fan, the statistician—
         nor is it valid
         to discriminate against "business docu-
         ments and

school-books"; all these phenomena are im-
         portant. One must make a distinction
     however: when dragged into prominence by
         half poets, the result is not poetry,
     nor till the poets among us can be
         "literalists of
         the imagination"—above
         insolence and triviality and can present

for inspection, "imaginary gardens with real
         toads in them," shall we have
     it. In the meantime, if you demand on the
         one hand,
     the raw material of poetry in
         all its rawness and
     that which is on the other hand
         genuine, then you are interested in
         poetry.

MARIANNE MOORE   (*1887–*)

❖ ❖ ❖

The Love Song of J. Alfred Prufrock

A persona che mai tornasse al mondo,
S'io credesse che mia risposta fosse
Questa fiamma staria senza piu scosse.
Ma perciocche giammai di questo fondo
Non torno vivo alcun, s'i'odo il vero,
Senza tema d'infamia ti rispondo.°

Let us go then, you and I,
When the evening is spread out against the
     sky
Like a patient etherized upon a table;
Let us go, through certain half-deserted streets,
The muttering retreats
Of restless nights in one-night cheap hotels
And sawdust restaurants with oyster-shells:
Streets that follow like a tedious argument

Of insidious intent
To lead you to an overwhelming question. . . .
Oh, do not ask, "What is it?"
Let us go and make our visit.

In the room the women come and go
Talking of Michelangelo.

The yellow fog that rubs its back upon the
    window-panes,
The yellow smoke that rubs its muzzle on the
    window-panes,
Licked its tongue into the corners of the
    evening,
Lingered upon the pools that stand in drains,
Let fall upon its back the soot that falls from
    chimneys,
Slipped by the terrace, made a sudden leap,
And seeing that it was a soft October night,
Curled once about the house, and fell asleep.

And indeed there will be time
For the yellow smoke that slides along the
    street,
Rubbing its back upon the window-panes;
There will be time, there will be time
To prepare a face to meet the faces that you
    meet;
There will be time to murder and create,
And time for all the works and days of hands
That lift and drop a question on your plate;
Time for you and time for me,
And time yet for a hundred indecisions,
And for a hundred visions and revisions,
Before the taking of a toast and tea.

In the room the women come and go
Talking of Michelangelo.

And indeed there will be time
To wonder, "Do I dare?" and, "Do I dare?"
Time to turn back and descend the stair,
With a bald spot in the middle of my hair—
(They will say: "How his hair is growing
    thin!")
My morning coat, my collar mounting firmly
    to the chin,
My necktie rich and modest, but asserted by a
    simple pin—
(They will say: "But how his arms and legs
    are thin!")
Do I dare

Disturb the universe?
In a minute there is time
For decisions and revisions which a minute
    will reverse.

For I have known them all already, known
    them all:
Have known the evenings, mornings, after-
    noons,
I have measured out my life with coffee
    spoons;
I know the voices dying with a dying fall
Beneath the music from a farther room.
    So how should I presume?

And I have known the eyes already, known
    them all—
The eyes that fix you in a formulated phrase,
And when I am formulated, sprawling on a
    pin,
When I am pinned and wriggling on the wall,
Then how should I begin
To spit out all the butt-ends of my days and
    ways?
    And how should I presume?

And I have known the arms already, known
    them all—
Arms that are braceleted and white and bare
(But in the lamplight, downed with light
    brown hair!)
Is it perfume from a dress
That makes me so digress?
Arms that lie along a table, or wrap about a
    shawl,
    And should I then presume?
    And how should I begin?

■

Shall I say, I have gone at dusk through nar-
    row streets
And watched the smoke that rises from the
    pipes
Of lonely men in shirt-sleeves, leaning out of
    windows? . . .

I should have been a pair of ragged claws
Scuttling across the floors of silent seas.

■

And the afternoon, the evening, sleeps so
    peacefully!

Smoothed by long fingers,
Asleep . . . tired . . . or it malingers,
Stretched on the floor, here beside you and me.
Should I, after tea and cakes and ices,
Have the strength to force the moment to its
    crisis?
But though I have wept and fasted, wept and
    prayed,
Though I have seen my head (grown slightly
    bald) brought in upon a platter,
I am no prophet—and here's no great matter;
I have seen the moment of my greatness
    flicker,
And I have seen the eternal Footman hold my
    coat, and snicker,
And in short, I was afraid.

And would it have been worth it, after all,
After the cups, the marmalade, the tea,
Among the porcelain, among some talk of you
    and me,
Would it have been worth while,
To have bitten off the matter with a smile,
To have squeezed the universe into a ball
To roll it toward some overwhelming ques-
    tion,
To say: "I am Lazarus, come from the dead,
Come back to tell you all, I shall tell you
    all"—
If one, settling a pillow by her head,
    Should say: "That is not what I meant at
    all;
    That is not it, at all."

And would it have been worth it, after all,
Would it have been worth while,
After the sunsets and the dooryards and the
    sprinkled streets,
After the novels, after the teacups, after the
    skirts that trail along the floor—
And this, and so much more?—
It is impossible to say just what I mean!
But as if a magic lantern threw the nerves in
    patterns on a screen:
Would it have been worth while
If one, settling a pillow or throwing off a
    shawl,
And turning toward the window, should say:
    "That is not it at all,
    That is not what I meant, at all."

■

No! I am not Prince Hamlet, nor was meant
    to be;

Am an attendant lord, one that will do
To swell a progress, start a scene or two,
Advise the prince; no doubt, an easy tool,
Deferential, glad to be of use,
Politic, cautious, and meticulous;
Full of high sentence, but a bit obtuse;
At times, indeed, almost ridiculous—
Almost, at times, the Fool.

I grow old. . . . I grow old. . . .
I shall wear the bottoms of my trousers rolled.

Shall I part my hair behind? Do I dare to eat
    a peach?
I shall wear white flannel trousers, and walk
    upon the beach.
I have heard the mermaids singing, each to
    each.

I do not think that they will sing to me.

I have seen them riding seaward on the waves
Combing the white hair of the waves blown
    back
When the wind blows the water white and
    black.

We have lingered in the chambers of the sea
By sea-girls wreathed with seaweed red and
    brown
Till human voices wake us, and we drown.

T. S. ELIOT   (1888–)

["If I thought my answer were to one who could
return to the world, I would not reply, but as none
ever did return alive from this depth, without fear of
infamy I answer thee" (Dante, *Inferno*, Canto XXVII,
lines 61-66).]

* * *

Ars Poetica

A poem should be palpable and mute
As a globed fruit

Dumb
As old medallions to the thumb

Silent as the sleeve-worn stone
Of casement ledges where the moss has
    grown—

A poem should be wordless
As the flight of birds

■

A poem should be motionless in time
As the moon climbs

Leaving, as the moon releases
Twig by twig the night-entangled trees,

Leaving, as the moon behind the winter
   leaves,
Memory by memory the mind—

A poem should be motionless in time
As the moon climbs

■

A poem should be equal to:
Not true

For all the history of grief
An empty doorway and a maple leaf

For love
The leaning grasses and two lights above the
   sea—

A poem should not mean
But be.

ARCHIBALD MACLEISH   (*1892–*)

* * *

if up's the word

if up's the word;and a world grows greener
minute by second and most by more—
if death is the loser and life is the winner
(and beggars are rich but misers are poor)
—let's touch the sky:
               with a to and a fro
(and a here there where)and away we go

in even the laziest creature among us
a wisdom no knowledge can kill is astir—
now dull eyes are keen and now keen eyes are
   keener
(for young is the year,for young is the year)
—let's touch the sky:
               with a great(and a gay
and a steep)deep rush through amazing day

it's brains without hearts have set saint against
   sinner;
put gain over gladness and joy under care—

let's do as an earth which can never do wrong
   does
(minute by second and most by more)
—let's touch the sky:
               with a strange(and a true)
and a climbing fall into far near blue

if beggars are rich(and a robin will sing his
robin a song)but misers are poor—
let's love until noone could quite be(and
   young is
the year,dear)as living as i'm and as you're
—let's touch the sky:
               with a you and a me
and an every(who's any who's some)one who's
we

E. E. CUMMINGS   (*1894–*)

* * *

In Memory of W. B. Yeats

(d. Jan. 1939)

1

He disappeared in the dead of winter:
The brooks were frozen, the airports almost
   deserted,
And snow disfigured the public statues;
The mercury sank in the mouth of the dying
   day.
O all the instruments agree
The day of his death was a dark cold day.

Far from his illness
The wolves ran on through the evergreen
   forests,
The peasant river was untempted by the
   fashionable quays;
By mourning tongues
The death of the poet was kept from his
   poems.

But for him it was his last afternoon as him-
   self,
An afternoon of nurses and rumors;
The provinces of his body revolted,
The squares of his mind were empty,
Silence invaded the suburbs,
The current of his feeling failed: he became
   his admirers.

Now he is scattered among a hundred cities
And wholly given over to unfamiliar affec-
    tions;
To find his happiness in another kind of wood
And be punished under a foreign code of
    conscience.
The words of a dead man
Are modified in the guts of the living.

But in the importance and noise of tomorrow
When the brokers are roaring like beasts on
    the floor of the Bourse,
And the poor have the sufferings to which
    they are fairly accustomed,
And each in the cell of himself is almost con-
    vinced of his freedom;
A few thousand will think of this day
As one thinks of a day when one did some-
    thing slightly unusual.
O all the instruments agree
The day of his death was a dark cold day.

2

You were silly like us: your gift survived it
    all;
The parish of rich women, physical decay,
Yourself; mad Ireland hurt you into poetry.
Now Ireland has her madness and her
    weather still,
For poetry makes nothing happen: it sur-
    vives
In the valley of its saying where executives
Would never want to tamper; it flows south
From ranches of isolation and the busy
    griefs,
Raw towns that we believe and die in; it
    survives,
A way of happening, a mouth.

3

Earth, receive an honored guest;
William Yeats is laid to rest:
Let the Irish vessel lie
Emptied of its poetry.

Time that is intolerant
Of the brave and innocent,
And indifferent in a week
To a beautiful physique,

Worships language and forgives
Everyone by whom it lives;
Pardons cowardice, conceit,
Lays its honors at their feet.

Time that with this strange excuse
Pardoned Kipling and his views,
And will pardon Paul Claudel,
Pardons him for writing well.

In the nightmare of the dark
All the dogs of Europe bark,
And the living nations wait,
Each sequestered in its hate;

Intellectual disgrace
Stares from every human face,
And the seas of pity lie
Locked and frozen in each eye.

Follow, poet, follow right
To the bottom of the night,
With your unconstraining voice
Still persuade us to rejoice;

With the farming of a verse
Make a vineyard of the curse,
Sing of human unsuccess
In a rapture of distress;

In the deserts of the heart
Let the healing fountain start,
In the prison of his days
Teach the free man how to praise.

W. H. AUDEN   (*1907–*)

* * *

The Fly

O hideous little bat, the size of snot,
With polyhedral eye and shabby clothes,
To populate the stinking cat you walk
The promontory of the dead man's nose,
Climb with the fine leg of a Duncan Phyfe
    The smoking mountains of my food
        And in a comic mood
    In mid-air take to bed a wife.

Riding and riding with your filth of hair
On gluey foot or wing, forever coy,
Hot from the compost and green sweet decay
Sounding your buzzer like an urchin toy;
You dot all whiteness with diminutive stool;
   In the tight belly of the dead
     Burrow with hungry head
   And inlay maggots like a jewel.

At your approach the great horse stomps and
   paws
Bringing the hurricane of his heavy tail;
Shod in disease you dare to kiss my hand
Which sweeps against you like an angry flail;
Still you return, return, trusting your wing
   To draw you from the hunter's reach
     That learns to kill to teach
   Disorder to the tinier thing.

My peace is your disaster. For your death
Children like spiders cup their pretty hands
And wives resort to chemistry of war.
In fens of sticky paper and quicksands
You glue yourself to death. Where you are
   stuck
   You struggle hideously and beg;
     You amputate your leg
   Imbedded in the amber muck.

But I, a man, must swat you with my hate,
Slap you across the air and crush your flight,
Must mangle with my shoe and smear your
   blood,
Expose your little guts pasty and white,
Knock your head sidewise like a drunkard's
   hat,
   Pin your wings under like a crow's,
     Tear off your flimsy clothes
   And beat you as one beats a rat.

Then like Gargantua I stride among
The corpses strewn like raisins in the dust,
The broken bodies of the narrow dead
That catch the throat with fingers of disgust.
I sweep. One gyrates like a top and falls
   And stunned, stone blind, and deaf
     Buzzes its frightful F
   And dies between three cannibals.

            KARL SHAPIRO (*1913–*   )

            * * *

Fern Hill

Now as I was young and easy under the apple
   boughs
About the lilting house and happy as the grass
   was green,
   The night above the dingle starry,
     Time let me hail and climb
   Golden in the heydays of his eyes,
And honoured among wagons I was prince of
   the apple towns
And once below a time I lordly had the trees
   and leaves
   Trail with daisies and barley
   Down the rivers of the windfall light.

And as I was green and carefree, famous
   among the barns
About the happy yard and singing as the farm
   was home,
   In the sun that is young once only,
     Time let me play and be
   Golden in the mercy of his means,
And green and golden I was huntsman and
   herdsman, the calves
Sang to my horn, the foxes on the hills barked
   clear and cold,
   And the sabbath rang slowly
   In the pebbles of the holy streams.

All the sun long it was running, it was lovely,
   the hay
Fields high as the house, the tunes from the
   chimneys, it was air
   And playing, lovely and watery
     And fire green as grass.
   And nightly under the simple stars
As I rode to sleep the owls were bearing the
   farm away,
All the moon long I heard, blessed among
   stables, the night-jars
   Flying with the ricks, and the horses
   Flashing into the dark.

And then to awake, and the farm, like a
   wanderer white
With the dew, come back, the cock on his
   shoulder: it was all
   Shining, it was Adam and maiden,
     The sky gathered again
   And the sun grew round that very day.

So it must have been after the birth of the simple light
In the first, spinning place, the spellbound horses walking warm
  Out of the whinnying green stable
    On to the fields of praise.

And honoured among foxes and pheasants by the gay house
Under the new made clouds and happy as the heart was long,
  In the sun born over and over,
    I ran my heedless ways,
  My wishes raced through the house high hay
And nothing I cared, at my sky blue trades, that time allows
In all his tuneful turning so few and such morning songs
  Before the children green and golden
    Follow him out of grace,

Nothing I cared, in the lamb white days, that time would take me
Up to the swallow thronged loft by the shadow of my hand,
  In the moon that is always rising,
    Nor that riding to sleep
  I should hear him fly with the high fields
And wake to the farm forever fled from the childless land.
Oh as I was young and easy in the mercy of his means,
  Time held me green and dying
  Though I sang in my chains like the sea.

          DYLAN THOMAS   (*1914–1953*)

* * *

Salem

In Salem seasick spindrift drifts or skips
To the canvas flapping on the seaward panes
Until the knitting sailor stabs at ships
Nosing like sheep of Morpheus through his brain's
Asylum. Seaman, seaman, how the draft
Lashes the oily slick about your head,
Beating up whitecaps! Seaman, Charon's raft
Dumps its damned goods into the harbor-bed,—

There sewage sickens the rebellious seas.
Remember, seaman, Salem fishermen
Once hung their nimble fleets on the Great Banks.
Where was it that New England bred the men
Who quartered the Leviathan's flat flanks
And fought the British Lion to his knees?

          ROBERT LOWELL   (*1917– *)

Lion

The lion, ruler over all the beasts,
Triumphant moves upon the grassy plain
With sun like gold upon his tawny brow
And dew like silver on his shaggy mane.

Into himself he draws the rolling thunder,
Beneath his flinty paw great boulders quake;
He will dispatch the mouse to burrow under,
The little deer to shiver in the brake.

He sets the fierce whip of each serpent lashing,
The tall giraffe brings humbly to his knees,
Awakes the sloth, and sends the wild boar crashing,
Wide-eyed monkeys chittering through the trees.

He gazes down into the quiet river,
Parting the green bulrushes to behold
A sunflower-crown of amethyst and silver,
A royal coat of brushed and beaten gold.

          WILLIAM JAY SMITH   (*1918– *)

* * *

Lion

In the bend of your mouth soft murder
  in the flints of your eyes
    the sun-stained openings of caves

Your nostrils breathe the ordained air
  of chosen loneliness

Magnificently maned as the lustrous pampas
  your head heavy with heraldic curls
    wears a regal frown between the brows

The wide bundle of your chest
　　your loose-skinned belly frilled with fur
　　you carry easily sinuously pacing on suede
　　　paws

Between tight thighs
　　under the thick root of your tufted tail
　　situated like a full-stoned fruit beneath a
　　　bough
　　the quiver of your never-used malehood is
　　　slung

You pace in dung on cement
　　the bars flick past your eyeballs
　　fixed beyond the awestruck stares of chil-
　　　dren

Watching you they remember their fathers
　　the frightening hairs in their fathers' ears

Young girls remember lovers too timid and
　　　white
.　and I remember how I played lion with
　　　my brothers
　　under the round yellow-grained table
　　the shadow our cave in the lamplight

Your beauty burns the brain
　　though your paws slue on foul cement
　　the fetor of captivity you do right to ignore
　　the bars too an illusion

Your heroic paranoia plants you in the In-
　　　dian jungle
　　pacing by the cool water-hole as dawn
　　　streaks the sky
　　and the foretaste of the all-day hunt
　　is sweet as yearling's blood
　　in the corners of your lips

MAY SWENSON (1919–)

* * *

For the New Railway Station in Rome

　　Those who said God is praised
By hurt pillars, who loved to see our brazen
　　　lust
　　Lie down in rubble, and our vaunting
　　　arches
　　　Conduce to dust;

　　Those who with short shadows
Poked through the stubbled forum pondering
　　　on decline,
　　And would not take the sun standing at
　　　noon
　　　For a good sign;

　　Those pilgrims of defeat
Who brought their injured wills as to a sol-
　　　diers' home;
　　Dig them all up now, tell them there's
　　　something new
　　　To see in Rome.

　　See, from the travertine
Face of the office block, the roof of the book-
　　　ing-hall
　　Sails out into the air beside the ruined
　　　Servian Wall,

　　Echoing in its light
And cantilevered swoop of reinforced concrete
　　The broken profile of these stones, defeating
　　　That defeat

　　And straying the strummed mind,
By such a sudden chord as raised the town of
　　　Troy,
　　To where the least shard of the world sings
　　　out
　　　In stubborn joy,

　　"What city is eternal
But that which prints itself within the grop-
　　　ing head
　　Out of the blue unbroken reveries
　　　Of the building dead?

　　"What is our praise or pride
But to imagine excellence, and try to make it?
　　What does it say over the door of Heaven
　　　But *homo fecit?*"

RICHARD WILBUR (1921–)

* * *

PART THREE

Between Prose and Poetry

The Old Testament: Isaiah I:1–31

1   The vision of Isaiah the son of Amoz, which he saw concerning Judah and Jerusalem in the days of Uzziah, Jotham, Ahaz, and Hezekiah, kings of Judah.

2   Hear, O heavens, and give ear, O earth: for the Lord hath spoken, I have nourished and brought up children, and they have rebelled against me.

3   The ox knoweth his owner, and the ass his master's crib: but Israel doth not know, my people doth not consider.

4   Ah sinful nation, a people laden with iniquity, a seed of evildoers, children that are corrupters: they have forsaken the Lord, they have provoked the Holy One of Israel unto anger, they are gone away backward.

5   Why should ye be stricken any more? ye will revolt more and more: the whole head is sick, and the whole heart faint.

6   From the sole of the foot even unto the head there is no soundness in it; but wounds, and bruises, and putrifying sores: they have not been closed, neither bound up, neither mollified with ointment.

7   Your country is desolate, your cities are burned with fire: your land, strangers devour it in your presence, and it is desolate, as overthrown by strangers.

8   And the daughter of Zion is left as a cottage in a vineyard, as a lodge in a garden of cucumbers, as a besieged city.

9   Except the Lord of hosts had left unto us a very small remnant, we should have been as Sodom, and we should have been like unto Gomorrah.

10   Hear the word of the Lord, ye rulers of Sodom; give ear unto the law of our God, ye people of Gomorrah.

11   To what purpose is the multitude of your sacrifices unto me? saith the Lord: I am full of the burnt offerings of rams, and the fat of fed beasts; and I delight not in the blood of bullocks, or of lambs, or of he goats.

12   When ye come to appear before me, who hath required this at your hand, to tread my courts?

13   Bring no more vain oblations; incense is an abomination unto me; the new moons and sabbaths, the calling of assemblies, I cannot away with; it is iniquity, even the solemn meeting.

14   Your new moons and your appointed feasts my soul hateth: they are a trouble unto me; I am weary to bear them.

15   And when ye spread forth your hands, I will hide mine eyes from you: yea, when ye make many prayers, I will not hear: your hands are full of blood.

16   Wash you, make you clean; put away the evil of your doings from before mine eyes; cease to do evil;

17   Learn to do well; seek judgment, relieve the oppressed, judge the fatherless, plead for the widow.

18   Come now, and let us reason together, saith the Lord: though your sins be as scarlet, they shall be as white as snow; though they be red like crimson, they shall be as wool.

19   If ye be willing and obedient, ye shall eat the good of the land:

20   But if ye refuse and rebel, ye shall be devoured with the sword: for the mouth of the Lord hath spoken it.

21   How is the faithful city become an harlot! it was full of judgment; righteousness lodged in it; but now murderers.

22   Thy silver is become dross, thy wine mixed with water:

23   Thy princes are rebellious, and companions of thieves: every one loveth gifts, and followeth after rewards: they judge not the fatherless, neither doth the cause of the widow come unto them.

24   Therefore saith the Lord, the Lord of hosts, the mighty One of Israel, Ah, I will ease me of mine adversaries, and avenge me of mine enemies:

25   And I will turn my hand upon thee, and purely purge away thy dross, and take away all thy tin:

26   And I will restore thy judges as at the first, and thy counsellors as at the beginning: afterward thou shalt be called, The city of righteousness, the faithful city.

27   Zion shall be redeemed with judgment, and her converts with righteousness.

28   And the destruction of the transgressors and of the sinners shall be together, and they that forsake the Lord shall be consumed.

29   For they shall be ashamed of the oaks which ye have desired, and ye shall be con-

founded for the gardens that ye have chosen.

30   For ye shall be as an oak whose leaf fadeth, and as a garden that hath no water.

31   And the strong shall be as tow, and the maker of it as a spark, and they shall both burn together, and none shall quench them.

Of Death

Men fear Death, as children fear to go in the dark; and as that natural fear in children is increased with tales, so is the other. Certainly, the contemplation of death, as the wages of sin and passage to another world, is holy and religious; but the fear of it, as a tribute due unto nature, is weak. Yet in religious meditations there is sometimes mixture of vanity and of superstition. You shall read in some of the friars' books of mortification, that a man should think with himself what the pain is if he have but his finger's end pressed or tortured, and thereby imagine what the pains of death are, when the whole body is corrupted and dissolved; when many times death passeth with less pain than the torture of a limb: for the most vital parts are not the quickest of sense. And by him that spake only as a philosopher and natural man, it was well said, *Pompa mortis magis terret, quam mors ipsa:* [it is the accompaniments of death that are frightful rather than death itself.] Groans and convulsions, and a discoloured face, and friends weeping, and blacks, and obsequies, and the like, shew death terrible. It is worthy the observing, that there is no passion in the mind of man so weak, but it mates and masters the fear of death; and therefore death is no such terrible enemy when a man hath so many attendants about him that can win the combat of him. Revenge triumphs over death; Love slights it; Honour aspireth to it; Grief flieth to it; Fear pre-occupateth it; nay we read, after Otho the emperor had slain himself, Pity (which is the tenderest of affections) provoked many to die, out of mere compassion to their sovereign, and as the truest sort of followers. Nay Seneca adds niceness and satiety: *Cogita quamdiu eadem feceris; mori velle, non tantum fortis, aut miser, sed etiam fastidiosus potest.* A man would die, though he were neither valiant nor miserable, only upon a weariness to do the same thing so oft over and over. It is no less worthy to observe, how little alteration in good spirits the approaches of death make; for they appear to be the same men till the last instant. Augustus Cæsar died in a compliment; *Livia, conjugii nostri memor, vive et vale:* [farewell, Livia; and forget not the days of our marriage.] Tiberius in dissimulation; as Tacitus saith of him, *Jam Tiberium vires et corpus, non dissimulatio, deserebant:* [his powers of body were gone, but his power of dissimulation still remained.] Vespasian in a jest; sitting upon the stool, *Ut puto Deus fio:* [I think I am becoming a god.] Galba with a sentence; *Feri, si ex re sit populi Romani:* [strike, if it be for the good of Rome;] holding forth his neck. Septimius Severus in despatch; *Adeste si quid mihi restat agendum:* [make haste, if there is anything more for me to do.] And the like. Certainly the Stoics bestowed too much cost upon death, and by their great preparations made it appear more fearful. Better saith he, *qui finem vitæ extremum inter munera ponat naturæ:* [who accounts the close of life as one of the benefits of nature.] It is as natural to die as to be born; and to a little infant, perhaps, the one is as painful as the other. He that dies in an earnest pursuit, is like one that is wounded in hot blood; who, for the time, scarce feels the hurt; and therefore a mind fixed and bent upon somewhat that is good doth avert the dolours of death. But above all, believe it, the sweetest canticle is, *Nunc dimittis;* when a man hath obtained worthy end and expectations. Death hath this also; that it openeth the gate to good fame, and extinguisheth envy. *Extinctus amabitur idem:* [the same man that was envied while he lived, shall be loved when he is gone].

SIR FRANCIS BACON   (*1561–1626*)

✶ ✶ ✶

The Chase—First Day

[from *Moby-Dick*, Ch. 133]

. . . Soon all the boats but Starbuck's were dropped; all the boat-sails set—all the paddles plying; with rippling swiftness, shooting to leeward; and Ahab heading the onset. A pale, death-glimmer lit up Fedallah's sunken eyes; a hideous motion gnawed his mouth.

Like noiseless nautilus shells, their light prows sped through the sea; but only slowly they neared the foe. As they neared him, the ocean grew still more smooth; seemed drawing a carpet over its waves; seemed a noon-meadow, so serenely it spread. At length the breathless hunter came so nigh his seemingly unsuspecting prey, that his entire dazzling hump was distinctly visible, sliding along the sea as if an isolated thing, and continually set in a revolving ring of finest, fleecy, greenish foam. He saw the vast involved wrinkles of the slightly projecting head beyond. Before it, far out on the soft Turkish-rugged waters, went the glistening white shadows from his broad, milky forehead, a musical rippling playfully accompanying the shade; and behind, the blue waters interchangeably flowed over into the moving valley of his steady wake; and on either hand bright bubbles arose and danced by his side. But these were broken again by the light toes of hundreds of gay fowl softly feathering the sea, alternate with their fitful flight; and like to some flagstaff rising from the painted hull of an argosy, the tall but shattered pole of a recent lance projected from the white whale's back; and at intervals one of the cloud of soft-toed fowls hovering, and to and fro skimming like a canopy over the fish, silently perched and rocked on this pole, the long tail feathers streaming like pennons.

A gentle joyousness—a mighty mildness of repose in swiftness, invested the gliding whale. Not the white bull Jupiter swimming away with ravished Europa clinging to his graceful horns; his lovely, leering eyes sideways intent upon the maid; with smooth bewitching fleetness, rippling straight for the nuptial bower in Crete; not Jove did surpass the glorified White Whale as he so divinely swam.

On each soft side—coincident with the parted swell, that but once laving him, then flowed so wide away—on each bright side, the whale shed off enticings. No wonder there had been some among the hunters who namelessly transported and allured by all this serenity had ventured to assail it; but had fatally found that quietude but the vesture of tornadoes. Yet calm, enticing calm, oh, whale! thou glidest on, to all who for the first time eye thee, no matter how many in that same way thou may'st have bejuggled and destroyed before.

And thus, through the serene tranquillities of the tropical sea, among waves whose hand-clappings were suspended by exceeding rapture, Moby Dick moved on, still withholding from sight the full terrors of his submerged trunk, entirely hiding the wretched hideousness of his jaw. But soon the fore part of him slowly rose from the water; for an instant his whole marbleised body formed a high arch, like Virginia's Natural Bridge, and warningly waving his bannered flukes in the air, the grand god revealed himself, sounded, and went out of sight. Hoveringly halting, and dipping on the wing, the white sea-fowls longingly lingered over the agitated pool that he left. . . .

HERMAN MELVILLE   (*1819–1891*)

* * *

A Haunted House

Whatever hour you woke there was a door shutting. From room to room they went, hand in hand, lifting here, opening there, making sure—a ghostly couple.

"Here we left it," she said. And he added, "Oh, but here too!" "It's upstairs," she murmured. "And in the garden," he whispered. "Quietly," they said, "or we shall wake them."

But it wasn't that you woke us. Oh, no. "They're looking for it; they're drawing the curtain," one might say, and so read on a page or two. "Now they've found it," one would be certain, stopping the pencil on the margin. And then, tired of reading, one might rise and see for oneself, the house all empty, the doors standing open, only the wood pigeons bubbling with content and the hum of the threshing machine sounding from the farm. "What did I come in here for? What did I want to find?" My hands were empty. "Perhaps it's upstairs then?" The apples were in the loft. And so down again, the garden still as ever, only the book had slipped into the grass.

But they had found it in the drawing-room. Not that one could ever see them. The window panes reflected apples, reflected roses; all the leaves were green in the glass. If they moved in the drawing-room, the apple only turned its yellow side. Yet, the moment after, if the door was opened, spread about the floor, hung upon the walls, pendant from the ceiling—what? My hands were empty. The shadow of a thrush crossed the carpet; from the deepest wells of silence the wood pigeon drew its bubble of sound. "Safe, safe, safe," the pulse of the house beat softly. "The treasure buried; the room . . ." the pulse stopped short. Oh, was that the buried treasure?

A moment later the light had faded. Out in the garden then? But the trees spun darkness for a wandering beam of sun. So fine, so rare, coolly sunk beneath the surface the beam I sought always burnt behind the glass. Death was the glass; death was between us; coming to the woman first, hundreds of years ago, leaving the house, sealing all the windows; the rooms were darkened. He left it, left her, went North, went East, saw the stars turned in the Southern sky; sought the house, found it dropped beneath the Downs. "Safe, safe, safe," the pulse of the house beat gladly. "The Treasure yours."

The wind roars up the avenue. Trees stoop and bend this way and that. Moonbeams splash and spill wildly in the rain. But the beam of the lamp falls straight from the window. The candle burns stiff and still. Wandering through the house, opening the windows, whispering not to wake us, the ghostly couple seek their joy.

"Here we slept," she says. And he adds, "Kisses without number." "Waking in the morning—" "Silver between the trees—" "Upstairs—" "In the garden—" "When summer came—" "In winter snowtime—" The doors go shutting far in the distance, gently knocking like the pulse of a heart.

Nearer they come; cease at the doorway. The wind falls, the rain slides silver down the glass. Our eyes darken; we hear no steps beside us; we see no lady spread her ghostly cloak. His hands shield the lantern. "Look," he breathes. "Sound asleep. Love upon their lips."

Stooping, holding their silver lamp above us, long they look and deeply. Long they pause. The wind drives straightly; the flame stoops slightly. Wild beams of moonlight cross both floor and wall, and, meeting, stain the faces bent; the faces pondering; the faces that search the sleepers and seek their hidden joy.

"Safe, safe, safe," the heart of the house beats proudly. "Long years—" he sighs. "Again you found me." "Here," she murmurs, "sleeping; in the garden reading; laughing, rolling apples in the loft. Here we left our treasure—" Stooping, their light lifts the lids upon my eyes. "Safe! safe! safe!" the pulse of the house beats wildly. Waking, I cry "Oh, is this *your* buried treasure? The light in the heart."

VIRGINIA WOOLF (*1882–1941*)

❖ ❖ ❖

Topics for Writing

Topics for Short Papers

The following topics are tied to specific essays or poems. Though designated as topics for short papers, some of them if explored deeply might well result in lengthy papers. The student should remember, therefore, that part of his task in writing any paper is so to limit his topic that he may treat it adequately in the space available. With a topic such as 23, for example, he would probably be unwise to attempt coverage of all the poems named; instead, he should select for discussion those poems which will best enable him to make a valid and meaningful point in the space assigned.

1. Does Plato's account of the process of poetic composition in the *Ion* harmonize with his account in the *Republic?* If not, explore the differences.

2. Both Plato (in the *Ion*) and Housman speak of madness in connection with the composition of poetry. Are they in essential agreement? Do they speak of the same kind of madness? Are their accounts of poetic inspiration similar or different?

3. Contrast the notions of poetic composition presented by Plato in the *Ion* and by Ransom in "Forms and Citizens."

4. Though Plato inveighs against poetry in the *Republic*, Sidney contends that Plato himself was a poet. What characteristics of the two selections by Plato, as translated into English, would qualify Plato for Sidney as a poet?

5. Plato and Shelley both use the metaphor of a mirror in speaking of art. Do they use this metaphor in similar or different ways?

6. Plato and Eliot have different notions of the effect of poetry on the state. Discuss.

7. Aristotle and Poe differ as to the proper length of a poem. Compare and contrast their views, and attempt to adjudicate between them, relying on your own experience, and on logic, and considering also what Coleridge and Wilson have to say on this topic.

8. Aristotle and Wordsworth have different theories of poetic diction. By applying each theory to selected poems in Part II, determine which you conceive to be more nearly correct.

9. Is a good poem complex or simple? Consult especially Aristotle, Coleridge, Warren, and Wimsatt on this point.

10. According to Aristotle, "the poet should prefer probable impossibilities to improbable possibilities." In the light of this principle, discuss Keats's "On First Looking into Chapman's Homer" in respect to Keats's mistake in making Cortez rather than Balboa the discoverer of the Pacific.

11. The object of poetry, says Sidney, is "to teach and delight." A good poet does ill, says Shelley, "to embody his own conceptions of right and wrong."—Are Sidney and Shelley opposed on this point, or can they be reconciled?

12. Sidney describes the poet as "a maker" who may make things "either better than nature bringeth forth, or, quite anew, forms such as never were in nature"; but he also describes poetry as "an art of imitation." Are the concepts of the poet as maker and as imitator contradictory, or does Sidney reconcile them?

13. Compare the ideas of Sidney, Shelley, and Mill on the relationship between poetry and primitive stages of society.

14. Compare the ideas of Pope and Ransom about the composition of poetry.

15. What are the qualifications of a good reader of poetry? Consult especially Wordsworth, Mill, and Macaulay (in the Definitions) on this point. Are they in agreement?

16. In what respect do Bradley, Frost, and Day Lewis differ from Shelley in their accounts of how a poem is conceived and composed? Which of these support Brooks's contention that "the poet is a maker, not a communicator"?

17. Can poetry be translated? Compare Shelley, Bradley, and Eliot on this point. Are they in agreement or disagreement?

18. Mill speaks of poetry sometimes as the "expression" or "utterance" of feeling, sometimes as the "representation" or "delineation" of feeling. Is he inconsistent, or does he reconcile these two ways of viewing poetry?

19. According to Mill, poetry "does not even require the instrument of words," but may speak through music, or even through sculpture, painting, and architecture. Would any other of the writers in Part I be willing to define poetry in this way? Discuss the issue involved.

20. Mill makes a sharp distinction between the faculty of the poet and that of the novelist. Would this distinction be supported by Aristotle? by Sidney? by Wilson? Discuss.

21. Apply Mill's discussion of poetry to an examination of the four prose selections. Would they qualify as poetry for him? Would he make any distinctions?

22. Apply Mill's remarks on descriptive poetry to James Stephens's "In Waste Places," page 215; William Jay Smith's "Lion," page 222; and May Swenson's "Lion," page 222. Do these poems bear Mill out?

23. Extend the foregoing discussion to include the following poems: William Blake, "The Tiger," page 198; Emily Dickinson, "A bird came down the walk," page 211; Karl Shapiro, "The Fly," page 220; and Carl Sandburg, "Fog," page 214.

24. In writing of descriptive poetry, Mill claims that a "lion may be described falsely or with exaggeration, and the poetry be all the better." Would Aristotle agree or disagree? Why? (The issue raised here is the issue sometimes referred to as that of "poetic license.")

25. In what respects are Mill and Yeats alike in their ideas about poetry?

26. Do Yeats, in "The Symbolism of Poetry," and W. H. Auden, in "In Memory of W. B. Yeats," page 219, agree or disagree in their ideas about poetry? Discuss.

27. Bradley and Brooks both insist that genuine poetry is not "the decoration of a preconceived and clearly defined matter." Discuss what they mean by this contention. Illustrate, if you can, by analysis or partial analysis of a poem in Part II.

28. Poe and Warren make different estimates of Shelley's "Indian Serenade." Explain the difference in light of their respective poetic theories.

29. "Poetry is not the thing said but a way of saying it," says Housman. "Poetry is one more art of having something to say," writes Frost. Which is right? Can these apparently contradictory views be mediated? How would Bradley or Warren approach this problem?

30. Compare the ideas of Warren and Wimsatt on the judgment of poetry. Are they essentially in agreement or essentially opposed in what they say?

31. Select any one of the essays and test its validity (or the validity of any part of it) by applying it to selected poems in Part II.

32. Select any one of the provided definitions or statements about poetry and test it by applying it to selected poems in Part II. Does it fit them all? If not, in what way is it defective? (Try especially definitions 3, 7, 11, 14, 17, 18, 19, 22, and 34.)

33. Test the validity of one of the following theories or assertions by applying it to selected poems in Part II:

A. Plato's theory that poetry is imitation.

B. Aristotle's contention that "the perfection of style is to be clear without being mean."

C. Sidney's theory that the end of poetry is "to teach and delight."

D. Wordsworth's theory that "not only the language of a large portion of every good poem, even of the most elevated character, must necessarily, except with reference to the metre, in no respect differ from that of good prose, but likewise that some of the most interesting parts of the best poems will be found to be strictly the language of prose when prose is well written."

E. The contention of Poe (advanced in "The Philosophy of Composition," an essay not included in this collection) that "Beauty is the sole legitimate province of the poem."

F. Poe's theory that poetry needs "efflorescence of language."

G. Poe's contention that "a certain taint of sadness is inseparably connected with all the higher manifestations of beauty."

H. Poe's idea that the noblest poetry is "at all times, the most ethereal,—in other words, the most elevating and the most pure."

I. Housman's theory that simile and metaphor are "things inessential to poetry."

34. Choose any essay and discuss its proper classification according to the scheme proposed by Winters.

35. Shelley's "Ode to the West Wind," page 202; O'Shaughnessy's "Ode," page 212; Marianne Moore's "Poetry," page 216; MacLeish's "Ars Poetica," page 218; Auden's "In Memory of W. B. Yeats," page 219; and Wilbur's "For the New Railway Station in Rome," page 223, are all poems to some extent concerned with poetry. What essayists advance ideas corresponding to the ideas implicit or explicit in these poems?

36. Are any common ideas about the nature of poetry or art to be found in Keats's "Ode on a Grecian Urn," page 203; Yeats's "Sailing to Byzantium," page 213; Marianne Moore's "Poetry," page 216; and Wilbur's "For the New Railway Station in Rome," page 223?

37. Discuss the meaning of George Herbert's "Jordan," page 190, and the means employed in expressing that meaning. Support or criticize Herbert's contention, using ideas or arguments furnished by the essayists (e.g., Ransom, Warren, Eliot, Wimsatt, Mill, Yeats, Housman, or others).

Topics for Long Papers

An extended paper on poetic theory may do a number of things: (1) it may study the development of a certain aesthetic idea; (2) it may simply arrange or classify the leading ideas on a specific issue; (3) it may, after summarizing different views, defend one among them; or (4) it may even, after summarizing previous theories, advance a new theory. The first two kinds of paper necessitate examination of the theories alone; the latter two kinds also entail use of poems in order to support one's own conclusions or to refute the conclusions of others. Whether its object be to study a development, to classify, to defend, or to assert, a paper should be clearly organized around its central purpose. It should be more than a simple listing. It should compare, contrast, associate, group, develop, and finally, by a discernible logic, reach a clear conclusion.

Some of the topics listed below are overlapping or even identical. Since they are stated in different terms, however, they may inspire different approaches though to similar topics. The questions in parentheses after the topics are meant to be suggestive rather than definitive.

1. Poetry and Truth

(What is the relationship between poetry and truth? Since poetry is frequently fiction—the presentation of imagined experience rather than of actual experience—is it therefore opposed to truth? Do all these writers mean the same thing by the term *truth?*)

2. Poetry and Knowledge

(What is the relationship—if any—between the modern theory that poetry presents *knowledge* and the ancient one that poetry presents *truth?* What kind of knowledge does poetry present?)

3. Poetry and Virtue

(Does poetry inculcate virtue in the reader? If so, by what means?)

4. The Object of Poetry

(What objects—i.e., goals, ends, functions, purposes—have been claimed for poetry? Is there any area of agreement between theorists?)

5. The Value of Poetry

(What does poetry do for the reader? Does it have any value beyond pleasure?)

6. Poet, Poetry, Poem

(What is the relationship between these three terms? Is it sufficient to say that a poet writes poems and that poems taken collectively constitute poetry?)

7. Should Poetry Teach?

(Does, can, or should poetry teach? If so, how?)

8. Pure Poetry

(What is meant by the term *pure poetry?* Is pure poetry desirable or undesirable, a superior or an inferior kind of poetry? What writers advocate the theory of pure poetry, what ones oppose it?)

9. Poetry and Practicality

(What is the use of poetry? What are its relationships to practicality?)

10. The Power of Poetry

(Arthur O'Shaughnessy, in his "Ode," page 212, and W. H. Auden, in "In Memory of W. B. Yeats," page 219, advance opposing conceptions of the power of poetry. What is their difference? Which essayists would support one poet or the other?)

11. Poetry and Pleasure

(What is the relationship of poetry to pleasure?)

12. The Subject Matter of Poetry

(Does poetry have a fixed or proper subject matter? Are there poetical and unpoetical subjects? Are some subjects more easily assimilated into poetry or more conducive to good poetry than others?)

13. Poetry and Ideas

(Are ideas properly a concern of poetry? If so, how should they be expressed, and what is the relationship between the merit of the ideas and the merit of the poetry? If not, why not?)

14. The Doctrine of Imitation

(The idea of art as "imitation" originates with Plato. What writers continue the idea, what ones reject it? Do they all mean the same thing by the term? Do they agree about what is imitated?)

15. The Universal and the Particular

(Is poetry specifically characterized by universality or particularity? Or both? How are they related in good poetry?)

16. Poetry, History, and Philosophy

(How is poetry related to history and philosophy? Critics used to be fond of comparing or contrasting poetry with philosophy; with what do they more frequently contrast it today?)

17. Poetry and Science

(In what ways is poetry related or opposed to science?)

18. Poetry and Religion

(What relationships are there, if any, between poetry and religion?)

19. Imagination and Poetry

(What is the role of imagination in poetic composition? Of what does imagination consist?)

20. Poetry and Emotion

(What is the relationship of poetry to passion, or emotion? As regards the poet? As regards the reader?)

21. Poetry and the Intellect

(What part do reason and intellect—logic, good sense, rationality—play in poetry and the composition of poetry?)

22. The Structure of Poetry

(What is meant by unity in a poem? How can unity be tested? Are any kinds of organization superior to other kinds?)

23. Form and Content

(What are the relationships in poetry of form and content? What is meant by each? Which is more important? Are they separable?)

24. Poetry and Music

(What is the relationship of poetry to music? What part does verbal music—the sound of language—play in poetry?)

25. The Role of Verse

(How important is verse—i.e., meter—to poetry? What function does it serve?)

26. Poetry, Prose, Verse

(What are the relationships of poetry to prose and verse? What writers would include the prose selections in Part III as examples of poetry?)

27. Alexander Pope—Poet?

(Ever since Aaron Hill in 1744 wrote of Pope that "He had a tune for verse without a soul for poetry," critics have debated hotly as to whether Pope was or was not a poet. What writers in this collection would admit or not admit "An Essay on Criticism" into the realm of poetry? What criteria would they apply?)

28. Familiarity and Novelty in Poetry

(How does the poet relate the familiar and the novel in his poetry? Is his business primarily with the former or with the latter or with both?)

29. The Diction of Poetry

(Is there any diction peculiar or proper to poetry? Are there poetical and unpoetical words? How should a poet choose his language? What are his responsibilities toward language?)

30. Metaphor

(How important is metaphor in poetry? How does it work?)

31. The Judgment of Poetry

(By what criteria may poetic merit be judged? What are the qualifications of a good critic?)

32. Bad Poetry

(What makes poetry bad? How can bad poetry be identified?)

33. Poetic Inspiration

(What is poetic inspiration? In what different ways has it been accounted for? What is the relationship between inspiration and craftsmanship?)

34. The Process of Poetic Composition

(How do poets compose poetry? Do the accounts of the creative process agree? Are all of them valid?)

35. Poetry and Madness

(Are poets mad? Must they be mad while in the process of composition?)

36. The Nature of a Poet

(What kind of person is the poet? How does he differ from other men?)

37. The Definition of Poetry

(Of the various writers, which have the broadest or most inclusive conception of poetry? Which have the narrowest or most exclusive?)

38. Definitions of Poetry

(Write a discussion of various definitions of poetry—both those in the list of definitions and those included in the essays—grouping or classifying them, and testing their validity by applying them to the poems in Part II.)

39. Philosophical Classification of Aesthetic Theories

(How many of the poetic theories advanced in these essays may be classified according to the scheme proposed by Yvor Winters? In which of Winters' categories do they fall? In so far as the essays state or imply their fundamental assumptions, is Winters' classification adequate?)

40. Indirection in Poetry

(What is meant by "indirection" in poetry? Does poetry achieve its effects directly or indirectly?)

B
C
D 5
E 6
F 7
G 8
H 9
I 0